GW00503809

King Charles III

The Leadership and Vision of a Modern Monarch

By Robert Jobson

*featuring photography
by Arthur Edwards MBE*

SJH

ST JAMES'S HOUSE

Printed by Kingsbury Press on Fedrigoni Symbol Silk 130gsm. This paper has been independently certified according to the standards of the Forest Stewardship Council® (FSC)®.

ISBN: 978-1-915558-01-5

A catalogue record of this publication is available from the British Library.

This publication includes sponsor content that has been paid for by third parties. The inclusion of sponsor content in this publication does not constitute an endorsement, implied or otherwise, by the publisher. Any readers wishing to use the products, services or facilities of the organisations featured in this publication should take up independent references in the normal manner.

All information in this publication is verified to the best of the authors' and publisher's ability. However, Regalpress Limited and the SJH Group do not accept responsibility for any loss arising from reliance on it. Where opinion is expressed, it is that of the author and does not necessarily coincide with the editorial views of the publisher. The publisher has made all reasonable efforts to trace the copyright owners of the images reproduced herein, and to provide an appropriate acknowledgement in the book.

St James's House
The Maple Building
39–51 Highgate Road
London
NW5 1RT

+44 (0)20 8371 4000
publishing@stjamess.org
www.stjamess.org

ST JAMES'S HOUSE

Foreword

The era of King Charles III's reign, the new Carolean age, commenced on 8 September 2022, when His Majesty ascended to the throne. It was subsequently ushered in with full pomp and pageantry on 6 May 2023, when Charles was crowned in Westminster Abbey in front of a watching world.

However, as a senior royal and statesman, our sovereign has been a figure of leadership and a servant to the nation and the Commonwealth throughout his adult life. The longest heir apparent in British history, his 70-year wait to become king has included many milestone moments that have seen him step away from what could have been a cosseted life and, in time, out of the shadow of his mother, Her late Majesty Queen Elizabeth II, to assume a place on the world stage.

It is an honour, then, to present the work of two of the most experienced and revered chroniclers of His Majesty's story in this beautifully illustrated book charting Charles's life, Coronation and burgeoning reign as monarch.

Author Robert Jobson has been a keen observer of the Royal Family and the history, traditions and changing persona of British royalty for more than 30 years. A royal editor and correspondent for major media outlets around the world, he has extensive first-hand experience of royal life – both in the glare of public scrutiny and behind the scenes – having toured with the royals on countless occasions. And as an internationally respected writer, his books have topped the best-seller lists on both sides of the Atlantic and include multiple biographies of Charles over the years.

Arthur Edwards, whose photography features within these pages, is a legend of royal reporting. From the mid-'70s onwards, wherever the senior royals have travelled, Arthur and his camera have accompanied them. Having documented over 200 royal tours to more than 120 countries, he was presented with an MBE by Queen Elizabeth in 2003 for "outstanding service to newspapers".

King Charles III: The Leadership and Vision of a Modern Monarch also includes a wider societal narrative, highlighting stories of success and progress during His Majesty's lifetime in social, cultural, technological and commercial spheres. The resulting book presents a celebration of Charles's life and achievements in the year of his Coronation and 75th birthday, and looks forward to how he intends to shape the future of the monarchy over the years to come.

Contents

Introduction   12

Chapter one
The young prince   14

A ROYAL ARRIVAL   16
EARLY YEARS AND EDUCATION   26
INVESTITURE   42
MILITARY SERVICE   52

Chapter two
Family life   64

MARRIAGE AND FATHERHOOD   66
A NEW CHAPTER   76

Chapter three
The new king   88

ACCESSION AND PROCLAMATION   90
THE CORONATION   102

Chapter four
The global leader   126

THE COMMONWEALTH   128
Commonwealth success stories
Zenith Bank   140
Barker College   144
BVI Finance   146
Aslan Renewables   148
Finance Incorporated Limited   149
Herconomy   150
Refilwe Monageng Trading Enterprises   151
GA R&D   152

ON THE WORLD STAGE   156
International leadership
Avanti Communications   166
Toucan Hill/Bouchaine Vineyards   170
Cole & Son   176
KogoPay   180
Poonawalla Group   184
Avuke   188
CATS Global Schools (CGS)   190
Esprit   192
International Curriculum Association   194
Alta Semper Capital   196
Chartwell International School   197
JTI UK   198
Instituto Superior de Engenharia do Porto (ISEP)   200
Kantar   202
Lady Primrose Fragrances   204
Concourse   206
Crown Goose   207
Linly Designs/Marge Carson   208
Minesoft   210
Pacha Group   212
Global PMI Partners   214
Jomadasupe   215
Resource Solutions   216
Dwi Emas International School   218
Yacht.Vacations   220
Oliver Wyman   222
Rheinmetall Defence UK   223
Spectrum Markets   224
Viberg   225
Kippa   226
Culture Trip   227
Vale Verde International School   228
Ensembl   229

Chapter five
An environmental pioneer — 230

CLIMATE CHANGE — 232

Eco-friendly products, services and innovation

Climate Strategy & Partners — 244

Fischer — 246

Advanced Hydrogen Technologies Group — 248

All Steels Trading — 249

Future Carbon Group — 250

Mpowa — 252

AquaSource — 254

Candriam — 255

Nephila Climate — 256

CarbonTRACC — 258

Climate X — 259

Corre Energy — 260

GB-Sol — 261

Hemswell Coldstore — 262

Mission Zero — 263

Oaro — 264

Offshore Solutions Group — 265

WMF Energy — 266

ESG360° — 267

SUSTAINABLE DEVELOPMENT — 268

Sustainability trailblazers

Alchemie — 276

K2 Corporate Mobility — 280

Megger — 284

abrdn — 288

Strix — 290

Copart — 294

Analucia Beltran Diamonds — 296

dbramante1928	298	Comte de Grasse	363
Enviroo	300	Sustainable Planet	364
Cepi	302	Jonathan Tole Consulting	366
Enviro-Point	303	Knowledge Cotton Apparel	367
epeaswitzerland	304	Matriark Foods	368
Faerch	306	Mosa Meat	369
FiRe Energy	308	Regrow Ag	370
Gabriela Hearst	310	Vita Coco	371
Eco Packaging Products	312	Unium Bioscience	372
GoJute International	313	Pearl Brasserie	373
Helm London	314		
Rimm	316		
Rouute	318		
GRIDSERVE	320		
Modern Synthesis	321		
Tri-Wall	322		
Climate Outreach	324		
Pulpex	325		
Titan Bioplastics	326		
WeVee Technologies	327		

Chapter six
A vision of modern Britain — 374

SOCIAL HARMONY	376		

Learning, wellness and charities

Evox Therapeutics	384
Recycling Lives	388
Skills and Education Group	392
Sue Ryder	396
Care Horizons	400
Compassion in Action	402
Academic Families	404
Ascot Rehabilitation	405
Electrical Safety First	406
Luckley House School	408
Association of Accounting Technicians (AAT)	410
AVORD	411
Plymouth Marjon University	412
Savage Cabbage	414
The British School of Monaco	416
Manchester Youth Zone	417
St Cloud State University	418
British University of Iraq	420
National Association for Able Children in Education	421

FOOD AND FARMING — 328

Agriculture, food and drink

Mooboo	336
ProducePay	340
Ahmad Tea	344
Shaniko Wool Company	346
Budweiser Brewing Group	350
BASF	352
Butlers Farmhouse Cheeses	354
Rodda's	356
EcofashionCorp	357
CGIAR	358
Solinftec	360
De La Tierra	362

St Lawrence College 422

Queen Ethelburga's Collegiate 423

Plenaire 424

British International School of Zagreb 425

Avernus Education 426

THE BUSINESS CHAMPION 428

Queen's and King's Award winners

ORCA Computing 434

Crystal Doors 436

Gray & Adams 440

Baird & Co 444

Auto Electrical Supplies 446

The Nutrition Society 447

Penman Consulting 448

Brian James Trailers 450

Brodie Cashmere 451

Shelforce 452

Cenin 454

DK Engineering 455

European SprayDry Technologies 456

JMDA Design 457

Smartleaf 458

LittlePod 459

NaughtOne 460

Simply Start 461

The James Hutton Institute 462

Vexo International 463

Wrapology 464

Xrail 465

THE MODERN MONARCH 466

British business success stories

Alcatel Submarine Networks (ASN) 474

AP Security 476

MEATER 478

City Pub Group 480

AKT London 482

Avant Garden 483

FatFace 484

National Windscreens 486

P&O Cruises 488

Solpardus 490

Cintamani Group 492

Fulton Umbrellas 493

Space Forge 494

Tea Cups London 496

Titan Security Technologies 498

Hubble 500

Kuflink 501

Twelve Oaks Software 502

Well-Safe Solutions 504

LEVC 506

Pragmatic Semiconductor 507

Really Wild Clothing 508

Pictorum Art Group 509

THE BUILT ENVIRONMENT 510

Architecture, design and engineering

CPW 518

4C Group 522

ChangeMaker 3D 524

Charlotte Findlater 526

Galliford Try 528

Appendices 530

About the publisher 532

Acknowledgements 534

Sponsors index 535

Introduction

This was the year that the nation watched, with a collective sense of anticipation and nostalgia, as King Charles III crafted his own chapter in the centuries-old story of monarchy.

On 6 May 2023, millions tuned in to witness his coronation at Westminster Abbey, which was followed two months later by the presentation of the Crown of Scotland on 5 July at St Giles' Cathedral in Edinburgh.

This year also heralds The King's landmark 75th birthday on 14 November, his official birthday having already been marked with the annual Trooping the Colour military parade earlier in June. And while making it to three-quarters of a century would, for most, be excuse enough for a party, King Charles wants no grand displays, preferring to keep things minimal and family orientated.

The cities of London, Edinburgh, Cardiff and Belfast will pay their respects with traditional gun salutes, and a military band will perform a rendition of Happy Birthday outside Buckingham Palace on the day.

Beyond the crown and the ceremonies, however, who is Charles III? To understand the man, one must examine his life through the prism of time, as this book attempts to do in words and photography.

From the proclamation of the arrival of Prince Charles Philip Arthur George in 1948 to the poignant moments of his upbringing under the watchful eye of his father, Prince Philip, and into adulthood, the world looked on as a self-effacing Charles rose to, and navigated, the challenges of his younger years.

The daunting confines of Gordonstoun boarding school, which he hated, were followed by the halls of academia at the University of Cambridge, where Charles read archaeology, anthropology and history at Trinity College. He then trained as a jet pilot at RAF Cranwell in Lincolnshire, before enrolling in the Britannia Royal Naval College in preparation for his years of service as a Royal Navy officer.

A man of vision, he went on to become a beacon of leadership for causes that transcended his royal duties and responsibilities as heir to the throne. From championing sustainable urbanism and organic farming to trumpeting holistic approaches in science, industry and business, he often knowingly went against the tide of popular and professional opinion.

The natural world resonated with Charles from a young age, and he would go on to use his public profile to sound the alarm on environmental concerns, even before the term "global warming" entered common parlance. Aged just 21, Charles made his first landmark speech about the environment, warning of the threats from plastic waste and chemicals dumped into rivers and seas, and from air pollution from industry, traffic and air travel.

His clarion calls, initially met with derision, have now become accepted truths, and he has been widely acclaimed around the world and honoured for his work in the field.

Today, Charles is not only the British sovereign but also monarch of the 14 Commonwealth realms, as well as Head of the Commonwealth, a role he takes extremely seriously. The leadership and service of the union of nations is integral to The King's daily life, and while the Commonwealth presents a significant legacy, it also presents a coalition of hope, one that can unite to change the world for the better.

Charles's dedication is evident in his travels, speeches and initiatives, such as the Blue Economy programme, which was set up to aid small island nations threatened by rising sea levels. Inevitably, the late Queen Elizabeth's long reign still looms large in the national psyche, but Charles has never been one to stand idly by.

Throughout his working life, he has striven to make a real difference and to enlighten others. For years, he has encouraged a more balanced approach to business and healthcare, and a more benign, holistic application of science and technology to global challenges. In his view, these areas are totally interrelated, and we must see what he often calls the "big picture" to better understand the problems that humanity faces.

Now more than a year into his reign, those close to The King are confident that he will not be suffocated by the limitations and restrictions of the "top job" and will continue to support the causes that he believes in. He will not be so outspoken, perhaps, but he will use his convening powers to bring influential people together to address the issues of the day.

As heir to the throne, Charles devoted his life to service and duty. Now that he is The King, as he wrote in a private letter in 1993, His Majesty is "entirely motivated by a desperate desire to put the 'Great' back into Great Britain".

CHAPTER ONE

THE YOUNG PRINCE

A royal arrival

The birth of Charles Philip Arthur George in 1948 was cause for celebration around the world and heralded a new chapter in the history of the Royal Family

The distinctive voice of BBC Presentation Director John Snagge, crackled onto the radio, just as it had when he delivered important announcements throughout the Second World War, with a late-night news item. It was 14 November 1948.

"This is the BBC Home Service," he said, in his familiar cut-glass tones. "It has just been announced from Buckingham Palace that Her Royal Highness Princess Elizabeth, Duchess of Edinburgh, was safely delivered of a prince at 9.14pm and that Her Royal Highness and her son are both doing well. Listeners will wish us to offer their royal congratulations to Princess Elizabeth and the Royal Family on this happy occasion." Patriotically, the national anthem was then played across the airwaves in honour of the as yet unnamed baby prince.

The British Empire may have been in irreversible decline by this stage, but the public's respect for the institution embodied by the baby's grandfather, George VI, and his family had never been stronger. The Countess Granville, the infant's great-aunt, could not contain her excitement when she first saw the little prince. "He could not be more angelic looking," she said. "He is golden-haired and has the most beautiful complexion, as well as amazingly delicate features for so young a baby."

Princess Elizabeth, then just 22, was less glowing about her first child. For some reason she fixated on his hands. "Rather large but fine with long fingers," said the future queen, "quite unlike mine and certainly not like his father's. It will be interesting to see what they become."

BIRTH OF A PRINCE

The news of Prince Charles's birth sparked celebrations throughout the British Empire. An editorial in *The Times* newspaper described King George VI as the nation's "supreme representative", which "in modern times is a more royal function than any duty of state", affirming that, "the representative monarchy has made every one of its subjects feel friend and neighbour to the Royal Family; and so it is that the simple joy which the coming of this child has brought to them is shared by all".

A month later, on 15 December 1948, the baby prince, second in line to the British throne, was baptised Charles Philip Arthur George in the Music Room at Buckingham Palace. The then Archbishop of Canterbury, Geoffrey Fisher, presided over the ceremony and used water from the River Jordan to anoint the baby's head. Pathé News reels showed footage of Princess Elizabeth holding Charles in her arms, sat alongside her mother, Queen Elizabeth, then 48, and grandmother Queen Mary, 81, consort to the late King George V. Baby Charles was swathed in a baptism gown originally worn by Queen Victoria's first-born in 1841, an intricate satin and lace robe, as he was admitted to the Church of England.

New parents Princess Elizabeth and Prince Philip moved out of their Buckingham Palace apartment a few hundred yards away along The Mall to the newly refurbished Clarence House. Two nannies, Helen Lightbody and Mabel Anderson, took charge of the royal nursery. In addition, Charles was watched over around the clock by Metropolitan Police officers. It was something he would have to get used to.

Charles's father, Prince Philip, was still a serving officer in the Royal Navy, while Princess Elizabeth was increasingly occupied with her role as heiress-presumptive and supporting her father, who was in frail health. Effectively, this meant the royal nannies took charge of the daily care of Charles – although Princess Elizabeth made sure whenever possible to attend bath time and would stay to read her son a bedtime story.

Previous page
Prince Charles in his mother's arms on his christening day, 15 December 1948, wearing the gown made for Queen Victoria's first-born

Right
Members of the Royal Family in an official christening portrait at Buckingham Palace, with Charles flanked by his great-grandmother, Princess Victoria of Hesse and by Rhine (left), and grandmother Queen Mary (right)

PUBLIC DUTY

In August 1950, Princess Anne was born and joined her brother in the nursery. By now, however, the heavy burden of public duty meant Princess Elizabeth could not spend as much time with her young children as she would have wanted. The king's health was in rapid decline and she had to step in to public engagements that he was not up to. Elizabeth was aware that she had to start preparing herself for the role as monarch. It may have been unspoken, but she knew her father was dying.

Within days of Charles's second birthday, she joined her husband in Malta without the children. Philip had just been promoted to the rank of Commander of a Royal Navy frigate, and his career was going from strength to strength. Charles and the four-month-old Anne remained at home in the care of their grandparents and nannies. At the time the king, gravely ill, was recuperating from the last of three operations. He celebrated Charles's third birthday and marked it with a special photograph of them together. Charles would later admit that this picture was one of his abiding personal memories of his grandfather.

The following month, the family was reunited for Christmas. Days later, the king waved his daughter off on a Commonwealth tour that he had been forced to postpone four years previously. The crowd gave the king a sympathetic cheer as he stood in the bitter cold as his beloved daughter left for Africa. He gave his customary wave of acknowledgement and turned to Margaret "Bobo" MacDonald, Princess Elizabeth's loyal assistant. "Look after the princess for me," he said. MacDonald later admitted that she had never seen the king so upset.

Elizabeth was not to see her father alive again. Six days after they had said goodbye, in the early hours of 6 February 1952, George VI died in his sleep of thrombosis at his Sandringham estate in Norfolk. He was only 56 years old and had reigned for 16 years.

Opposite
Princess Elizabeth and Prince Philip with the baby prince

Above
Charles with his grandparents, Queen Elizabeth and King George VI (far left), at Ballater station, en route to Balmoral

Right
Members of the Royal Family pictured in the grounds of Balmoral Castle in 1951

"The king celebrated Charles's third birthday and marked
it with a photograph of them together"

Opposite
The prince pictured
on his birthday in 1951
– one of Charles's
abiding memories of
his grandfather

Above
Moments of joy for
the royal prince and
princess, playing
in the grounds of
Balmoral Castle

A NEW SOVEREIGN

Buckingham Palace officials held up the announcement of the monarch's passing for three hours while they desperately attempted to contact Elizabeth. Oblivious, the royal couple had just returned from the Treetops hotel and observation tower to Sagana Lodge in Kenya. They could not be reached.

A telegram sent to Government House in Nairobi could not be decoded because the keys to the safe holding the codebook were unavailable. Meanwhile, "Operation Hyde Park Corner" – the code name for arrangements for the death of the king – was well underway. But Elizabeth still did not know that she was already Queen.

Prime Minister Winston Churchill had been informed of the king's death. When his staff tried to console him, saying he would get on well with the new Queen, Churchill replied that he barely knew her and she was "only a child".

The widowed Queen Elizabeth set out her thoughts in a letter to Queen Mary, in which she worried about the burden that would fall on the 25-year-old Elizabeth. "My darling Mama, what can I say to you – I know that you loved Bertie dearly, and he was my whole life, and one can only be deeply thankful for the utterly happy years we had together. He was so wonderfully thoughtful and loving, and I don't believe he ever thought of himself at all ... I cannot bear to think of Lilibet, so young to bear such a burden – I do feel for you so darling Mama – to lose two dear sons, and Bertie still so young and so precious – it is almost more than one can bear, your very loving Elizabeth."

Elizabeth was now Queen. Charles, at just three years of age, a sensitive and somewhat shy boy, was given the title the Duke of Cornwall upon his grandfather's death. He was now the direct heir to the throne.

> "Charles was given the title the Duke of Cornwall upon his grandfather's death. He was now the direct heir to the throne"

Below
The prince's aunt, Princess Margaret, holds his hand as they arrive for a horse show at Windsor Great Park in 1953

Opposite
With sister Anne and his parents at Balmoral in 1953, by which time Princess Elizabeth had acceded to the throne as Queen Elizabeth II

Early years and education

Charles's school days were a testing time, but the future monarch found his feet as he stepped out into the world beyond the classroom

A little over a year after the death of his grandfather King George VI, the four-year-old Charles attended his mother's magnificent Coronation at Westminster Abbey – the first to be televised. Afterwards, he was brought out onto the Buckingham Palace balcony as Her Majesty acknowledged the cheers of the huge and enthusiastic crowd below. By now, the prince was starting to comprehend that his life was very different to that of other children.

More than 8,000 guests attended Queen Elizabeth II's Coronation. When she took the Coronation Oath, binding her to serve the people and maintain the laws of God, millions around the world tuned in to witness the historic moment. Some had bought television sets – then a rarity in Britain and much of the world – purely for this occasion. This glamorous new Queen was quite possibly just what the war-weary British people needed. The image of the youthful Elizabeth with the heavy crown on her head was one of the most iconic photographs of the age.

COMMONWEALTH COMMITMENTS

Within months, Queen Elizabeth II was handed a colossal diplomatic mission – to lead the transformation from British Empire to Commonwealth over a marathon six-month tour, to cement her position as symbolic leader of much of the free world. It was her chance to stamp her personality on the Commonwealth. It meant her young children would be left without their parents again as the Queen toured 13 countries in the West Indies, Australasia, Asia and Africa, covering a staggering 43,618 miles. Many of the countries had never before seen

Previous page
The prince on his eighth birthday, in 1956, photographed in a State Room in Buckingham Palace

Above
On the balcony of Buckingham Palace after Elizabeth II's Coronation in 1953, when Charles was four

Opposite
Charles and Anne with their mother, who was often away performing state duties during their childhood

their monarch. The tour included 10,000 miles by plane, 2,000 miles by car, 2,500 by rail and the rest by sea, most of it on board the Royal Yacht SS *Gothic*. The final leg home was on the newly commissioned Royal Yacht *Britannia*.

When the Queen and Prince Philip completed their final leg home on the new Royal Yacht, from Tobruk on the North African coast, Charles and Anne were waiting patiently for them. Her Majesty later joked, "They were extremely polite. I don't think they knew who we were at all!" The queen was their mother and her dedication to duty was something that the two children would have to bear.

Shortly before Charles's fifth birthday, one of the rooms of the nursery was converted to a classroom and Catherine Peebles was engaged as a governess to teach the heir to the throne some primary-school skills. Peebles – who had previously worked with the Baroness Darcy de Knayth and the Duchess of Kent's children – soon discovered that the way to get the best out of the young Charles was to be encouraging. He excelled at drawing and also enjoyed singing. The prince's affectionate nickname for Peebles was "Mipsy".

On 14 April 1954, a five-year-old Prince Charles and his sister, Anne, boarded the Royal Yacht *Britannia* to join their parents in Malta before continuing on to Gibraltar, their first official overseas visit. Charles took his sister's hand as she patted down the steps, shepherded her carefully into the car and turned to wave to the press.

EARLY SCHOOLING

Just before his eighth birthday, Charles broke with the royal tradition of being home-schooled and joined Hill House pre-preparatory school in Knightsbridge, west London. This enabled the prince to play sports with other boys, and he even travelled on public transport. He mixed

with the pupils and made reasonable progress as a student. Away from school, his father, Prince Philip, was determined to introduce his son to the adventures of rural life. He taught his son to fish and shoot, but the duke's blunt manner and attempts to mould the boy into his idea of a son to be proud of stifled their relationship.

In September 1957, the prince had to face a new challenge when he was sent to Cheam School in Hampshire. Founded in the 17th century, this boarding school housed around 80 boys between the ages of eight and 14. Prince Philip, a former Cheam pupil himself, felt the school had helped to toughen his character and wanted the same for his son.

Headmaster Peter Beck said that, while the school was honoured to have the prince as a pupil, he would be treated the same as any other boy. His parents dropped him off, amid a media frenzy, and stayed long enough to see where Charles would sleep, then left. At first, Charles struggled with homesickness and found it difficult to mix. "It was not easy to make large numbers of friends," he recalled, many years later. "I'm not a gregarious person so I've always had a horror of gangs … I have always preferred my own company or just a one-to-one."

The rough and tumble of boarding shook him into action and, quite wisely, the prince taught himself to wrestle and box. He was, as a result, able to take care of himself in a playground fight, although it did result in the future king receiving corporal punishment, which he later admitted worked for him. "I didn't do it again," he said.

In the summer term of 1958, headmaster Beck summoned Charles and a group of boys to his study. It was the last day of the British Empire and Commonwealth Games in Cardiff and the boys were allowed to watch the closing ceremony on his television. The Queen was unable to attend in person due to an attack of sinusitis, but a pre-recorded message was played. She appeared on the screen with

Opposite
The royal siblings In the grounds of the Royal Lodge, Windsor, with the Queen Mother

Left
Charles and Anne wave goodbye on the Royal Yacht *Britannia*, in Portsmouth in 1954, before sailing to join their parents in Malta

Above
The prince and
princess receive much
public attention as
they are driven from
Buckingham Palace

Opposite
As part of his early
schooling, the future
king was encouraged
to play sport with
other children

"I'm not a gregarious person so I've always
had a horror of gangs ... I have always preferred
my own company or just a one-to-one"

a simple message: "The British Empire and Commonwealth Games in the capital ... have made this a memorable year for the principality. I have therefore decided to mark it further by an act which will, I hope, give much pleasure to all Welshmen as it does to me. I intend to create my son, Charles, Prince of Wales today. When he is grown up, I will present him to you at Caernarfon."

He had now become His Royal Highness Prince Charles Philip Arthur George, Prince of Wales and Earl of Chester, Duke of Cornwall, Duke of Rothesay, Earl of Carrick and Baron of Renfrew, Lord of the Isles, and Prince and Great Steward of Scotland. His school friends all congratulated him. The newspapers, too, were enthusiastic about the decision.

Two weeks later, the Royal Family visited Anglesey in the Royal Yacht en route to Scotland. Once ashore, Charles was greeted with great enthusiasm. The principality had a new prince, and it was clearly delighted. Cheering crowds broke through the police cordons. An excited dog nearly knocked the heir to the throne to the ground. The prince kept his composure and patted the dog. Prince Philip put a reassuring arm around his son's shoulder in an act of paternal care and both father and son waved to the crowd.

In 1962, after five years at Cheam, he was made head boy. Although he was later to say he loathed his time there, it had certainly helped him develop as a person. He was academically competent, had discovered a love for acting, and had also captained the school's first XI at football, and played in the first teams at cricket and rugby.

"COLDITZ WITH KILTS"

Where the future king should be educated next became a source of constant speculation. Eton College was the popular choice, favoured

> "A warning was sent out to other boys that anyone caught bullying the heir to the throne risked immediate expulsion"

Left
Charles as a pupil at Cheam in 1958, the year he learned he would become the Prince of Wales

Opposite
With Prince Philip and the Queen in a family portrait at Windsor Castle in 1959

Opposite, top
Accompanied by his father, Charles arrives at Gordonstoun in 1962 and is greeted by staff, including headmaster Robert Chew (far left)

Opposite, bottom
The prince takes to the slopes on a ski holiday in Liechtenstein in 1964, under the gaze of the media

Left
An enthusiastic welcome from schoolchildren while visiting North Bondi Beach, Sydney, in 1966

too by the Queen Mother, but Prince Philip had other ideas. The Queen left the decision to her husband and his choice was his old boarding school, Gordonstoun.

Established in 1934 on the shores of the Moray Firth in northeast Scotland, Gordonstoun was the brainchild of headmaster Dr Kurt Hahn, a refugee from Nazi Germany who was inspired by Plato. He believed that good and wise government could only occur when philosophers become rulers or rulers become philosophers. This, in turn, could only be achieved through education: not just through academic learning, he believed, but also the moral and physical training of the mind, the body and, in particular, the character.

Charles was delivered into this spartan world by his father and allocated to Windmill Lodge, one of seven houses scattered through the grounds. Like the other houses, Windmill Lodge was a wooden hut that had been acquired from the Royal Air Force as temporary accommodation years before, but never replaced. At night, the windows were kept open by order, even if the weather was poor, which it often was. If a student was unlucky enough to have been allocated a bed near one of these windows, as Charles was, he would invariably awake to a rain-soaked bed in spring, summer or autumn, or one covered in snow in the winter.

When Charles arrived at the school, Hahn had recently retired and been replaced by Robert Chew. A warning was sent out to other boys that anyone caught bullying the heir to the throne risked immediate expulsion. This had the opposite effect, however, to that intended. Charles was picked upon at once, "maliciously, cruelly and without respite".

The prince endured this thuggery without complaint. But he was in private despair. "I hate coming back here and leaving everyone at home," he wrote in one of his letters. "I hardly get any sleep at the house because I snore and get hit on the head the whole time. It is absolute hell."

For Prince Philip, his time at Gordonstoun had been an edifying and character-building experience. But, as the school tottered into the Swinging Sixties, many of the students were a law unto themselves, and Charles found himself at the receiving end of some brutal treatment from his peers. "A prison sentence", was how Charles later described it. "It's Colditz with kilts."

TROUBLED WATERS

One infamous event unfolded while he was a pupil, which made headline news. Charles developed his sailing skills and in his second year, he joined the crew of *Pinta*, one of two ketches owned by the school. On his first outing in the summer of 1963, he sailed into Stornoway Harbour on the Isle of Lewis. He and four other boys were given shore leave to have dinner and see a film. Charles was accompanied by his policeman, Donald Green. As they walked towards the Crown Hotel, they began to attract a small crowd. By the time they were in the lounge, a larger crowd had gathered outside the main window and flash bulbs were going off as folk jostled to get a photograph. Embarrassed by all the attention, Charles retreated from the room and, followed by his detective, found himself in the public bar.

"Everybody was looking at me. And I thought, I must have a drink – that's what you are supposed to do in a bar," he later recalled. "I went and sat down at the bar and the barman said, 'What do you want to drink?' I thought that you had to have alcohol in a bar, so I said, 'Cherry brandy'." At that very moment, a female journalist walked into the bar and the incident went on to become headline news.

At first, the Palace denied the story was true. But it wouldn't go away. Two days later, the Palace was forced to withdraw its denial with Press Secretary Richard Colville claiming that he had been initially misled by the prince's detective and sincerely regretted giving the newspapers incorrect information. The consequences of this were serious for both the prince and Donald Green. Once back at school, Charles was sent for by the headmaster and was demoted a rank in the school system. Green was unfairly removed from royal duties, which horrified the prince.

NEWFOUND CONFIDENCE

In 1964, teacher Eric Anderson, who in later life would become headmaster of Eton, set about putting on a production of Shakespeare's *Henry V* and asked for volunteer actors. Charles applied and proved to be a fine character actor. However, Anderson didn't cast him in the lead role. Instead, he gave the young prince the part of Exeter. The play was a success, but the audience of locals commented that it was a pity Charles, the best actor, didn't play Henry.

Encouraged by this, Anderson persuaded the headmaster that there should be a winter play as well. That November, a production of *Macbeth* was hastily planned and the prince was offered the title role. His performance was sensitive, regal and convincing, and impressed the producer, the staff, the pupils and even his father, who came to watch.

Charles was sent to Timbertop school in Australia in 1966 to help with his development. At first the prince feared the worst but, to his amazement, he found the boys and masters friendly, and got on well with his room-mate. He started to enjoy school life without being stricken by fearful bouts of homesickness, and his letters told of what he was doing rather than expressing the bitter pain of missing his family.

"Charles left Australia with sadness. In a statement, he thanked the Australian people for their kindness, adding that he was sorry to be leaving"

Left
The prince meets North Bondi Beach lifeguards on his royal engagement

Opposite
At Trinity College, Cambridge in 1967, with college master Lord Rab Butler (left)

In between his outdoor adventures of long walks and climbing, Charles was expected to teach himself A-level French and history. This he did, but he often found it more congenial to go trout fishing in a nearby stream. Prince Charles left Australia with sadness. In a statement, he thanked the Australian people for "a marvellous and worthwhile experience" and for their kindness, adding that he was very sorry to be leaving. He meant it. He has loved visiting Australia ever since.

The prince did not look forward to returning to Gordonstoun, but he was now approaching 18 and his stay in Australia had given him newfound confidence. To his surprise, he was appointed head boy, an appointment that gave him the chance to help reform Gordonstoun's bullying culture.

In July 1967, Prince Charles became the first British heir to the throne to sit A-level examinations with a view to studying at university. He received a grade B in history and a grade C in French. He also took a special paper in history, designed for high-flyers to test their judgement, initiative and acumen. According to the secretary of the examining board, he had shone.

HIGHER EDUCATION
It was decided that the prince should attend university first and then serve in one or more of the armed forces. But which university? After nine months of discussion, Trinity College, Cambridge, was decided upon. Charles elected to read anthropology and archaeology, and then history, and wanted to do so via a full three-year tripos, to be judged entirely on his own abilities.

He arrived at university and buckled down to his studies, conscious that his results would be subject to the scrutiny of the press. After four terms at Trinity, the prince was sent to the University College of Wales, Aberystwyth, to learn Welsh before his formal investiture as Prince of Wales. This was very much a political decision: in the late 1960s, a wave of nationalism was on the rise in Scotland and Wales. More seriously, fanatics calling themselves the Free Wales Army were causing police and security services concern.

Upon his arrival at Pantycelyn Hall, where he was to share accommodation with 250 other students, he encountered a crowd of some 500 cheering locals. He experienced an incident-free spell at the university. At the end of his eight-week term, he was invited to close the Urdd National Eisteddfod, the annual Welsh youth festival for poetry, drama and music, before an audience of some 6,000 people. It would be his first public speech of any significance in Welsh, a language that he had studied for just two months.

As he got to his feet, demonstrators screamed abuse at the prince. Charles stood his ground and simply stared back at them. The natural sympathy of the rest of the audience was aroused and mayhem broke out. "It was extraordinarily warming to have so many people applauding and cheering and, as a result, my nerves were dissipated by the time that I was allowed to get anywhere near the microphone," he noted later. The end of his speech was greeted by a roar of approval and a standing ovation.

By May 1970, the prince was back at Cambridge to face the moment of truth – his history finals. He was awarded a lower second-class degree, which, given all the disruption to his studies through royal duties, was deemed a major achievement by the college – an assessment that was echoed by the national press. The prince finished his academic education full of self-confidence. At times it had been a testing journey, but his strength of character had seen him through.

Investiture

Charles was created
Prince of Wales at the
age of nine and formally
invested 11 years later,
establishing a lifelong
fealty to, and affection
for, the principality

On 26 July 1958, the headmaster of Prince Charles's preparatory school at Cheam, Peter Beck, asked a small number of pupils to join him in his sitting room. The prince was among them. The British Empire and Commonwealth Games in Cardiff was being broadcast on the BBC and the boys were allowed to watch the closing ceremony on his television. It was announced that, while Her Majesty the Queen was not in attendance, she would address the stadium and the television audience in a recorded message. Her Majesty then appeared on the screen and read out a message that would have huge implications for the young prince.

"The British Empire and Commonwealth Games in the capital… have made this a memorable year for the principality," announced the Queen. "I have therefore decided to mark it further by an act that will, I hope, give much pleasure to all Welshmen as it does to me. I intend to create my son, Charles, Prince of Wales today. When he is grown up, I will present him to you at Caernarfon."

Charles's friends turned and congratulated him on his elevation in status, which made the prince a touch uncomfortable as he hated being the centre of attention.

At a dinner in Caerphilly Castle in July 2008, held to celebrate his half-century as the Prince of Wales, Charles spoke of the moment. "I remember with horror and embarrassment how I was summoned with all the other boys at my school to the headmaster's sitting room, where we all had to sit on the floor and watch television," he said. "To my total embarrassment I heard my mama's voice – she wasn't very well at the time and could not go. My father went instead and a recording of the message was played in the stadium saying that I was to be made the Prince of Wales. All the other boys turned around and looked at me and I remember thinking, 'What on earth have I been let in for?' That is my overriding memory."

The prince said later it was one of the greatest privileges possible to be the 21st Prince of Wales. "I have tried my best," he said. "It may not be very adequate to live up to the motto of my predecessors, 'Ich Dien – I Serve'."

A WARM RECEPTION

Eleven years after the Queen's announcement, on 1 July 1969 Charles was sworn in as the Prince of Wales in an Investiture at Caernarfon Castle – a ceremony based on the one held for his great-uncle David (later Edward VIII) in 1911. On the eve of the initiation, the prince joined the Queen and Prince Philip on the Royal Train and headed for North Wales. All three of them felt it was essential that this royal pageant had to go to plan and all were eager for a positive reaction from the public, especially in Wales.

After completing four terms at Trinity College, Cambridge, the prince was sent to the University College of Wales, Aberystwyth, to learn Welsh before his formal Investiture as the Prince of Wales. This was a political decision rather than a cultural one, amid a revival of nationalism in Scotland and Wales. Prior to his departure to the Welsh college, Charles recorded his first radio interview and, not surprisingly, he was asked about his attitude towards the hostility in the principality. "It would be unnatural, I think, if one didn't feel any apprehension about it," he said. "One always wonders what's going to happen … As long as I don't get covered in too much egg and tomato I'll be alright. But I don't blame people demonstrating like that. They've never seen me before. They don't know what I'm like. I've hardly been to Wales, and you can't really expect people to be overzealous about the fact of having a so-called English prince to come amongst them."

To cancel the university term in Wales would have been a public-relations disaster for the government and, indeed, for Charles himself.

Previous page
A portrait of Charles wearing the Prince of Wales's regalia – the sword, rod, ring, coronet and mantle

Left
Local people form a guard of honour for the 20-year-old prince at Caernarfon Castle before the Investiture on 1 July 1969

It was decided it would be a weakness to bow to extremist threats. So they went ahead regardless. Upon his arrival at Pantycelyn Hall, where he would share accommodation with 250 other students, Charles was met by a 500-strong cheering crowd. The welcome raised his spirits. In the end, the prince enjoyed his time in Aberystwyth and was treated kindly. His period of study there passed without incident.

He wrote to a friend: "If I have learned anything during the last eight weeks, it's been about Wales ... they feel so strongly about Wales as a nation, and it means something to them, and they are depressed by what might happen to it if they don't try and preserve the language and the culture, which is unique and special to Wales, and if something is unique and special, I see it as well worth preserving."

Many years later, the prince recalled that the time he spent studying in Wales was among his fondest memories. "Memorable times spent exploring mid-Wales during my term at Aberystwyth University," he said with pleasure, "and learning something about the principality and its ancient language, folklore, myths and history."

NATIONALIST THREAT

Despite this preparation in fealty to Charles's status within the principality, more radical factions within the Welsh nationalist movement had started a disturbing campaign of terrorism. Fanatics had formed what they called the Free Wales Army and had finally gained the attention of the police and security services after an RAF warrant officer was seriously injured in an incident. The gang then planted a bomb that destroyed the Temple of Peace in Cardiff. Another bomb was found in the lost-luggage department of the railway station.

On 30 June – the eve of the Investiture – two members of a paramilitary organisation called Mudiad Amddiffyn Cymru (MAC – Movement for the Defence of Wales) were killed while placing a bomb outside government offices in the North Wales coastal town of Abergele. On the day of the Investiture, two other bombs were planted in Caernarfon, one in the local police constable's garden, which exploded as the 21-gun salute was fired. Another was planted in an iron forge near the castle but failed to go off. A final bomb was placed on the Llandudno Pier and was designed to stop the Royal Yacht *Britannia* from docking – this also failed to explode.

In addition, it was announced, anonymously, that the Prince of Wales was on their target list. This threat left Charles understandably concerned. The Royal Family was powerless in this regard and had to trust in the competency of the security services and the measures the police had already put in place to ensure the safety of both Charles and the Queen.

CROWNING MOMENT

Thankfully, the streets of Caernarfon were peaceful during Charles's instalment as the Prince of Wales, on 1 July 1969. Charles was driven through the town in an open carriage on his way to the castle past cheering crowds. As the guests and choir sang "God Bless the Prince of Wales", he was conducted to the dais and knelt before the Queen. He would later write that he found it profoundly moving when he placed his hands between his mother's and spoke the Oath of Allegiance.

Her Majesty then presented the prince to the crowd at the King's Gate and at the Lower Ward to the sound of magnificent fanfares. He was then paraded through the streets once more before retiring aboard the Royal Yacht at Holyhead for a well-deserved dinner, an emotionally exhausted but very happy prince. Buoyed by the experience, Charles noted, "As long as I do not take myself too seriously I should not be too badly off."

The next day, the prince embarked on a week of solo engagements around the principality. He recalled being "utterly amazed" by the positive reaction he received. As the tour progressed south, the crowds grew even

"The message was played saying that I was to be made the Prince of Wales ... I remember thinking, 'What on earth have I been let in for?'"

Below
The prince at the University of Wales, Aberystwyth, where he spent a term studing the Welsh language

Opposite
Charles is appointed Colonel-in-Chief of the new Royal Regiment of Wales on the day of his Investiture

"Charles was driven through the town past cheering crowds. He would later write that he found it profoundly moving when he placed his hands between his mother's and spoke the Oath of Allegiance"

Opposite
The newly invested
Prince of Wales is
presented by the
Queen to the public
in the castle grounds

Above
After the ceremony,
the Royal Family
ride through the
streets of Caernarfon
in an open carriage

THE YOUNG PRINCE

49

"[The Welsh] feel so strongly about Wales as a nation … and they are depressed by what might happen to it if they don't try and preserve the language and the culture"

bigger. At the end of it, Charles arrived exhausted but elated at Windsor Castle. He retired to write up his diary, noting the silence after the day's cheers and applause, reflecting that he had much to live up to and hoped that he could do something constructive for Wales.

COMMUNITY CONNECTION

During his time as the Prince of Wales, Charles cultivated close contacts within the principality. He purchased, through his Duchy of Cornwall trust, a 192-acre estate near the village of Myddfai to the south of Llandovery in Carmarthenshire, called Llwynywermod (also known as Llwynywormwood). Adapted from a former model farm and located just outside the Brecon Beacons National Park, it bears witness to Charles's philosophy of sustainable building with a structure traditionally made from existing and locally sourced materials, an ecologically sound heating system and elegant interiors that harmonise perfectly with the architecture.

Charles used the estate, which has since passed on to William, the current Prince of Wales, for meetings, receptions and concerts, and as the base for his regular visits to Wales, including the annual week of summer engagements, known in his schedule as "Wales Week". In his words, Charles helped establish it as "a showcase for traditional Welsh craftsmanship, textiles and woodwork, so as to draw attention to the high-quality small enterprises, woollen mills, quilt-makers, joiners, stonemasons and metalworkers situated in rural parts of Wales".

During a January 2015 interview with Visit Wales, Charles was asked how important it was for him to have a retreat in Wales. "Very important!" he replied. "It enables me to be part of the local community around Llandovery and to have a base for entertaining and meeting people from throughout the principality."

Opposite
The prince walking in Snowdonia, Wales, where he has fond memories as a student

Below
With Camilla outside their Carmarthenshire home on a visit during "Wales Week" in 2009

Military service

Having completed
his academic studies,
Charles's education
continued in the military,
with the young prince
serving in the airforce
and on the high seas

Prince Philip passed up on a most promising naval career when he married Princess Elizabeth, the future queen. It is no great surprise, then, that once Charles had completed his academic education, Philip was keen for his eldest son to follow in his footsteps and embark upon a career in the Royal Navy. Officially, Charles would sign up for three years, but it was expected he would stay for at least five so that he could gain command of his own ship.

Charles was to enter the Royal Naval College, Dartmouth, in autumn 1971, but before that it was decided that he should undertake an intensive four-month attachment to the Royal Air Force at Cranwell to gain his wings as a jet pilot. It was to herald the start of the "action man" image that the media was determined to create for him. He flew to the college at RAF Cranwell in March 1971 at the controls of a twin-engine aircraft from the Queen's Flight.

Two aircraft were assigned to the prince for his use only. They were separated from the others and maintained only by a special team and guarded by RAF police. While Charles was allowed to undertake the course, anything that involved any high-risk elements was ruled out.

FLYING HIGH

The prince loved his time at Cranwell and wrote to his great-uncle, Lord Mountbatten, enthusing about the lectures on jet engines: "To my amazement I find I am beginning to understand some of it and I am convinced that the secret is continuity all day every day. They certainly keep you busy here and I am up early and in bed fairly early as well."

After only two weeks of ground training, he was allowed to take the controls of a Jet Provost and, while he found navigation tricky, he was soon permitted to make his first solo flight, on 31 March 1971 – just three weeks after arriving at Cranwell. "I did one circuit and managed to bring off a very passable landing," he wrote. "The feeling of power, smooth unworried power, is incredible." Later, he was allowed to fly solo aerobatics at 25,000ft, which he found "breathtaking". His next adventure was to fly in the rear seat of a Phantom Jet from 43 Squadron. They flew twice over Balmoral at 400ft, which he noted was an "unforgettable experience".

After five months, the prince was awarded his wings and left the RAF. On his last evening, he was called upon to make a speech at a guest evening in the officers' mess. When he finished, his fellow officers rose as one in a genuine, heartfelt standing ovation. In September, he headed to the Royal Naval College at Dartmouth to start his Royal Navy training.

NAVAL TRAINING

Charles found learning seamanship and naval technology intense, especially as he had once again been put on a fast-track course, a six-week one in this case – half the usual allocated time. After passing his exams at Dartmouth, he joined the destroyer HMS *Norfolk* in Gibraltar. On his second day aboard, Charles recorded that he was looking forward to "my first day at sea in one of Her Majesty's finest warships".

On the *Norfolk*, he was expected to gain a Bridge Watchkeeping Certificate in nine months, when a year would be more usual, and he felt the pressure. "I believe in being well-occupied and busy but I expect more is learned and accumulated by midshipmen who have longer to explore and investigate," wrote the prince. "However, I did obtain my wings reasonably fairly ... and I passed the exams

Previous page
The prince in uniform on his arrival at the Royal Naval College, Dartmouth, in 1971

Opposite
For his 21st birthday picture, Charles chose to be at the controls of a Basset aircraft at RAF Oakington

Right
Father and son both in RAF uniform on the day of Charles's passing out ceremony at Cranwell in 1971

at Dartmouth, but I lacked that touch of professionalism which only comes after longer periods."

Despite his obvious talent and leadership qualities, he suffered periods of self-doubt. In one private letter to Lord Mountbatten, he wrote: "I've been made to work extremely hard since I set foot in this mighty vessel. I stumble around the ship, falling down hatches and striking my head against bulkheads in an effort to find my way about ... I have been 'thrown in at the deep end' in the most obvious manner ... I'm afraid that I tend to suffer from bouts of hopeless depression because I feel that I'm never going to cope." But he did not let his insecurities show and proved popular with his peers.

In the autumn of 1971, Charles was based ashore at Portsmouth for several weeks. He stayed, at the invitation of his great-uncle Lord Mountbatten, at Broadlands, the stately home of the Mountbattens in nearby Hampshire. By this time Mountbatten, now in his seventies, was quite prepared to spend as much time as was required helping his great-nephew develop into a man fit for kingship. At this time Charles took to referring to Mountbatten as "honorary grandfather" and Mountbatten responded by calling Charles "honorary grandson".

AN AFFAIR OF THE HEART

Mountbatten also became the young prince's confidant in matters of the heart. Among the young women in Charles's circle was Lucia Santa Cruz, a friend from Cambridge, who contacted the prince and said she had found "just the girl" for him and went on to make the arrangements for Charles to meet her – one Camilla Shand. Camilla was attractive and, crucially, shared Charles's sense of humour. Like him, she loved *The Goon Show* and Spike Milligan. She was individual, not too intense or serious, and smart.

> "I've been made to work extremely hard since I set foot in this mighty vessel ... I have been 'thrown in at the deep end' in the most obvious manner"

Below
Charles remains in the public eye during his six weeks of fast-track training at Dartmouth

Opposite
The Queen visits HMS *Norfolk* and is shown around by her son, in 1972

> "On his last evening, [the prince] was called upon to make a speech. When he finished, his fellow officers rose as one in a genuine, heartfelt standing ovation"

It wasn't long before Charles was smitten. He felt at ease with her and felt sure that she could be the friend that he would want to love and spend his life with. Even better, she seemed to have the same feelings for him. By the late autumn of 1972 they had become inseparable.

Camilla, while single and clearly fond of the heir to the throne, had previously been going out with a cavalry officer some nine years older than her, named Andrew Parker Bowles, who she had dated since she was 18. In the autumn of 1972, Parker Bowles was posted to Germany and it appeared to Camilla that the relationship was over. She therefore felt free to enter into a new relationship with the prince.

In the new year of 1973, Charles's next posting in the Royal Navy was due to separate them for eight months. In early December, he had joined his new ship, the frigate HMS *Minerva*, which was bound for the Caribbean in January.

Prior to sailing, he invited Camilla to make a tour of inspection and then have lunch on board. She returned the following weekend – "The last time I shall see her for eight months," he observed, sadly, in a letter to Mountbatten. But it was to be far worse than that. Andrew Parker Bowles and Camilla rekindled their relationship and became engaged in March 1973 – just two months after Charles had set sail. When the prince came to hear of this he was deeply upset. Andrew and Camilla wed in July 1973 in a large service that was attended by Princess Anne, Princess Margaret and the Queen Mother.

AIRBORNE ONCE MORE

Once in the Caribbean, Charles combined the roles of lowly junior naval officer and heir to the world's most famous throne. As a result, he was to attend scores of cocktail parties and, despite the "alcoholic haze", the prince navigated these diplomatic mazes with aplomb.

Opposite
With his helicopter flying instructor at the Royal Naval Air Station, Yeovilton, in 1974

Below left
Charles in 1975 on a military commando course as part of his Royal Navy training

Below right
The prince takes command on his first ship, HMS *Bronington*, based in Rosyth

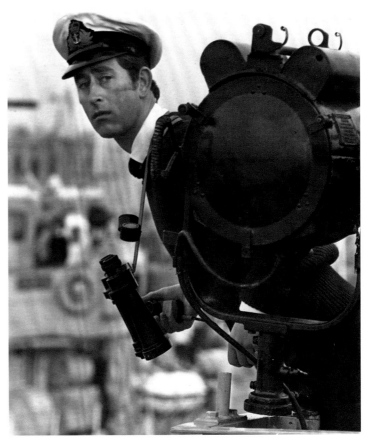

"On 9 February 1976, Charles took command of his first ship. 'The great and terrifying day had arrived at last', he recorded"

Charles's duties with the Royal Navy were becoming ever more varied and challenging, and in the autumn of 1974 he joined the Fleet Air Arm. After completing a helicopter conversion course in Yeovilton, Somerset, he was assigned to 845 Naval Air Squadron as a pilot on board the commando carrier HMS *Hermes*. There he was to spend the happiest four months of his naval career. He loved flying and, thanks mainly to Mountbatten, he had great affection for and loyalty to the Royal Navy.

He was duly assigned two helicopters, both with bright red nose- and tail-markings to denote that they were for his exclusive use and were to be maintained to the unique standards of the Queen's Flight. Once the Marines discovered this, Charles became their favourite pilot – hardly an endorsement of their confidence in the rest of the fleet's maintenance!

The prince was a naturally gifted pilot. Towards the end of his time on HMS *Hermes* he wrote: "I had more fun flying than I ever had before. The flying was extremely concentrated, but there was masses of variety and interest; troop drills, rocket firing, cross-country manoeuvres (day and night), low-level transits, simulated fighter-evasion sorties, parachute-dropping flights and commando exercises with the Marines. There were no interruptions from any other source and as a result I ended up Hog of the Month with about 53 hours in May!"

A CAPTAIN'S CALLING

Charles thought his next posting in the Royal Navy would be catastrophic, but Mountbatten assured him otherwise. On 9 February 1976, he took command of his first ship – the coastal minehunter HMS *Bronington* at Rosyth in Scotland. "The great and terrifying day had arrived at last," he recorded. "The whole prospect weighed heavily upon me as I drove across the Forth Bridge. There seemed so many things to worry about, particularly as I am not the sort of person who

is endowed with supreme self-confidence." For the next nine months the prince sailed his command, fulfilling the duties that concerned a minesweeper's modest role in the Royal Navy. He remained mindful that any slip-up would be seized upon by the press and lead to not only personal embarrassment, but also shame for the Royal Family.

No such incident emerged and with no disasters to report the press persisted with the prince's "action man" image. Having spent five years in the Royal Navy, the public's perception of the prince had been completely transformed from that of a shy young man to that of a services hero. Headlines in the press spoke to the nation of: "Fearless, Full of Fun Charlie", "The Get-Up-and-Go Prince Charles" and "Charles, Scourge of the Seas". This pleased the Palace, the Royal Navy, Mountbatten and, therefore, the prince. It may also have gratified his father, but if it did, it does not appear to have been recorded.

The Royal Navy's final report on Charles was written in December 1976 by Commander Elliott. "In spite of enormous outside pressure," it read, "Prince Charles has attained an excellent level of professional competence as a Commanding Officer. He has a natural flair and ability for ship handling and consequently his manoeuvres have been a pleasure to witness. Charles showed a deep understanding for his sailors, their families and their problems and as a result the morale of his ship has been of an extremely high order." There may have been better navigators and finer sailors in his generation, but, as a captain, Prince Charles was a natural.

On his last day, the officers and crew of his ship threw a lavatory seat around his neck and pushed him ashore in a wheelchair. As they proceeded down the quay at Rosyth, crews from every ship cheered as the prince waved farewell to an institution that had embraced him. He had come a long way from his bleak schooldays at Gordonstoun.

CHAPTER TWO

FAMILY LIFE

Marriage and fatherhood

Despite a picture-book wedding and the joy of fatherhood, Charles's first marriage went from fairy tale to acrimonious reality

It was described as "the wedding of the century" and a fairy-tale romance. But sadly it was to end in acrimony and, ultimately, tragedy.

Prince Charles married Lady Diana Spencer in St Paul's Cathedral on 29 July 1981, with Diana becoming Her Royal Highness the Princess of Wales. A global audience of 750 million watched as the Glass Coach, pulled by two bay horses, arrived at the steps of St Paul's Cathedral and Lady Diana Spencer, looking every inch the radiant princess, stepped out in her billowing bridal train. The pomp, pageantry and sheer spectacle of the occasion are unmatched to this day.

THE ROYAL WEDDING

Expectation had been building since the prince and "Lady Di" announced their engagement five months previously. More than £100 million in souvenirs had flooded onto the market. An estimated million people lined the wedding route from St Paul's to Buckingham Palace. Many had camped overnight and, on the eve of the wedding, had been treated to an extravagant pyrotechnic display in Hyde Park, set to Handel's *Music for the Royal Fireworks*. Charles had lit the first of 101 beacons and bonfires that blazed across the night's sky.

When, through loudspeakers, the crowd heard the Archbishop of Canterbury, Robert Runcie, sum up their hopes with the words "this is the stuff of which fairy tales are made – the prince and princess on their wedding day", there were huge cheers that continued until long after the newly married couple glided past in the 1902 State Landau towards Buckingham Palace. In all, the ceremony cost an estimated £600,000 – the most expensive in British history.

Diana Spencer came from an aristocratic lineage with long links to the Royal Family. She was born on 1 July 1961, at Park House on the Queen's estate at Sandringham, Norfolk, and lived there until the death of her grandfather, the 7th Earl Spencer, in 1975. It was then that the family moved to the Spencer family seat, Althorp, in Northamptonshire.

When the young Lady Diana was romantically linked with the prince, she immediately became the darling of the media. To the world, the marriage seemed to be a happy one. They had two sons: Prince William, born on 21 June 1982, and Prince Harry, on 15 September 1984.

Often consumed by work, Charles did not have the opportunity to spend as much time with the boys as he would have wanted. But he tried his best, sometimes spending time with his sons at Highgrove, their Gloucestershire country home, or Balmoral, the Queen's family estate in Scotland.

His sons revealed that Charles used to laugh "in all the wrong places" at their school plays and send them handwritten notes – apparently, his penmanship was so appalling that they couldn't tell if he was writing to praise them or to tell them off.

A BROKEN RELATIONSHIP

The couple became the most famous double act on the world stage. Titled the Prince and Princess of Wales, they went on overseas tours and carried out many engagements together in the UK. Diana's photograph was rarely off the front pages. But the princess's new-found fame brought with it tremendous stress and the return of a debilitating eating disorder.

Nobody outside the royal inner circle knew of the problems in the marriage. Charles sought professional help for his wife but it was all

Previous page
Charles and Diana outside St Paul's Cathedral after their momentous wedding ceremony, held on 29 July 1981

Right
Crowds of well-wishers line the streets as the fairy-tale wedding procession heads to Buckingham Palace

> "The couple became the most famous double act on the world stage ... they went on overseas tours and carried out many engagements together"

in vain. After the birth of Prince Harry, the marriage had irretrievably broken down and the couple began to live separate lives.

A book by Andrew Morton called *Diana, Her True Story* was published on 16 June 1992. Shrewdly, Diana had never met with its author face to face, which gave her plausible deniability. But it was clear to Charles and the Queen that Diana had colluded with the author, and the book proved damaging to both Charles and the Royal Family.

In the book, Diana depicted herself as a lamb to the slaughter on her wedding day – a 19-year-old virgin victimised by a bloodless cabal of royals. She exposed Charles's affair with his long-term love Camilla Parker Bowles, while choosing to ignore her own affairs with a string of suitors, including army officer Captain James Hewitt, who she later admitted she "loved and adored". In fact, Diana refused to take any blame for the collapse of her marriage to the prince or to acknowledge that her own behaviour had any impact on the doomed relationship.

On 9 December 1992, the Prime Minister, John Major, announced to the House of Commons that the Prince and Princess of Wales had agreed to separate. It took Charles two years to give his version, agreeing to an interview with heavyweight journalist Jonathan Dimbleby, whose accompanying biography had the full co-operation of the prince. This was an unprecedented move for a future king of England, and Charles, looking and sounding uncomfortable, admitted to cheating on Diana only after the marriage had "irretrievably broken down, us both having tried". But Charles couldn't win. The British public felt no sympathy for him; instead, they felt he had debased himself and the monarchy.

Diana retorted in 1995, granting a wide-ranging interview to the BBC journalist Martin Bashir. Dressed in a smart black suit,

"Often consumed by work, [Charles's] time with his sons was limited, but he tried his best, spending time with them at Highgrove or Balmoral"

Opposite
Charles and Diana with young princes Harry and William in a wildflower meadow at their country home, Highgrove, in 1986

Above
The prince and his sons on holiday together at Balmoral in the summer of 1997, shortly before Diana's death

eyes rimmed with kohl, Diana sought to blunt her own infidelity by volleying right back at Charles and Camilla. "There were three of us in this marriage," she said, damp eyes looking up from a bowed head. "So it was a bit crowded."

More than 25 million people watched the interview, which was announced on Charles's 47th birthday and aired on the Queen and Prince Philip's 48th wedding anniversary. In it, Diana also claimed to be a victim of Palace backstabbing and of orchestrated attempts to depict her as mentally ill, and a target of sinister plots to get her to "go quietly". In a twist of the knife, Diana claimed her husband wasn't fit for the British throne – his sole purpose in a life otherwise spent in purgatory. As for herself, Diana said she had no more humble aspiration than to be "a queen of people's hearts".

DIVORCE AND TRAGEDY

The couple divorced at the Queen's insistence in 1996, although the princess, as mother to the heir to the throne, was still regarded as a member of the Royal Family. She continued to live at Kensington Palace and to carry out her public work for a number of charities. Diana reinvented herself as a globetrotting humanitarian with a focus on sick children and landmines, and on meeting with the likes of Mother Teresa rather than movie stars – but still, she fought hard to retain her title.

In the summer of 1997, Diana allowed paparazzi to catch her on vacation with Egyptian playboy Dodi al-Fayed, although she was fresh out of a secret, two-year relationship with Hasnat Khan, a heart surgeon she called "the love of her life". She had even visited Khan's extended family in Pakistan in May 1996 – proof that she could live a private life when she chose.

When the princess was killed in a car crash in Paris on 31 August 1997, it fell on Charles to break the news to his young boys. "One of the hardest things for a parent to have to do is to tell your children that your other parent has died," Prince Harry said in a BBC documentary. "How you deal with that, I don't know."

Charles flew to Paris with Diana's two sisters to bring her body back to London. The princess lay in the Chapel Royal at St James's Palace until the night before the funeral. On the day, Charles accompanied his two sons, aged 15 and 12 at the time, as they walked behind the coffin from The Mall to Westminster Abbey. With them were the Duke of Edinburgh and the princess's brother, Earl Spencer.

In the weeks and months after Diana's death, the media came under much scrutiny, with many people blaming tabloid journalists and photographers for hounding the princess to death. Even today – despite those who knew Diana admitting that she used the press to cover her romance with al-Fayed, hoping to make Khan jealous – the prevailing narrative paints Diana as a pure victim, hounded by a soulless media consumed by its own prurient interests. Why couldn't we all just leave her alone?

The Prince of Wales asked the media to respect his sons' privacy to enable them to lead a normal school life. In the following years, William and Harry joined their father on a limited number of official engagements in the UK and abroad.

Although Prince Harry later questioned the decision that led him to participate in his mother's funeral procession as a 12-year-old, he did not hold his father at fault for what was undoubtedly a traumatic childhood experience. "[Our dad] was there for us," said Harry. "He was the one out of two left, and he tried to do his best and to make sure that we were protected and looked after."

A new chapter

Charles's marriage to Camilla, his future Queen Consort, in 2005 brought closure to the questions that had hounded the couple for many years

More than two emotionally turbulent decades after Charles had stood before the altar at St Paul's Cathedral and married Lady Diana Spencer, he made his vows to Camilla Parker Bowles. This time the ceremony was a civil one, in a room in Windsor Guildhall.

The church's involvement was not required for the legal ceremony, but given the monarchy's links with the established church – especially with Charles as the prospective Supreme Governor of the Church of England – the civil service was followed by a religious one of prayer and dedication. This took place at St George's Chapel, within the grounds of Windsor Castle, and was officiated by the sitting Archbishop of Canterbury, Dr Rowan Williams. Following the wedding, Camilla became known as Her Royal Highness The Duchess of Cornwall.

The couple were joined by around 800 guests and the service was followed by a reception at Windsor Castle hosted by the Queen. The date of the wedding coincided with the Grand National in which the Queen had a horse running, and she began her speech by saying she had two important announcements to make. The first was that Hedgehunter had won the race at Aintree; the second was that, at Windsor, she was delighted to be welcoming her son and his bride to the "winners" enclosure. "They have overcome Becher's Brook and The Chair and all kinds of other terrible obstacles," said the Queen. "They have come through and I'm very proud and wish them well. My son is home and dry with the woman he loves." There was hardly a dry eye in the house.

EARLY ROMANCE

The couple were originally introduced in 1971 by Charles's old university friend Lucia Santa Cruz, who was living in the apartment above Camilla's in London at the time. The prince was visiting Lucia and she invited Camilla up for a drink, believing she and Charles would hit it off. It was then that Lucia heard reference to the fact that Camilla's great-grandmother, Alice Keppel, had once been a mistress of Charles's great-great-grandfather, Edward VII, which amused them both. "Now, you two, watch your genes," she said with a smile, referring to their ancestors' adultery.

Charles recognised Camilla as a woman with the strengths needed to handle the job of being his royal partner. She was not fazed by him or his royal status, and by late autumn of 1972 they had become inseparable. Unfortunately for Charles, however, Camilla wasn't as devoted to him as he was to her. While extremely fond of the prince, she had previously dated cavalry officer Andrew Parker Bowles, nine years her senior, since she was 18 and was still captivated by him. When he was posted to Germany in 1972, she felt that the relationship was over for good and that she was free to enjoy her liaison with Charles.

But in the new year of 1973, Charles's new Royal Navy posting was to prove fatal for the romance. In early December, he had been assigned to the frigate HMS *Minerva* and he was due to sail on her to the Caribbean the following month. He would be gone for eight months. Camilla joined him on a tour of the ship before it sailed and they had lunch on board. She returned the following weekend and he bemoaned the fact that it would be "the last time I shall see her for eight months".

It would be much worse than that. Andrew Parker Bowles had returned, and Camilla and Andrew rekindled their relationship and became engaged in March 1973. It left the sensitive prince emotionally drained. He wrote to a friend that it seemed so cruel that fate should be this way. "Such a blissful, peaceful and mutually happy relationship ... I suppose the feelings of emptiness will pass eventually." Charles and Camilla remained friends and she became one of his most trusted confidantes.

"Given the monarchy's links with the established church, the civil service was followed by a religious one of prayer and dedication"

Opposite
The blessing at
St George's Chapel,
Windsor, following
the civil wedding for
the two divorcees

Above
Prince Charles and
his new wife Camilla,
who went on to be
named Queen Consort
in September 2022

When the Parker Bowles's first child, Tom, was born in 1974, Camilla asked the prince to be his godfather and he happily accepted. The intimacy between Charles and Camilla returned after the birth of Camilla's daughter Laura in 1978, and following the continued deterioration of her relationship with Andrew.

Camilla was drawn to the prince again and an adulterous affair ensued. She was not the first married woman to move in royal circles and have an affair, nor was she to be the last. Charles knew fully the dangers of conducting an affair with a married woman but was prepared to take the risk. He knew that, in time, he would have to marry a woman who was suitable to be his consort.

He was later to comment, "I've fallen in love with all sorts of girls and I fully intend to go on doing so, but I've made sure that I haven't married the first person I've fallen in love with. I think one's got to be aware of the fact that falling madly in love with someone is not necessarily the starting point to getting married. Marriage is basically a strong friendship, so I'd want to marry someone whose interests I could share."

A ROYAL ENGAGEMENT

The watershed moment on the so-called "Camilla question" came for Charles when he announced that his relationship with her was "non-negotiable". He laid down a marker in the late 1990s that sent a message not only to the general public but also to the mandarins at the Palace and to the Queen herself. He felt aggrieved at the way his "darling Camilla" was being treated and made it clear he was not going to go along with it.

"All my life people have been telling me what to do," he said when asked about his relationship with her in a 1998 interview with trusted journalist Gavin Hewitt. "I'm tired of it. My private life has become an industry. People are making money out of it. I just want some peace."

When I broke the world-exclusive story of the royal engagement of Charles and Camilla in the *London Evening Standard* – and, according to the prince's biographer and friend Jonathan Dimbleby, "bounced" Clarence House into issuing a formal announcement – the courtiers were ill-prepared. The wording of the statement that was released, long after the *Evening Standard* had broken the scoop, was simple enough. "It is with great pleasure that the marriage of HRH The Prince of Wales and Camilla Parker Bowles is announced," read the statement. "It will take place on Friday 8 April."

My inside source had been right on the money and we were both elated and relieved. In the weeks that followed, the extent to which my scoop had caught Charles's team off-guard was woefully apparent. My story marked the start of a torrid time for Clarence House officials, whose grasp on the finer and legal points of this royal wedding was exposed as being tenuous at best – if not altogether incompetent.

It started well enough. The ring, £100,000 worth of platinum and diamonds, had been a gift from the Queen. It was a 1930s Art Deco design, a central square-cut diamond with three smaller ones on either side, which had belonged to the Queen Mother and was one of her favourites. When asked how she felt, Camilla said she was just coming down to earth.

The Prime Minister sent congratulations on behalf of the government. The Queen and the Duke of Edinburgh were "very happy" and had given the couple their "warmest wishes". The Archbishop of Canterbury was pleased, too, that they had taken "this important step".

MEDIA RESPONSE

However, critical newspaper headlines soon followed. The legality of the marriage was called into question; the impossibility of a church wedding turned Camilla into the House of Windsor's first "town-hall bride"; and, for a while in the early spring of 2005, barely a day passed

Right
On overseas duties with the Queen and Prince Philip for the Commonwealth Heads of Government banquet in Kampala, Uganda, in 2007

"Camilla, through hard work and the fact that time heals, has cemented her place in the Royal Family in recent years"

Left
Harry and William with their father in Klosters in 2005 during a photocall in which they were quizzed about the upcoming marriage

Opposite
The prince and family attend the Braemar Gathering in 2006

without the revelation of some apparent monumental oversight or error on the part of Charles's team.

While they struggled to control the situation, they were also forced to address one key question they might rather have ignored: what did William and Harry think about their father marrying the woman who ostensibly helped break up their mother's marriage, a woman their mother loathed with a passion? William gave his blessing, saying that both he and Harry were "delighted" at their father's happiness. Privately, their mood was more of acceptance than undiluted joy at the prospect of having Camilla as a stepmother.

Charles, William and Harry faced down the press when their father was challenged in public at a prearranged photocall during a skiing holiday in Charles's favoured resort of Klosters, Switzerland. "How did he feel about the wedding?" a TV reporter asked. Charles knew the question was coming, as it had all been cleared with his communications team.

"Your Royal Highnesses," began the seasoned broadcaster Nicholas Witchell, shouting from behind the barrier separating the royals from the media. "It's eight days now to the wedding."

"You've heard of it, have you?" Prince Charles interrupted, with a fake smile. Caught a little off-guard, Witchell valiantly continued. "Can I ask how you are feeling and how, in particular, Princes William and Harry are feeling at the prospect of the wedding?"

"Very happy," replied Prince William. "It'll be a good day."

"And Prince Charles, how are you feeling?" continued Witchell after a second or two of silence.

"It's a very nice thought, isn't it?" said Prince Charles, eventually, without a smile, then added somewhat sarcastically, "I'm very glad you've heard of it, anyway."

With that, he turned his head slightly away and, in a very quiet aside aimed solely at his sons, added, "Bloody people. I can't bear that man. He's so awful. He really is."

Charles, who hadn't seen the microphones in the snow before he had spoken so loosely, had been unaware that his curmudgeonly remarks were being picked up. It was a gaffe more befitting of his father, Prince Philip, than the usually media-savvy and careful prince. It proved another low point in Charles's relationship with the British media. During the collapse of his marriage to Diana he had grown to loathe the cynicism of the tabloids for the blatant commercialisation of his personal misery.

A HAPPY UNION

As far as the Palace was concerned – and Charles, too – the marriage was a triumph. Camilla's deeply respected father, Major Bruce Shand, aged 88 at this time and ailing, stalled going to the doctor until after the wedding. He knew something was very wrong but was desperate to see his daughter, so often maligned, remarried.

The marriage was the beginning of the end of the "Camilla question" that had dogged the heir to the throne throughout his adult life. Camilla, through hard work and the fact that time heals, has now cemented her place in the Royal Family.

On the occasion of her official 90th birthday in 2016, the Queen chose to tidy up plans for her passing and elevated the duchess to her most senior advisory body, the Privy Council. It was, as ever, all done with the utmost discretion and showed the esteem in which Her Majesty held Camilla. It also pre-empted the duchess's subsequent elevation to the title of Queen Consort upon Charles's accession in September 2022.

CHAPTER THREE

THE
NEW
KING

Accession and proclamation

The death of Her Majesty The Queen was cause for mourning around the country and the world, and called for Charles to dedicate himself to his new role as the nation's sovereign

A longside a portrait of Queen Elizabeth II, an official statement on the Royal Family website, posted at 6.30pm on 8 September 2022, confirmed the sad news that the monarch had passed away. It read, "The Queen died peacefully at Balmoral this afternoon. The King and the Queen Consort will remain at Balmoral this evening and will return to London tomorrow." Her late Majesty's death certificate, made public later, officially recorded that she had died at 3.10pm, aged 96, of old age. It marked the end of the second Elizabethan era and the beginning of the reign of King Charles III, known as the Carolean age (so called because Carolus is Latin for Charles.)

The following day, our new king and his Queen Consort, Camilla, returned to Buckingham Palace, where the large, gathered crowd applauded and cheered him as he stepped from his car and went on an impromptu walkabout. Some people shouted, "God bless you Charles" and "God save the King", from which the grieving monarch seemed to take strength. One woman, a visitor from Cyprus, hugged and kissed him on the cheek. The royal couple then surveyed the flowers left in tribute to the Queen before walking onto the palace forecourt.

THE PROCLAMATION

At 10am on 10 September, Charles was officially proclaimed king before the Accession Council in the red-carpeted Throne Room at St James's Palace. The council, comprising around 670 senior Privy Counsellors, senior politicians, and Lords Spiritual and Temporal – bishops of the Church of England, including the Archbishop of Canterbury, and the secular peers of the realm – gathered to witness history unfold. The Lord Mayor of London, senior civil servants, and High Commissioners from the 14 other realms that have the monarch as their head of state also sat on the council, alongside the Prime Minister, Liz Truss, and the Lord President, Penny Mordaunt.

The King then read the proclamation, a historic act that was televised and broadcast live for the first time and watched by millions in the UK and around the world. "It is my most sorrowful duty to announce to you the death of my beloved mother, the Queen. I know how deeply you, the entire nation – and I think I may say the whole world – sympathise with me in the irreparable loss we have all suffered," he said in a short speech, witnessed by his wife, Camilla, and his son and heir, William. His pain of grief was etched on his face.

He went on, "It is the greatest consolation to me to know of the sympathy expressed by so many to my sister and brothers, and that such overwhelming affection and support should be extended to our whole family in our loss. To all of us as a family, as to this kingdom, and the wider family of nations of which it is a part, my mother gave an example of lifelong love and of selfless service.

"My mother's reign was unequalled in its duration, its dedication and its devotion. Even as we grieve, we give thanks for this most faithful life. I am deeply aware of this great inheritance and of the duties and heavy responsibilities of sovereignty which have now passed to me. In taking up these responsibilities, I shall strive to follow the inspiring example I have been set in upholding constitutional government and to seek the peace, harmony and prosperity of the peoples of these islands and of the Commonwealth realms and territories throughout the world."

Looking tired but determined, he continued, "In this purpose, I know that I shall be upheld by the affection and loyalty of the peoples whose sovereign I have been called upon to be and that in

Previous page
The King speaks during the proclamation on 10 September 2022 at the Accession Council in St James's Palace

Left
Crowds gather at the gates of Buckingham Palace upon hearing the news of Queen Elizabeth II's death

Opposite, top
From the palace, Charles delivers his first address as king to the nation and the Commonwealth

Opposite, bottom
The Queen Consort, Camilla, stands at her husband's side for the proclamation ceremony

the discharge of these duties, I will be guided by the counsel of their elected parliaments. In all this, I am profoundly encouraged by the constant support of my beloved wife.

"I take this opportunity to confirm my willingness and intention to continue the tradition of surrendering the hereditary revenues including the Crown Estate to my government for the benefit of all in return for the Sovereign Grant which supports the official duties as head of state and head of nations. And in carrying out the heavy task that has been laid upon me, and to which I now dedicate what remains to me of my life, I pray for the guidance and help of Almighty God."

The new King Charles III then made a separate and required oath relating to the Church of Scotland. "I understand that the law requires that I should, at my accession to the Crown, take and subscribe the oath relating to the security of the Church of Scotland," he said. "I am ready to do so at this first opportunity.

"I, Charles III, by the grace of God of the United Kingdom of Great Britain and Northern Ireland and of my other realms and territories, King, Defender of the Faith, do faithfully promise and swear that I should inviolably maintain and preserve the settlement of the true Protestant religion as established by the laws made in Scotland in prosecution of the Claim of Right and particularly by an act intituled 'An Act for securing the Protestant Religion and Presbyterian Church Government' and by the acts passed in the Parliament of both kingdoms for union of the two kingdoms, together with the government, worship, discipline, rights and privileges of the Church of Scotland. So help me God."

Clearly fatigued, his ill temper got the better of him for a split second, as he gestured to his Private Secretary, Sir Clive Alderton, to remove a box for his pen and an ink pot, a gift from his sons, from the small desk where he signed one of two copies of the proclamation documents.

A ROYAL RECEPTION

At 11am the Garter King of Arms, David Vines White, stepped out to a trumpet fanfare from the Friary Court balcony at St James's, with gun salutes fired in Hyde Park and at the Tower of London, and began the proclamation ritual. As is convention, a second proclamation would be read at the Royal Exchange in the City of London at 12pm and further proclamations took place over the coming days when the King travelled to Scotland, Wales and Northern Ireland.

In Belfast, the King, who had shown his steely resolve throughout, displayed signs of his fatigue and frustration once again, this time when signing the visitors' book at Hillsborough Castle. After being told that he had signed the wrong date, his fountain pen started to leak, causing him to complain, "Oh, God, I hate this [pen]." He then walked out of the room, rubbing ink from his fingers and mumbling, "I can't bear this bloody thing ... every stinking time." The Queen Consort calmed him, clearly aware of the pressure her husband was under.

On the death of the Queen, Charles was immediately King of the UK and 14 other realms, including Canada, Australia, New Zealand, Papua New Guinea and Jamaica, where separate ceremonies took place. In Australia, Charles III was proclaimed with hundreds of people lining the forecourt and streets around Parliament House, Canberra, to watch the formal ceremony before the Federal Executive Council where the Prime Minister, Anthony Albanese, recommended the accession to the Governor-General, David Hurley. Albanese said that there had been "an outpouring of grief" after the death of the Queen.

In Canada, at Rideau Hall, Ottawa, Governor General Mary Simon met with the Prime Minister, Justin Trudeau, surrounded by members of cabinet, to sign an order in council and a proclamation of accession that

"I am deeply aware of this great inheritance and of the duties and heavy responsibilities of sovereignty which have now passed to me"

Opposite
The funeral cortege, with Elizabeth II's coffin draped with the Royal Standard of Scotland, moves along the Royal Mile in Edinburgh

Above
Charles receives a warm welcome on his visit to Northern Ireland, part of his UK-wide tour following his accession to the throne

officially announced the Queen's death and proclaimed King Charles III as the nation's new monarch. "We … proclaim that His Royal Highness Prince Charles Philip Arthur George is now, by the death of our late sovereign, Charles III, by the grace of God with the United Kingdom, Canada and his other realms and territories, King," Canada's Chief Herald Samy Khalid read aloud followed by a 21-gun salute.

In New Zealand, the proclamation of Charles as monarch took place in the parliament in Wellington. The then Prime Minister, Jacinda Ardern, said the event acknowledged the Queen's son, "His Majesty King Charles III as our sovereign".

Ardern told a crowd that in the wake of the Queen's death, New Zealand had entered a time of change. "King Charles … has consistently demonstrated his deep care for our nation," she said. "This relationship is deeply valued by our people. I have no doubt it will deepen."

Elsewhere, in the Caribbean, the Queen's passing has focused the minds of politicians about the future, with some realms wanting to follow the example of Barbados and become a republic. Antigua and Barbuda have said it will hold a referendum on removing the monarchy in the next three years, as has the Bahamas. Despite this push from some realms to become republics, the monarchy's "soft power" helped deepen the respect and appreciation of many.

The process was repeated in all the Commonwealth realms with the Governor-Generals taking the lead. Elsewhere, from Gibraltar to the Antarctic, British Overseas Territories – all of which have the British monarch as head of state – marked Her Majesty's death and recognised the new King.

The Queen's death was marked with a 96-gun salute on Victory Green in the capital of the Falkland Islands, Port Stanley, where,

40 years earlier, Argentina surrendered to Major General Jeremy Moore, marking the end of the Falklands War.

Tristan da Cunha – a tiny volcanic island in the South Atlantic and one of the world's most remote settlements – was garrisoned by Britain in 1816 and is now home to 238 British citizens. Chief Islander James Glass paid tribute to the Queen after she "graciously welcomed" refugees from the island to Buckingham Palace in 1962, for which "her kindness will never be forgotten".

"Tristan da Cunha was the remotest inhabited part of her realm, but we proudly fly the Union Flag, and Queen Elizabeth's portrait in our Council Chamber inspired all our deliberations, reminding us of a life devoted to public service," he said, as her son and heir was recognised as the new monarch.

Back in London on 12 September, Charles addressed MPs from the Commons and peers from the House of Lords in Westminster Hall for the first time as monarch. In a poignant speech from the gilded lectern, he said his beloved mother had "set an example of selfless duty which, with God's help and your counsels, I am resolved faithfully to follow." He went on, "As Shakespeare said of the earlier Queen Elizabeth, she was a pattern to all princes living. As I stand before you today, I cannot help but feel the weight of history which surrounds us and which reminds us of the vital parliamentary traditions to which members of both Houses dedicate yourselves with such personal commitment, for the betterment of us all."

The King looked deeply emotional as the Speaker of the House of Commons, Sir Lindsay Hoyle, expressed his condolences, and said, "Deep as our grief is, we know yours is deeper." He also seemed close to tears as the hundreds of dignitaries then stood for the national anthem for the first rendition of *God Save the King* in 70 years.

Left
The King, his sister Anne and son William take part in the procession of the coffin from Buckingham Palace to the Palace of Westminster

Opposite, top
Floral tributes for the late Queen laid outside the Sandringham Estate in Norfolk

Opposite, bottom
The public queue to pay their final respects to the Queen who lies in state across the river in Westminster Hall

A NATION BIDS FAREWELL

The following day, the Princess Royal and her husband, Vice Admiral Sir Timothy Laurence, accompanied the Queen's coffin by hearse in the funeral cortege of seven vehicles on the 170-mile, six-hour long procession to Edinburgh from Balmoral Castle, where the coffin had been resting in the ballroom. Thousands of people packed the streets to watch it pass before it went on public view.

The convoy of cars made its way through the small village of Ballater in Deeside. On the way, Scottish farmers paid their respects by lining the procession route with dozens of tractors; some had their front loaders raised in salute as the Queen's coffin passed by them. After following a scenic route that also took in the River Forth and Edinburgh's Royal Mile, the coffin received a guard of honour as it entered the Palace of Holyroodhouse, the official residence of the monarchy in Scotland.

The following afternoon, a bagpipe lament was the only sound as kilted soldiers from the Royal Regiment of Scotland bore the casket from the palace. Then a gun salute boomed out from a battery on Edinburgh Castle as the hearse moved off, on its way up the Royal Mile. A single round was fired each minute of the procession as the royal party walked to St Giles's Cathedral, where the coffin would remain for 24 hours.

King Charles and his siblings, Anne, Andrew and Edward, held a silent vigil at the side of their mother's coffin as it lay at rest in Edinburgh's historic cathedral, with thousands queuing for hours to pay their respects to Britain's longest-serving monarch. With his head bowed, Charles, wearing a kilt, stood solemnly for ten minutes next to the oak coffin, which was draped with the Royal Standard of Scotland and had a wreath of white flowers and the Crown of Scotland on top of it. The late Queen's four children then left the cathedral to the reverential applause of those gathered.

Her late Majesty was subsequently taken from Scotland to England by RAF C-17 plane, accompanied by the Princess Royal and her husband. When the plane carrying her coffin landed at RAF Northolt in west London, her daughter Anne issued a moving tribute, saying she was "fortunate" to be able to share "the last 24 hours of my dearest mother's life", adding, "it has been an honour and a privilege to accompany her on her final journeys. Witnessing the love and respect shown by so many on these journeys has been both humbling and uplifting."

The state funeral of Elizabeth II, watched by an estimated 4.1 billion people globally, making it the biggest television audience in history, was held at 11am on Monday, 19 September at Westminster Abbey. The congregation of 2,000, including royals and their foreign cousins, presidents and prime ministers, was the largest gathering of world leaders in a generation, but among them were those selected by the Queen for their contribution to society.

Her late Majesty's coffin was then carried from the abbey by a gun carriage, passing an estimated two million well-wishers who had lined the streets as the cortege drove from London to Windsor. The final service, in St George's Chapel at Windsor Castle, was private, for members of the Royal Family only. There, Her Majesty joined her father, mother and sister Margaret. Prince Philip, whose casket had been in the Royal Vault since his funeral in 2021, was later moved to lie beside his wife in the chapel at her final resting place. The stone now reads, in list form, "George VI 1895– 1952" and "Elizabeth 1900–2002", followed by a metal Garter Star, and then "Elizabeth II 1926–2022" and "Philip 1921–2021".

King Charles's moment of destiny had arrived, and he rose to it.

Opposite
Pallbearers from the Grenadier Guards carry the Queen's coffin into Westminster Abbey, accompanied by the Royal Family

Right
The crowds gather along the Long Walk at Windsor Castle, before the Committal Service at St George's Chapel and private burial

The Coronation

King Charles III's crowning moment ushered in the new Carolean age with a blend of tradition and inclusivity befitting of a modern monarchy

It was a touching moment for father and son, one of love amid the pageantry and ritual of the time-honoured ceremony. After the 22-carat gold St Edward's Crown, weighing 2.23kg and decorated with 444 precious gemstones, had been placed upon The King's head by the Archbishop of Canterbury Justin Welby, Charles III glanced up at his heir, William, Prince of Wales, who had stepped forward. With pride in his eyes, the monarch quietly mouthed "Thank you" after his eldest son had sealed his coronation with a kiss on his father's cheek.

Resplendent in his Order of the Garter robe over his ceremonial Welsh Guards uniform, Prince William had knelt before his father, who sat on the Coronation Chair – also known as St Edward's Chair (the ancient wooden seat dating back to 1399, from which British monarchs are invested with regalia and crowned at their coronation) as his eldest son pledged his allegiance to him.

King Charles's second son, Prince Harry, watched on from the third row in Westminster Abbey, alongside his cousins Princess Beatrice and Princess Eugenie, as his estranged older brother declared before the congregation, "I, William, Prince of Wales, pledge my loyalty to you, and faith and truth I will bear unto you, as your liege man of life and limb. So help me God." Then he touched the crown. William, now first in line to the throne, had earlier helped his father put on the golden Supertunica coat as part of the two-hour ceremony, held before 2,300 guests and a global television audience of millions, who looked on as history unfolded before their eyes in a service that experts liken to "the king marrying the state".

HISTORY IN THE MAKING

The Coronation was steeped in 1,000 years of religious symbolism that incorporated several significant elements. Firstly, the Recognition entailed The King turning to each of the four points of the compass so he could be recognised as the true monarch: to the east, by the Archbishop of Canterbury; to the south, by Lady Elish Angiolini, a Lady of the Order of the Thistle; to the west, by Christopher Finney, a holder of the George Cross; and finally to the north, by Baroness Amos, a Lady of the Order of the Garter. After each made their declaration, the abbey audience replied, "God save King Charles."

The King was then presented with the new coronation *Bible*, which he kissed before taking the Oath, which included a new line in which he pledged to "foster an environment in which people of all faiths and beliefs may live freely". The most sacred and symbolic part of the ceremony took place behind screens, where The King removed his Robe of State before sitting in the Coronation Chair. Shielded from view, holy oil was then poured from the eagle-shaped ampulla into the 12th-century coronation spoon for the Archbishop of Canterbury to anoint King Charles on his "hand, breast and head".

At the outset, Charles had put on a red velvet surcoat – worn by his grandfather George VI at his coronation in 1937 – underneath the Robe of State, trimmed with lace and ermine. For the Anointing, he changed

Previous page
The King and Queen on the balcony of Buckingham Palace after the Coronation on 6 May 2023

Right
Members of the Armed Forces march along the ceremonial route from Westminster Abbey to Buckingham Palace

into a sleeveless, white linen *Colobium sindonis* (or "shroud tunic"), following which he donned the Supertunica and the coronation sword belt, called the Girdle. Lastly, The King was presented with his regalia – the 1661 gold spurs, then the jewelled Sword of Offering followed by a small velvet bag holding 100 newly minted 50 pence pieces featuring His Majesty. He was also presented with the armills, or bracelets, the coronation glove and the golden orb.

The homage, led by the Archbishop of Canterbury and William, ended the ritual. Each part of the Oath was framed as a question to The King, who, having answered, kissed the *Bible* and declared, "The things which I have here before promised, I will perform and keep. So help me God."

Outside the abbey, giant TV screens had been set up so that people could watch the proceedings. When Charles and Camilla emerged to cheers from the gathered crowd, they looked every inch a king and queen in the gold and red of their ceremonial regalia.

The Coronation had been carried out with military precision – not surprising, as it was the largest military ceremonial operation in 70 years. Across the UK, including at firing stations in Edinburgh, Cardiff and Belfast, gun salutes sounded to celebrate the historic moment. More than 400 personnel in 13 locations fired 21 rounds, apart from at the Tower of London and Horse Guards Parade, where a 62-round salute and a six-gun salvo were fired, respectively.

One thousand members of the Armed Forces lined The King's route from Westminster Abbey back to Buckingham Palace and another 6,000 service men and women took part, including representatives from some 35 Commonwealth countries. All the military personnel on parade proudly displayed The King's new cypher on their uniforms, featuring his initials, the reginal number

"…2,300 guests and a global television audience of millions looked on as history unfolded before their eyes in a service that experts liken to 'the king marrying the state'"

III and the Tudor Crown. This helped create a moment of historic and breathtaking splendour that will live long in the memory.

THE BUILD-UP

The eve of The King's coronation – the first to take place over a weekend since 1902 when Edward VII was crowned – was marked by a glittering Buckingham Palace reception. More than 1,000 guests, along with most senior members of the Royal Family, attended the event, which was more like an annual diplomatic reception than a state banquet – a mix of majesty, family and friends.

In the weeks before the big day, the "Harry" question had dominated the news pages of the national press. Would he snub his father's invitation? Would he be accompanied by his wife? What about the children? *The Daily Telegraph* reported that Harry had held "positive" peace talks with The King ahead of confirming he would be attending without his wife and family, although the relationship was said to still be strained. He did not, however, speak to Prince William, they claimed. It was reported, too, that he would not be sitting with the working royals but relegated to a seat with his York cousins three rows back.

Ahead of the coronation day, the media also seemed fascinated with Charles's apparent "levelling up" of the occasion with its planned inclusive ceremony and congregation making it "meritocratic not aristocratic". His decision to exclude many of the nation's nobles, along with their robes and coronets, would dilute one of the more colourful and moving aspects of previous coronations, it was argued by some. Financier Ben Goldsmith, whose grandfather the Marquess of Londonderry was a senior member of the aristocracy, was prompted to warn that Charles was at risk of giving in to "dullards and drips" by "watering down" his coronation. "Britain," he said, "does these kinds

"William led the nation's salute to King Charles III, with the message that, for his 'Pa', being king was all about serving his people"

Previous pages
The Diamond Jubilee State Coach carries the royal couple to the abbey, with the King's Guards lining The Mall

Above
Five-year-old Prince Louis, and Princess Charlotte, eight, on their grandfather's coronation day

Opposite
Wearing his Order of the Garter robe, the Prince of Wales arrives at the abbey with Kate, Louis and Charlotte

"The King was presented with his regalia – the 1661 gold spurs, the jewelled Sword of Offering, the armills, or bracelets, the coronation glove and the golden orb"

of celebrations so well, and they matter to a huge number of people, not just here but around the world."

When, at last, the day of the Coronation arrived, Saturday 6 May, the heavens opened. However, the rain didn't deter tens of thousands of loyal supporters from wanting to be part of history. From the early hours of the morning, people lined the route of the procession – many sporting red, white and blue outfits and waving Union flags and umbrellas – and waited patiently behind barriers. Some were given special treatment, with almost 4,000 veterans and NHS and social care workers invited to watch the Coronation from special viewing spaces in front of Buckingham Palace. In addition, some 350 uniformed Cadet Forces watched the procession from Admiralty Arch.

Away from the centre of London, the British public were still determined to enjoy a four-day "knees-up" holiday weekend, which included music concerts, street parties and afternoon teas. The nation embraced the milestone ceremony and lapped up all the tiny details that were drip-fed by the Palace communications department. The Pope, we were told, had even given The King two splinters of wood said to have been taken from the cross on which Jesus was crucified, which had been arranged in the shape of a cross at the centre of the Cross of Wales behind a rose crystal gemstone. Multifaith individuals were to attend, too, at His Majesty's behest.

The night before the Coronation, Great Britain's Chief Rabbi, Sir Ephraim Mirvis, who had been knighted by The King in January, and his wife stayed nearby at Clarence House as Charles and Camilla's guests to observe the Sabbath and be able to walk to the ceremony. Another first was the Welsh-language performance of Paul Mealor's "Coronation Kyrie", which was sung by bass-baritone Sir Bryn Terfel and the Westminster Abbey Choir in the main part of the service.

> "The King remained stern-faced but clearly moved by the experience. He was now truly wedded to his people"

Above
The future heir to the throne kisses his father on the cheek after Charles receives the St Edward's Crown

Opposite
Dressed in the golden Supertunica, The King bears the regalia used in coronations over the centuries

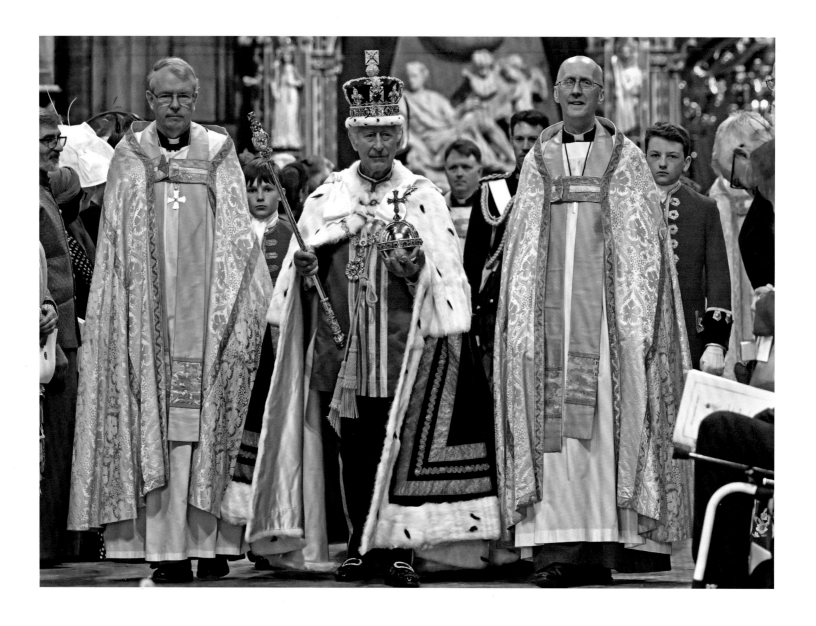

Above
The closing stage of the ceremony, at which The King now wears the Imperial State Crown and carries the sceptre and golden orb

Opposite
A final display of pomp and pageantry as the newly crowned king and queen return to Buckingham Palace in the Gold State Coach

"When Charles and Camilla emerged to cheers from the gathered crowd, they looked every inch a king and queen in the gold and red of their ceremonial regalia"

The Ascension Choir, a group of eight "handpicked" singers from the choir that performed at the Duke and Duchess of Sussex's wedding, was also chosen for The King's ceremony. Led by Abimbola Amoako-Gyampah, they sang "Alleluia (O Sing Praises)", becoming the first gospel group to perform in Westminster Abbey for a coronation.

As with every monarch since the coronation of King James II in 1685, the King's (or Queen's) Scholars of the Westminster School had the privilege of acclaiming the monarch by shouting "Vivat" during the monarch's procession from the Quire of Westminster Abbey towards the Coronation Theatre in front of the High Altar. The Latin version of the monarch's name was used – "Vivat, Rex!/Vivat, Rex Carolus!/Vivat! Vivat! Vivat!"

A RAPTUROUS RECEPTION

Throughout the deeply religious ceremony, which was steeped in centuries-old traditions, The King remained stern-faced but clearly moved by the experience. He was now truly wedded to his people. When the newly crowned king and queen returned to the palace and stepped onto the famous balcony, their relief was palpable. They, along with their family and the ceremony's pages, were given a rapturous reception as they acknowledged the crowds with a wave.

But one key figure chose not to join the party. Prince Harry did not return to the palace but instead made his way to Heathrow Airport to catch his return flight to Los Angeles. If the royal rift was to heal, it was for another time.

Back at the palace, the Royal Family and their guests enjoyed a post-ceremony lunch. The King, the Queen and the royal party posed for official photographs taken by the French-born Hugo Burnand, a royal favourite who Charles and Camilla had commissioned previously to

"The following day at the Coronation Concert, it was clear just how determined the British Royal Family is to remain a relevant force for good in the modern age"

Above
Katy Perry performs at the star-studded Coronation Concert, held in the grounds of Windsor Castle

Opposite, top
VIPs, politicians and dignitaries watch the concert from the royal box alongside the Royal Family

Opposite, bottom
Some of the 20,000 concert-goers in front of the stage, with the castle a backdrop to a special lightshow

"When the newly crowned King and Queen returned to the palace, they, along with their family and the ceremony's pages, were given a rapturous reception as they acknowledged the crowds with a wave"

Previous pages
A balcony appearance
at the palace for close
members of the Royal
Family and those
who took part in the
coronation ceremony

Opposite
Pages of Honour (from
left to right) Lord Oliver
Cholmondeley, Prince
George, Nicholas
Barclay and Ralph
Tollemache

Above
King Charles III
emerges to wave
to the crowds from
the balcony, with his
reign marking a new
Carolean age

chronicle their wedding. Queen Camilla wore Queen Mary's Crown and posed with the train of her lengthy embroidered Robe of Estate spread in front of her. In a sweet detail, Camilla's Bruce Oldfield-designed coronation gown paid tribute to her two Jack Russells, who were honoured in gold thread. The white fabric was intricately embellished with other designs, including a variety of flowers and the names of her grandchildren. The floral stitching was a tribute to her husband, incorporating garlands and leaves in honour of the couple's mutual love of the great outdoors.

After many months of planning, led by the Duke of Norfolk, Edward Fitzalan-Howard, the Earl Marshal, the first coronation to take place in Britain for 70 years was over as The King ushered in the new Carolean age.

CELEBRATING A NEW ERA

The following day at the Coronation Concert in Windsor, which featured performances from pop stars including Katy Perry, Lionel Ritchie and Take That, it was clear just how determined the British Royal Family, led by King Charles, is to remain a relevant force for good in the modern age. The night's sky was lit up by a spectacular lightshow against the backdrop of Windsor Castle to the delight of the crowd. When William, Prince of Wales addressed his sovereign and the 20,000 attendees lucky enough to get a ticket for the concert, it felt that the monarchy was in safe hands.

William led the nation's salute to King Charles III, with the message that, for his "Pa", being king was all about serving his people. Up in the royal box alongside Queen Camilla and family, Charles acknowledged the crowd with a broad smile.

On the final day of the long weekend of celebrations, Prince Louis turned into a labourer as he joined Prince George, Princess Charlotte and the Prince and Princess of Wales shovelling dirt and operating a digger as they helped at a Scout hut in Slough as part of the national volunteering drive to mark the Coronation. The King hoped "The Big Help Out", as the initiative was called, would create a volunteering legacy, inspiring the public to become involved in their communities throughout the summer.

When it was all over, official photographs of The King in full regalia were issued to the media, along with a written message. It said that he and Queen Camilla gave their "most sincere and heartfelt thanks" to "countless people" who helped make coronation celebrations across the UK a success. They also rededicated their lives "to serving the people of the United Kingdom, the Realms and Commonwealth". The warmth of the people had touched him deeply.

From now on The King's focus, sources close to him say, is on making the monarchy fit for purpose over the next five years. He is working closely with his son and heir William to achieve this. Gone, too, is that sense that he has something to prove. Now the paterfamilias of "the firm", he is no longer in the shadow of his late mother's mystique or his father's dominant personality. The decisions are coming from him; and he is slowly but surely shaping the institution he leads with pride.

CHAPTER FOUR

THE GLOBAL LEADER

The Commonwealth

As the Head of
the Commonwealth,
King Charles is a firm
believer in channelling
the combined strength of
the "family of nations"
for the common good

Previous page
King Charles delivers his first Commonwealth Day message in March 2023 from the pulpit of Westminster Abbey

Above
Charles attends the opening ceremony of the Commonwealth Heads of Government Meeting in Rwanda, 2022

Left
A procession of flags from member states form part of the annual Commonwealth Day celebrations

Opposite
Charles and Camilla host dignitaries from across the Commonwealth at Buckingham Palace

nside Westminster Abbey, King Charles III took to the Great Pulpit on his first Commonwealth Day as the head of the international organisation and paid tribute to Queen Elizabeth II's pride in the "family of nations". Speaking in front of the congregation of 2,000, he described the Commonwealth as a force for good in areas such as climate change and biodiversity loss, as well as in economic co-operation and health.

Charles, who succeeded his mother as Head of the Commonwealth and 56 independent nations, and as king of 14 realms including the UK, spoke of how the voluntary association of nations promotes "tolerance, respect and solidarity". And whereas his mother chose not to speak at the annual celebration, instead having her words appear in the event programme, Charles decided to share his message in person, perhaps aware that his soundbite would get much more traction if it could be shown in TV news bulletins across the Commonwealth.

With limited opportunities available to speak out publicly on the issues that really matter to him, The King did not waste his chance. After receiving a traditional New Zealand Maori greeting of touching noses on his arrival at the service, he made an impassioned speech in which he highlighted the association of nation's "indispensable role in the most pressing issues of our time".

A COMMON PURPOSE

He drew on the Commonwealth Day theme for 2023 – "Forging a Sustainable and Peaceful Common Future" – and stressed the organisation's core values, from "peace and justice" to "care for our environment", all embodied in the Commonwealth Charter, which was signed a decade ago.

"Whether on climate change and biodiversity loss, youth opportunity and education, global health or economic co-operation, the Commonwealth can play an indispensable role in the most pressing issues of our time," he said. "Ours is an association not just of shared values, but of common purpose and joint action. In this we are blessed with the ingenuity and imagination of a third of the world's population, including one-and-a-half-billion people under the age of 30. Our shared humanity contains an immensely precious diversity of thought, culture, tradition and experience. By listening to each other, we will find so many of the solutions that we seek."

The King sees the Commonwealth, which covers almost 21 per cent of all land masses and more than 33 per cent of the population on the planet, at around 2.6 billion individuals, as a voluntary association that can make a real difference. The Commonwealth is made up of independent member countries, almost all of which were formerly under British rule. And while the role of heading it up is a purely symbolic one that carries no formal powers, during the twilight years of her reign, the Queen worked quietly behind the scenes to ensure that Charles succeeded her on her passing. It was a position and responsibility that she cherished and that, in the eyes of many, is perhaps her greatest legacy.

A WEALTH OF EXPERIENCE

Since 1969, Charles has visited 45 Commonwealth countries. Even before leaving the military in 1976, Charles stepped up and toured Australia and New Zealand with the Queen, the Duke of Edinburgh and Princess Anne. He made solo visits to Fiji's centenary celebrations in 1974 and, the following year, represented the Queen at the independence celebrations of Papua New Guinea.

"There was little doubt, after years of tireless and distinguished service, that few were better qualified for the important role of Head of the Commonwealth"

Opposite
With Indian Prime
Minister Indira Gandhi
in New Delhi in 1980,
on one of his early
visits to India as prince

Above
Immersed in local
culture at a temple
in Penang, Malaysia,
during the South East
Asia tour in 2017

His foreign forays increased after his active military service ended, and he visited the 1976 Olympics in Montreal, Canada, along with other members of the Royal Family, to see his sister Princess Anne compete in the three-day equestrian event on the Queen's horse Goodwill. In 1977, the year of the Queen's Silver Jubilee, Charles made solo visits to Kenya, Ghana, Ivory Coast, Canada and Australia, following which visits to Commonwealth nations around the globe on behalf of the Queen would become a core part of his work.

Over the past 10 years, Charles has led the charge for member island states that face being wiped out by a rise in sea levels with his Blue Economy initiative, which presents a sustainable approach to the conservation of marine ecosystems in a way that drives economic growth and supports coastal communities. In growing the Blue Economy, he hopes to combat poverty and accelerate prosperity in these under-threat regions.

Recent years also include the major, 11-day Commonwealth tour to South East Asia in 2017. Taking in Singapore, Brunei, Malaysia and India, Charles attended nearly 50 engagements that showcased the breadth and depth of the UK's relationship with those key Commonwealth partners. Speaking to an assembly of Malaysia's leaders about the challenges of climate change, urban overpopulation and the threat to the world's oceans, he said that "for the resolution of all these issues, the Commonwealth should, and does, have a pivotal role to play.

"Representing a third of the world's population and a fifth of its landmass," he added, "it can draw on a uniquely wide range of national contexts, experiences, traditions and, above all, professional associations – something, of course, which makes the Commonwealth unlike anything else in the world – for the solutions that we all so desperately need now."

STEPPING UP

There was little doubt, after years of tireless and distinguished service, that few were better qualified for the important role of Head of the Commonwealth. On 19 April 2018, as Her late Majesty spoke at the official opening of the Commonwealth Heads of Government Meeting (CHOGM) at Buckingham Palace, she spelled out for the first time her hopes for the future of the Commonwealth and offered her support to her son in the role.

She made her position clear to the Commonwealth leaders attending the London and Windsor summit. "It is my sincere wish that the Commonwealth will continue to offer stability and continuity for future generations," she told the assembly, "and will decide that one day the Prince of Wales should carry on the important work started by my father in 1949."

Her words galvanised the world leaders to push through their decision. "We are certain that, when he will be called upon to do so, he will provide solid and passionate leadership for our Commonwealth," Joseph Muscat, the Prime Minister of Malta, said of the prince in response to the Queen's address. Later that day, Malcolm Turnbull, the Australian Prime Minister, confirmed that his country "strongly supports the continuation of the king or queen of the United Kingdom as the Head of the Commonwealth … Prince Charles in time will succeed his mother."

Speaking to the media, Justin Trudeau, the Canadian Prime Minister, said, "I very much agree with the wishes of Her Majesty that the Prince of Wales be the next Head of the Commonwealth." Ralph Regenvanu, the foreign minister of the Pacific state of Vanuatu, concurred, "We see it almost naturally that it should be the British Royal Family, because it is the Commonwealth, after all."

"Through the unprecedented global challenges of these past seven decades, the Commonwealth remains as vital today as it has ever been"

Opposite
In Brunei, on a leg of the 2017 South East Asia tour, Charles attends a reception with members of the Gurkha community

Above
The Queen and her son arrive for the opening of the Commonwealth Heads of Government Meeting in 2018 in Buckingham Palace

The next day, Charles took another step closer to the chalice when Commonwealth leaders backed the Queen's "sincere wish" to recognise that her heir, the Prince of Wales, would one day succeed her as the next Head of the Commonwealth. Theresa May, the British Prime Minister at the time, announced the decision after private deliberations among Commonwealth leaders at Windsor Castle. When the formal announcement was made, Charles was typically self-effacing. "I am deeply touched and honoured by the decision of Commonwealth heads of state and government that I should succeed the Queen, in due course, as Head of the Commonwealth," he responded. "Meanwhile, I will continue to support Her Majesty in every possible way, in the service of our unique family of nations.

"The Commonwealth has been a cornerstone of my life for as long as I can remember," he continued, "and, through all the unprecedented global challenges of these past seven decades, it seems to me that the Commonwealth remains as vital today as it has ever been."

Leaders of the Commonwealth nations said, however, that the decision to make a hereditary appointment was a one-off and that the ruling did not apply to Charles's direct heirs, Prince William and Prince George, who will not be automatically in line to hold the office. They decided it would remain a non-hereditary position.

RENEWED RELEVANCE

A year later, in March 2019, Charles backed his words with action when he embarked on a major tour of Caribbean Commonwealth realms, as well as a historic visit to communist Cuba, the first by a British royal. Speaking at an open-air event in St Lucia on the first stop of his 12-day tour, Charles said the Commonwealth was "as vital as ever". This was, of course, a thinly veiled reference to Britain's post-Brexit prospects.

Three years later, in a speech to Commonwealth leaders in Rwanda, Charles spoke of the importance of acknowledging the past and his "personal sorrow" at the suffering caused by the slave trade. It was up to individual states to decide whether to remain monarchies or became republics, he added.

There will be questions about whether the Commonwealth will remain such an important diplomatic priority for Britain during Charles's reign. But his first Commonwealth Day service address acknowledged the strength of bringing together the different cultures within the Commonwealth. "By listening to each other," he said, "we will find so many of the solutions that we seek."

For Charles, being Head of the Commonwealth is not about applauding past successes but galvanising the modern association of nations to play a vital role in building bridges between countries, fairer societies within them, and a more secure world around them. It is a fundamental feature of his life, and those close to him say he hopes his role will unlock the "extraordinary potential" of the Commonwealth and enable member states not only to revitalise the bonds with each other, but also to give the Commonwealth a "renewed relevance to all citizens", finding practical solutions to their problems and giving life to their aspirations. That way, he believes, the Commonwealth will be a cornerstone for the lives of future generations.

The King summed up his commitment to the Commonwealth and what it can achieve in his 2023 Commonwealth Day address. "The myriad connections between our nations have sustained and enriched us for more than seven decades," he said. "Our commitment to peace, progress and opportunity will sustain us for many more. Let ours be a Commonwealth that not only stands together, but strives together, in restless and practical pursuit of the global common good."

Zenith of success

Zenith Bank was founded on the principle that technology could transform banking, and the company's rapid success has proved this maxim right

The title of Jim Ovia's autobiography says it all: *Africa, Rise and Shine*. Part-memoir, part-business guide, it tells the story of Ovia's huge success with Zenith Bank, which he founded in 1990 and rapidly turned into one of the largest banks in Africa. Zenith was one of the first to embrace digital banking and continues to act as a pioneer today, becoming the first Nigerian bank to set up a branch in London.

"We started in 1990 when I was a young man in my thirties," says Ovia. "We are successful because planning is done very efficiently. Discipline has also been important. To be successful, you have to be disciplined, you have to respect the rule of law, and you have to be consistent in your discipline. You need to respect the rules and regulations of the environment wherever you operate. We had to go through a very tough process to obtain a licence to operate in the UK and become the first Nigerian bank to achieve a licence to practise in London. When we came to the UK, we knew there was a very strict legal system, so we worked very carefully and respected that system."

There was something meaningful about Zenith's appearance in London. It was born into a Nigerian banking system that was still dominated by the old European and American banks – and now a triumphant Ovia was taking his thriving, exciting young bank back to England. Part of Zenith's success was down to the fact that Ovia understood the flaws of the old banks. An alumnus of Harvard Business School, he had worked at the International Merchant Bank in Lagos, a subsidiary of what was then called the First National Bank of Chicago. That gave Ovia the confidence, insight and contacts to strike out on his own. He developed a strategy and then wrote a feasibility study that he sent to potential investors, raising the required $4 million and obtaining a licence from the federal government.

That strategy was based on Ovia's insight that customers wanted something new from banking that modern technology was able to provide. "You need to look at global standards, what the business

"It was also easy to win over customers, who loved the new technology we were using"

imperatives are," says Ovia. "People are discussing fintech and mobile banking, so you need to understand what society needs. Nobody wanted to go to a branch to do a transaction, they wanted to bank with their mobile phone. It was very clear that individuals would prefer to do banking in their homes using their own computers without physically having to go into a banking hall. We knew that was the way forward and it allowed us to grow very quickly. We introduced digital technology to Nigeria – the older generation of banks did not understand technology and the internet and they were reluctant to learn. We saw that things were changing."

Ovia founded Zenith with three principles in mind: people, technology and service. He believed it would be a success if it had good initiatives, exceptional customer service and was driven by IT. This was revolutionary at a time in Nigeria when most banks were still using ledgers and requiring customers to make an appointment if they wished to make a deposit or see their balance. "From the moment we started, we never used paper and pen," explains Ovia. "We used computers for all our transactions and that immediately gave us an edge. There were very big banks in Nigeria, but they were not digitalised, they were analogue, so it was easy for us to scale up with our computerisation and digital technology. It was also easy to win over their customers, who loved the new technology we were using."

This meant customers no longer had to spend much time on transactions at the bank. It also freed up valuable time for staff to provide customers with exceptional service. The transparency, control and ease of use Zenith gave customers exceeded anything else available. The bank took Nigeria by storm at Civic Tower, Lagos (pictured on the previous page) and with its Lagos head office (opposite, above). It expanded with branches in Ghana, Sierra Leone and The Gambia, as well as in London, UK (opposite, below), the United Arab Emirates and China. "We were able to leapfrog our rivals by becoming computerised when the older banks were still expecting their customers to come to the branch," says Ovia. "We wanted to use digital technology. This was very forward-thinking, but it was what our customers wanted."

Ovia also has a personal connection to the UK. "It is an important market for us, and we employ staff in the UK and pay taxes, so we are invested in that economy," says Ovia. "My children were educated in the UK, so I have benefitted from the environment and am pleased to contribute in terms of employment and tax. It is a symbiotic relationship."

The success of Zenith has seen it receive a string of awards over the years, including 2022's Best Commercial Bank in Nigeria at the World Finance Banking Awards, and has allowed Ovia to invest in his belief in a sustainable society, one that supports those who need it most. The Bank has undertaken social responsibility initiatives in line with the UN's Sustainable Development Goals to help eradicate poverty and encourage skills development and employment. This has included the donation of ten mobile cancer centres and the building of a healthcare centre to meet the primary healthcare needs of Lagos residents, while the Jim Ovia Foundation offers scholarships to indigent students and has built and renovated learning institutions, IT centres and science laboratories. Zenith's Adopt-a-School initiative, meanwhile, has targeted primary and secondary schools in Nigeria with the donation and renovation of classroom blocks, providing laboratories, computers and accessories, power-generating sets and libraries.

Alongside these social investments, Zenith Bank is committed to using its financial products to help SMEs grow – supporting and nurturing a new generation of Nigerian entrepreneurs and demonstrating the vast potential of the African continent.

www.zenithbank.com

Call of duty

Barker College in Australia nurtures
its students to become responsible
citizens – creators of the future rather
than consumers

The first thing new arrivals to Barker College glimpse are its resplendent mint-coloured gates. Made of twisted wrought iron, they have become symbolic for this co-educational independent school on the outskirts of Sydney, Australia – a constant reminder for the faculty and student body of the sense of possibility inherent in the act of teaching. "Our purpose," says the school's Head, Phillip Heath AM, "is to look outwards and beyond ourselves and try to do a good and important thing in the world – and to do that without arrogance."

Duty is central to that sense of mission at Barker College, which was founded in 1890. This is evidenced most literally by the school's war memorial chapel, built in 1957 to commemorate the 60 alumni who lost their lives in the Second World War, but also in the daily exhortation to the student body to make a meaningful contribution to the world. That is what distinguishes the ethos of Barker College from so many other independent schools in Australia and beyond. "We want to deliberately and intentionally put our students in connection with the world and its most important issues, namely sustainability, climate, ecology and responsible citizenship," says Heath.

The school's edge, he says, lies in its culture of kindness, of excellence without arrogance and a purposeful connection to some of the more profound questions of life. "These questions, of personal responsibility, of duty to country and our natural environment, cannot be left to other people, much less the state, to fix. We want our students to become creators of the future, not its consumers – and that's a goal that's built into everything we do, inside the classroom and out."

Above all, that means respecting Aboriginal and Torres Strait Islander peoples, principles that are inculcated in the students and the institution itself. "We want to open our arms to people who cannot otherwise afford to be here," says Heath. Under his tenure Barker College set up three Indigenous school campuses, two of which are in New South Wales: Darkinjung Barker in Wyong, which opened in 2016 in partnership with the Darkinjung Local Aboriginal Land Council; and Ngarralingayil Barker in Wollombi, which opened in 2020 and works with the Kiray Putjung Aboriginal Corporation. In the Northern Territory, Dhupuma Barker opened in 2021 as a bilingual primary school for Yolŋu children from the Gunyangara community in North East Arnhem Land.

Many students of these campuses show a flair for robotics, with the Dhupuma Barker students becoming the first Yolŋu team to enter a robotics competition and the first Northern Territory team to compete nationally and at the 2023 World Robotics Championship in Dallas, Texas. "We're launching our own robotics experience and competition in Arnhem Land," says Heath. This is especially important, he adds, as the region becomes a hive of activity for Australia's nascent satellite launch industry. "They need young people with the skills in automation and robotics who are local to that part of the world. It's a win-win."

While the college has its traditions, it has thrived for more than a century precisely because it has embraced the world beyond its mint gates. "We want to remain loyal to our own heritage and celebrate that without shame or regret," says Heath. "But there's no future in the past. And so, we must find a new story, for a new generation."

www.barker.college

The big issues

A global financial-services big hitter, the British Virgin Islands is also punching above its weight when it comes to climate change

The archipelago of the British Virgin Islands (BVI) is around 60 square miles in size, which makes the jurisdiction similar in area to a city such as San Francisco – but with a total population of just over 30,000, it is more in keeping with one of that city's suburbs. Despite such tiny dimensions, the BVI manages to wield an outsized influence on the world stage thanks to its position as an international finance centre for four decades.

This status has allowed the BVI to develop a global reputation, which it can leverage into impactful conversations on subjects that affect the entire planet. One such issue is climate change – and the most recent climate shock to affect the BVI itself came in 2017, when Hurricane Irma damaged 80 per cent of the buildings in the jurisdiction.

"When it comes to climate change and other areas that concern King Charles, we have had direct experience of the consequences," says Elise Donovan, CEO of BVI Finance, the organisation responsible for the marketing, promotion and brand reputation management of

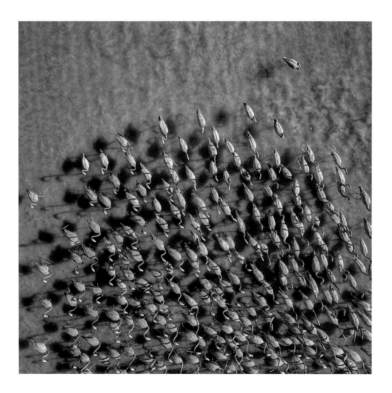

the BVI's financial services. "We are very resilient as a people, and our financial services industry survived Hurricane Irma just as we survived Covid. We were able to survive and thrive."

When the BVI became an international finance centre in 1984, it placed this Caribbean jurisdiction at the heart of globalisation. It has since developed a vast international network, with BVI companies recognised as dependable, efficient, transparent and responsible legal vehicles to facilitate cross-border trade, investment and finance.

There are more than 375,000 active BVI businesses with a combined estimated value of $1.4 trillion in assets, conducting business in markets all over the world, including a significant presence in Latin America, Europe, China and the rest of Asia. Hundreds of trained experts in BVI law and legislation work in these host markets to ensure the smooth and reliable execution of business. The BVI also offers efficiency and ease of business, with a collective capacity to enhance financial stability and confidence while supporting prosperity and employment across the world. "We are very experienced and one of the most advanced nations at having a global understanding of what a business requires to facilitate globalisation," says Donovan.

As a result of this, the BVI wields a disproportionate impact, punching well above its weight. Using the BVI gives businesses security, but only because the BVI maintains a careful balance between international regulatory standards and innovation. This creates trust and demonstrates responsibility. By ensuring transparency and delivering a level playing field, the BVI has been able to contribute to international debate on subjects from tax and banking to money laundering. It can also use its global standing to increase understanding and decision-making around environmental issues.

"There is a place for our jurisdiction as an international finance centre, but also as a country and a people with experience of the climate issue when looking at areas of environmental and social governance," says Donovan. "These are important issues for King Charles, and they are certainly aligned with the priorities of the BVI. We want to serve as a model for sustainability, inclusivity and innovation. These are complex issues that will require complex solutions, and the BVI has that experience as part of a global ecosystem. We want to be part of the next phase in the conversation around climate."

www.bvifinance.vg

Bringing power to people

Harnessing the power of water, Aslan Renewables is bringing energy to communities on Prince Edward Island, with sights set on the world

On Canada's Prince Edward Island, a renewable energy revolution is under way that is returning hydroelectric power to local people. Andrew Murray, founder and CEO of Aslan Renewables, is leading the march.

"When people think of hydro power, they tend to think of huge hydroelectric plants," says Murray. "But imagine a hydro generator that could simply be put in a container and shipped to a small community anywhere in the world, along with the instructions to install and operate it themselves. That's the Aslan approach."

Aslan is pioneering sustainable hydroelectric solutions on the island's waterways. It has developed a scalable modular concept that can be tailored to the environment, ecology, waterway, flow rates and energy requirements of the installation location.

Aslan's generators can harness energy from rivers and tidal waterways, as well as from wastewater from industrial sites, waste processing and agriculture. They can be used anywhere in the world with sufficient running water and a drop in height to power the generator. Costing from just £50,000, they can power around 30 homes, a business, or a facility such as a school or hospital.

The idea came to Murray when he realised there were many abandoned hydroelectric dams across Canada. "While everyone was thinking global and looking to the future for renewable energy solutions," he says, "I realised the answer could lie in the past." Historically, watermills powered industry, then towns developed around those mills. "Not only did the mills provide a proof of concept for hydro power, but those riverside towns are still there today, in a prime position to utilise hydro power again. All that is needed is a little modern innovation and community spirit – that's where Aslan comes in.

"Some of our first hydro dams were developed for use on crown land so we have always met the highest environmental standards," he continues. Aslan undertook extensive environmental consultations and worked with indigenous groups to fully understand the ecology of the rivers. Local university students and businesses helped with the design and manufacturing, "so the concept evolved within the community, for the community. Having proven our concept here in Canada, we are now ready to help power – and empower – other communities all over the world."

www.aslanrenewables.com

A new way to pay

Malta-based fintech Finance Incorporated Limited has woven together the best digital technologies to help transform financial services electronically

"We were one of the first to sign the Terra Carta and the only one so far in Malta," says Cenk Kahraman, CEO of Maltese financial transaction experts Finance Incorporated Limited (FIL). It is clear the company takes its social responsibility seriously, the Terra Carta being the guiding mandate for the Sustainable Markets Initiative created by King Charles to provide a set of principles for the private sector to put "nature, people and planet at the heart of global value creation".

The 70-strong team, says Kahraman, is "multitalented and driven to create really good, innovative tech". FIL's products and services, rival to Revolut, PayPal and other financial technology companies, can be tailored to individual, corporate and institutional clients and is the basis of an infrastructure that can process transactions with enormous scalability, undertaking more payments than any EMI (electronic money institution) in Malta.

"When we started to change Finance Incorporated Limited, what connected the team was the desire to do things well," says Kahraman, who joined the firm in 2017. "There is a difference between running a company well and running a good company. We wanted to do both. We look at the markets we serve and attempt to do right by them in every way possible and we look at the products that we deliver to our customers with the intent of making their lives better – wherever and whenever they make a transaction."

As the business expands – with plans to enter mainland Europe and the UK – FIL is taking steps towards becoming carbon neutral, which the company aims to achieve by summer 2025. "We are keen to make environmental, social and corporate governance a foundational matter. This means that we go beyond sponsoring the odd activity here and there. We make decisions at every level, taking into account the needs of all stakeholders."

Happiness in the workplace is also a key performance indicator at FIL. "Early on, we made a commitment to each other," says Kahraman. "We decided we would look out for everyone, develop the team in a nurturing way and accept each other's differences so that the company would ultimately grow into a model for the world we want to see."

www.financeincorp.com

On the money

With her community-building fintech startup, Herconomy, Ife Durosinmi-Etti
is empowering Nigerian women to gain financial independence and thrive

Like most women signed up to her female-focused fintech startup, Herconomy, Ife Durosinmi-Etti started out with nothing – just a big idea. "I was so broke after leaving my job, I had to take money from my pension to keep afloat. But something inside me said, 'Stick with it'," says the author, entrepreneur and Young Global Leader from her home in Nigeria. And that is what she did.

"I quit my job in 2017 and I'm so grateful for how much my business has grown," she says. Her ambition to empower Nigerian women towards financial independence has flourished, with over 60,000 signups since she posted her first Instagram Story inviting new recruits to earn, grow and connect.

Durosinmi-Etti's foray into entrepreneurship opened her eyes to the challenges women face. She knew that beyond the training offered to women by organisations and government, raising capital remained a problem. It led her to write her book *Accessing Grants for Startups*, which birthed the AGS Tribe, before transitioning to Herconomy. "There is a huge gender gap because women are not financially empowered, but they can't be empowered through a single one-size-fits-all solution," she says. "They need access to financial services, community and capacity building, and we've built just that."

More than 57 per cent of women in Nigeria have no access to bank accounts and few have access to savings. Some do not earn, while others do not earn enough to warrant a savings account. "But if you're earning, you need to know how to save, so you can avoid things like Ponzi schemes," says Durosinmi-Etti. From investment opportunities to entrepreneur grants and smarter savings, Herconomy's mission is clear: "We're creating a better economic future for women and women-owned businesses."

One way to achieve this is by building the first bank for women in Nigeria with an ecosystem in which women can thrive. It is an ambitious goal that Durosinmi-Etti is determined to achieve, and Herconomy has concluded fundraising to facilitate it.

There are systemic hurdles to issues faced by women, from economic abuse to financial illiteracy in matters such as insurance. But with Herconomy's community-led approach, outlooks are being rewired for a new generation," she says. "It is a strong narrative as women's attitudes are changing. We are seeing so many women coming to believe in what we are doing. It is a ripple effect for change."

www.herconomy.com

Ethical investment

Refilwe Monageng is a South Africa-based businessman and a champion of responsible practice in fields ranging from mining to commodities and construction

"Often, the international perception of making a difference in South Africa is associated with sending aid," says Refilwe Monageng, founder of Refilwe Monageng Trading Enterprises (RMTE). "But investing in, sourcing from, or partnering with South African businesses is a far more sustainable and effective way to have a positive impact on communities and the environment."

A participant in the Johannesburg Stock Exchange Enterprise Acceleration Programme, which supports the sustainable growth of medium-sized companies, Monageng is a fervent advocate for the abundant business opportunities in South Africa. A successful entrepreneur with an interest in mining, commodities, energy, construction and infrastructure, he has worked with the Minerals Council South Africa and been part of the Commonwealth Enterprise and Investment Council. He also helped to organise the 2018 Commonwealth Business Forum.

Monageng is actively raising the profile of the country's mineral assets and their potential utilisation in medical, engineering and scientific fields. "Minerals have immense value," he says. "South Africa is rich in minerals and they play an important role in our economy, so I want to encourage investment that supports more ethical and sustainable operations, for the benefit of local people and the future of the planet."

South Africa is a leading source of the six platinum-group metals, with platinum already having applications in anti-cancer drugs, electric vehicles and clean energy. Alongside this, the climate of the Northern Cape is ideal for clean energy solutions, which creates investment opportunities in solar and wind power. Monageng is, however, adamant that a responsible approach should be taken to investment and the sourcing of assets, with an open, equitable and collaborative spirit.

"I believe in two key principles: putting people first and working collaboratively," says Monageng. "These principles underpin many Commonwealth campaigns and initiatives – there is a lot to be gained from working together for the greater good, rather than competing against each other for the sole benefit of ourselves. I'm keen to collaborate with organisations in the Commonwealth to drive progressive and sustainable agendas that will have a positive impact on people in South Africa for generations to come."

www.rmte.co.za

Positive energy

From its Aberdeen base, GA R&D is designing innovations
in cleaner, cheaper energy production for the world

"We are very dynamic," says Yerasimos Angelis, founder and Managing Director of GA R&D, a small technology design and development company with a big mission to deliver cleaner, cheaper energy to the UK and the world. "Our idea is to develop technology in the UK as a global hub, then distribute this technology out through the countries of the Commonwealth."

The company is well placed to do so. It is located at the centre of the UK's energy industry in Aberdeen, which is also a significant location for King Charles III through its proximity to the royal estate of Balmoral. Angelis draws inspiration from The King both in developing novel, sustainable approaches to energy production and in delivering them with a Commonwealth focus.

"It gives us at least 56 countries to support," says Angelis. "We are setting up hubs in every continent – in 2022 we opened an office in Ghana, and we have others, including in Mumbai, Singapore and Mexico." Angelis's idea is to take GA R&D manufacturing to other countries to create value for them, then transfer on the technology and knowledge. "We can help countries grow their economies and deliver a huge return for the UK," he explains.

Founded in 2010, GA R&D has developed two innovative products with a view to creating cleaner and more efficient global energy production. The first is the GARD U-Line, a next-generation technology developed to extract oil and gas more efficiently, safely, cleanly and cheaply, while global energy production is in transition. Production and decommissioning processes are expensive in these industries, but the company's universal modular mechanical tool reduces the cost of operations by up to 95 per cent. The U-Line roller system can be used for the deployment of all tools in deviated and shallower wells, reducing risk when carrying out standard operations. The U-Line system is the first all-in-one multifunction tool for intervention conveyance, offering unmatched flexibility and minimising the use of power-rich electrical systems.

"We can help countries grow their economies and deliver a huge return for the UK"

It is an innovative technology that is quickly becoming a global market leader. "It's coming to the point where this is a national technology in India, for example, where they are asking specifically only for our product in the tendering process," says Angelis. It is the same story in Malaysia. "We are helping them with production and they are saving so much money compared with our rivals," he says. "Countries use our device; it costs them less money and creates jobs in the process."

Inspired by how the Royal Family has nurtured a strong and resilient global network through the Commonwealth, GA R&D has focused attention on territories with a historic connection to the UK. India has been a particularly fruitful partner, with GA R&D building a partnership with the nation's biggest oilfield tool manufacturer to export the U-Line technology. GA R&D has further developed its Commonwealth footprint in Asia by partnering with SubSea Pressure Controls, Singapore – subsea specialists with more than 20 years decommissioning experience. "These are huge milestones," says Angelis. "It is important to maintain relationships and build bilateral bridges – something the Royal Family is so good at doing."

The company's other innovative technology is the 3C-Steam. This new steam-turbine technology has been designed as a clean energy-technology solution to combat the rise in global temperatures by decarbonising and reducing emissions in power plants. The modular 3C (Compress-Cool-Condense) turbine design can be retrofitted to existing plants, significantly lowering costs, enabling the elimination of high-maintenance carbon-emitting cooling towers, and allowing for their reinvention through capturing renewable energy, for example, from industrial waste. It thus generates cost-effective, efficient and clean electricity from existing steam sources that account for over 60 per cent of global power production.

For Angelis, this is a potential game changer and an example of the type of step change he has been striving to develop since his youth, when he invented a trailblazing hydrogen car. That vehicle was ahead of its time and is now in a museum, but it represents the positive application of imagination and resources that GA R&D was founded to harness.

"I don't give up on things – you have to meet a challenge if you want a return," says Angelis. "Our 3C-Steam Turbine is a significant development, but we need to understand how the UK as a nation would like to see the technology implemented. We want to collaborate and work with the government. We need to develop a unique plan to drive the development of this technology so we can provide what the world needs. You have to innovate in the process, and in how to implement and introduce it."

This focus on innovation and collaboration has underpinned how GA R&D has grown its business globally, developing regional hubs and giving countries control over the manufacture and implementation. "Our first goal was to demonstrate that our technology is needed in these different countries," explains Angelis. "Then the goal is to nationalise the technology in each country. That is the way forward. We are not here to manufacture and produce forever, so we stand out as unique in this landscape as none of our competitors are willing to hand over manufacturing rights. The best thing about this approach is we still own everything. We have evolved our business model and created a framework in which we have minimum liabilities, significantly minimising risk."

Angelis seeks to maintain and extend this collaborative approach, which he believes is essential to fix the challenges presented by climate change. "There are a lot of good technologies to fix the problems, but none will work on their own – you need many of them," he says. "What we are trying to do at GA R&D is to provide one good British tech that can address one area of concern, and which is exportable, so it can work in any country regardless of climate. It is not wind-dependent or solar-dependent or geothermal-dependent. This is what makes the difference."

www.ga-rd.co.uk

On the world stage

King Charles has
established himself as
a distinct and respected
voice among the world's
influencers and decision-
makers, following
a lifetime of state
visits and impassioned
campaigning

Previous page
Against a backdrop of St Peter's Basilica, Vatican City, where Charles attended a reception at the Pontifical Urban College in 2019

Above
With Emperor Hirohito and Empress Nagako at the Imperial Palace, Japan, during Expo '70

Left
Pictured in the White House Oval Office with US President Ronald Reagan in 1981

Opposite
Charles is met by Sheikh Isa bin Salman al-Khalifa, Emir of Bahrain, as he arrrives in the Gulf state in 1986

he world has watched on over the course of Charles's life as the once reticent young man has emerged from his role as a royal touring-party extra to that of leading man – his nation's representative on the international stage and, increasingly, a principal player in the tackling of global issues, such as international co-operation, climate change and sustainable development.

While Queen Elizabeth II undertook more than 260 official overseas visits during her reign, making her the most internationally recognisable British monarch in history, her heir has gone even further. Charles travelled to the far-flung reaches of the earth and visited 45 of the 56 Commonwealth countries, several of them multiple times, in his late mother's stead. He has also toured many other nations on behalf of the Foreign Office, all in the name of duty.

A GROWING GLOBAL PRESENCE

As a child, Charles made his first overseas trip in 1954, sailing to Malta abroad HMY *Britannia* on her maiden voyage with his sister Princess Anne to greet their mother and father, following the royal couple's exhaustive round-the-world Commonwealth tour.

He enjoyed a more extended foreign visit in 1966 when, aged 17, he lived in Australia as a schoolboy, spending two terms at the prestigious Geelong Grammar School's Timbertop in Victoria's High Country. The experience was one that he has since recalled fondly, telling an audience during a subsequent visit down under that "part of my own education took place here in Australia. Quite frankly, it was by far the best part."

Although many of Charles's early visits were to current and former British colonies and Commonwealth states, his schooling in

international diplomacy was taken to the next level in 1970 when he visited Strasbourg, France, representing the Crown with his father, Prince Philip, at the Council of Europe conference. He went on to attend Expo '70 in Osaka, Japan, before embarking on his most important overseas engagement to date that same year – a visit to Washington DC with his sister Princess Anne as the guests of US President Richard Nixon's two daughters and son-in-law.

Having graduated from the University of Cambridge in June 1970, Charles went on to serve in the Royal Navy. He continued to fulfil his royal duties, however, accompanying his parents on a state visit to France in 1972 and visiting West Germany several times over the course of the decade, as well as attending colourful gatherings such the centenary celebrations in Fiji in 1974 and the coronation of King Birendra of Nepal in 1975. After completing his active service in the Navy in 1976, he made high-profile visits to South America in 1978, taking in Brazil and Venezuela, and to Norway and Yugoslavia that same year.

In the 1980s, Charles stepped up his international presence even further. He made several visits to the US, including one to New York in 1981, flying by Concorde for the first time. Four years later, he returned to America with his wife, Diana, Princess of Wales, as the guest of President Ronald Reagan. Charles undertook his first visits to the Middle East in 1986, when he made official trips to Oman, Qatar, Bahrain and Saudi Arabia, where he forged close ties with the ruling families, and his interest in Islam was sparked.

In 1990, following visits to Nigeria and Cameroon, Charles and Diana toured Hungary – the first royal tour to a Warsaw Pact country. That same year, they attended the enthronement of Emperor Akihito in Japan. The first Gulf war dominated the headlines in the latter

months of 1990, and in December Charles visited Saudi Arabia, where he met with British forces who had been deployed to the conflict zone.

The royal couple toured India and South Korea in 1992, engaging in charity and business activities. The visit to India was made famous by the image of Diana sitting alone in front of the Taj Mahal in Agra. When Charles and Diana travelled to South Korea, on what turned out to be their last joint tour, they became the first members of the British royal family to visit the country.

Both tours were remembered for the deteriorating state of the royal couple's relationship, and they separated formally at the end of the year. From then on – apart from those rare occasions when he was joined by one or both of his sons – Charles travelled alone, until he married his second wife, Camilla, Duchess of Cornwall.

CHARLES THE DIPLOMAT

In 1995, Charles attended the funeral of Israeli Prime Minister Yitzhak Rabin on his first visit to Jerusalem. In total, he has made three visits to the country, also attending the funeral of former president Shimon Peres in 2016 and the World Holocaust Forum in 2020. During this most recent visit, he paid tribute to his paternal grandmother, Princess Alice of Greece and Denmark, who was honoured as "Righteous Among the Nations" by Israel's Holocaust memorial institution for having hidden a persecuted Jewish family in her house in Athens during the Second World War to avoid them being captured by the Nazis.

Charles played an important part in building relations with former Soviet states, which included his key visit to the Baltic states of Estonia, Latvia and Lithuania in 2001, where he was attacked by a communist sympathiser in Vilnius. He also paid important visits to Basra in Iraq in 2004 to meet British troops and went on to visit Tehran, where he held talks with Iranian President Mohammad Khatami.

His influence in the region grew with further highly successful visits, including his 2006 tour to Saudi Arabia, accompanied by Camilla. The couple visited Kuwait, Qatar, Bahrain and the United Arab Emirates the following year, and undertook further tours to the region in 2014 and 2015.

In March 2009, Charles visited the South American countries of Chile, Brazil and Ecuador, taking in the ecological treasure of the Galapagos Islands. The natural world was firmly on the agenda for his trip to Denmark later that year, where he delivered a powerful address to the UN Climate Change Conference in Copenhagen, telling the assembled delegates that "the eyes of the world are upon you".

"As our planet's life-support system begins to fail and our very survival as a species is brought into question, remember that our children and grandchildren will ask not what our generation said, but what it did," he concluded. "Let us give an answer, then, of which we can be proud."

In March 2015, Charles and Camilla made a major visit to the US, taking in Washington DC, where they met President Barack Obama, as well as Virginia, where they visited Mount Vernon, the family estate of George Washington, and Kentucky.

That same year, the royal couple made an official visit to Ireland. They met President Michael Higgins and attended an ecumenical service of peace and reconciliation in Drumcliffe. They also visited Galway and Mullaghmore, where Earl Mountbatten of Burma was assassinated by the IRA in August 1979.

Charles and Camilla toured the Balkans in 2016, visiting Croatia, Serbia, Montenegro and Kosovo. A few months later, Charles made an

"Charles is perhaps most commonly associated with his powerful speeches warning of the devastating impact of climate change"

Opposite
On a state visit to
Germany in 2020,
Charles takes part in
the country's Central
Remembrance
Ceremony at the
Bundestag, Berlin

Above
At the UN Climate
Change Conference
(COP26) in Glasgow,
where Charles calls
for urgent action on
the climate and
biodiversity loss

official visit to Romania, where The King is a regular visitor on private holidays as he has property there.

THE ELDER STATESMAN

In recent years, Charles has fully assumed the mantle of global statesman. On a visit to Berlin in November 2020, Charles spoke, partly in German, at the Central Remembrance Ceremony, acknowledging past conflicts while highlighting the bonds between the two countries.

"As our countries begin this new chapter in our long history, let us reaffirm our bond for the years ahead," he said. "Let us reflect on all that we have been through together, and all that we have learned. Let us remember all victims of war, tyranny and persecution; those who laid down their lives for the freedoms we cherish, and those who struggle for these freedoms to this day. They inspire us to strive for a better tomorrow – let us make this our common cause."

Charles is perhaps most commonly associated with his powerful speeches warning of the devastating impact of climate change, but he is no doom-monger. In June 2020, at the opening of the virtual meeting of the World Economic Forum, usually held in Davos, Switzerland, Charles gave a speech in which he called for a Great Reset initiative in response to the Covid-19 pandemic and an urgent transformation of the global economy to avert climate catastrophe.

Demanding "nothing short of a paradigm shift, one that inspires action at revolutionary levels and pace", he nodded to electric vehicles, space travel, mobile technology and online streaming as examples of rapid industry transformation.

Charles went on to explain that with "bold and imaginative action" together with "decisive leadership", the green economy offers "new employment opportunities, entire new industries and markets rooted in sustainability … with the potential for unprecedented economic growth".

Introducing his Sustainable Markets Initiative, Charles said that "sustainable markets generate long-term value through the balance of natural, social, human and financial capital.

"Systems-level change within sustainable markets is driven by consumer and investor demand, access to sustainable alternatives and an enhanced partnership between the public, private and philanthropic sectors," he continued. "Sustainable markets can also inspire the technology, innovation and scale that we so urgently need."

He ended the memorable address by warning that, to make sustainable markets a reality, urgency, systemic change and collaboration were critical. "Do we want to go down in history as the people who did nothing to bring the world back from the brink in time to restore the balance when we could have done?" he challenged the assembly. "I don't want to. And just think for a moment – what good is all the extra wealth in the world, gained from 'business as usual', if you can do nothing with it except watch it burn in catastrophic conditions?"

The following year, in a speech on climate change at COP26 in the host city of Glasgow, Charles issued an urgent call for action at the opening ceremony, telling world leaders that time had "quite literally run out" and that the Covid-19 pandemic had "shown us just how devastating a global, cross border threat can be".

"Climate change and biodiversity loss are no different," he said. "In fact, they pose an even greater existential threat to the extent that we have to put ourselves on what might be called a war-like footing."

> "The natural world was firmly on the agenda during Charles's trip to Denmark, where he delivered a powerful address to the UN Climate Change Conference in Copenhagen"

FUTURE VISION

Charles's first state visit as king came in March 2023, a few weeks before his coronation, when he and the Queen Consort travelled to France and Germany. He was invited by the French President, Emmanuel Macron, and the German President, Frank-Walter Steinmeier, to help restore frayed relations in the aftermath of Brexit – a role that illustrates how, working with his government, King Charles hopes to shape the monarchy's relationship with the wider world.

The tour celebrated the nations' shared histories and cultures, and reflected on past conflicts and the sacrifices made on both sides, as well as the legacy of reconciliation that followed. One of the highlights came when The King addressed the Bundestag in Berlin, making him the first British monarch to make a speech in the German parliament.

A skilled figurehead of Britain's soft power diplomacy, Charles addressed the assembly in English and German. Setting out his aspirations for the two countries, he also presented the wider world with an insight into his vision for a mutually strong, stable and successful tomorrow. "Heeding the lessons of the past is our sacred responsibility, but it can only be fully discharged through a commitment to our shared future," he said. "Together we must be vigilant against threats to our values and freedoms, and resolute in our determination to confront them. Together we must strive for the security, prosperity and wellbeing that our people deserve.

"In the long and remarkable story of our two countries, there are many chapters yet unwritten. Let us fill these with the restless pursuit of a better tomorrow. The legacy of our past, and the great promise of our future, demand nothing less."

Opposite
A Commonwealth leaders reception at COP26 co-hosted by Charles and the British prime minster

Above
German politicians applaud The King after his speech in the Bundestag on his first state visit as monarch

Reaching the unconnected

With state-of-the-art satellite technology and support of educational programmes in Africa, UK company Avanti Communications brings life-changing internet connectivity to hard-to-reach places

When it comes to internet connectivity, the continent of Africa is like the final frontier. It has been estimated that up to 60 per cent of its population is without a reliable connection, denying people access to government services and the information and communication networks that those in the rest of the world take for granted. This includes citizens of the 19 African countries that form part of the Commonwealth, including Kenya, Nigeria, South Africa and Rwanda. Seeking to improve the situation is Avanti Communications, a British satellite-communications company that was formed in 2002 with a vision to bring high-power, low-cost communications to Africa.

"This company was originally founded with one vision – to bring connectivity to Africa via satellite," explains CEO Kyle Whitehill. "Africa is notoriously underserved when it comes to connectivity. The founders' view was, you will never get mobile or fixed networks to stretch into Africa's rural and isolated communities. They started their journey by developing their first satellite, HYLAS 1, part funded through the European Space Agency. Move forward a few years and around 75 per cent of our capacity is over sub-Saharan Africa."

Avanti recognised a potentially groundbreaking idea. Through applying its innovative technology, it was able to challenge a market that had previously been dominated by huge companies. Its success came through its use of Ka-band satellites, which offer high speed, high capacity and high connectivity, making them ideal for the growing demands of internet-based, data-driven applications. Today, Avanti has four HYLAS geostationary-orbit, high-throughput satellites (HTS) covering Europe, Africa and the Middle East. The vision has been well and truly realised.

With its focus on sub-Saharan Africa, Avanti is perfectly placed to boost its connectivity. The company was selected by the Department for International Development (now the Foreign, Commonwealth and Development Office) to assist with a UK government commitment to support the development of marginalised schoolchildren in Africa.

"Over the past eight years, we have been providing connectivity to 245 schools in rural Kenya," says Whitehill. "This individualised programme provided digital access to maths, literacy and life skills, and when a child has access to maths for one hour a week, it has been shown to increase their maths age by 18 months per year."

In addition, Avanti has developed relationships with education ministries in several countries across East Africa, none more so than Kenya where it has continued to fund satellite connectivity in the 245 schools. The ambition is to connect 5,000 schools in hard-to-reach remote areas where digital connectivity would otherwise not be possible. Avanti is also a partner of the Girls Education Awareness Programme (GEAP), a social marketing collaboration for business and foundations communities, ministries of education, donor governments and other strategic partners, "who work together to change harmful social norms that keep girls from school," says Whitehill.

Education is only one aspect of Avanti's mission. With its HTS network, it partners with other companies and organisations to roll out connectivity for some of sub-Saharan Africa's most remote communities, including refugees. Working with the Social Innovation Academy, the company supplies free solar-powered satellite broadband technology and laptops at three refugee settlements across East Africa. This enables people to access everything from self-learning to information and job applications. It does similar work with the UN Refugee Agency (UNHCR), supporting connectivity in four refugee settlements across Uganda. As with education, these projects are centred on Avanti's grounding principle, "Be More". "We look at how we can help people develop so they can go on to have a more successful life," says Whitehill. In 2020, Avanti won the Better Satellite World Awards by Space & Satellite Professionals International (SSPI) for its part in the project.

Another area of Avanti's work is with the UK's military and emergency services. As well as providing connectivity for British emergency services in rural parts of the UK, Avanti enables UK Special Forces to stay

connected in the field; for this branch of the military to be effective when mobile, secure and reliable communication is essential. The armed forces have had a deep impact in the way Avanti operates, with the company supporting military charities and employing former service personnel. These are causes dear to Whitehill's heart, as he came close to joining the Royal Marines before opting for a career in communications, working at Vodafone for many years prior to joining Avanti.

"When I joined Avanti, I wanted to build a military business working with US and UK armed forces. We provided connectivity to them to ensure they can have contact in very difficult terrain," he says. "I was then invited to a charity dinner and sat next to a young guy who had been injured on active service. As a company we became interested with that as an issue and agreed to support former service personnel through the Armed Forces Covenant. We want to help veterans return to the civilian world and have made ex-military personnel one of the first channels we look to when hiring new people. They make excellent employees, as the military gives people enormous responsibility at a very young age."

Avanti's approach to connectivity now focuses on increasing existing capacity to meet customers' needs. Whitehill credits Elon Musk with transforming the way satellite companies operate, by showing how much customer appetite still exists for connectivity. Today, Avanti talks to customers to ask them what they need. "It's not about building more satellites as such, which is very expensive, it's about being more customer focused, seeing what people want and adjusting our capacity to solve problems – because there is a lot of capacity around," explains Whitehill.

"We are a small company, so we can be nimble and react quickly. We will solve a problem for customers, and they don't need to worry how it works. We ask what they want to do, and we make sure it happens."

www.avantispace.com

Two of a kind

With Toucan Hill on the island of
Mustique and Bouchaine Vineyards
in Napa Valley, Tatiana Copeland has
created two luxury dream destinations

Magic, fantasy and romance are three words often uttered by guests staying at Toucan Hill. "I call it a fantasy but paradise is another good word for it," says Tatiana Copeland, businesswoman and philanthropist, who is talking about her unforgettable house, Toucan Hill. "It's the most fanciful, improbable villa on one of the world's most fanciful, improbable islands."

The Copelands were guests in Mustique before they were owners and were introduced to the island by none other than Colin Tennant, Lord Glenconner, a friend of Princess Margaret. "Princess Margaret was given a plot of land there by Colin as a wedding gift, which is where she built her own villa. When we first visited in the 1980s, there were only about 30 houses on the island," says Copeland. "Princess Margaret lived a life of fantasy down here. She would come for the months of February and November and always had fascinating house guests and costume parties. The island felt like a private club back then."

Copeland's villa is a jaw-dropper. The domed dining pavilion has a floor covered in rare blue tiles from Brazil that pick up the sapphire sea beyond, as does the 360-degree view – a limitless horizon of lush gardens and beautiful blue ocean and Caribbean sky. "I wanted to create a wow factor when you first come in," says Copeland of her concept for the house. Inspired by the *Thousand and One Nights*, "I set about designing a Moorish fantasy that would transport visitors to a place whose beauty defied imagination, rich in opportunities for romance.

"I envisioned it to be completely different from what rational people have in their lives. Once guests enter, they are greeted by an infinity pool framed by arches. Most people have left a cold environment and have been travelling a long time. I would like them to walk in and say 'wow' out loud." Visitors have included British comedian John Cleese, who was married on the property (an effusive tribute from him is scrawled in the guest book). "I want people to relax here," says Copeland, "but I also want them to have fun. I sign my emails 'Lady Touc'," she says with a smile.

> "I set about designing a Moorish fantasy that would transport visitors to a place whose beauty defied imagination, rich in opportunities for romance"

Available for short or long-term rental, the villa is over 10,000 square feet in size. It has four luxurious, air-conditioned king-sized suites, all with en-suite bathrooms and private terraces or balconies. There is a tiled courtyard with a fountain, a rooftop "mirador" deck and a large terrace surrounding the infinity pool, perfect for viewing glorious sunsets. The Master Pavilion Suite, complete with gold-leafed bed, separate private infinity pool and lush gardens, is also available for rent on limited occasions. Guests have the use of two vehicles and are looked after by an attentive staff of seven: an estate manager, butler, chef, two housekeepers, a houseman and gardener, who pride themselves on delivering special experiences for guests.

In the gardens, bougainvillea and hibiscus provide glorious fragrance and add splashes of bright colour against the cool white walls. By day, sunshine floods the terraces and turquoise infinity pool; by night, the glow of lanterns and the scent of jasmine predominate.

Mustique is unique in the Caribbean in that it is harder to reach than other islands and so offers a real sense of escape. The easiest way to travel there is by private jet or a commercial flight to Barbados, St Lucia or St Vincent. Then it is a short hop by private or shared charter to Mustique. Once there, visitors can party at the famous Basil's Bar, enjoy beach barbecues, picnics, snorkelling, scuba diving, sailing, fishing, tennis and horse riding, or opt for privacy and seclusion, if that is their preference – which Copeland believes may be the attraction for royal visitors, such as the Prince and Princess of Wales. "They love Mustique because people on the island simply let them be. Mustique lets people take a breath and be themselves, so they can go out with the family and have something closer to a normal life than they can manage at home."

Copeland herself is travelling to London for King Charles's 75th birthday celebrations at Claridge's, where guests will have the opportunity to sample wines from Bouchaine Vineyards. She will also bring members

"I love to warmly welcome the world to the unique Napa views of rolling hills and vineyards, so one of my ideas was to design our newest Tasting Room in the form of an embrace"

of her vineyard management team to thank them for their work during the year. A great admirer of the Royal Family through her friendship with Princess Margaret, Copeland has previously met The King as the Prince of Wales and the late Duke of Edinburgh through her charitable work.

Together with her husband, Gerret, she owns Bouchaine Vineyards in Napa Valley, California. Bouchaine is one of the few family-owned vineyards still operating in the valley, one of the most popular tourist destinations in the US. Sitting on 104 rolling acres, it showcases an award-winning 5,000-square-foot tasting and dining space built in the shape of a half-moon. The winery also includes a terrace and gardens that provide guests with unspoilt views of the landscape as far as the eye can see. "I love to warmly welcome the world to the unique Napa views of rolling hills and vineyards, so one of my ideas was to design our newest Tasting Room in the form of an embrace," says Copeland. "Our vineyard gazes towards San Francisco, but there are no buildings in sight. We can still provide a feeling of Napa as it used to be – friendly faces, no crowds, fabulous views and great wine."

Many Bouchaine wines have won gold medals, including the Chardonnay, Pinot Gris, Pinot Meunier and Pinot Noir. Run on sustainable farming principles, the vineyard holds Napa Green certification. As decisions are made

by Copeland and her husband, "we can make our goals happen without going through layers of management, and those goals are to make the best wine possible. I am President and Chief Financial Officer, and my husband is Chairman. We joke around as to who is the top boss.

"The wine world is male dominated for the most part, so when you find women in wine, they are exceptional. Our winemaker is a woman, our assistant winemaker is also a woman, and our farming crew comprises an all-woman team, who I think are more careful and more detail-orientated than the usual male-only teams."

Fluent in Russian, French, Italian, Spanish, German and English, Copeland is a huge lover of art and classical music. Her mother's uncle was the famous composer and pianist Sergei Rachmaninoff, and she is named after his daughter Tatiana. Drawing on this connection to music, Copeland is a long-time major sponsor of Festival Napa Valley, which each July hosts performances of renowned artists. "We love to combine wine with food and music, and we are very involved with classical music. I love that world and I love to bring music to the vineyard, as it is a fantastic combination – beautiful music, beautiful views and beautiful wines."

www.toucanhill.com
www.bouchaine.com

Heritage at home

Cole & Son has almost 150 years of wallpaper design expertise
and its vibrant pieces demonstrate a uniquely British sensibility

Wallpaper can be more than just decorative; it can be a distinct piece of design. Few companies understand that as well as Cole & Son, a London-based designer of the finest wallpaper, which produces lively, brightly coloured hand-painted designs that hang in some of the most prestigious buildings in the country. These include several historic royal palaces, with Cole & Son earning a Royal Warrant from Queen Elizabeth II in 1961 following decades of experience working with the Royal Family.

"In the early 20th century, when Queen Mary was redecorating Queen Victoria's former bedroom in Kensington Palace she chose our Hummingbirds pattern," says Marie Karlsson, Cole & Son's Creative and Managing Director. "It features 28 colours, which meant you needed to use a combination of block and hand-painting across numerous wooden blocks to print it. It was introduced to that historic room and it's something we are still very proud of.

"We are an ambassador for historic buildings. We have our deep knowledge and expertise and are passionate about the history as well as the art and craft of what we do. That's why so many stewards of buildings with historic character still turn to us for help when they want to dress their homes."

Cole & Son was founded in London in 1875 by John Perry, an artisan wallpaper printer who used wooden blocks for printing and made wallpaper for the upper classes. Perry was both creative and innovative, inventing a process to imitate silk using a solution of ground mica, a natural mineral that is still used for a pearlescent effect today. As the printing block business declined, he began to acquire other companies that would otherwise have gone out of business, incorporating their collection of wooden blocks into his own. In this way, the Cole & Son portfolio began to expand, providing a huge archive from which to draw upon. It currently contains around 2,000 block print designs and 500 screen print patterns, as well as a vast quantity of original drawings and wallpapers. This library of wallpaper

"We have our deep knowledge and expertise and are passionate about the history as well as the art and craft of what we do"

has unprecedented historic value. It includes exclusive pieces that were designed for a single room and will never be used elsewhere.

Over the decades, Cole & Son has worked with some of the most prestigious buildings in the UK, such as Chatsworth House, Blickling Hall, Audley End, Buckingham Palace, Windsor Castle and the Palace of Westminster. This unique and extensive portfolio is a source of inspiration for new designs within contemporary collections, which are made with all the care that historically made Cole & Son the wallpaper of choice for generations of British aristocracy. "We are art and craft – as much craft as we are art," says Karlsson, "and we think that accounts for our success. Traditionally, the block would be hand-painted and crafted, creating the product in the same way for clients wishing to beautify their home, whether it was a palace or apartment."

While wood blocks are no longer frequently used, newer techniques employed by Cole & Son's craftspeople replicate the feel and appearance of that old method. "We use 'surface print' design, so you can feel every single layer of ink," says Karlsson. "Tangible and tactile, the process emulates the old technique, creating the same sensation with metal rollers much like those used in newspaper printing. The texture and the quality is still there, and some of the rollers we use are now more than 100 years old themselves."

Cole & Son's collection includes iconic designs developed in the 1950s. These are the most striking wallpaper prints of the contemporary post-war design movement and include classics such as "Woods" and "Palm Leaves", which remain popular today. Like many Cole & Son patterns, these utilise aspects of the natural world, bringing some of the colour and magic of the outdoors into the home. "People are drawn to the beauty of nature and it is something that is very important to them," says Karlsson. "We have a collection called 'The Gardens', but we also have designs based on hot air balloons, ornaments, buildings,

all sorts of things. The idea is to bring a sense of magic or English quirk into the home. People want their homes to be full of joy and Cole & Son would like to be part of that."

The company releases a handful of new collections each year, working with in-house designers, as well as Italian and South African ateliers and notable collaborators such as fashion designer Stella McCartney, who developed a "Fungi Forest" mushroom-patterned toile de Jouy in 2022 that was created to spread a message of sustainability. "Mushroom [which has fibres that can be made into an eco-friendly fabric] has the potential to challenge leather, so we felt there was no way we could do anything other than put it on a really good sustainable material made from 79 per cent renewable fibres," says Karlsson. "That was interesting for Cole & Son as it persuaded us to move some of our portfolio over to a different base. Our wallpaper lasts for many years, so it's not a wasteful business, but the young generation very rightly care about what they buy. They want to make sure it's ethical."

Customers can select from just over a thousand different designs, all different but unmistakably the work of Cole & Son. The company also has a limited range of complementary and co-ordinating fabrics and furnishings that can be mixed and matched, delivering the same joie de vivre and sense of impeccable craftsmanship that is detectable in every single inch of wallpaper.

"I am so proud of the ability of our team," says Karlsson. "We still do things the way we did 100 years ago. We hand-paint, we archive. We feel that we are preparing for the next generation of Cole & Son so that in 50 or in 100 years' time, somebody will look at what we have done and take inspiration to create something new themselves. That is our core business, and we will continue to do that for years to come."

cole-and-son.com

Payment with purpose

KogoPay's QR-code payment system is ahead of the curve, putting fast, secure transactions in the hands of everyone, while doing good for society

Almost one million people visit Thailand from the UK each year. There are countless cultural differences between the two countries, but one of the most surprising is how to pay for things. While people in the UK tend to favour debit and credit cards, in Thailand they increasingly use QR codes via their phones, particularly in smaller shops and on market stalls. This is also true in other South East Asian countries such as Singapore and Malaysia.

The popularity of QR-code payments in the region is one reason why, in 2017, Thai-born, UK-based entrepreneur Narisa Chauvidul-Aw founded KogoPay – an app that uses QR codes backed by blockchain technology. As KogoPay unfolds across the UK, it also presents an opportunity to do good for society, as Chauvidul-Aw intends to build into the platform the ability to pay for food and drink for the homeless.

Before setting up KogoPay, Chauvidul-Aw completed a PhD at the London School of Economics and was employed by major companies in a finance capacity. Even then, she often worked on her own businesses alongside her main job; in 2000, she founded *ThaiSmile*, a magazine for the Thai community in Europe.

"When I came to the UK in 1997, I started a website about Thailand and the official tourist office in Thailand began using it as their own," she explains. "I love to celebrate the country and encourage people to visit. Then we published a free magazine for the Thai community in the UK, which was available in Thai temples and supermarkets."

Despite her experience in tech, finance and business, Chauvidul-Aw had to overcome multiple barriers to make KogoPay such a success. "An Asian woman in fintech?" she says. "It was not easy." Even after getting potential investors to the table, it was difficult to find people who shared her commitment to social justice. But as a Christian who had worked as a missionary among the homeless in Japan and with children's charities in the UK and Thailand, this was non-negotiable.

"What's the point in having a business that doesn't inspire people or make a difference?" she says. "I wanted to donate ten per cent of

182

"What's the point in having a business that doesn't inspire people or make a difference?"

profits to social-impact causes, but my investor said his dream was to give 33 per cent. Throughout my journey, these are the sorts of investors and partners I have found – people who share my way of thinking and my sense of purpose."

Chauvidul-Aw's dream is for people to use KogoPay so that, when they go to a cafe to buy themselves food and drink, it is easier for them to also donate money to help homeless people buy themselves a meal. "I can do these small-scale things with my own business," she says. "But with the support of bigger companies I can do even more."

For KogoPay, environmental sustainability works hand in hand with social sustainability. Chauvidul-Aw is interested in the idea that, given the right direction by leadership, businesses can progress values, wealth-sharing and human welfare across all sections of society, while working to protect the planet.

"To this end, I have signed a deal with the Estate (Thailand) which is part of MQDC group, one of the biggest family businesses in Thailand," she explains. "It is a property company and we are its payment partner. I wanted to work with MQDC because its interests align with ours regarding sustainability and social enterprise."

The partnership arose after Chauvidul-Aw won several awards for her work with KogoPay. In 2019, she won the Women in Tech Global Award in the startup category and, in 2021, she won the WinTrade Global Award for Women in Banking and Finance. Other accolades and awards have followed. As a result of these successes, she was invited to speak at the Bloomberg Business Summit at APEC 2022 in Bangkok to discuss her experiences as a female entrepreneur.

"At the Bloomberg Summit, every speaker around the table was very famous in their field except for me," she recalls. "Included were the Thai Minister of Finance, chairmen of the big banks, presidents of multinational corporations – and me. The founder of MQDC was there and she heard me speak about my experiences. This is how our partnership started."

The KogoPay system can now be used to purchase MQDC property, or make instant cross-border payments between Asia and Europe, and it will soon have a digital banking platform and crypto wallet. The QR payment method is already gaining popularity in Europe and, in 2022, KogoPay was the official sponsor for Berlin's renowned Thaipark food market. The market was first established in Wilmersdorf many years ago by Thai women who wanted to share their cooking in Germany, and it has now grown into a weekly celebration of Thai and other South East Asian cuisine. For such small businesses, debit-card readers are expensive and unnecessary – KogoPay offers the same service and

security through an app. "You scan somebody's QR code and send them money instantly. You can even send it to another country just like that – it is very fast," she says.

Chauvidul-Aw is now exploring similar opportunities in the UK. She has been in conversation with a number of high-profile charities, including one that offers financial support to survivors of UK disasters. "I would love to work with them so that, when they are raising funds, they use KogoPay," she says. "Corporate partners could match public donations." Chauvidul-Aw would like more people in Europe to start using QR-code payments and believes this will happen in the next five years. "Everybody should have the option to pay by cash, card or QR code – in Europe, Asia and around the world," she says.

Above all, financial inclusion is at the core of KogoPay's culture. "To us, this means giving every single person on the planet the opportunity to access financial and banking services," she says. "It's an achievable goal."

www.kogopay.com

Labour of love

Entrepreneur Yohan Poonawalla continues the family legacy of business and philanthropy, adding his own niche as a world-renowned collector of classic cars

Indian billionaire industrialist Yohan Poonawalla comes from an entrepreneurial family that made its fortune through engineering and an array of business ventures, from biotech to finance. As such, Poonawalla pursues a wide range of interests while being Chairman of India's highly respected and reputed Poonawalla Engineering Group. He has built one of the world's finest collections of vintage Rolls-Royces and Bentleys, alongside running the family's prestigious stud farm for racehorses and carrying out pioneering work with his eponymous foundation.

In 2022, Poonawalla received the prestigious accolade Business Leader of the Year at the Gravittus Foundation's URJA Award 2022. "The award bears testimony to our companies, focusing on various businesses like engineering, finance, exports, real estate, investment and horse breeding," says Poonawalla. "Our vision has always been to strive for excellence by constantly pushing our boundaries and taking every challenge as an opportunity to meet our business goals. We have been involved in various philanthropic activities, and I feel privileged to carry on the legacy to make our surroundings a better place to live. While we all strive to excel and create wealth, giving back to society is equally important. This is because it is that same society that we make our own living with."

The Poonawalla Group was established in 1946 and operates in diverse sectors, including engineering, biotech, real estate, hospitality and finance, with a strong emphasis on quality, innovation, dedication and customer support. Successful subsidiaries include Intervalve Poonawalla, which manufactures valves for the oil and gas industry, exporting to countries in Europe, North American, Asia, South America, Africa and the Middle East; and El-O-Matic India, which makes international-quality pneumatic actuators and valve automation systems for valve control. Both businesses have helped advance Indian engineering while ensuring safe and effective performance.

Through the Yohan Poonawalla Foundation, Poonawalla has become personally involved in various social and charitable activities,

"While we all strive to excel and create wealth, giving back to society is equally important"

such as funding and supporting schools, hospitals and public gardens. The foundation is well-known for its contribution towards improving access to education and healthcare for the underprivileged in Pune, Maharashtra state, where the Poonawalla family live. Donations encompass the state-of-the-art Zavaray Poonawalla Cancer Building, for the treatment and care of cancer patients, and centres of education for the underprivileged, including the Soli Poonawalla Memorial High School and Shri Sant Gadge Maharaj Vidhyalay.

The Poonawalla Group supports several Corporate Social Responsibility initiatives in Pune, among them the Poona Leprosy Committee, which for decades has played an important role in eradicating the disease. The group created the Gool Poonawalla Garden in Salisbury Park, providing ongoing maintenance; and has contributed towards the widening and resurfacing of the Hadapsar Road – now known as the Soli Poonawalla Road. It also helped fund a new modern police station in Pune and regularly donates vehicles for police use. Further investment projects include sports ground development and sponsorship of the Indian Mixed Martial Arts team for World and All-India championships.

One of the Poonawalla Group's most successful enterprises is Poonawalla Stud Farms, established in 1946 by Yohan Poonawalla's grandfather, Soli A Poonawalla. The business began with a dozen mares and one stallion, producing the Group 1 Indian 2000 Guineas winner, Fitzcall. Poonawalla Stud Farms is now Asia's leading thoroughbred stud farm, having won 15 Champion Breeders Awards and bred some 373 All-India Classic winners, including winners of ten Indian Derbies and 70 Indian Classics. Internationally, horses owned and bred by the group have won accolades in Hong Kong, Singapore, the US and Malaysia, as well as back-to-back wins at the Dubai World Cup.

Poonawalla's wife, Michelle, is a successful businesswoman who utilises her skills in her role as Managing Director of both Intervalve Poonawalla and EL-O-Matic. Through her work, she is one of the most respected and influential female role models in India today, and is also an acclaimed artist who has exhibited at prestigious galleries. Michelle's love of heritage conservation has seen her personally supervise the renovation of the historic Pune Turf Club, a building visited by Queen Elizabeth II and Prince Philip during their visit to India in 1961.

Business success has enabled Poonawalla to become an Indian ambassador of classic cars, indulging is passion to build from scratch what is today one of India's leading car collections. The Yohan Poonawalla Collection features pre-war, post-war, modern classics and supercars, with a particular focus on provenance and pedigree. This means he preserves automobiles with special histories such as those owned by erstwhile maharajas and nawabs, as well as presidents, sheikhs and the British Royal Family. His children, Tania and Zayan, also share his passion for motoring.

The highlight of the collection is a carefully curated selection of bespoke Rolls-Royces, Bentleys and Ferraris, which has made Poonawalla one of the most renowned names in the classic car world. He is the first Indian to be nominated as the finalist for the Classic Car Ambassador of the Year Award in the UK and, according to The Classic Car Trust (TCCT), is the first and only Indian to feature in the list of Top 100 Classic Car Collectors of the World.

"Each vehicle is unique owing to its features and has its own story to tell," says Poonawalla of his collection, which includes several cars that are well-known around the world, such as the Rolls-Royce Phantom II owned by Sir Malcolm Campbell, the Maharaja of Mysore's Bentley Mark VI and the Lincoln Continental custom-built for Pope Paul VI.

"When one is driven by passion and is always on the lookout for a car one wants, they are always available," he says. "[But] the collector's hobby is not a race to hoard the finest and most expensive cars, it is about enjoying the cars one owns and sharing and showing them to others. Rebuilding, restoring and reviving great cars, and being part of the heritage motoring movement, gives just as much joy to the true enthusiast."

www.poonawallagroup.com

The bigger picture

Management consultancy Avuke focuses on business compliance with a uniquely global outlook, thanks to the multinational backgrounds of its talent

Growing up in Sweden, Simo Kubheka was aware of his South African heritage even though he could not visit the country of his birth. His father was a member of the ANC (African National Congress) and had fled apartheid South Africa in exile before moving to Germany and then settling in Scandinavia. By the time Kubheka reached university age, the ANC was in power and, having grown up in Sweden, Kubheka opted to study and practice law in South Africa before settling in the UK as an expert in strategic compliance and risk management. After his father passed away from Covid, Kubheka decided to build a business that would create formal links between Africa and Europe while supporting disadvantaged communities in South Africa. He called it Avuke, which means "Rise Up" or "Rising" in Zulu.

"We are a management consultancy specialised in ethics and strategic compliance, legal and risk management, and we help businesses to navigate complex situations and change," explains Kubheka, Chief Compliance Officer, who set up the company in 2019. "We work with

businesses that are seeking to expand, often tech companies dealing with human capital." Kubheka's experience as an in-house head of legal and compliance has given him an understanding of how businesses move into new territories and how they raise more capital. "We worked with CEOs to help them navigate through business impacting the blind spots and help them to identify opportunities through compliance. Our associates have a unique repertoire of skills that are not limited to typical legal and compliance skills. This is something that allows us to work with small and medium companies – and even some large ones – who don't have the time, the skills, the resources or the capital to make the investment on their own."

An essential element of Avuke's business plan is to identify, develop and train talent in South Africa. Access to this support allows individuals from poorer backgrounds to contribute to Avuke, while there is the added advantage that South Africa and London share a timezone and have almost identical legal systems. Not only does this approach provide essential social value for South Africans, but it also enables Avuke to compete financially with larger firms while ensuring customers receive an excellent service.

Avuke has clients in the UK, continental Europe and South Africa and is seeking to expand within Scandinavia before leveraging existing contacts in the US. "We do business orientated compliance, navigating key concerns when scaling up, looking at things such as tax issues and GDPR," says Kubheka. "The key difference is, we don't just provide a laundry list of things that our clients need to do; we develop strategic solutions that enable them to expand and grow, whether it's providing an outsourcing solution, partnering with other companies or doing it ourselves. If a company cannot afford a large legal department, we will do that for them. We like companies with a similar value proposition around driving change – companies that think the same way as us and try to do the right thing."

Kubheka is excited about the potential of this relationship between Africa and Europe, and feels that he is following his father's legacy. "This is a two-way partnership between Europe and Africa with opportunities for both," he says. "After the end of apartheid in South Africa, my father became ambassador to Denmark and my auntie and uncle were also in foreign affairs. Although I went into commerce, I see myself and Avuke in a very similar position – we connect companies and people around the world to create opportunities for growth."

www.avukegroup.com

Inspiring the next generation

CATS Global Schools (CGS) is a pioneering education group committed to equipping students with the skills they need to thrive in tomorrow's world

In a rapidly changing world, the need for forward-thinking education has never been more crucial. CATS Global Schools (CGS) stands as a beacon of inspiration, a network of UK and US boarding schools, arts institutions, and English language schools, all united in inspiring the next generation of world shapers.

The foundation of CGS is rooted in history. It brings together 13 distinguished schools, dating back to 1899, each with a legacy of academic excellence. These institutions form the foundation upon which CGS is built, today welcoming 18,000 students of more than 100 nationalities.

Among the portfolio of schools, St Michael's in Llanelli stands tall, earning the prestigious title of Welsh Independent School of the Decade 2021, according to The Sunday Times Schools Guide. Guildhouse School, London, is proud to be the only school in Europe with a Bloomberg Business Lab, helping those who aspire for a career in finance. Meanwhile, Cambridge School of Visual & Performing Arts (CSVPA)'s partnership with Hearst Magazines UK, opens doors for students to gain invaluable work placements at renowned publications such as *Elle*, *Harper's Bazaar* and *Cosmopolitan*.

At the heart of CGS lies a commitment to prepare students for the challenges and opportunities of the future. Its mission is clear: to equip each student with the knowledge, skills and attributes necessary not only for academic success, but also for thriving in their personal and professional lives.

The group values of "Pioneering, Persevering, People" form the essence of CGS's teaching philosophy. Central to its success is its dedicated education committee, comprised of experienced educationalists who are actively engaged in research. Their work empowers teachers to continuously develop their pedagogy, ensuring students receive a world-class educational experience.

CGS stands apart from the competition through its expansive, global network of schools. Operating in multiple countries, CGS accommodates a multitude of nationalities, providing a truly international perspective.

CGS was the original pioneer of the University Foundation Programme (UFP), a qualification developed in 1985 to help international students progress to a UK university. Today, 95 UK universities accept the UFP, including 21 from the Russell Group. "Our approach to education enables students to progress to the top world-ranked universities, including Oxbridge and those belonging to the Ivy league, Russell Group, Top 10 UK Universities and UK G5," says CGS CEO Christopher Stacey.

In keeping with its pioneering spirit, CGS continues to push the boundaries of education. Its AI committee is exploring the integration and ethics of artificial intelligence for teaching and assessment, to enhance the student learning experience. It is all part of aligning its mission with the demands of future careers.

"Our active research culture and continuous professional development for teachers are integral to enhancing our teaching practices. As we look forward, we remain steadfast in our commitment to providing exceptional education," says Stacey.

CGS is dedicated to inspiring its students to meet the demands of the future, ensuring they are well-prepared to shape the world and make a positive impact on society. "Our schools have been in operation since 1899, and they will be here long after me," says Stacey. "I recognise the significance of their legacy and history, and plan to continue their commitment to providing exceptional education for generations to come."

www.catsglobalschools.com

Spirit of enterprise

Following a major global relaunch and rebranding, fashion label Esprit is bringing its pioneering edge to the digital age

Esprit is one of the world's most iconic clothing brands. Since forming in California in 1968, this international fashion label has always been one step ahead of its competitors, from its distinctive bold logo and store design to its "Real People" campaign in the mid-1980s and its first "ecocollection" in the early 1990s, featuring organic cotton long before it was fashionable to do so.

Cut to today and the company has undertaken a major rebranding, relaunching the shopping experience with New York, London and Amsterdam as its base. "It is ESPRIT 3.0," says William Pak, Esprit CEO. Esprit's new global flagships will be "customer experience innovation centres", combining a high-street store with a company headquarters. "The physical store uses a futuristic interface to deliver to the senses – touch, smell and sight – what you can't experience online," says Pak. "We are taking high technology and manifesting it physically in the store, like a reverse metaverse. The experience is an 'online, offline' integrated omnichannel approach to customer interaction."

Prior to the opening of the global flagships, the plan is to roll out the concept stores across the world throughout 2023. New York, the company's creative centre, has an opening, as does Los Angeles, followed by Canada, Asia and Australia. "Our retail stores are the best ambassadors of the brand, so to expand globally we need them to be modernised."

Esprit's new "online universe" for customers, especially the younger generation, is designed to offer unique experiences as well, involving not only shopping, but also community and education. As with the physical stores, the concept includes tech innovations such as the metaverse and NFTs.

The rebranding also includes fresh style guidelines, which are being applied to Esprit's full product lines.

"Our new designs go in the direction of playful, modern and cool," says Pak. "A metropolitan, outdoors and elevated chic look, based on cool and effortless style with rich textures and powerful details using premium quality materials." This focus on classic and exceptional quality items that last longer demonstrates Esprit's commitment to tackling the problem of disposable fast fashion. "It goes hand in hand with the economic circularity of fashion."

Green policies are not a recent development, though. Esprit sets trends rather than following them. "Esprit was one of the first eco-friendly fashion brands," says Pak. "From the very beginning in California, environmentalism was at the forefront of people's minds." Esprit chose London for its new initiative because the UK itself is at the forefront of global awareness and sustainability, with a very educated consumer base in terms of the environment.

"But we also try to understand patterns and behaviour at a regional, localised level, where some groups prefer different aspects of sustainability to others. For example, at a recent event in Berlin, we were educating consumers about sustainability in terms of upcycling, and using new and better materials such as mycelium, a form of mushroom product, to make sustainable fibres."

With inclusivity and progressive ideas high on the agenda, Esprit is spearheading change in the fashion industry once more. "As opposed to just buying clothing for how it looks and feels, we want to convey that fashion is an attitude as well," says Pak. "The Esprit attitude is to be positive, playful and joyful. We celebrate real people, self-expression and togetherness. It's about embracing how you feel."

www.esprit.com

On the right course

The teacher-founded International Curriculum Association has built a
global educational network on the principle of improving learning for all

It was the Princess of Wales's passion for early years education that inspired her to create The Royal Foundation Centre for Early Childhood. Its aim is to drive awareness of the extraordinary and transformational impact of learning and development in the early years. The International Curriculum Association (ICA), evolved from its origins in 1984 and – being founded by teachers – has the same understanding of and commitment to the power of learning.

Over time, the ICA has developed its International Curriculum, built on researched best practices and integrating a pedagogical framework aligned to learning and development for its three stages: early years, primary and middle years. The International Early Years Curriculum (IEYC), International Primary Curriculum (IPC) and International Middle Years Curriculum (IMYC) are now being implemented successfully across schools in more than 90 countries

"The evolving landscape of international education means that schools may use one or all of our curricula and combine them with a national

curriculum, delivering either in English, bilingually or trilingually," explains Sarah Blackmore, Director of the ICA. "International Curriculum plays a crucial role in preparing learners to navigate an increasingly complex world, engaging with and addressing global challenges, engendering global perspectives and developing global competencies."

Building on the impact of the IPC, the ICA launched the IEYC in 2016. "While early years education is not compulsory education in many countries, it is recognised as a critical phase of learning and development," says Blackmore. "The experiences and interactions in any learning environment are the key to enabling young children to start building their identity as a learner – crucial first steps on a journey of lifelong learning."

The IEYC offers an holistic approach to learning and development structured around thematic units. The underpinning pedagogy combines four approaches: nurturing, responsive, playful and brain-based. In the primary curriculum, thematic units offer interdisciplinary content around personal goals, subject goals and international goals. In the middle years, the approach evolves to a more conceptual "big idea", underpinned by research about the needs of the teenage brain.

In the latest review of the International Curriculum, the ICA has deepened its focus on international learning, with discrete elements of international mindedness and global competence. The latter emphasises the importance of taking action and the development of learner agency within all three programmes. This enables learners to engage – through both challenge and choice – with a learning environment and learning experiences that support the development of knowledge and understanding, skills that are future facing, and sustainable personal dispositions such as adaptability, resilience and collaboration.

The ICA works alongside its learning community to improve learning, champion quality and unlock potential. "We recognise the potential that sits within our schools and harness that by engaging our teachers to deliver training through our professional development pathway, and to peer mentor through our ICA accreditation framework," says Blackmore.

Unlocking potential in the quest to improve learning is what the ICA exists to do. "You know it's working,' adds Blackmore, "when a student in Kathmandu engages with a teacher working in Brazil during our annual conference to explain the impact of a recent learning experience. Or when a kindergarten teacher in New Delhi arranges a virtual exchange with a nursery in London to provide Indian dance lessons and English interactive storytelling."

www.internationalcurriculum.com

Investment with impact

Alta Semper Capital makes strategic, impactful interventions in the healthcare sector in Africa, investing in both business and people

Having visited more than 50 countries during her career, Afsane Jetha, CEO and founder of Alta Semper Capital, has noticed that wherever she goes, one thing is constant: everyone wants access to healthcare and education for their families. "It's a globally unifying theme, and we should not lose sight of the fact that humanity ultimately wants the same thing," she says.

Alta Semper (meaning "always rising") is a leading impact investment fund worldwide, focusing on providing healthcare solutions in rapidly developing economies where there is massive unmet demand. Since its founding in 2015, the firm has achieved investment returns in the top decile for investments across the African continent. Its diverse portfolio includes Morocco's largest group of cancer hospitals and East Africa's leading online pharmacy.

The firm has an innovative approach to distributing quality and affordable healthcare services in regions with limited investment in the sector, which is tailored to meet the unique necessities of growing regions. "We build health ecosystems that are fit for the emerging markets," says Jetha. "Our interventions are impactful but lucrative. They are an investment, not aid, using technology to bring best-in-class healthcare to people everywhere."

Alta Semper "can make a huge impact with a relatively small amount of capital, and we work with local entrepreneurs to help them scale and regionalise. We have taken businesses public in local markets or sold them to multinationals, working with young, ambitious, tech-savvy and optimistic entrepreneurs who want to change the world."

While the company works alongside the World Bank and philanthropic organisations such as the Gates Foundation, its two major investors are well-known, impact-minded US families who understand the importance of economic sustainability. By investing in human capital (doctors and nurses), the businesses can develop sustainable healthcare infrastructure alongside economic reliability, avoiding "bubble-wrap capitalism", as Jetha puts it.

"In many of these countries it might take decades to develop enough doctors and nurses, but with our partners we can now use technology to reach and train large parts of the population. By investing in edu-tech, we can train disenfranchised populations, particularly women, and that has powerful, positive ripple effects for the wider society and economy."

www.altasemper.com

A holistic education

Chartwell International School in Belgrade is more than a school – it is
a caring, progressive environment for students to develop healthy minds

"Our goal is to provide the best possible education not only in this part of the world, but worldwide," says Nenad Gazikalovic, founder of Chartwell International School in Belgrade, Serbia.

Along with its sister school in Santiago, Chile, Chartwell has become a highly reputable and respected British curriculum school and was named as one of the top 10 International Schools in Central Europe for four years consecutively. It offers education from pre-school through to secondary school for ages two to 18, and has been growing since it was founded some 25 years ago. It now has more than 1,000 students, including 60 different nationalities, and around 180 members of staff. "Every year, we invest in new teaching methods, new books, new facilities and more people," says Gazikalovic, "along with improving and implementing new technologies."

The Belgrade site is located in a quiet residential area and stretches across seven buildings. The school prides itself on its vast and varied number of options for study. "Students have a wide range of choices," says Gazikalovic. "We try to give them a broad education and then narrow down their field of interest. We offer 20 different options for A-level. We have a full-blown music studio, art studios and science laboratories. Many of the things that are usually only offered at the universities, we offer here in school."

This applies to after-school activities, too, which is a huge focus for Chartwell. "Every day of the week there are extracurricular activities, including languages, music, arts, drama, debate club, chess, games, 3D design and more. We also have our own catering service that prepares nutritious meals for students. Parents know that when they send their children to us in the morning, they return home safe and healthy, having been given the best possible education."

The results speak for themselves, with alumni going to a variety of prestigious universities across the world. "We are there to help parents as well as students and guide them into further education," says Gazikalovic. "Our aim is to provide a caring environment tailored to the academic and personal needs of each child. Chartwell is more than an academic institution. Our philosophy encompasses the student's whole personality and emphasises balanced development."

www.chartwell.edu.rs

Investing in people

For JTI UK, success means investing in employees, local communities and veterans, as much as in the business itself

From humble origins in 1850s Northern Ireland, Japan Tobacco International has grown to become a multinational tobacco and vaping company with operations in more than 130 countries. In the UK, its roots can be traced back to the hand-rolled tobacco sold from a cart on the streets of Belfast by Tom Gallaher, who later opened a tobacco factory. Fast-forward to the acquisition by Japan Tobacco Group in 2007 and its place as one of the largest tobacco companies in the world was cemented.

Today, JTI is committed to making its business not only the fastest growing of its kind, but also the most sustainably run. There's a real focus on becoming a fully inclusive business that breaks down barriers and creates a safe environment for everyone: consumers, suppliers, employees and wider society.

"We want to give our people the best possible working environment, so they can reach their full potential" says Louise Harris, Communications Manager for JTI UK, which has 550-plus employees. "And we want to mirror that in our communities, too, so we have significantly grown our community investment programmes over the past 15 years." All JTI employees can dedicate 50 hours each year to volunteer with local charities. This can include tea parties with the elderly, job coaching for those who face barriers to employment and charity events such as sponsored walks.

Team spirit is at the heart of the company culture and JTI UK employees have volunteered more than 44,000 hours and raised more than £500,000 since 2008 – while JTI itself has contributed £43 million to good causes. The employee-led community investment programme addresses some of the most pressing social issues, such as homelessness, isolation and food poverty,

while bringing employees together, away from their usual roles, for a good cause.

This is an example of the positive working culture that has seen JTI certified Global Top Employer by the Top Employers Institute for the ninth consecutive year in 2023. JTI UK was also rated UK Top Employer by the same organisation for the eleventh consecutive year, and was the first company to win two platinum awards from the employment standards accreditors, Investors in People, for its track record of investing in people and wellbeing.

One of JTI UK's chosen causes is The Not Forgotten, a charity it has partnered with since 2009, which works to restore dignity, confidence and independence in wounded serving personnel and disabled veterans. Last year, JTI UK employees raised £140,000 for the charity by taking part in the Big Walk event and walking 10 miles with service veterans. The funds raised will be used to address isolation and loneliness among veterans in care homes across the country, in addition to a series of outdoor events bringing veterans together to socialise amongst like-minded company. This reflects JTI UK's wider commitment to the Armed Forces; the company holds a gold rating in the Armed Forces Covenant Employer Recognition scheme, offering programmes that are designed to support veterans and their spouses.

"We started our Inspiring and Hiring programme in 2018 with the goal of widening our talent pools by supporting veterans, their partners and spouses into fulfilling work, which could be at JTI or elsewhere," says Catherine Guilfoyle, HR Business Partner. "The expertise these individuals can bring to businesses like ours is astounding, and we want to inspire other organisations to do the same."

www.jti.com

Studies in sustainability

At Portugal's prestigious Instituto Superior de Engenharia do Porto,
the engineering students are finding solutions to a greener future

The future of the planet depends on people today finding innovative solutions for tomorrow, with the world's younger generations having a particular motivation in the endeavour. It is one reason why sustainability is at the heart of operations at Instituto Superior de Engenharia do Porto (ISEP), the storied engineering institute at the Polytechnic of Porto, Portugal, which invites students to "interpret and solve the issues of tomorrow".

Founded in 1852 as the Porto School of Industry, the institute's 7,000-plus students are trained as the engineers of the future in state-of-the-art programmes that encourage critical thinking and individual and teamwork, as well as an understanding of the needs of industry, the local community and the planet itself. "We are one of the top engineering schools in Portugal, and in 2022 we celebrated 170 years, so we have a great history," says Maria João Viamonte, a professor of computer engineering who became President of ISEP in 2018.

ISEP ensures that its degree and master's students have access to a wide range of courses, covering everything from established subjects such as civil engineering and mechanical engineering to contemporary disciplines including AI and sustainable engineering. "We offer a range of courses in many different areas, implementing a series of courses that match the profile of young, modern students," says Viamonte.

The institute has also developed close relationships with industry to ensure students have the skills and opportunities required to make an impact in the world of work. ISEP also incorporates sustainability research carried out by different groups into the running of the campus. Recent research and development work includes co-ordinating ProEMiBiL, an EU-funded project exploring the use of sugarcane and microalgae biomass to produce ethanol for use as a clean, renewable fuel. "One of the most important issues is that we know we must be creators of sustainable products," says Viamonte. "It is very important that we act sustainably to have a better future for ourselves and the generations after us."

On the principle that sustainability begins at home, the institute's carbon footprint has been improved by reducing reliance on plastic and eliminating water waste. In 2021, ISEP was rewarded with a prestigious Green Heart certification, the first educational establishment in Portugal to achieve the commendation. "The name of our sustainability campaign is Act Local, Think Globally," says Viamonte. "We are proud that our campus itself is an example of sustainability."

As well as its involvement in projects to benefit the planet, such as developing a method to detect plastic in shallow water using drones, ISEP projects also help its local community. "We are developing an aquaponics project in the Botanical Garden to produce food for the students and the community," says Viamonte. "We want Porto to be a leading city for climate action and we are helping the city achieve climate neutrality by 2030."

The professor explains that ISEP students and faculty fully embrace their responsibilities on the campus, working with local institutions and supporting activities and campaigns that benefit the community. "Being the first institution of higher education in Portugal to obtain green certification is a great achievement, and it is one that involved all the institute community – the students and the teachers from every part of the university. It is a great opportunity to commit academia to our green-future objective, which is so important for our students and for everyone."

www.isep.ipp.pt

Understanding people

Combining artificial intelligence and human insight, global market research and data analytics company Kantar finds the truth behind customer behaviour

At a time when we are bombarded with more information than ever, sifting good data from bad is essential if people are to make informed decisions. This is something Kantar has been helping companies do since it was formed in 1992. Kantar is now the world's leading data analytics and brand consultancy, sourcing and sorting through billions of pieces of data to deliver the most reliable, accurate and valuable insights for clients across the globe.

"Our purpose in Kantar is to shape the brands of tomorrow by better understanding of people everywhere," explains Caroline Frankum, Kantar's Global Chief Executive Officer, Profiles Division. "We want to deliver the most meaningful data, and we want to be an indispensable brand partner."

The company gathers data from 179 million people in more than 100 markets across the world and then uses a combination of AI and human insight to identify trends and ensure accuracy. "We validate

our data through technology and human expertise, which means we can be more confident that we are sourcing truthful data," says Frankum. That data helps brands shape strategy – as well as helping Kantar evolve its own culture, one that ensures employees know they are valued. This was recognised at the 2023 British Diversity Awards, when Kantar was named Company of the Year. The company has also set ambitious targets for gender parity and the environment.

"We are a people-driven business and our values are clear and simple," says Frankum. "They focus on always getting better, winning together, and making today count." This attitude resonates with Kantar's clients and with those who provide their data.

"It means people are willing to share their time as well as their data, and that ensures we deliver a sense of hope and purpose to the business world through these insights. We have found that people need a sense of hope. They want to find a way forward and to think positively. That's why the Platinum Jubilee and the Coronation have been important. Occasions such as these represent continuity, tradition and hope."

Kantar works on local and multinational projects with world-leading brands, spanning industries such as tech, energy, finance, retail, and automotive and mobility. The company needs to demonstrate a knowledge of both global scale and local relevance to provide a clear vision of growth opportunities. To do this accurately, it works with the differences in data in numerous markets, identifying patterns. "That means getting the right balance between human and machine collaboration, using AI and machine learning as a purpose for good to automate the things we can automate, but not losing sight of the times we need to be personal and empathic," says Frankum. "One of the things I loved about the Coronation is that it provided a sense of community – when we source data, we remember that we are dealing with human beings. At a time of great challenges, giving people a sense of worth, purpose and value is very important."

For Kantar, to be sustainable is to be multidimensional. It means being financially sustainable, but also being a force for good in the world. "People don't care how much you know until they know how much you care," says Frankum. "Sustainability for any brand – including ourselves – is hugely important. It's important for our clients and for their customers, as well as employees who will be the future leaders of tomorrow."

www.kantar.com

Fine fragrance

Lady Primrose Fragrances is a legacy brand founded on fragrance recipes that date back centuries, now relaunched to bring luxurious scents to homes and hotels alike

When she worked as a magazine publisher, Michelle Balaz often stayed at the Rosewood hotels in Dallas, Texas, where she treated herself to the exquisite Royal Extract fragrance that was a part of the hotel amenity programme there. With notes of creamy milk, sweet golden honey, apple blossoms and orange, with base tones of precious woods, it was her favourite.

One day, she went to buy some Royal Extract oil diffusers online but discovered the company – Lady Primrose Fragrances – was closing down. "My heart sank, because it wasn't just about me not being able to get this fragrance," says Balaz. "I knew this was a special company with a story behind it."

Lady Primrose Fragrances started life in Texas in 1990, but its scents were based on centuries-old formulas from perfume houses in London and Paris. Balaz was determined not to let that tradition die. She and her sister decided to buy the company, and a restyled version of Lady Primrose Fragrances was launched in 2021.

"We wanted to keep the packaging and the core audience but embrace a new audience as well," says CEO Balaz. The company targeted a male demographic for the first time as part of this fresh approach. The Gentlemen 1677 Collection was born, with a profile described as "noble, warm and bold", with notes consisting of white lavender, plum, anise, black pepper and an amber base highlighting vanilla. "We created a scent that was neutral and could be appreciated by women but was marketed towards men. I wanted to bring gentlemen back." The name highlights the year 1677, paying tribute to archival scent recipes dating back to that year which launched Lady Primrose brand's original scents.

Gentlemen 1677 was an instant success, and the collection was expanded to include lotions, shower gels, grooming powders and other related products. Now, Lady Primrose is looking at adding other products to the range, such as beard oil. Alongside the men's range, Lady Primrose offers five core scents: Tryst, Royal Extract, Momentous, Celadon and Necture. After Gentlemen 1677, Balaz's next task was to make sure that all these collections had the same level of investment and were supported by the same variety of choice, spanning products for the body and home, all imbued with the fragrances. "We don't want to be big," says Balaz. "We take a boutique, sentimental approach, linking the past with the present. It has been a balancing act between paying our respects to tradition and appealing to a new demographic."

Packaging that includes crowns and decanters lends a regal, heritage look to Lady Primrose products – many of which form part of the amenities in luxury hotels worldwide, in a nod to the brand's beginnings at The Lanesborough in London. "We are trying to capture that emotion," says Balaz. "We like to tap into that because history can be mesmerising." For instance, the body-cream jars have ornamental silver lids reminiscent of those in the Victorian era, while the dusting-silk body powder shakers are inspired by vintage English sugar shakers from the 1800s. The candles come in a glass crown, and Royal Extract bath gel, found at Waldorf Astoria, Los Cabos Pedregal, is in a honey pot-shaped container complete with a bath gel drizzler.

As the company expands, Lady Primrose has partnered with Fortnum & Mason – a brand Balaz sees as a well-appointed collaboration that aligns nicely with her own values. "It costs more to make things special, but that's what makes us stand out."

www.ladyprimrose.com

Navigating retail success

With its focus on creativity, efficiency and sustainability,
Concourse is helping airport stores reach new heights

Each day, millions of airline passengers fly for business or leisure, and airport security and procedures mean they often have time for pre-flight retail therapy. Display management company Concourse helps brands create stores that maximise this experience with minimum environmental impact.

"Creating and managing retail spaces in airports can be a complicated process, involving lots of stakeholders, design and engineering complexities, and logistical challenges," says Rob Penn, CEO of Concourse. "Our business evolved to handle the whole process for our clients." Concourse co-ordinates everything from initial budgeting, planning and design to manufacturing, installation and ongoing maintenance, while working with clients to adopt the most sustainable approach whenever possible.

Since its first assignment for a client in Switzerland in 2007, Concourse has completed around 7,000 projects. It now has offices in London and Singapore, with hubs in 14 locations across the world. It is trusted by the biggest retail brands and is proactively engaging with innovative startups in the field. Concourse's use of remote technology and its digital travel retail asset management system enable the company and clients to connect and manage projects online, helping to facilitate effective global collaborations and lower carbon footprints. Sustainability has always been a core tenet of the business, so Concourse has welcomed the industry's shift towards environmentally friendly solutions.

"We've been presenting sustainable solutions to clients since 2012 but, for many, it's only recently that corporate social responsibility has become a major priority," says Penn. "We have established partnerships with community programmes local to our projects which reuse and recycle retail furniture. Our office in Singapore, for example, works with the government and charities to recycle old display furniture into school desks and chairs." While working on the refurbishment of around 20 stores for Apple in India, Concourse used furniture donated by the computer giant to create 650 desks and chairs for the country's schools.

Concourse bridges the desires of the passenger, the needs of the retailer, the vision of the designers and engineers, and the requirements of the airport. By bringing together these stakeholders to deliver projects effectively and efficiently, Concourse has charted its way to success while protecting the planet.

www.concoursedm.com

Jewels in the crown

From ethical eiderdown and goose down to the finest cotton, Crown Goose's
quality bedding brings conscious luxury to the modern bedroom

Around a third of our life is spent in bed. This means the quality of our bedding can significantly impact not just our sleep, but also our wellbeing. Natural materials are unquestionably superior – the pinnacle of which is eiderdown.

"Eiderdown bedding has been the privilege of European royalty and nobility for centuries," says Douglas Humble at Crown Goose, the luxury bedding specialist. "The down is hand-gathered in limited quantities each year from the former nests of eider ducks in remote locations such as protected sites in Iceland. This makes it scarcer than gold, platinum and diamonds combined. It has no quills, so it's the softest, most lightweight and insulating of downs. It's known as the 'jewel of down' and remains popular with our royal patrons and affluent clients today."

Crown Goose has a strong presence in Asia and the US, where international clients can visit its prestigious boutiques in Seoul and Los Angeles. The brand's luxurious duvets, pillows, linens and bedding accessories are also available online. Guests of five-star hotels such as Hilton, Marriott and Grand Mercure can enjoy its bedding in the exclusive Crown Goose suites. As well as designing and creating its own collections, Crown Goose accepts bespoke bedding commissions and will also partner with carefully selected luxury brands and celebrities on limited-edition collections.

Crown Goose takes ownership of the design, development, manufacture and sales of its bedding, to uphold the highest standards. In its boutiques, clients can have private consultations with bedding experts, by prior appointment, so they can explore the science behind superior sleep and discover their personal preferences. The combination of natural fabrics, innovative designs and an informed, individualised buying experience has garnered the loyalty of many discerning clients.

"Alongside Icelandic eiderdown, which is one of the most ethical and sustainable sources of down, we use ethically sourced European goose down," says Humble. "Goose down is much lighter than standard duck down, with more air pockets, which are crucial for warmth and temperature regulation. And we only use the extra-long staple cotton, so-called Supima cotton, as it is extremely soft and breathable. At the end of the day, when our clients go to bed, we want to rest easy, too, knowing we've done everything possible to ensure they sleep well and wake refreshed."

www.crowngooseusa.com

Leader in luxury

Thanks to her entrepreneurial leadership and the acquisition of a prestigious global furniture brand, Janet Linly is taking the design industry to a new level

When Janet Linly acquired US furniture manufacturer Marge Carson in 2022, it was an exciting opportunity for her to expand her already extensive portfolio. Janet founded Linly Designs in 2002 in the Chicago area, and has spent the past 21 years assiduously building the company into one of the largest and most successful luxury interior design firms. Now leading two prestigious complementary companies from her Chicago headquarters, Janet explains which aspect of her growing empire provides her with the most enjoyment. "It's our teamwork and the collaborative environment we have created," she says. "Whether it is with our designers, artisans or clients, everything we do is a team endeavour. One individual can accomplish a lot, but with a team of creative, passionate and ambitious people there are endless possibilities, and that is what I find truly inspiring."

When working with the team at the Marge Carson factory in Mexico, Janet recognises that she shares with them an excitement and passion

for exceptionally crafted bespoke furnishings. "These pieces are unique and made by true craftspeople. They are artists. I appreciate their skills and their pride in what they create," she says. The Marge Carson brand is recognised around the globe for the quality and beauty of its furniture, which is made with premium materials and the finest textiles in the industry. "Our goal is to elevate the Marge Carson brand to even greater heights," Janet explains. "Marge Carson is a lifestyle, and we understand our discerning clientele's refined taste and expectations."

What differentiates Janet from other manufacturers is personal experience in the luxury interior design industry. Along with astute leadership skills, Janet's experience in design, retail and space planning gives her an elevated perspective on manufacturing, which coincides with the expectations of Marge Carson's dealers and clients alike.

After Janet founded Linly Designs, she quickly developed a reputation for her impeccable design eye and accomplishments in leadership. Among her accolades, Janet's work has been featured in numerous prestigious publications chronicling the Royal Family as well as world-recognised brands such as Rolls-Royce and Bentley Motors. In 2007, Janet was named one of the top entrepreneurs in the US by American Chronicle and was later invited to join the exclusive Forbes Chicago Business Council, the foremost organisation for successful entrepreneurs and business leaders. When the opportunity arose to acquire the Marge Carson brand, Janet knew her background and experience as an entrepreneur would elevate this 75-year-old global brand, while honouring its legacy.

Marge Carson was founded in 1947 by a female interior designer and entrepreneur with a vision of grandeur, luxury and sophistication. With perfect synchronicity, the storied company is once more under the stewardship of a woman entrepreneur. Marge was an innovative designer with a keen eye for detail and a commitment to craftsmanship – which remains a brand focus to this day.

"We create exceptional pieces of furniture that are comfortable, luxurious and are considered timeless pieces of art," says Janet. "When referring to luxury watches, brands such as Rolex come to mind. When speaking of luxury furniture, the name that comes to mind is Marge Carson. We have positioned ourselves among other global, bespoke high-end brands. These are the brands that represent a lifestyle of timeless design and uncompromised quality."

www.margecarson.com
www.linlydesigns.com

Brain power

With more than two decades of practice, Minesoft is the go-to global patent database for innovators and collaborators

Information is the catalyst of innovation. That is something Ann Chapman-Daniel has proudly embraced in the 25 years she and her husband have been running Minesoft, a company that collects, analyses and stores patents from around the world in multiple languages. Its database provides companies with access to an unmatched, searchable library of the latest technological, engineering and chemical inventions, many of which are related to sustainability, green energy and the environment.

"We know that sustainability and stewardship of the planet have been very dear to Prince Charles's heart, and this is an area in which so many of our big corporate clients are patenting right now, whether that's in the automotive industry to try to create electric vehicles, or among the big fuel companies seeking to invest in the clean energies of the future," says Chapman-Daniel. "We have developed software that allows our clients to manage the information. It's not just tools to search the data. We host patent archives and work with their engineers on how they should classify and manage that information."

Chapman-Daniel's background was in publishing, business and languages, while her husband, Ophir Daniel, was a software engineer. By forming Minesoft, back in 1996, they merged their individual skills and interests to develop a searchable database for intellectual property, taking advantage of their knowledge and the sudden growth of the internet. Their company went on to win The Queen's Award for Enterprise in International Trade, in 2009 and 2015.

Minesoft's software uses AI and machine learning to index and translate, clean and store that information, making it easily accessible for innovators. As patents are often filed at the earliest stage of any research and development project, the software allows companies to see the areas in which their rivals are operating. It prevents the infringement of intellectual property, and partners can be found for collaboration, using inventions already in existence.

"We have one of the largest patent databases in the world with around 150 million documents," explains Chapman-Daniel. "These are generally in science and technology. The innovations need to be described quite carefully, so they are full of chemical patterns or electronical and engineering drawings. Our customers are the corporate innovators around the world with big patent departments sitting around figuring out the next revolution and how to make it happen. What sets us apart is that we have a huge amount of data, and it is very clean – we are constantly using our AI to improve the quality. We have been doing this for so long and have accumulated so much expertise we are in a better position than the competition."

As well as helping seed innovation and collaboration in the world's leading markets, Minesoft brings opportunity to developing countries, allowing them free access to the database. Sustainability is only possible through global co-operation, with developing economies given access to the sort of information richer countries take for granted. "We work with the World Intellectual Property Forum and make some of our biggest databases available for free in some underdeveloped countries. That is another part of sustainability – spreading knowledge," says Chapman-Daniel.

"Increasingly, we find people all over the world have the same issues as we move towards a zero carbon economy. They don't necessarily need to innovate; they just need to see what is out there. We give them the opportunity to access what is essentially a gigantic brain."

www.minesoft.com

Beyond the Balearics

Renowned Ibiza club Pacha is still stealing the limelight after 50 years, bringing its heritage, music and glamour to London through its iconic Lío experience

"Pacha was always a manifestation of the real Ibiza – the bohemian nature, the creativity, the glamour," says Sanjay Nandi, CEO of Pacha Group, the iconic nightclub brand which has branched into hospitality with restaurants and hotels. "Even at the beginning, back in 1973, we were at the forefront of new music, new party concepts, and we made sure we always brought in the community – the island – as part of that."

Fifty-year-old nightclubs are rare. "Our heritage is based on our music and artists, whether it is the dancers, the DJs or our production teams," says Nandi (above, in Pacha Ibiza's main room). "Keeping that at the core of what we do allows us to remain relevant. Whether you were at the club 50 years ago, 30 years ago or today, you're not going to be seeing a bunch of old acts. DJs worldwide still consider it a rite of passage or as having achieved the pinnacle of success when they take on a DJ residency at Pacha."

That capacity to evolve and adapt translated into a 30 to 40 per cent increase in Pacha's profit at the end of 2022, and the outlook is equally positive. As Nandi and his team take this global brand with

a local feel around the world, he remains steadfastly confident. "Investing when everyone else is not, when you believe in your product and when other people are running away from investment, that is the time to focus and deliver."

Pacha strives to maintain its originality when opening venues outside of Ibiza. "When we branch out, we find similar venues. When we expanded to London, we found a 90-year-old locale, the Café de Paris, which has always been a cabaret venue. We want to reinvest in iconic places and bring them back to their original glory."

Indeed, Lío London – part of Pacha's modern cabaret and restaurant concept – opened to much fanfare in March 2023 at the Café de Paris, which "has many levels and is vast, with capacity for 700 people," says Nandi. "Lío is a traditional dinner show that is totally immersive with a very strong cast of 24 artistes split equally between guys and girls. Those performers have won awards and have been gymnasts."

A night at this new venture for Pacha is multifaceted. "As the show ends at 11.30pm, it changes into a club. New people join and the energy increases, so you end up staying many more hours and having a full experience of the night."

As interaction is key to the Pacha experience, the brand's venues are not ultra-modern, boxy or in the warehouse style. "We prefer to use venues that engage with the client in a different way," says Nandi. "In Pacha Ibiza [whose experiential Wednesday residency, SAGA by Bedouin, is above], you walk through the kitchen to get to the VIP area, so you feel like it is your house. That interaction builds a sense of family."

Nandi sees Pacha as leading the way when it comes to environmental, social and governance matters – working with charities and cleaning up the beaches. "Outside our extremely extravagant hotel, you don't see a line of supercars, you see a line of electric cars being charged. Because it's part of what we are. Personally, as CEO it is not just about driving growth and taking over the world, it is also about understanding the world in a sustainable way."

www.grupopacha.com

Merging interests

With its global team of expert M&A practitioners, Global PMI Partners offers clients a bespoke and market-leading route through post-merger integration

"When companies go through mergers, acquisitions, divestments or carve-outs, our expertise and research has shown us the same thing: boards and executives are very involved up until the point where the deal is signed," says Chris Charlton, Managing Partner and UK CEO of Global PMI Partners. "At this point, they may think 'job done'. In fact, it's just the beginning. They must go on to deliver the value of the deal and that doesn't happen by itself."

Charlton joined Global PMI Partners in 2017, taking the UK helm in 2018. He was later joined by Mark Bevan, Managing Partner & UK COO, in 2020. Both were convinced the business could deliver original, more effective consultancy to companies undergoing the complex process of PMI (post-merger integration) than that offered by traditional consultancies. "Of course, no one is going to walk into a boardroom and get fired for hiring a well-known company," says Charlton. Their belief, however, was that opting for such consultancies was not only playing it safe, but also incurring needless expense and often not delivering expected results.

"Many companies operate with an old pyramid model," says Charlton. "They bring a few expert partners and senior directors – and often many junior consultants working at five times cost. Juniors can be brilliant and should be involved in such projects, but not for the prices clients are charged."

Global PMI Partners, founded in 2013, offers clients a customised approach, drawing on a team of rigorously selected professional M&A consultants, hired for their proven specialist industry and business functional expertise. "Our team of 400 people averages 24 years' experience each," says Bevan. It means the company can offer clients all around the world flexibility and specialist knowledge in all industry sectors. "We've spent 10 years investing in our process. It's battle-tested, refined."

Global PMI Partners' wide range of services, including operational due diligence, integrations and carve-outs, are all underpinned by its market-leading proprietary playbooks, approaches and toolsets. "These are honed specifically for clients to maximise the deal value they want," says Charlton. "We innovate and enhance these after every project, which number over 500 across all sectors and transaction scales."

The company also continues to set standards in its own field. "This is what we do, this is the market we serve, and our collective capability to support clients' M&A projects is unsurpassable," he says. "There isn't a better team globally, all available to our clients on demand."

www.gpmip.com

Philanthropy in action

Jomadasupe's philanthropic approach to investment aims to bring health and wellbeing at a local level and to the wider world

"When you approach programme management from a philanthropic perspective, it leads to a different way of thinking," says Peter Coker, OBE. "Goals relate to community value and outcomes, rather than corporate profit and output, which results in a positive impact that extends far beyond the original scope of the project."

Coker founded programme management company Jomadasupe in 2022, primarily to manage the humanitarian and philanthropic investments of a high-net-worth individual. The enterprise, which also has its own investment portfolio, was a natural progression after three decades of strategic management experience in the aerospace, military and technology sectors.

Having lived and worked abroad during a distinguished career in the Royal Air Force and the corporate world, Coker has developed strong professional connections among many cultures, and he appreciates the need and potential to work together altruistically. This belief is shared by his client, who is investing in a series of sustainable projects around health and wellbeing.

Jomadasupe has subsidiaries in the regions in which the projects are focused. The programme aims to develop jobs, training and businesses not only in those place, but also in the UK where the company is headquartered. An office in Kenya is the hub of its work in Africa, starting with a medical park in Uganda. Globally, subsidiaries in Thailand, the Philippines and the Bahamas are set to manage the development of high-end wellbeing resorts.

"We hope the first medical park will become a blueprint for others, which will be adapted to the needs of the local communities," says Coker. "It will include a hospital, medical and nursing training facilities, research and development laboratories, and production capabilities for medical items such as PPE, as well as additional facilities such as schools to support the local community.

"When you're not constantly focused on the bottom line, you can be more innovative, creative and forward-thinking. Our programme involves the development of supporting technology around long-term sustainability, as it is vital to integrate this from the outset. This optimises our immediate solutions for communities while supporting the environment.

"Philanthropical investment in innovation such as this is a fantastic way to make a significant and enduring difference at a local level and globally to people and the planet."

Creating opportunity

Resource Solutions makes diverse hiring central to its recruitment and
consultancy practice, ensuring workforces meet the challenges of tomorrow

"Our ambition is to redefine work so everyone has a lifetime of opportunity," says Norma Gillespie, CEO of Resource Solutions, a global provider of outsourced recruitment and consultancy services. The company has won multiple industry awards for its work, in recognition of the quality of its consultancy and its effort to address a lack of diversity in the workplace. "We want to help everyone find meaningful and enjoyable work, whatever their background or stage in their career," she says.

To realise this ambition, Resource Solutions pioneered a unique new hiring model for the company, the Recruiter Academy, driven by the need to create a more diverse talent pool of recruiters, to tackle the competitive employment market that emerged post-pandemic. The Resource Solutions team devised a training scheme, blending theory and practical elements with on-the-job shadowing. The application process was open to all socio-economic backgrounds, using attraction channels such as social media. "We were looking for attitude and work ethic, recruiting on potential rather than specific background or work experience," says Gillespie. "I'm very proud of the way the Recruiter Academy builds people's skills and encourages them to stay with our organisation in the long term."

The initial cohort attracted an exciting breadth of diverse candidates, including a healthcare assistant, a technical support engineer, a music agent and an anti-money laundering analyst. Recruiter Academy graduate Addy Iqbal was a prison officer before applying. "A lot of people wouldn't even consider my CV when I applied for other roles, but Resource Solutions saw past the stigma attached to working in a prison. The company gives people from all walks of life a chance to explore a new professional avenue."

Resource Solutions pursues five core values: being client-focused, dedicated, inclusive, proud, and united. Alongside these, it practises the strategic behaviours "Start with why" and "Dare to do different". This approach empowers people to respond to societal shifts. Following the Black Lives Matter movement, in 2020, the Resource Solutions Innovations Team reviewed more than 100 academic and industry papers identifying ways in which recruitment processes perpetuate bias. The result was the Recruitment Inclusivity Audit, which supplies clients with rigorous, data-led "to-do lists" of actionable recommendations to reduce bias in the hiring process. "For example, asking job applicants their current salary was found to perpetuate pay gaps and disadvantage Black women in particular," explains Gillespie. "Job application processes that can't be completed on a mobile device impact people living in digital poverty. And some game-based assessment technologies can disadvantage neurodiverse talent."

Resource Solutions partners with clients to ensure they are positioned to attract the most talented jobseekers, who increasingly look for roles in companies with well-defined ethical profiles. "Applicants are looking for purpose and transparency around what a company does and how it fulfils its environmental, social and governance obligations." In addition, clients can partner with Resource Solutions to craft hiring strategies that make the best of freelance and contract talent, as well as knowing when to take advantage of government-sponsored apprenticeships or training schemes. It is a consultative approach and key to what Resource Solutions does, says Gillespie. "Our ambition to redefine work is driving business performance for ourselves and our clients, but it's also encouraging meaningful societal change – and that gives us tremendous satisfaction."

www.resourcesolutions.com

Resource Solutions

Growing green heroes

Dwi Emas International School is undertaking the challenge of converging the 3Es: Environment, Education, Entrepreneurship

Dwi Emas International School, located in the Malaysian state of Selangor Darul Ehsan, is much more than just a school. ACE EdVenture, of which Dwi Emas is a part, was founded in 1995 by teacher Anne Tham after she noticed that the students studying English where she worked were neither achieving mastery of the language, nor gaining the skills necessary to succeed at college, university or in real life. Fearful that her own daughters would be held back by the same system, she began teaching classes from her living room and devised the ACE Method – an acronym for Adapt, Create and Experience.

This unique method seeks to redefine the role of education. The success of the methodology – which incorporates real-world skills into the syllabus – saw Tham's practice expand from her home to become two schools: Sri Emas International School, founded in 2012, and Dwi Emas International School in 2015.

It is within the latter, a pioneering school for entrepreneurs, that the ACE EdVenture Biosphere is located. The latest development within the ACE schools, it applies Tham's groundbreaking teaching techniques to the environment, offering students a hands-on approach to learning about the world – and the problems it faces – with the express idea of creating solutions to fix them. "For the Biosphere, we started focusing on what the kids are going to need, the DNA of environmental regeneration and sustainability," says Tham. "But we're also teaching them the DNA of entrepreneurship at the same time. Otherwise, it remains a school project, when what we need is for them to be able to solve the problems out there in the world. This is because of what my generation is leaving them – an environmental mess."

For the school, teaching environmental regeneration and entrepreneurship goes hand in hand. It should not only help the world become a better, safer, greener place, but also significantly increase the potential earning power of its students. Focusing on those things at a much earlier age than in traditional schools greatly increases the students' chances of success. "If you have academic skills alone," explains Tham, "everybody has that. That's the baseline in an incredibly competitive world. But with exponential entrepreneurship, not just entrepreneurship, the children learn to multiply the value of a company by ten within the space of two years, because these are the critical skills the children need for the future."

By converging education, environment and entrepreneurship, the ACE EdVenture Biosphere is elevating the school's already innovative approach to education. Importantly, by eschewing traditional teaching methods, it can instead deliver a much more valuable type of education – one designed to influence the students outside the classroom and positively impact their lives. This bold vision is very much in keeping with Tham's original intentions and ambitions for the school.

"Nobody gave us permission to do all this, we just decided that it needed to be done," says Tham. "But it's not us driving this, it's the kids. As educators, we don't understand how people can keep education in the past, because our responsibility is to the children and their future. It's a disservice to them if we are planning to just teach them until they graduate. You have to give them skills and tools for the rest of their lives. And if we don't do that, we are not doing the right thing."

www.dwiemas.edu.my

Sailing away

For the ultimate bespoke getaway, Yacht.Vacations draws up dream yacht-based holidays for its clients in destinations far and wide

"It's about creating perfection in paradise," says Nick Porter, one of three founders of luxury charter company Yacht.Vacations. The trio's mission is to create unforgettable yacht-powered holidays for clients, whether it is sailing to the Pacific North West to go whale watching on a solar-powered boat, or cruising around the Caribbean on a superyacht in search of the ideal beach.

"You are in this beautiful part of the world, alone, surrounded by nature and with nothing to do except relax," says Porter. "It's so different to a hotel. You are entirely self-sufficient, with a crew who spend every moment thinking of ways to improve your experience. These are moments you can't replicate." Indeed, he points out, yachting has many similarities to the experience of luxury cars. "There are very few times in people's lives when they feel such absolute euphoria as when they drive a classic car or step on to a private yacht."

Formed in 2020, and based in Delaware in the US, Yacht.Vacations has gone from strength to strength thanks to the expertise of the founders and the company's commitment to customer service. Many clients have taken their first-ever yachting holiday through Yacht.Vacations – and returned for more. The company has access to more than 25,000 yachts internationally and organises holidays in destinations around the globe, from skiing holidays in northern Norway (off-piste skiing by day, après-ski on deck each evening) to the uninhabited magic of the Virgin Islands. Greece, Croatia and the Balearics are popular destinations, as clients benefit from the freedom to move easily between secluded beaches and perfect coastal towns.

Crucially, clients only liaise with one personal consultant at the company – a sole point-of-contact who will take care of all their needs. Following discussions with the client, the consultant will draw up their dream holiday on the perfect yacht with the best crew and be available throughout to deal with any complications. "That develops a certain level of trust between ourselves and our clients," says co-founder Nick Snow. "It's the reason we get so much repeat business. We like to think you have your lawyer, your doctor, your accountant – and now you have your yacht broker. Just like them, we are there to solve a problem: a client needs a magical experience – how can we help?"

Crews are chosen as carefully as the boat, ensuring their interests match the clients', from a love of extreme sport to a fondness for early-morning yoga. Yacht.Vacations has a presence on the ground in every key location to identify regional highlights. "We don't use Google as a resource, we rely on local knowledge so we can really get to know the best things to do and the best times to go," says Snow. "We encourage our staff to be out experiencing these things themselves rather than sitting in an office."

As the third member of the founding team explains, the result is a holiday you will never forget. "On a yacht, you can combine so many experiences," says Miguel Zapatero. "You can swim with turtles, eat fresh lobster on a beach and go to one of the best nightclubs in the world. I have never felt as relaxed as I do when I step on a yacht. By the third day, all your stress has gone and you can't stop smiling."

www.yacht.vacations

Challenging convention

By mixing entrepreneurial spirit with strong core values and specialist insight, management consultancy Oliver Wyman helps clients deliver impactful breakthroughs

"There has never been so much change in the world," says Nick Studer, CEO of management consulting firm Oliver Wyman. "Our goal is to be right there with clients, supporting them in the moment that they initiate the breakthroughs they need to respond to that constant change. This requires much more than deploying the best analytics and modelling; it means deeply understanding clients as human beings, sharing the entire journey."

Part of Marsh McLennan, a global leader in professional services provision, Oliver Wyman came together as a single multi-specialist business a decade ago, assembled from a series of boutique acquisitions, some of which had up to eight decades of experience. With offices in more than 70 cities across 30 countries, the company fuses industry knowledge with a range of key capabilities, in areas spanning everything from finance and energy to retail and industrial products.

Hitting that sweet spot where industry knowledge intersects with relevant capabilities is what counts, says Studer. "If you're consulting with a client going into a merger, it really helps to know the industry, but it also really helps to have supported many mergers before and be agile enough to adapt your knowledge to the client's specific situation."

Five core values define Oliver Wyman: "Be Brave", "Lead with Heart", "Strive for Breakthroughs", "Work as One" and "Own Our Impact". That last one is particularly important for Studer. "The destination does not justify the journey. You must demonstrate sound ethics throughout any project, balancing the needs of the client, yours and those of society."

Each value propels its employees to aspire to a signature consultancy style that thrives in the company's relatively flat hierarchy. "We worked with the whole company to talk about who we are on our best days. There is no better feeling than hearing our clients talk about how different working with us feels. They say we have deeper knowledge, we are more committed to solving their problem with them, equipping their teams to succeed, and we are collegial to work with."

Studer believes there is further growth potential for Oliver Wyman and wants it to expand its activities. "A third of our work is focused on that moment when the client makes a transformative breakthrough in their business. Our view is that this should make up at least half of the work we do. We want to be more embedded with our clients and their industries, building more relationships and gaining more trust."

www.oliverwyman.com

Defence for tomorrow

While working with the Armed Forces on national security, Rheinmetall Defence UK is also building a fairer, more sustainable business

"As the military's Commander-in-Chief who has a long-standing relationship with the Armed Forces, King Charles's future focus is definitely aligned with ours," says Rebecca Richards, Managing Director of Rheinmetall Defence UK. The Bristol-based arm of the historic German company upholds a powerful presence in UK defence. Following the Boxer and Challenger 3 contract awards to Rheinmetall's joint venture, RBSL, the company continues to invest in the UK and deliver follow-on contracts from these programmes, developing a long-term partnership with the Ministry of Defence. Rheinmetall is also aiming to attain carbon neutrality by 2035.

"To support the UK's environmental goals, we're developing future mobility technologies including hybrid and full electric drive military vehicles," Richards explains. "We are also developing alternative power solutions that could be used for commercial or domestic purposes – including hydrogen generation, storage and fuelling solutions." Rheinmetall's hybrid diesel concepts leverage advanced electric drives to reduce environmental impact, increase power output and improve reliability.

"Like King Charles, Rheinmetall takes ecology and sustainability very seriously," says Richards. "Globally, we are implementing steps to improve our carbon footprint. For example, we've introduced an e-vehicle scheme for employees."

Founded in 2009, Rheinmetall Defence UK is abreast of long-term megatrends while working towards a safer planetary future. One focus is in creating opportunities for young people. "We're working alongside schools and universities to promote STEM careers within Defence and capture wider expertise to work on our technological developments, as there are so many versatile avenues within the industry," says Richards. An apprenticeship scheme began in January 2023, with four engineering apprentices starting on key projects and learning from the vast experience in the team.

In January 2022, Rheinmetall signed the Women in Defence Charter. "This shows our commitment to providing opportunities for women to succeed at all levels," says Richards. "We're aiming for 30 per cent female representation in our workforce by 2030." The company publishes its annual progress, which currently shows female representation is 24 per cent.

"We are continuing to provide the very best technologies and vehicles to the Armed Forces," says Richards, "while innovating sustainable development."

www.rheinmetall-defence.com

On the money

Non-professional investors can take control of their finances and explore new investment opportunities with Spectrum Markets

Investment is no longer the preserve of specialised City gatekeepers and large financial institutions. Retail investors – non-professional investors – comprise an ever-increasing segment of the market, taking advantage of changes in technology and communication to seize control of their financial futures. Spectrum Markets was launched in 2019 with a desire to make it even easier for retail investors to explore a wide range of products across Europe.

"People relying on pension funds for their retirement are starting to feel that is not sustainable," says its founder and CEO, Nicky Maan. "They want to control and invest their money themselves. This is the democratisation of financial markets. We have built a pan-European trading venue that can work seamlessly throughout Europe, 24 hours a day, five days a week. We have experienced very good growth – 50 per cent year on year – with a notional turnover of €1 billion each quarter. We are still expanding the range of products on the venue through partnerships with big institutions around Europe, and we're enabling more retail investors to access those products through our partnerships with banks and brokers."

Maan worked as an international corporate lawyer before launching Spectrum Markets. The strategic investor is the IG Group, which has 50 years of experience with retail clients globally. To increase credibility and ensure stable foundations, Spectrum Markets was launched in the highly regulated German market; this secure base allows the company to innovate without unnerving a traditionally conservative industry. It allows increased flexibility for the issuers of financial products, enabling them to rapidly roll out new products to retail investors, with round-the-clock access and support from the venue.

"We wanted to establish ourselves first," says Maan. "It is about introducing innovation at the right time without ignoring the environment in which we operate. Now we need to build on what we have created and increase the range of products available on Spectrum Markets. Our other area for growth will be international. We are primarily in Europe, but we can go beyond. That works for us because we are already 24/5, so time zones don't matter to us. It is all about how quickly tech can adapt to the demands of retail customers. We want to be the dominant retail exchange in Europe, and we are on the way to that goal. There is no reason why we can't take this model to other markets, with similar success."

www.spectrum-markets.com

One small step

As the need increases to lighten our global footprint, Canadian footwear brand Viberg is making strides in the right direction

"We've always had a reputation for beautifully crafted, enduring footwear," says Brett Viberg, third-generation owner of the family-owned Canadian footwear brand Viberg. "I'm passionate about sharing this ethos with a new generation and highlighting the ergonomic, economic and environmental value of high-quality repairable shoes and boots."

It is a particularly relevant ethos as humanity strives towards a light planetary footprint. Founded in 1931 by Viberg's grandfather, the company creates footwear collections crafted in British Columbia from entirely natural materials sourced from the finest international suppliers. These include custom-made, rust-resistant brass nails from Japan; vegetable-tanned leather from Italy; and leather heel bases, a by-product of the US cattle meat industry. Where possible, the company also sources within Canada and is exploring vegan-friendly materials, such as mushroom leather.

Brett is a fervent advocate of Viberg's shoemaking legacy. "Each Viberg shoe represents our craftmanship and supply chain," he says. "I feel a responsibility to nurture and share these through brand stories, raising awareness of ethical producers and skilled, sustainable manufacturing techniques."

From its responsibly sourced wild antelope-suede slides and calf-suede sneakers to exquisitely fashioned men's ankle boots and limited-edition collections, every item is meticulously crafted by Viberg's shoemakers and is fully repairable by authorised repairers. For Viberg, the company's shoemaking legacy is more important than ever. "For the next generation to continue our legacy, they need to recognise the importance of these timeless and enduring values in a fast-paced, technology-centric society," he explains. "If we don't support them, they will be lost to history."

Viberg is equally as protective of Canada's natural resources, heritage and communities, a reverence reflected in the footwear. "Our footwears' quality and comfort has evolved because of the tough Canadian environment it has to work in, rather than through a conscious drive towards luxury," he says. "This organically evolving quality blends with a sense of British sophistication in our design and craftmanship, such as our intricate stitched detailing influenced by Savile Row brogues."

It is a quality that has seen Viberg's brand presence expand among luxury stockists in Europe. On every level, each step taken in a Viberg shoe is increasingly akin to putting one's best foot forward.

www.viberg.com

Finance made easy

Kippa is harnessing the latest in financial technology to help make business simple for people around the world

Africa is experiencing a revolution. Technology is enabling the continent to fulfil its vast potential, with smartphones putting considerable power and control into the hands and pockets of people across the continent. One technology company that is making a huge difference in Nigeria is Kippa, which was set up in 2021 by Kennedy and Duke Ekezie and Jephtah Chidozie-Uche.

The company, founded in Lagos, has developed an easy-to-use payments platform for small businesses, which also enables small and medium-sized enterprises (SMEs) to manage complex financial affairs, helping them to compete with far bigger businesses. This takes much of the stress and difficulty out of running a small business and has led to Kippa already being used by more than 400,000 clients.

It is a success story that speaks of the huge hunger in Nigeria for technological solutions that make it quicker and easier for small businesses to conduct financial transactions and manage their affairs. The company offers a business incorporation software suite as well as allowing merchants and SMEs to record and track payments made by customers. Kippa also provides an automated inventory management and debt collection system and promises exceptional levels of privacy and security across its portfolio of products.

Kippa started out with a simple, mobile bookkeeping app for SMEs, which, with many Nigerians using a phone as their main tool for computing and communication, has helped make the lives of its customers much easier. This has since been supplemented by a second product, Kippa Payments, which enables customers to send transfers and payments for bills, as well as invoices with embedded payment links. Kippa Payments is sophisticated enough to automatically detect, record, synchronise and validate users' business data – information that was previously self-recorded by merchants on the app.

"We are very proud to be launching our new digital payments solution, which comes at a key time for Nigeria's fintech sector, as demand from SMEs for digital payments solutions continues to rise," said Chidozie-Uche. "Kippa Payments will also enable us to have a deeper understanding of our customers through transactional data, so that we can offer more tailored and bespoke products over time, unlocking deeper value within the Kippa ecosystem alongside our existing solutions."

www.kippa.africa

The good in travel

By connecting with its customers, Culture Trip taps into
what travellers really want from a unique, cultural holiday

Culture Trip launched with a simple yet passionate mission: to inspire people to go beyond their boundaries and experience what makes a place, and its culture, special. What started as a site for providing award-winning travel guides has evolved into a provider of small-group insider-led, curated trips.

"We curate these incredibly interesting trips in a respectful and responsible way," says Ana Jakimovska, Culture Trip's CEO. "We use local guides who know their locations and really lean on that knowledge to ensure people have a meaningful and memorable experience."

Culture Trip's website and social media platforms attract a combined monthly audience of around 15 million users who explore the thousands of travel tips and ideas from travel experts, and create a rich variety of insights for the team when devising new trips. Trips are curated by local experts on the ground and are aimed at travellers who appreciate premium four- and five-star accommodation and good food, but want to be sustainable, authentic and respectful, too, when immersed in local customs and traditions. Trips are arranged as small tours, allowing solo travellers, friends and couples to enjoy the experience with like-minded travellers. "We obsess about the group dynamic. Most people end up making lifelong friends," says Jakimovska.

Culture Trip focuses on lesser-explored destinations, such as Taiwan, or a particular flavour of popular destinations, such as visiting Scotland by train, allowing enough time to both explore and relax while on the trip. Other trips range from staying in a Buddhist temple in South Korea, to feeding and bathing elephants in a rescue sanctuary in Thailand, to tasting mezcal and making tortillas in Oaxaca, Mexico. "Our trips are very highly rated with lots of repeat customers," says Jakimovska. They are also curated with care for the planet without using internal flights and are carbon offset as part of the company's path to net zero.

"From our travel guides, we know what is popular and we know what sort of trips our users are looking for," says Jakimovska. "We are also looking to create interest-based holidays, such as hiking, as this is something our community has said they want. It's all about creating culture-based, sustainable but authentic experiences that draw on the knowledge of our passionate local creators."

www.theculturetrip.com

Bright futures

Vale Verde International School in the Algarve provides its pupils
with a first-class education in a beautiful and inspiring setting

The Algarve is home to almost half a million permanent residents, around 10 per cent of whom are expats – a number expected to rise due to the popularity of this idyllic, sun-drenched corner of Portugal. Vale Verde International School was created to meet the educational needs of that community, providing academic education, as well as first-class pastoral support, in a beautiful setting.

The school aims to prepare young people in the Western Algarve to take their full place in society. That means developing academic, social, physical and interpersonal skills, as well as a sense of personal responsibility and a joy for learning that will stay with them forever.

The school delivers a balanced, quality education to ensure that all students achieve their potential. The principal focus is on academic achievement, with the school welcoming students for admission to primary (key stages 1 and 2) and secondary (key stage 3) level education, an offering IGCSE, AS and A-level curricula. The school is widely recognised for its exceptional teaching of the sciences, but it is also the Algarve's leading school for the arts and humanities.

Vale Verde takes a proactive approach to its students' cultural development, providing an extensive grounding in Portuguese history, culture and traditions as part of the bilingual primary curriculum. Students are also encouraged to develop an appreciation of classical music, art, language and aesthetics, and the school boasts a theatre with state-of-the-art electronic and lighting equipment for performing arts and music. It also offers a range of after-school sports, with excellent facilities for football and basketball, and participates in interschool activities, regularly hosting events for local and regional schools.

A sense of community and social responsibility are essential attributes for a modern citizen, and older students are expected to undertake voluntary and charitable work, ranging from hosting Christmas parties for the local orphanage to involving primary schoolchildren in sports tournaments. The overall feeling is of a first-class international school that takes pride in its setting; one that combines a global outlook with local traditions and values.

www.vvis.org

Pots, pans and purpose

Ensembl's stackable, space-saving cookware collection is
redefining the modern kitchen one sustainable pot at a time

Like many groundbreaking ideas, Kate Swanson's lightbulb moment came to her quite unexpectedly. "It was an awful moment at the end of a long day," says the founder and CEO of high-performance cookware brand Ensembl. She is recalling the night she returned home from work, opened the cupboard door – and everything came crashing down. Looking down at the jumble of pots and pans on her kitchen floor, she thought to herself: what terrible product designs, there must be a better way.

It was in that same small kitchen in Toronto, Canada, that Ensembl's ethos was born. "By engineering beautiful multifunctional products that are built to last and designed to fit any space, we create tools for the modern home that will inspire performance for decades to come," explains Kate, six years after the kitchen mishap led her to her original idea for Stackware. "It is the first product that can be used to cook, serve and store."

Inspired by the camping pots Kate would use on hiking trips, Ensembl's high-quality stainless-steel vessels are not only efficient in design, they are sustainable, too. "I was shocked at the waste in the legacy cookware industry," says Kate. "Sustainability seemed to be an afterthought for many producers." Ensembl's environmental innovation includes compact design that means Stackware takes less transportation space than competitors, and uses plastic-free recyclable packaging. All components of Stackware are easily repairable and backed by a lifetime warranty, ensuring Stackware never needs to go to landfill.

The past inspires Ensembl's modern concept. "I believe in things that are designed to be repaired, used and reused. We need to ask, if one part fails after ten years because of wear, how can we repair it?" These questions matter to Kate, both personally and professionally. A trained lawyer, she has an eye for detail.

The advancement of sustainability is in such details. "How can we ensure that we're not using plastics? How can we optimise the size of the shipping containers so we're not incurring extra sea fuel?" says Kate. The Stackware Collection is just the start of things. "There's a better way to make products, and that's what we will continue to do."

www.getensembl.com

AN
ENVIRONMENTAL
PIONEER

Climate change

The environment has always been a passion for Charles, whose ideas have gone from being derided to being hailed as visionary

C harles's longstanding role as a pioneer on environmental issues has earned him the respect and admiration of leaders and activists around the world. For more than half a century, he has championed the battle against climate change and the erosion of biodiversity loss.

It is a passion that his father, Prince Philip, inspired his eldest son to pursue, urging Charles to do his research and be well-informed if he planned to speak out on the subject. The young prince soon developed an interest in the environment to match his father's. And although the pair didn't always see eye to eye, their shared work on the subject is something that Charles's mother, the late Queen, spoke of with deep feeling towards the end of her life.

"It is a source of great pride to me that the leading role my husband played in encouraging people to protect our fragile planet lives on through the work of our eldest son Charles and his eldest son William," she said in a pre-recorded message for delegates at the UN Climate Change Conference (COP26) in Glasgow in November 2021. "I could not be more proud of them."

Her Majesty followed this up with unusual candour in that year's Christmas speech, saying that she was "proud beyond words" that Philip's environmental advocacy has been "taken on and magnified by our eldest son Charles and his eldest son William."

As king, Charles has already encountered a number of conflicts, especially as his role now requires him to "rubber-stamp" his government's decisions in major speeches, rather than give voice to his own opinions. To his frustration, despite being listed to speak at the UN's COP27 conference in Sharm el-Sheikh, Egypt in 2022, the

Previous page
On a visit to the Harapan Rainforest conservation project on the Indonesian island of Sumatra in 2008

Above
At the opening of COP26 in Glasgow, Charles gives a speech in which he calls for a "war-like footing" against climate change

Opposite
A reception at Buckingham Palace ahead of COP27, with guests including Prime Minister Rishi Sunak and Stella McCartney

"Charles was happy to confirm himself as an environmental radical
– a stance that has been at the core of his life's work ever since"

Prime Minister at the time, Liz Truss, advised for him not to attend, and it was "unanimously agreed" that he would not do so.

Any suggestion of tension between the sovereign and his government was played down, however, with the Palace stating it was "entirely in the spirit of being ever mindful as king that he acts on government advice".

That said, Charles had already adapted his stance and found a way of making his point ahead of the Egypt gathering by hosting a pre-conference reception at Buckingham Palace for key COP27 figures, inviting more than 200 guests, including his new Prime Minister, Rishi Sunak. The PM went on to reverse his own decision and skipped the UN climate-change meeting.

THE YOUNG ACTIVIST

Charles entered the world of green activism as a young adult. He gave his first speech on the environment in 1968 – years before the phrase "global warming" was in common use or taken seriously. It was at this time in his life, while still an undergraduate, that his "inner dissident" began to surface.

Within months of his investiture as Prince of Wales in 1969, Charles, still only 20, penned a letter to Prime Minister Harold Wilson, expressing his concern about the decline of salmon stocks in Scottish rivers. "People are notoriously short-sighted when it comes to questions of wildlife," he noted.

On 19 February 1970, Charles felt emboldened enough to make his first landmark speech about the environment at the Countryside Steering Committee for Wales conference, warning of the threats from plastic waste and chemicals dumped into rivers and seas, and of air pollution from industry, vehicle use and air travel.

Such ideas were dismissed as unproven back then, but Charles was having none of it. "We are faced at this moment with the horrifying effects of pollution in all its cancerous forms," he said. "There is the growing menace of oil pollution at sea, which almost destroys beaches and certainly destroys tens of thousands of seabirds. There is chemical pollution discharged into rivers from factories and chemical plants, which clogs up the rivers with toxic substances and adds to the filth in the seas.

"There is air pollution from smoke and fumes discharged by factories and from gases pumped out by endless cars and aeroplanes," he continued. "The list is longer, but what I am getting at is that it is going to be extremely expensive to cut down this pollution. To install a filter plant at a factory is going to increase the production overhead costs, which in turn are going to be added to the price of the product. In the end, it will be the general public, as consumers, who will have to pay. Are we all prepared to accept these price increases for the sometimes-dubious advantage of seeing our environment improved?"

Charles also highlighted one of his father's major themes, the overpopulation of the planet. "In many places, the number of people is increasing faster than the resources of the local environment can cope, thereby exaggerating the problems of conservation."

His robust language raised eyebrows among the political class and in the corridors of Whitehall. He did not hold back, happy to confirm himself as an environmental radical – a stance that has been at the core of his life's work ever since.

A GLOBAL MESSAGE

In an impassioned address to the European Parliament in 2008, Charles told MEPs that it was their clear duty to show a more "determined" lead on the issue. Standing in the parliament building, he claimed that the world was "sleepwalking its way to the edge of catastrophe".

Above
The prince talks to a member of the team cleaning up after the *Sea Empress* oil spill off the Pembrokeshire coast in 1996

Opposite
In the tropical forest of Cameroon in 1990, at a time when Charles was already an active campaigner against climate change

"Ultimately, many of his 'dotty' ideas would prove to be spot on and have been embraced fully by the mainstream"

Above
With naturalist Sir
David Attenborough
at an event in London
for the Rainforests
Project, which Charles
launched in 2007

Opposite
Charles listens to
permaculture expert
Ali Sharif as he walks
through the rainforest
near Manaus during
his 2009 visit to Brazil

"Charles gave his first speech on the
environment in 1968 – years before the phrase
'global warming' was in common use"

He warned MEPs of the grave danger of climate change. "For me, the crux of the problem is – and I only pray I will be proven wrong – that the doomsday clock of climate change is ticking ever faster towards midnight.

"We are simply not reacting quickly enough," he added. "We cannot be anything less than courageous and revolutionary ... In this sense, it is surely comparable to war. The question is whether we have the courage to wage it. If military policy has long been based on the dictum that we should be prepared for the worst case, should it be so different when the security is that of the planet and our long-term future?" His speech caught the attention of media outlets across Europe and beyond.

In Copenhagen a year later, he spoke out again, saying it was critical that humanity changed its ways to save the planet. "Reducing poverty, increasing food production, combating terrorism and sustaining economic development are all vital priorities," he said, "but it is increasingly clear how rapid climate change will make them even more difficult to address.

"Furthermore, because climate change is intimately connected with our systemic, unsustainable consumption of natural resources, any decline in the ecological resilience of one resource base or ecosystem increases the fragility of the whole," he continued. "The simple truth is that without a solution to tropical deforestation, there is no solution to climate change. That is why I established a Rainforests Project to try to promote a consensus on how tropical deforestation might be significantly reduced."

After he retired from active service in the Royal Navy in December 1976, Charles had developed a reputation for being outspoken, and faced media criticism as he called for harmony and balance in society.

"Most critics imagined that I somehow wanted to turn the clock back to some mythical golden age when all was a perfect rural idyll. But nothing could be further from the truth," he wrote in his 2010 book *Harmony: A New Way of Looking at Our World*. Bold and courageous, in many ways the book is Charles's blueprint for a more balanced and sustainable world. He described it as his "call to arms to save the planet from ecological devastation".

"Some of these ideas were radical and literally decades ahead of their time," said his co-author Tony Juniper, Chair of Natural England, a fellow at the University of Cambridge Institute for Sustainability Leadership and formerly the Executive Director of Friends of the Earth and President of the Wildlife Trusts. "Some you could reprint today and they would be very much of the moment. It's hard to overstate the role he played in putting these subjects on the agenda."

Charles has received many significant honours for his ecological work over the course of his life, none more so than the GCC Global Leader of Change Award, which he was presented with in May 2017, and which was first established at COP21 in Paris, for his outstanding contribution to environmental preservation and protection. He followed it up in November of that year by delivering another keynote speech at the Our Ocean conference in Malta about the conservation of the oceans and the circular economy.

In September 2018, Charles received a special Lifetime Achievement Award from *GQ* magazine for Services to Philanthropy. Talking about the importance of sustainable fashion, he said, "I have always believed that living on a finite planet means we have to recognise that this puts certain constraints and limits on our human ambition in order to maintain the viability of the planet."

"Charles was happy to confirm himself as an environmental radical
– a stance that has been at the core of his life's work ever since"

"The King is a convener, connecting people and organisations in ways that open up possibilities and create solutions"

Climate change and the environment have been a major part of Charles's work for decades now, and in 2020 he set up the Sustainable Markets Initiative, which is supported by the World Economic Forum, to help financial markets become more sustainable.

"Everything we are doing has been to destroy our own means of survival, let alone the survival of everything else we depend on," he said in an interview for the Sustainable Markets website. "But at the same time, we seem to be unable to understand that there is an alternative way of doing it, which is to put nature back at the centre, value everything she does and build from there, and now there is an amazing amount that can be done through the circular bioeconomy."

Reflecting on the first speech he gave on environmental concerns, 50 years on from the event, he added, "I was considered rather dotty, to say the least, for even suggesting these things, rather like when I set up a reed-bed sewage treatment system at Highgrove all those years ago – that was considered completely mad."

Ultimately, of course, many of his "dotty" ideas would prove to be spot on and have been embraced fully by the mainstream.

CONNECTED THINKING

Having campaigned on environmental issues as the Prince of Wales for decades, now that he is king, Charles has acknowledged that he is subject to different rules. After all, British monarchs are obliged to remain politically neutral to avoid conflicting with their government. As Robert Hazell, an expert on British constitutional affairs at University College London, has observed, Charles's speeches will be vetted by government ministers and he will have to be "far less outspoken" than he has been in the past.

There is no doubt that Charles is clear about his constitutional responsibilities, having said that he will not continue to lobby parliamentarians, dismissing such suggestions as "nonsense". As he has admitted, it will "not be possible for me to give as much of my time and energies to the charities and issues for which I care so deeply". But his passion about environmental issues still burns.

"The King is a convener, connecting people and organisations in ways that open up possibilities and create solutions," his former press secretary Julian Payne told the BBC. Charles, he said, would invite "the best brains and the most experienced people and listen to their ideas and advice. I suspect it is a modus operandi that will continue as he takes on this new role."

He is unlikely, therefore, to totally abandon his wide-ranging interests, such as saving the tropical forests, reducing plastic pollution in the world's oceans and calling for the introduction of sustainable farming practices. Behind closed doors, he will no doubt discuss such matters with political leaders in the UK and further afield as Head of State and Head of the Commonwealth.

Guiding business to net zero

Climate Strategy & Partners is leading the way in helping companies and governments along the path to decarbonisation

When Peter Sweatman was 30, he reached a fork in the road. He had a successful career in finance at JP Morgan and he knew he could continue on that route, working long hours in a high-pressure environment for large financial rewards. Or he could make a genuine difference to the world. His decision to take the latter path led to him founding Climate Strategy & Partners in 2009. The consultancy advises multinational companies, international organisations and governments in their journeys towards decarbonisation. "I have never regretted my decision," he says. "I chose the right path."

Sweatman went on to create Charity Digital (then Charity Technology Trust) in 2001, which helps charities undergo digital transformation – to date, 68,000 charities have used the service, saving £260 million. Working alongside leading environmental charities, he developed an early interest in climate change. Next, he joined the founding team of Climate Change Capital, one of the first fund managers to specialise in climate-themed investment.

Based in Madrid, Climate Strategy & Partners brings together Sweatman's knowledge of finance, NGOs and climate change. There are three strands to the firm's work. The first involves helping large companies across various sectors achieve sustainability. "We don't repeat work we have already done or use the same framework on multiple clients – our approach is tailored to the exact needs of each client," says Sweatman. "This means we usually deliver first-of-a-kind projects that involve resolving complexity and answering difficult questions for companies trying to establish a decarbonisation strategy while operating all over the world." For example, since 2010, Climate Strategy has worked with Ferrovial, one of the world's largest infrastructure groups, implementing the first group-wide climate-change strategy, setting emissions targets,

undertaking climate risk and opportunity assessments, and setting science-based targets for 2030. Ferrovial is now committed to reduce its emissions by 35 per cent by 2030.

The second element involves advising on government policy development. Sweatman led the G20's Energy Efficiency Finance Task Group for five years, promoting energy efficiency investment principles, with the aim to help the world's largest emitting countries join forces to invest to reduce energy demand. This resulted in the G20 Energy Efficiency Investment Toolkit. "This is a compendium of all policies used by G20 countries to spur energy efficiency investments, backed by over 140 leading financers making specific promises for private-sector delivery," he says. "We also helped Mexico develop its Long Term Political Framework for Energy Efficiency. We work across the world because governments face similar challenges in our area and there is a lot to learn from the policy frameworks that work. You can effect change by identifying successful policies and tailoring them to fit different national environments."

Finally, Sweatman launched Energy Efficiency Capital Advisors, working mainly with Spanish cities to refinance €60 million of energy-savings contracts for long-term investors, enabling dozens of cities to decarbonise.

"These three strands all connect because each activity informs the other," he says. "Our policy insights come from working closely with businesses in the field, and our strategic judgement is improved by being at the cutting edge of policy development. We are mission-orientated and we only take on projects that will have a positive climate impact and make a difference. Time is our most valuable asset, and – in climate – there isn't enough of it left."

www.climatestrategy.com

Making the switch

For the owners of Fischer, providing households with electric heating systems makes sense for people and the planet

"It started because I wanted to use a cleaner form of energy such as electricity, which could be created without using fossil fuels," says Keith Bastian, CEO of Fischer Future Heat. "It was a personal passion." He is talking of the time he changed the heating in his house from traditional gas-powered central heating to clay-core electric radiators by the German company Fischer – and was so impressed with the results that he bought the company.

"Fischer's system was very easy to install and to use, it didn't require any maintenance and was flexible and reliable," explains Bastian. Along with his wife Maria, Bastian brought Fischer Future Heat to the UK in 2009, becoming the UK face of the 75-year-old German brand, which specialises in producing electric boilers, water heaters and EV chargers, as well as radiators that allow for room-by-room temperature control. With the Fischer Future Heat HQ now in Leicester, manufacturing continues in Germany, as well as in the UK and Spain.

Bastian believes a switch from gas to electric is essential if the UK is to meet its carbon targets. A combination of electric radiators and renewable energy will enable heating to become environmentally cleaner, he maintains, while homeowners will benefit from the resulting efficiencies.

Fischer Future Heat radiators give the user complete and precise control over the temperature in each room. Bastian explains that this mitigates the inefficiencies caused by gas central heating in the UK, where every room is usually heated according to a single thermostat that does not compensate for heat loss, nor the fact that heat rises, nor the fact that different rooms can be kept at different temperatures. With Fischer Future Heat, homeowners can maintain different temperatures, secure in the knowledge that heating through electricity can be done without using fossil fuels.

"You can now get 100 per cent clean electricity, so if you switch to our radiators you can have zero emissions and room-by-room control," says Bastian. "We can change the entire house to electric heating in one or two days."

Customers initially went to Fischer Future Heat because they had inadequate and cumbersome systems and they could see the company's system made sense. "Today, we are more relevant than ever," says Bastian, "because our message of energy efficiency and energy security has come true." It is a message the UK government supports, offering grants towards the installation of heat pumps and biomass boilers. While Bastian welcomes the principle, he is not convinced that the focus is correct. "The government's attitude should be to push all solutions," he says. "It has to be heat pumps and electric boilers and electric radiators – people should be allowed to choose what works for them. Up to 54 per cent of UK homes don't meet the insulation standards required for heat pumps, so we need other solutions involved."

Bastian's vision is to see every home in the UK converted to a zero-emission system so that people can see the effectiveness of room-by-room heating and how it can deliver comfort and economy. "That will be a great step for the planet and the homeowner," he says. "We feel that we are doing our bit. We are totally committed, we have been for more than 10 years, and we will continue to be for the foreseeable future."

www.fischerfutureheat.com

Hydrogen powered

With its team's Formula 1 experience, Advanced Hydrogen Technologies has groundbreaking solutions to reduce carbon emissions and provide affordable, sustainable domestic fuel

"Our initial work helped reduce carbon emissions in internal combustion engines in the transport sector. Our most recent challenge was to find an affordable, effective heating system to incorporate easily into new builds and retrofit in existing housing. Our Engine Carbon Clean Technology and Chimera products provide both these solutions," says Ben Kattenhorn, CEO of Advanced Hydrogen Technologies (AHT) Group.

Launched in 2021, AHT Group is at the forefront of breakthrough intellectual property for the automotive and energy industries. The hydrogen experts' Chimera system is an off-grid replacement for natural gas that can be safely integrated into a domestic central-heating system, using the pure hydrogen it generates from tap water via electrolysis.

Extracted using the same hydrogen-generation method, the medical-grade gas can be used to clean internal combustion engines (petrol or diesel) of carbon build up, which restricts airways. This restores engine efficiency, cutting carbon emissions by up to 65 per cent. Trials of AHT's Engine Carbon Clean Technology with industry leaders are nearing their conclusion, with game-changing initial results.

"I was working in motor racing when I met my now business partner Den Karmal, a highly successful engineer," says Kattenhorn. "Den was generating and controlling hydrogen to clean internal combustion engines to restore lost power and maximise efficiency. We now work in a different competition: the race to net zero!" The pair stayed in touch when Kattenhorn returned to a career in the city, managing and assisting start-ups with strategy and investment. Later, he joined Den in business and, following fundraising, Den adapted his original machine to generate and pump hydrogen into a gas boiler.

"Since then, the company has grown; we've fine-tuned the concepts and will soon report on advanced trials with some big names. Of course, we're also securing all the necessary approvals before going to market," explains Kattenhorn.

AHT Group was named the best brand in the Domestic category at the 2023 Hydrogen Awards. It is an active advocate for British engineering talent and also tries to source parts from UK supply chains. Where possible, the company uses recyclable and biodegradable parts in the generator. "Our vision," says Kattenhorn, "is that the pioneering technology of tomorrow should be kind to the planet today."

www.ahtgroup.co.uk

Trading strengths

All Steels Trading is one of Europe's fastest growing steel-trading companies, with a focus on green steel and cutting emissions

When Laurence McDougall founded All Steels Trading in 2006, he was determined to do things differently. All Steels Trading represented a clean slate – a chance to develop a new type of steel trading company – and McDougall quickly set about distinguishing the company from its competitors. This meant keeping the core business lean and agile.

McDougall found partners to handle stock management and transport, which allowed the company to concentrate on buying and selling steel. "We focus on modern producers and quality suppliers, the people who are using the best and latest gear," explains McDougall. "Turkey is a big supplier and it's one of the biggest producers of re-melted steel – this is what we call 'green steel'. It uses 75 per cent less energy and is very environmentally friendly as it is just recycling old steel. This is now a prerequisite when quoting for a lot of jobs, and we have been ahead of the curve on getting access."

Additionally, the company's facilities are equipped with solar panels and ground source heat pumps. With clients seeking to reduce emissions in their supply chain, this gives All Steels Trading an important advantage. As a result of such forward thinking, the company has become one of the fastest growing steel-trading companies in Europe and is preparing to open a facility in Ghent, Belgium, further building relationships on the Continent.

Through alliances with other companies, All Steels Trading offers a processing service and can supply niche market products. "We have beaten all expectations, but we can never be complacent. We have one of the largest stocks of structural steel and the vastest range of products, but we also have the skill to develop new products. So, if somebody is looking for a new shape or a new grade, we are the experts at finding a solution that works for them."

In terms of sustainability and community, "we try to do the right thing," says McDougall, "and have supported The Prince's Trust for the past eight years as we really believe in this organisation and enjoy giving back to society. There has been great satisfaction in seeing All Steels Trading succeed and allowing our workforce to enjoy the journey."

www.allsteelstrading.co.uk

An Amazonian task

With its carbon-credit generation, the Brazil-based Future Carbon Group
is operating at the fore of climate-change mitigation

"Our goal is to have one million hectares of protected land in Amazonia within five years," says Gabriel Junqueira Sciotti Elias, Chief Financial Officer of Future Carbon Group. "We currently have more than 100,000 hectares of land in the Amazon, which we protect to mitigate the impact of climate change, and to generate positive impact for the Indigenous communities who live there."

In operating globally from a country where more than 60 per cent of the Amazon basin is located, the Brazil-based Future Carbon Group is a vital stakeholder in climate-change mitigation. The Amazon basin covers 2.6 million square miles across nine South American countries and stores around 100 billion metric tonnes of carbon. With over half of the Amazon within its borders, Brazil is one of the most important places on the planet for the protection of the climate and meeting climate targets.

The Future Carbon Group, founded in (YEAR), helps drive transformation towards a sustainable future through the generation of carbon credits. This involves funding projects that reduce greenhouse gas emissions in exchange for internationally accredited credits that companies around the world can buy to offset their carbon emissions. It is an important step for companies working towards operating more sustainably. "We are the biggest lender of carbon credits in the energy sector in Brazil and help companies and governments to reach their net-zero targets," says Elias. "We also have offices in London, making us the first Brazilian carbon company with a London office."

Elias came to Future Carbon Group from a career in private equity and venture capital. It was after an encounter with a Tibetan healer that he began to think more carefully about the impact humanity was having on the planet. His interest and work combined on projects around climate and ESG (environmental, social and governance) for multinationals such as Parmalat, which produces and distributes diary and food. This led him to create the first sustainable milk producer in Brazil, which was a major breakthrough for the country regarding action on the climate.

Future Carbon Group works with partners to generate and share carbon credits over a range of areas, encompassing forest restoration; low-carbon agriculture and livestock; renewable energy; ESG programmes and climate-related training courses; carbon investment and financial products; future carbon technology; and solutions to support companies in their net-zero strategies and carbon-generation portfolios. This means that the company is a one-stop shop for climate mitigation and carbon credits, able to support partners from around the globe in a variety of ways to meet the most robust standards.

"We want to have the biggest portfolio of climate solutions for major companies, so they can start to become net zero without having to completely transform their business model," says Elias. "They can buy carbon credits or have an ESG strategy or compensate for damage by planting trees and looking after communities. We are also starting to generate credits for biodiversity and water protection."

The company, staffed by executives with decades of experience in carbon, sustainable investments and corporate governance, is focused on long-term partnerships where everyone profits by working together for the good of the planet. "We don't have the final answer, but the ideas are there and we have a commitment to deliver solutions for the future of the Earth," says Elias. "Profit is important, but it's not enough. We need to work for the planet and for future generations to leave them with a better world."

www.futurecarbon.com.br

The power of innovation

Pioneering blockchain platform Mpowa wants to transform the world of investment by harnessing the power of zero-carbon digital tokens

When Ryan Lavelle founded blockchain platform Mpowa in 2019, he saw it as an opportunity to apply all the experience he had acquired during an international career of software development within finance. After witnessing systematic barriers within the industry, he was determined to address these issues with a particular focus on supporting enterprises that wanted to create a greener, brighter future.

"We are creating a platform that will showcase and train passionate, driven people who want to make their communities better and source funding through business sponsorship," says Lavelle. "Our technology is designed for purpose to help these change-makers solve the world's biggest problems, including in hard to reach, marginalised communities such as refugee camps."

Already well established in creating transparency for money and data, blockchain digital ledgers ensure trust so that Mpowa can monitor how money is spent within projects and track and share what social and environmental impact the money makes in these communities. "We are even creating a sustainability demonstrator and training centre here in the UK, so we can openly share learnings," says Lavelle. "Working closely with Mpowa's sister arm Mpowa Impact – itself a social enterprise run by Bushra Burge – the team has identified a number of mutually beneficial, innovative ways in which international corporations and social enterprises can work together using our robust, transparent framework."

Mpowa helps businesses find a project relevant to its needs, and provide the most green, efficient way to fund the project: a zero-carbon digital token. These are ideal for a business that wants to put something back into communities in which it already has supply chains.

"We can help take an idea from conception to execution by curating bespoke projects for people to invest in and support," explains Lavelle. "I'd like to have supported a few thousand successful projects over the next few years, which is doable because we are focused on scale and automation, building platforms that enable large numbers of people to invest with teams on the ground that scale out horizontally."

Mpowa is now a growing international opeartion that has begun developing a network and building a community in Africa over the past two years to find the right investment opportunities. It is important to Lavelle that projects are financially as well as environmentally sustainable, hence the commitment to zero-carbon digital payments mined on a global network of clean data mining facilities. An alternative to charitable donations, Mpowa's technology allows investors to put money into businesses that have a long-term financial plan.

For example, rather than just donating money to an orphanage in Uganda, Mpowa's blockchain software allows businesses to safely invest funds to buy land which can then be used for agriculture, or training people in a skill, while providing the orphanage with a long-term, sustainable form of income.

Lavelle is also exploring alternative energy sources. "Along with our non-profit side, raising funds to allow businesses to make a positive impact, we are also looking at energy and infrastructure, developing a portfolio of smart cities across Africa using hydrogen and other alternative energies," he explains. "It is about creating a movement to become independent. We know that there is more work to be done but we are very inspired by the innovation, hope and unity we are discovering and attracting through our community."

www.mpowa.io

A source for good

Putting people and the planet above profit is the ethos of health and wellness company AquaSource and its community of independent distributors

Arthur Spurling was working as a fruit and vegetable merchant, when, in 1991, he discovered the nutritional value of blue-green algae and embarked on a transatlantic algae-sourcing adventure, driven by his pursuit of optimum quality ingredients. What started with the algae – sourced from the fresh water of the Upper Klamath Lake in Southern Oregon in the US – gradually expanded to a range of nutritional products that ticked biodynamic, organic, vegan and sustainability boxes long before they were *de rigueur*.

In 1994, Spurling joined UK health and wellness company AquaSource as a business consultant, later becoming Managing Director. Alongside his unwaveringly energetic hunt for hero ingredients, he inspired others to consume high-quality nutrition from natural sources. This evolved into a business of likeminded individuals across the UK and Europe. "It has grown organically, not because of what we say, but because of what we do," says Spurling. "Distributors and customers aren't attracted to our products by marketing claims, but by the recommendations of people who have actually experienced them."

Charity work is equally important to Spurling. The LightSource Charity was founded in 2014, and he and his wife, charity trustee Albena Spurling, are genuinely passionate and proactive about the cause it supports. "LightSource helps to create positive and motivational environments in schools," he says. The focus of their work began in Bulgaria, but they are now working with schools elsewhere in Europe – helping to bring bright colours, positive affirmations and images, and educational information to schools through the use of photo wallpaper. "The transformations and feedback have been incredible and extremely moving."

LightSource's life-changing work is predominantly supported by funds from AquaSource, which donates 10 per cent of its profit after tax to the charity. The company is also committed to planting trees in honour of new distributors, as well as protecting wild bees through an initiative to supply seeds and grow wildflower reserves, supporting habitats for pollinating insects. Spurling encourages independent distributors with their charitable causes. Many share the company's values of putting the health of people and the planet above profit. "It's wonderful that our quality products are the reason we can pursue this positive work," he says. "It's all about giving back."

www.aquasource.net

Green governance

With 25 years of ESG experience, Candriam invests responsibly to add value while shaping a better future

The roots of responsible investment at Candriam run deep, dating back to 1996 when this global, and pioneering, multi-specialist asset manager from New York launched its first sustainable fund. "Conviction and responsibility in asset management" is even embedded in the name.

"Sustainable and responsible investing has been at the heart of Candriam for 25 years," says Naïm Abou-Jaoudé, Chairman of Candriam and CEO of New York Life Investments International. The company leads the way in Environmental, Social and Governance (ESG), managing more than €100 billion in ESG-related assets and offering over 30 sustainable products covering all asset classes and global markets.

For Candriam, conviction means believing in the value of its work to deliver superior investment returns, solutions and services to clients, while managing its impact on society, the environment and stakeholders. As a long-term thinker, the company strives to be the best corporate citizen it can be.

In 2017, the Candriam Academy was launched. The industry's first free-to-access accredited training platform, it raises awareness and educates people about sustainable, responsible investing. Today, it has over 13,000 members across 50 countries.

Additionally, Candriam is pursuing a philanthropic commitment to donate 10 per cent of net management fees across its sustainable strategies to social and environmental projects. This is carried out through the Candriam Institute for Sustainable Development, which, since 2001, has helped over 140 organisations. "Our efforts towards achieving an inclusive and sustainable society don't stop at our investments. Through the institute, we seek to effect meaningful social change, deliver a positive environmental impact and, ultimately, play our part in leaving a better world for future generations," says Abou-Jaoudé.

The fight against climate change is another of the company's commitments. In 2021, it joined the Net Zero Asset Manager Initiative to support reaching net zero by 2050. "We are convinced that today's climate issues are so important that they call for our collective responsibility in order to accelerate sustainable development and respond to the many challenges facing the world's population and environment."

By including stakeholders, clients, providers, employees and communities, while taking care of the environment, Candriam is hoping to help shape a world that people really want to live in.

www.candriam.com

Pricing climate transition

By overseeing investment for renewable energy, Nephila Climate
is reshaping the insurance market in the transition to net zero

The long and difficult journey to net zero is not going to be possible without unprecedented levels of investment. While banks and pension funds have the pockets and potential to unlock exciting and impactful renewable projects, investments must be bolstered by new insurance solutions. Nephila Climate is a specialist in climate-related insurance, with the experience, scale and technical know-how to analyse risk so that capital providers can make decisions with confidence and invest in renewable projects with security.

"Insurance will be critical in the transition to net zero in a way people haven't yet imagined," says CEO Maria Rapin. "We are essentially building a new market. I think of the transition to net zero as our modern-day version of the industrial revolution. It will fundamentally change the shape of our economy and, of course, it will require new forms of risk transfer. There is demand for the development of large-scale clean-energy projects, and investors require new insurance solutions. Solving these risk-management challenges is Nephila Climate's core competency."

As one example, Nephila Climate provides minimum revenue protection for wind and solar power to enable these projects to grow at scale, which is crucial if the world is to meet net zero targets. The company provides similar insurance products to battery storage developers to unlock more affordable finance and accelerate growth in this important new sector. Another aspect of the company sees Nephila Climate work in Brazil and India to provide the insurance that protects smallholder farmers against extreme climactic conditions, ensuring they still have access to the seeds and machinery they need in difficult times. "Agriculture makes up a material portion of GDP in these countries and is therefore critical to their economic stability. The crop insurance schemes aim to give farmers in the region the stability they need to keep planting year after year, especially as weather patterns become more unpredictable. Our hope is that it will also give them the confidence to try more sustainable farming techniques."

Nephila Climate is part of Nephila Capital, which was co-founded in 1998 by Frank Majors and Greg Hagood, at the time two London-based US financiers. The company was the first to focus on the convergence of catastrophe reinsurance and weather risk transfer markets with capital markets, creating "catastrophe bonds", a high-yield debt instrument designed to indemnify companies in the insurance industry in the event of a natural disaster. Nephila Capital has more than $7 billion under management, as of September 2023, and Rapin believes the potential for Nephila Climate is comparable given the scale of investment required to meet net zero targets.

"We have a duty to not just provide solutions to the industry, but to be selective and price these risks correctly in order to reward our own capital providers," says Rapin. "We don't have the capacity to do everything we are asked about, so we focus on projects with the biggest impact and sound fundamentals."

Ultimately, Nephila Climate is "in this space to solve problems, support the transition to net zero and develop new insurance products for a greener world," says Rapin. "We are fortunate to interact with curious people with a huge passion for their mission on a daily basis. We are helping to make change happen by putting a price on risk and helping unlock capital flows into a very important new sector."

www.nephila.com/climate

Carbon accounting

Underpinned by the principles of honesty and transparency, CarbonTRACC's carbon consultancy service helps ethically minded businesses reduce greenhouse gases

"Right now, it's not just that we are rearranging the deckchairs on the Titanic. It's like we have got people in the first-class casino on the Titanic after it's hit the iceberg and the ship is going down, still trying to make a few shillings." Fergal Mee, CEO of CarbonTRACC – a company that delivers consultancy and training in measuring and cutting greenhouse gas (GHG) emissions and removing carbon dioxide from the atmosphere – is talking about the unethical efforts of many businesses to urgently mitigate climate change.

After decades of experience in various business sectors offering environmental protection advice, Mee founded CarbonTRACC in 2023. The company has already worked with various governments, as well as in both the Republic of China and the People's Republic of China, quantifying GHG emissions and training organisations in ways to reduce them. CarbonTRACC conforms to standards set by the ISO (International Organization for Standardization). "These experts from 190 countries have given their time and experience voluntarily – we can trust their unpaid, nonvested independence and expertise," says Mee.

Mee knows the difference it can make to sustainability when businesses make small changes. He wants to deliver "high quality, robust and greenwash-free" services that will lead to quantifiable improvements for businesses. He is also aware of the possible perils of lengthy, globalised supply chains, "a big contributor to environmental damage. If you buy an iPhone in London, it's made in China and sent on a container to Felixstowe. The emissions from that supply and manufacturing chain are huge."

When it comes to his own business practice, "we are fundamentalists and we are a little unorthodox in the way we select the organisations we work with," says Mee. The company values "transparency, relevance, accuracy, completeness and consistency" (TRACC), which he sees simply as "trying to stay honest and ensuring our work is authentic and ethical". Mee will not do business with organisations, large or small, that do not strive to meet these standards. For those that do, he provides bespoke advice, helping them find opportunities to reduce their carbon footprint.

Ultimately, CarbonTRACC seeks "to do the right thing by working on projects that have a real, positive effect on tackling climate change because the threat is civilisational. People are realising they can make a difference, and we're here to help them do that."

www.carbontracc.com

Climate risk assessment

Climate X is helping businesses to identify their exposure
to extreme weather events – and to prepare for change

Climate change is here, and it is clear that while decarbonisation remains of paramount importance, mitigation and adaptability are essential. Even if net zero were reached tomorrow, the climate would not return to "normal" overnight. But to build adequate resilience, we need information. Climate X, a British startup, quantifies the impacts of climate change decades in advance, allowing organisations to prepare for change with confidence.

With banks, mortgage lenders and investors increasingly asking businesses to identify their exposure to climate risk, Climate X's platform, Spectra, is already essential within the world of finance. "While the human contribution towards climate change is essential to tackle, we must also consider how climate change affects us," says founder and CEO, Lukky Ahmed. "I came from the finance world, where we still treated extreme weather events as isolated incidents even though they occurred yearly. We needed to accept these things happening more frequently and consider how they would affect businesses."

Climate X's team of climate scientists draw on numerous pieces of data to model the effect of climate change on very specific geographies. It can show what might happen to soybean crops in Illinois, in the US, in the event of extended drought, or which parts of London would be affected by subsidence or flood. Armed with that information, financial institutions can quantify their physical exposure to climate risk and make the required transitional changes. The impact of climate change on the entire global economy, from food to mortgages to insurance, will be vast – but forewarned is forearmed.

Climate X's platform visually shows how the world is changing. "This will help to show where people should live and help organisations adapt, but it doesn't stop there," says Ahmed. "Our data can be used to identify areas at risk of climate migration, or anything that might be affected by extreme weather events, such as biodiversity and nature.

"We work with financial institutions and commercial realtors, but climate risk is affecting everything everywhere," he concludes. "Our purpose as a company is to move the direction of change. Even if it is a tiny bit, it will allow all of us to make better decisions."

www.climate-x.com

The renewable revolution

Corre Energy's game-changing energy storage concept unlocks affordable
green electricity at scale, and is ready to be replicated worldwide

Conventional wisdom has long been that renewable energy cannot be stored at scale, but Keith McGrane has never cared for conventional wisdom. After studying geophysics at university and holding various successful financial roles, he began to develop a product that would allow energy produced by the wind or sun to be stored for days at a time. Today, a pioneer and thought leader in energy storage, he is Executive Director and CEO of Corre Energy.

Founded in 2018, Corre Energy uses an innovative compressed air energy storage system, taking renewable energy and storing it in subterranean salt caverns. "The tech was first demonstrated in the 1970s. Corre Energy has brought this solution into the 21st century by designing it for long duration by optimising salt cavern sizing and operation, with above-ground equipment for compressing and generating electricity," explains McGrane. "We use the air to drive a turbine that returns 100 per cent green energy from the cavern straight back into the grid, complemented by green hydrogen fuelling. We have optimised a design that allows us to produce continual output for 84 hours by going underground, where we can store larger volumes of energy and achieve scale."

With several sites already in Europe, McGrane wants to create further investment opportunities, and recently secured an opportunity in the huge US market. He sees Corre Energy as delivering a product as much as individual projects – the overall concept, now perfected, can be standardised and replicated across the world on multiple sites to suit any grid. Such storage has economic, environmental and national security advantages, with studies by Imperial College London estimating the value of compressed air energy storage to the UK system into the future to be between £2 billion and £5 billion per installation.

"We are seeing increased demand for this solution," says McGrane. "The targets being set for renewable energy are significant and difficult to achieve without multi-day storage such as our solution. Governments are beginning to realise how important it is to generate and store your own electricity in your own system."

McGrane is also keen to point out the multifaceted, positive societal impact of this product, while the list of benefits "goes on and on". "It enables more renewables, accelerates their deployment, increases their value and enhances security of supply," he says. "It also displaces fossil fuel plants, thereby greatly reducing carbon emissions. What's not to like!"

www.corre.energy

Solar gain

Seamlessly integrated into a roof, GB-Sol's solar slates are not only aesthetically pleasing, but are also homegrown, too

As a spin-out from Cardiff University, South Wales-based GB-Sol had proudly showed a prototype for roof solar panels to Queen Elizabeth II seven years before the company was founded in 1999. GB-Sol now installs PV Slate, one of its many product innovations. It has been fitted seamlessly with natural slate on a listed building at York Minster, for example, as well as on many of the new houses at the Duchy of Cornwall's Nansledan development, near Newquay, generating solar power yet looking like a traditional roof.

Initially, says Director Mark Candlish, who joined the company in 2007, solar-panel clients were pioneers, willing to "spoil" the look of their roofs for the sake of cost-effective greenness and feed-in tariffs. Today, a second wave of customers seeks the aesthetic quality and durability offered by GB-Sol in such products as its edge-to-edge, glass and aluminium Infinity solar roof, which not only looks sleek, but also offers huge power generation. "The solar industry has been slightly obsessed with cheapness and payback, which is not the case with other building materials," says Candlish. "Most people choose their bricks, windows and paint with an eye to making their house look better, not just choosing the cheapest. Now, we find people are more demanding in what they want in terms of solar power, too."

GB-Sol has had to overcome setbacks. A few years ago, the River Taff burst its banks and flooded the factory in a metre of water. The team had only just cleaned the mess when lockdown hit. This, says Candlish, was a "grow or die" moment for the company. It took stock, reviewed its manufacturing processes, expanded its team and is now in a perfect position to fulfil the ever-increasing demand for solar-powered products.

As well as its flexibility in meeting demand by making the product in Britain rather than importing, Candlish highlights the social benefit GB-Sol provides. "It's not just the direct employment that a British manufacturer generates, we're connected to dozens of other support businesses – metalworkers, glass tougheners, electricians, plumbers – the factory is quite an organism. Plus, we have generations of workers in the electronics tradition of the Valleys, since the coal-mining industry was replaced. That brings a great deal of goodwill and enthusiasm."

www.gb-sol.co.uk

Forward thinking

Cold storage facility Hemswell Coldstore has high standards,
not only in food safety, but also in the use of renewable energy

"Even small businesses can do green well," says Stephen Hill, owner and Managing Director of Hemswell Coldstore in rural Lincolnshire. The business might be small in comparison to other cold stores, but this tight ship delivers large-scale operations for the UK and beyond.

Freezing 600 tonnes of produce a week in their blast freezers, Hill and his team deal with nearly 5,000 pallets of chilled or frozen food at any one time. It is essential produce that is waiting to be imported across the country and exported around the world.

With such an energy-expensive business, Hill says it is important to demonstrate their green credentials. This 35-year veteran of the meat and poultry industry has ensured that Hemswell Coldstore holds an AA grade – the highest accreditation for food safety standards – from the British Retail Consortium. He employs all his staff from within a 15-mile radius of the site and is constantly updating and maintaining the plant, ensuring it is leak free.

"The biggest impact our business has on the environment is energy usage and loss of refrigerant gasses, which contribute to global warming," says Hill. "The latter is something we have tackled by constantly maintaining our refrigeration plant."

Most significant is the leap Hill took in 2016 to symbiotically team up the business with an anaerobic digestion plant (AD) as a source of energy. The plant, which converts food waste to biogas, just so happens to be built on the same industrial estate. "It's fair to say, when I initially spoke to customers and staff about this project, I was mainly met with scepticism," he says. "I was determined to encourage the company to build their plant on this site. I guaranteed we would buy our energy from them, as well as being a source of raw materials: if our customers have waste food they need to dispose of, it goes to the plant."

This forward thinking in partnering with the AD plant means Hemswell Coldstore is playing a part, says Hill, in protecting the environment for future generations. "King Charles III was an early outlier, bringing people's attention all over the world to the issue of global warming," he adds. "It is clear he was a forward thinker, too."

www.hemswellcoldstore.com

On a mission

By scaling cutting-edge carbon capture technology, Mission Zero
is racing to mitigate the effects of man-made climate change

"A lot of climate technology startups scale breakthroughs over decades", says Dr Shiladitya Ghosh, Chief Product Officer of Mission Zero. "They commercialise incrementally, secure grant funding collaborators, and finally develop a profitable project. With the climate crisis, we don't have decades left." With fellow co-founders Dr Nicholas Chadwick and Dr Gaël Gobaille-Shaw, Ghosh is pursuing a radically different model to help to urgently rebalance the world's atmosphere.

The trio are pooling their expertise to pioneer direct air capture (DAC) technology to recover historic waste CO_2 from the air at a fraction of the cost and energy of the few alternatives currently available. In just three years, they have completed vital research and development and are already delivering commercial-scale technology to international clients.

"Traditionally, carbon capture has had to use a lot of heat or thermal energy," says Ghosh. "This is inefficient and counter-productive if you're burning fossil fuels to obtain that energy. As we are focusing on a method that doesn't produce heat, and only requires electricity, we have something that is future-proofed for the transition to renewables taking place around us."

Rather than developing new hardware from scratch, Mission Zero's model works by leveraging existing off-the-shelf options. The team seek to grow quickly by focusing purely on their product. "We see ourselves as suppliers of an incredibly flexible keystone product that empowers customers to easily integrate DAC into their operations, wherever they may be based," explains Ghosh. It is an approach that has won them the backing of the world's foremost climate venture capital firm Breakthrough Energy Ventures, as well as the XPRIZE foundation, Anglo American, Stripe and the UK government.

By scaling to provide a reliable, abundant, and cost-effective source of sustainable CO_2, Mission Zero sees its technology as vital to help fossil-dependent industries decarbonise and tackle historic emissions. With net zero goal deadlines drawing ever closer, Mission Zero's founders know that time is of the essence. "Carbon removal is a conduit for enabling critical climate transitions. We need DAC to become a staple industrial technology all around the world, as highly visible and impactful as solar panels are today."

www.missionzero.tech

Chain reactions

With its secure and eco-friendly blockchain technology, Oaro is enabling a host of imaginative digital authentication opportunities

"I'm super-proud to be running a carbon net-zero blockchain vendor," says Garry Harrison, CEO of technology company Oaro. "It's a unique concept with a huge impact on how we use tech." Oaro's eco-friendly blockchain and identity solutions aim to place trust and opportunity at the heart of business, government and consumer interaction, enabling safe, secure connections. And where blockchain technology usually requires heavy energy consumption, Oaro's Eco-NFT (a non-fungible token or unique digital certificate of authenticity) is powered by the company's own private blockchain cloud platform, one of the most sustainable in the world.

Founded in 2017, the Canadian company's platform is enabling innovative applications in digital security across sectors including pharmaceuticals, sports, retail, finance and government. NFT-generated airline tickets and advanced identity technology, using Oaro's blockchain, are even transforming air travel. "Oaro offers a secure, seamless travel experience. Once you've authenticated yourself using our face recognition and blockchain technology, you can enjoy a frictionless airport journey from kerbside to departure gate." For vendors, legal ownership of airline tickets resides in crypto tokens. These can be resold securely, with profits applied to each seller and the original vendor.

Oaro is also working with sports federations and elite teams. "With tokenisation blockchain technology, vendors can attach memorabilia, collectables and media to each secure unique ticket, to enrich fan experience and eliminate fraud." Similarly pioneering interventions include the world's first loans secured by NFTs related to agricultural commodities. Using tokenised digital assets, which represent real crops, rural farming communities can access a new loans and trading landscape.

As Oaro develops its services, more applications follow. Tokenisation of the property market using Oaro's technology, for example, creates new opportunity. "We want to open up real-estate markets, making them more accessible for everyone," says Harrison. "We've partnered with a real-estate company to tokenise a significant area of the Amazon rainforest so anyone can buy and protect a piece of it. This also helps us meet our carbon-offset goals. It's a fundamentally different, imaginative approach."

www.oaro.net

Winds of change

Offshore Solutions Group solves the challenge of building and installing giant
floating offshore wind turbines, bringing green opportunities to the UK

The skills and space needed to build the next generation of gigantic floating offshore wind (FLOW) units – each the size and weight of the Eiffel Tower – presents challenges and opportunities; both of which Will Rowley, Group Chief Executive of Offshore Solutions Group, which was set up in 2020, believes the UK is well placed to embrace.

"Some older wind turbines produced less than a megawatt of energy, but the new FLOW units can produce 18 megawatts. They're much bigger and most of the forthcoming projects feature 40 to 60 units," he says. "Their scale and engineering complexity puts them beyond the current capacity and skillset of most ports and shipyards in the UK, so their construction, transportation and storage (while awaiting a weather window for anchorage in their intended location) present new and interesting challenges. Our team of experts work with clients to solve these challenges, so they can make the most of the opportunities."

The Crown Estate and Crown Estate Scotland have already engaged in the exploration of solutions in the sector and Rowley expects other partners, collaborators, investors and developers in the UK to follow suit swiftly, in order to establish a world-leading presence. "There are around 1,500 turbines in planning around the UK and 12,500 in planning worldwide. For context, in tonnage, that's about the same amount as the entire UK shipping fleet," he explains. "The task is huge and new, which makes it both challenging and exciting.

"We're working internationally with developers on new engineering solutions for the next generation of units, such as building them in 2,000-tonne modules, which can be joined together using aerospace technology adapted to the marine environment. Major innovations like this require new skills, technology and infrastructure – all of which are opportunities we'd like to see the UK seize upon and excel in."

A proposal for a £300 million floating unit module factory on Teesside in the North of England has already put the UK on the map. It shows that with the commitment, investment and concerted action to develop the expertise that Rowley talks about, the UK could establish itself as a leader in a sector that not only promises to secure energy, but also secures a brighter future for people and the planet.

www.offshoresolutionsgroup.com

An eco-friendly vision

WMF Energy is working to mitigate the impact of huge
infrastructure projects on the Amazon and its communities

Before he formed WMF Energy, Alexandre da Rosa worked with leading FTSE 100 and Fortune 500 companies designing and building more than 50 data centres around the world. As a Brazilian, however, he was acutely aware of the importance of maintaining the fragile ecological balance of the Amazon rainforest. He began to contemplate the huge negative environmental impact of these enormous data centres, which emit vast quantities of heat and consume large amounts of often fossil fuel-derived energy.

He decided to act and formed WMF Energy in 2004. His focus was to develop technological solutions to mitigate the impact caused by the construction of data centres and other huge tech infrastructure projects. His work focuses on the scientifically advanced care of forests, the generation of clean energy and the transformation of waste into clean energy or reusable and sustainable fuels. Da Rosa became one of the ten largest owners and administrators of private Amazon forestlands in the world, using WMF Energy as an environmental remediation company to develop and implement projects for forest conservation with social impact.

WMF Energy offers services in four areas: forest management, carbon credit, clean energy and tokens, each of which are targeted at improving three specific socio-environmental areas – forests, energy and waste. The company believes that tackling deforestation is not enough; instead, it advocates for sustainable intervention to maintain the integrity of the forest. This is now recognised as the most effective way to protect both the forest and the local and indigenous communities that depend on it. Through the application of active management practices, carbon can be sequestered and dead or dying trees emitting methane gas can be removed.

Such interventions can be supported through carbon credits – financial instruments used to help reduce greenhouse gas emissions. WMF Energy provides a range of verified and internationally accepted carbon credits. The company also supports the development and implementation of clean sources of energy, focusing on hydroelectric plants, hydrogen, wind and solar. Finally, all investment and projects are valued and paid for in tokens in the form of definitive blockchains, to provide transparency and security for all involved.

www.wmfenergy.com

The path to progress

ESG360° provides its client organisations with all-round expertise in the implementation of environmental, social and governance priorities

For a modern company, the bottom line is no longer enough. A successful business places as much importance on its environmental, social and governance (ESG) priorities as it does its commercial concerns, recognising that all these elements are intimately connected. Such organisations understand the importance of confronting the global environmental challenges to ensure a successful future for everyone.

However, for many business leaders, this is a process that takes them outside their comfort zone. ESG360° was created to support this transition, helping businesses to understand the challenges and opportunities of ESG so they can adjust their focus accordingly.

"Today, ESG is a business imperative," states the company. "We exist to enable all companies to build self-sufficiency in ESG within the whole organisation. We also help our clients to understand the interplay across the E, the S and the G components of ESG. From collecting Scope 3 primary data [which relates to the indirect emissions that occur in the upstream and downstream activities of an organisation] through our platform and automating reports, all the way to understanding the financial impact of net zero decisions across the value chain, we help our clients to become autonomous in data collection and in strategic decision-making on ESG."

Founded in 2022, ESG360° is an enterprise platform designed to help listed and large private companies enhance value by managing ESG as a strategic asset. This means that ESG360° will handle the complexity of ESG compliance, reducing the strain on the executive team. The company quantifies financial ESG impacts for FTSE 100 and FTSE 250 clients, analysing more than 50,000 datapoints per company.

The company can automate the collection of primary Scope 3 data directly from suppliers and engage all relevant teams within an organisation into a collaborative ESG process.

ESG360° will also automate reporting to align with a huge range of international standards, while analysing the impact of ESG transition and physical risks. Using ESG360°, a company can execute strategic scenario planning to analyse the impact of potential net zero paths.

In a nutshell, ESG360° aims to translate the complexity of real-world challenges into simplicity so that its clients can focus on taking effective action.

www.esg360.io

Sustainable development

Action plans such as his Sustainable Markets Initiative and "earth charter" demonstrate the commitment of King Charles to the future of the planet and its people

King Charles has made it clear that he believes a healthy, sustainable future can only be achieved when global capital markets unite to reverse the damage to the planet's oceans, atmosphere and soil. He has repeatedly stressed publicly that sustainable – rather than profitable – investment is key to preserving our biodiversity.

In an interview with myself for the *London Evening Standard*, he urged big business and the city to step up by investing "trillions of pounds" into schemes that protect the environment and promote a sustainable economy. He emphasised the need for investors to be more open-minded and to look at the potentially lucrative investment opportunities in the burgeoning sustainable markets, and complained that the previous reluctance of financiers to back green ventures had undermined his efforts to raise levels of environmental responsibility.

"The problem that I've found is that after 35 to 40 years of trying my best with corporate, social and environmental responsibility with the private sector, and countless seminars and workshops, trying to get people to recognise the huge challenges we face, we could never actually crack the real problem," said Charles, "which was the lack of real understanding on the part of the financial services and capital markets sector to understand why there was such a need to invest."

He went on to explain, however, that interest had "suddenly taken off" as investors have come to realise that "the returns on investment on sustainable investing are greater now than many of the conventional ones, such as stranded assets like fossil fuels".

"There are many more people wanting to look for sustainable investment opportunities, which would direct the money to the most effective things – whether it is regeneration, reforestation, sorting out fisheries and ocean issues to make them more sustainable," he continued. "Or agriculture and how to rebuild soil fertility, which is completely degraded around most of the world. Because if you can get the soil fertility back again, you can capture carbon much more quickly."

SUSTAINABLE MARKETS

Putting his words into action, Charles established the Sustainable Markets Council, with the support of the World Economic Forum, in September 2019, bringing together companies, governments and major financial institutions to "transform our market mechanisms to work for, not against, sustainability".

Charles believes the council will provide the financial muscle to raise far bigger sums than has been possible in the past to go into schemes such as the greening of the transportation systems in the Commonwealth Caribbean countries. "The money is now at last beginning to become available," he said, "because there are trillions of pounds out there, particularly in the private sector, which can now potentially be harnessed to drive real change. The key is the private sector, which has to lead, then you can create a partnership with the public sector.

"But you see there is no good waiting until it is a complete crisis because then it is terribly difficult to rectify the situation. So often in the history of humanity we've waited until something becomes a total catastrophe, before doing something about it. This time it is more critical than ever.

"The most important thing is the rapid decarbonisation of the whole of our economies and the development of this circular approach, which means that nothing is thrown away" he added. "You don't need to go on digging everything up because you can recycle it."

> "Charles's leadership in this field has helped change the narrative on sustainability, encouraging people to rethink their position on the issue going forward"

Increasingly, investors are taking a longer-term view and off-loading shares in fossil-fuel energy firms. The King believes this trend will continue as the planet's needs outweigh the hunger for short-term gain.

In an address he made at the World Economic Forum in Davos, Switzerland, in January 2020, Charles launched his Sustainable Markets Initiative, outlining his ten-point action plan for tackling these issues and driving the sustainable markets approach:

• Put nature's capital at the centre of business models, decisions and actions.

• Outline responsible transition pathways to decarbonise across sectors and nations.

• Reimagine industries using a sustainable markets framework, based on a circular bioeconomy.

• Identify game-changing technologies, as well as policy, regulation, infrastructure and investment barriers to transition.

• Reverse fossil-fuel subsidies and improve sustainable incentives.

• Invest in STEM projects and research and development into innovative technologies and solutions.

• Invest in nature as a "true engine of our economy" with nature-based solutions, including in agriculture, forestry and fisheries.

• Adopt common global metrics and standards for goods and services.

• Make the sustainable option the "trusted and attainable option" for consumers.

• Connect investors to sustainable projects.

Charles believes that the Sustainable Markets Initiative will encourage major market transformation. The initiative includes the need for a co-ordinated global effort to enable the private sector to accelerate the transition to a sustainable future. It also aims to ensure that the natural assets upon which we all depend – soil, water, forests, a stable climate and fish stocks – endure for future generations. True economic and social development, Charles believes, will best succeed when it works in harmony, rather than in conflict, with nature.

LEADING BY EXAMPLE

He has put his money where his mouth is, too. Charles divested his personal holdings from fossil fuels in 2015 and now, as monarch, he is hoping that Coutts and other leading banks will speed up the disconnection of royal holdings from all fossil fuels.

His Majesty is also behind a global sustainability revolution to persuade world leaders, indeed every one of us, to take personal

responsibility for the damage that is being done to the planet and consider how each of us can live in harmony with nature.

Charles's leadership in this field has helped change the narrative on sustainability, encouraging people to rethink their position on the issue going forward. As he has said repeatedly in his speeches, "Right action cannot happen without right thinking".

As king, he will continue to lead on sustainability, but with an even greater awareness of his position. This was demonstrated shortly after his accession when in January 2023 he gave up the opportunity to benefit from a £1 billion-a-year windfall from a major expansion of green energy, 25 per cent of which would have gone directly to the royal household as part of the annual Sovereign Grant.

Mindful of the cost-of-living crisis facing the UK, he asked the Government to change the way the monarchy is funded in order to ensure that the extra revenue from six new offshore wind-farm projects, which was estimated to bring the Crown Estate an extra £250 million annually and almost quadruple his current income from the taxpayer, is used for the "wider public good" instead.

The wind farms – three in the North Sea off the Yorkshire and Lincolnshire coast and three off the north Wales, Cumbria and Lancashire coasts – are expected to bolster Britain's efforts to reach net zero greenhouse gas emissions by 2050. Examples such as this illustrate Charles's determination to still have a positive influence on the areas that he has been passionate about all his life.

CHARTER FOR THE FUTURE

In sustainable markets, the economy operates for the benefit of people and the planet, while contributing to growth and prosperity. The 17-page Terra Carta – meaning "earth charter" – that Charles launched in 2021 provides a clear roadmap to 2030 for businesses to move to sustainable markets. It asserts that the "fundamental rights and values of nature" must be placed at the core of the global economy.

It is not only a rallying call to action, but also a roadmap to recovery. King Charles is convinced that if it is adopted globally, it will harness the power of nature combined with the transformative power, innovation and resources of the private sector.

His message at the time of its launch was a familiar one – that "time is fast running out". But what make Charles stand out is that he has solutions, too. "We are rapidly wiping out through mass extinctions many of nature's unique treasure trove of species, from which we can develop innovative and sustainable products for the future," he said at the One Planet Summit in Paris in 2021. "It is critical that we accelerate and mainstream sustainability into every aspect of our economy.

"To that end, I am launching the Terra Carta as the basis of a recovery plan for nature, people and planet. The fundamental rights and value of nature lie at the heart of the Terra Carta and represent a step change in our 'future of industry' and 'future of economy' approach," he continued. "Timelines for change must be brought forward if we are to make a transformative shift by the end of the decade and before it is, quite literally, too late."

The "charter" may never reach legal status in the UK or elsewhere. However, it provides a framework that holds companies accountable, with firms that have signed up to it so far including such leading names as Bank of America, AstraZeneca, HSBC, Heathrow Airport and BP.

Slowly but surely, the message is reaching companies large and small that what they do matters for the communities in which they operate, for now and for tomorrow. As King Charles has emphasised time and time again, they can make a real difference.

"So often in the history of humanity we've waited until something becomes a total catastrophe, before doing something about it. This time it is more critical than ever"

Technology for good

Using novel textile dyeing and finishing technologies that reduce energy and wastewater emissions, Alchemie is striving for a greener planet

It was while touring dye houses in China that Alan Hudd began to see the negative impact the archaic dye industry had on the environment. Hudd had spent a career in digital inkjet technology and, having recently sold his previous company – which won a Queen's Award for International Trade in 2010 – was seeking new opportunities. In his role as a consultant for one of the five largest dye companies in the world, he came face to face, for the first time, with the negative impact of dyeing in industrial textiles, an industry that is responsible for more than 3 per cent of global CO_2 emissions and over 20 per cent of global water pollution.

"The light bulb moment came when I was touring one of 50 or 60 dye houses in China," says Hudd. "They are terrible places in so many ways, especially from a pollution point of view, with all the chemicals they dump in the river. It's a dinosaur industry. I showed the owner of the dye business a video of the technology I was developing, and he said it had the potential to transform textile dyeing. That was when I realised the technology had the power to change this industry."

The result was Alchemie, a company Hudd founded in 2013, which has developed two breakthrough technologies: Endeavour Waterless Smart Dyeing and Novara Digital Textile Finishing. These two innovations can collectively deliver a dramatic reduction in energy consumption and eliminate contaminated wastewater emissions. The Endeavour dyeing process utilises Alchemie's proprietary jetting technology to penetrate microdroplets of dye deep into fabric fibres and infrared energy to activate dye fixation, which removes the water requirement and high-energy fabric washing relied on by traditional dyeing techniques. The Novara digital finishing solution features a unique technology and digitally controlled nozzles to deliver precise, high-quality finishes, such as water resistance, just where they are needed on a fabric – for example, the exterior of a raincoat. Together, these processes aim to massively reduce waste, while shortening the supply chain and production time. This makes it easier for textile

"The light bulb moment came when I was touring one of 50 or 60 dye houses in China"

manufacturers to manage their stock and ensure less is destroyed at the end of each season.

"We have invented, developed and created our own patented tech, which is very left-field compared with traditional inkjet," says Hudd. "It took nine years and £20 million in terms of research and development to get to where we are now. This problem started 175 years ago in the cotton mills of Lancashire. It was exported to the US and then sent to China, where it became a lucrative business. Our efforts are about reshoring: bringing this industry back to the West with a clean-tech solution. It is revolutionary and it will disrupt."

The technology is already being deployed in Taiwan, where five major fashion brands are using Alchemie to produce their 2023 winter fashion lines. When adopted by the textile industry more widely, Alchemie's clean-tech solutions will not only reduce the negative impact on the environment of highly polluting processes, but also deliver five times more production from a smaller factory footprint. This means that companies will achieve higher revenue and lower operating costs following the initial outlay. In an industry of fine margins, this also makes good business sense. Indeed, in recognition of the company's business-led innovation, Alchemie received support from the UK government's Innovate UK fund in 2020 to develop Novara in order to apply protective coatings to medical textiles.

This sort of sustainable innovation is something that King Charles has long been advocating as essential to secure the future of the planet. "Most people, even informed people, don't understand how bad the problem is," says Hudd. "They don't know how old-fashioned the industry is and nobody wants to advertise that. Even at the brands themselves, fashion designers don't understand the problem. When you tell them, they are shocked and horrified. But we can change this within The King's reign if we just get on with it. And we have no better person than The King to lead the way."

Apart from their success in Taiwan, Alchemie's products have also drawn interest in Turkey, Portugal and India, where many Western fashion brands house their production plants. For Hudd, it is essential to get the big brands onside, as they are the ones in the industry with the weight to make positive change. "There's no joined-up evidence that governments want to make any change yet – it's a classic SEP (someone else's problem)," says Hudd, "but there is from some leading brands that are getting behind it. They know that the younger generation is not going to put up with this, and that the general public needs to understand that cheap solutions are not sustainable ones. Brands are going to invest, and then it's down to them to lobby

government to bring about change. We are too small, but the big Western brands can do that."

Hudd likens events to the dawn of the computer age, which started slowly but built momentum rapidly as the benefits and opportunities became clear. He extends the metaphor, likening Alchemie to Intel – a brand name that adds value to existing products as a stamp of environmental quality and assurance. "We want people to know that clothing uses Alchemie technology and will make a point of celebrating it on the packaging," says Hudd. "We want people to associate Alchemie with a clean-tech green label process.

"There are 50,000 dye houses in the world, and we sell our machines for £1.5 million so there is a massive opportunity as we scale up to supply hundreds of these machines a year. Brands are committing, as they can see it's not just marketing hype. This is our window of opportunity. We can gain market accessibility and build engagement, and as soon as that happens the floodgates will open."

www.alchemietechnology.com

Making the move

K2 Corporate Mobility settles talented
employees into new locations globally
by practising a personalised, empathetic
and ground-up approach

When, in 2002, Nick Plummer borrowed £3,000 from his mother to start a business, she was sceptical. More than 20 years later, her generosity has been rewarded through the success of the company Plummer began with that loan: K2 Corporate Mobility. A business-to-business global relocation specialist with over 300 staff in 12 offices across nine countries, K2 helps companies large and small relocate their employees, working alongside HR departments to manage everything from removals to school-finding to immigration. From its Guildford, Surrey headquarters, K2 can create personalised support packages for short-term mobility needs, long-term international assignments, permanent transfers, group moves and domestic assignments, providing a single point of contact and reducing the stress on individuals and their parent companies.

"When I started K2, I couldn't have imagined what we'd achieve," says Plummer, "but looking in the rear-view mirror, there's a lot of hard work – but also science. Business people understand a lateral approach to problem-solving and this is what K2 is about."

As the founder of a global company, Plummer takes a huge interest in sustainability. K2 has made a series of commitments to reduce its carbon footprint – and in 2022 it became a participant of the UN Global Compact (UNGC), the world's largest responsible business initiative. This means the company is committed to the UNGC's principles regarding human rights, labour, environment and anti-corruption, incorporating these into wider strategy, culture and daily operations.

Plummer also understands the value of human talent and the benefits of having a happy and motivated workforce. The Kinetic Cash Plan was launched in 2022, followed by The Great Place to Work Certification in January 2023. The plan, through which each employee effectively becomes a partner in the business, receiving an equitable profit share every year, is just one of the reasons why K2's employee satisfaction rate sits at 96 per cent. "When you have passionate and motivated employees, you can achieve anything. At the core of our success is our ability to

"Business people understand a lateral approach to problem-solving and this is what K2 is about"

attract the right people in the right positions, and then retain and reward that key talent," says Plummer.

K2 prides itself on understanding the personal concerns of individuals – and their families – who are moving to a new country to start a new job. The company takes on the burden of responsibility and ownership, removing much of the administrative and logistical stress as possible. It manages all aspects of the process, such as finding temporary or permanent accommodation; securing school places; managing the immigration process; arranging the packing, transportation and unpacking of personal effects; creating tailored insurance products; providing post-service KPI (Key Performance Indicator) feedback; and even supporting the spouse as they contemplate their own career.

"It's a complete service. We work alongside our valued customers for up to three months, potentially a very testing period for them, and help them acclimatise when they are starting a job in another country with a different culture, new neighbours and new schoolfriends. We recognise it is essential that the family is happy and settled, otherwise the individual moving jobs won't be. We work with about 50 per cent of the companies in the FTSE 100, all of which have a focus on talent management. K2 places great value on talent management, so we dovetail with the corporations that share our talent management ethos."

The company's success is, in great part, due to a company culture defined by "Q", a combination of IQ and EQ (Emotional Intelligence). Q gives staff a shared sense of identity and purpose, across the company and internationally. Staff with Q recognise that moving can be stressful for clients, so they require a committed, empathetic service.

In 2022, K2 launched a new five-year plan for growth and development, the Kinetic business strategy, which has six pillars: Sustainability, People and Culture, Commercial, Technology, Marketing, and Partner Network. The sustainability element is

particularly dear to Plummer. He was raised in Norfolk as the son of a farmer, spending his formative years outdoors and learning to appreciate the importance of nature. "In 2022, we embarked on our ESG (Environmental, Social and Governance) and sustainability drive. Some of the highlights include signing up to the UNGC and developing a great relationship with the Sustainable Supply Chain team at Bath University, who are helping us to future-proof our supply chain process.

"We also created the K2 Foundation, to focus on supporting good causes such as children's education around the world; we engaged with EcoVadis, a trusted provider of business sustainability ratings; and we are being rated in relation to our Scope 1 and Scope 2 carbon emissions, and have invited all our service partners to be rated as well. The aim is to get 70 per cent of our global partners EcoVadis-accredited by the end of 2024. Our next step is to remove all plastics from our supply chain."

K2 continues to evolve, expanding overseas in the locations that offer clients the greatest value. Offices in Houston, Miami, Pittsburgh, São Paolo, Paris, Stockholm, Malmö, Dubai, Singapore, Cape Town and Sydney allow companies to relocate staff almost anywhere in the world. Where K2 does not have a direct presence, it still offers the services of fully vetted, accredited and trusted expert partners who deliver the same K2 experience across 186 countries worldwide. In addition, K2 Bespoke was launched in 2021 to focus on C-suite, or executive-level, individuals. The K2 Bespoke team work with the boards of ten FTSE 100 businesses to offer an even more individualised and expansive service. "We live and breathe our customers," says Plummer. "We have seen competitors grow too fast and lose focus and become disconnected from the customer. That's why we set high standards for client and employee satisfaction. If we get that right, everything else will follow."

www.k2corporatemobility.com

Safe and sound

A market leader in the manufacturing of electronic test equipment for over 100 years, Megger knows the true value of sustainability

S cience, safety and sustainability have been central to the work of Megger for more than a century. The UK-based company can trace its history back to the 19th century and is named after its most famous invention – the megohmmeter, or Megger – invented by Sydney Evershed in 1889 as the first portable insulation tester for what was at that time the new industry of electricity. Over the decades, numerous other companies were absorbed into the Megger family, without deviating from that original core mission of ensuring the safety of electricity infrastructure, which includes everything from plug sockets to underground cables and power stations.

"There is a very rich heritage of Megger leading the world in electrical test and measurement," says the company's CEO, Jim Fairbairn, who received an OBE from then Prince Charles for services to business and charity in 2007. "Megger invented the insulation test that is used worldwide. A lot of the British inventions in electricity that made us the envy of the world were actually by Megger. We have gone from a £70 million business to one of more than £300 million in the past 15 years, and our goal is to achieve £500 million."

This target will be achieved through the application and understanding of science – a process that includes encouraging young people to engage with STEM (science, technology, engineering and mathematics) subjects – and the implementation of technology designed to support sustainability. Megger provides the tests and equipment that allow solar power and wind farms to join the National Grid, ensuring that renewable forms of electricity are safe, efficient and effective. For this reason, Fairbairn sees Megger as an essential enabler of sustainability, helping drive the rapid transformation required in the race towards net zero.

"Our sustainability strategy has three pillars," explains Fairbairn. "We have our internal goals to reduce waste and reach net zero, just as every other company does. We have our green product line, which is to assist the renewable energy industry, using our skills to support solar

"We enable the progress of renewable energy by keeping it safe and ensuring the grid is reliable"

power and wind farms. And our third angle is, we invest regionally to help other countries around the world. We go to places such as Brazil and China, anywhere we can put our people on the ground to work with and educate customers, provide them with the right equipment and, ultimately, try to do good for the planet. We have set ourselves targets around what we want to achieve, and we believe that we can help others achieve their targets."

Megger's products span a wide range of electrical test equipment. They incorporate cable tests and diagnostics; protection relays and systems; circuit breakers; transformer testing and diagnostics; low voltage installations; general electrical testing, and motor and generator testing. The company's success, meanwhile, is built on consistency of service, and it has seen off numerous competitors that have been unable to match its high standards in terms of assurance, integrity and repeatability. When dealing with high-voltage electrical components, nobody can afford to take risks and Megger's equipment has proven itself to be the best at delivering the sort of safety checks and safeguards that are essential in the industry. This demand for consistency is compounded by the increased complexity of the National Grid, which has to incorporate renewable energy alongside traditional oil and coal, as well as the ageing infrastructure, much of which continues to be in use a number of years after its expected lifespan.

The company's focus is now about anticipating problems that could be triggered by this combination of age and complexity. "We have made 11 acquisitions over the past five years, but these haven't been in the UK," says Fairbairn. "We've bought companies in Europe, North America and Israel to support our strategy of trying to anticipate and get ahead of the current agenda. One of the trends we recognised two or three years ago is around asset health, where our customers want to anticipate failure before it happens. That means taking AI and machine learning and applying it within this environment – nobody else is using this technology in the way we do."

Just as Megger takes a proactive approach towards asset life, the company is determined be at the forefront of the use of future technology, such as batteries. "We need to be aware of the implications of change and hire the talent. Over the past five years, we have reanalysed our business strategy several times to understand that."

When it comes to horizon scanning, Fairbairn can draw a parallel with his personal hobby of mountain climbing. He recently travelled to Tanzania to scale Mount Kilimanjaro and says leadership is like climbing "a mountain without a summit", where there will always be

another ridge beyond the one you can see in front of you. "Business success for me is going beyond what you can see ahead of you, knowing that the journey is going to continue after that. What we are really thinking of is the goal behind the goal."

One thing Fairbairn is particularly proud of is the culture within the company. "We have a really supportive atmosphere and a belief that it will always be better tomorrow. That creates a lot of positivity and passion for the brand. People are proud to be part of this company because if you are forward-looking and people understand the vision and the strategy, and believe that they can contribute to our army of problem-solvers, then they will have something they can really buy into."

Part of that vision is supporting sustainable, green energy. "We enable the progress of renewable energy by keeping it safe and ensuring the grid is reliable and maintains its integrity. That is very important for us, as it aligns to the values we hold dear."

www.uk.megger.com

Tomorrow's world

Embodying a modern approach to planning, saving and investing for tomorrow's financial futures, abrdn champions the client's agenda and the transition to sustainability

Evolution in business requires a combination of stability and innovation – a mix that has sustained abrdn, formerly Standard Life Aberdeen, for two centuries. The company celebrates its 200th anniversary in 2025 and has changed dramatically over the decades. It started in life insurance in the UK, becoming Europe's largest mutual insurer, before transitioning again to focus on managing investments for global businesses, organisations and individuals.

"While governments come and go and establishments such as the monarchy provide both heritage and continuity, all businesses need to evolve and adapt to changing practices" says Stephanie Bruce, Chief Financial Officer. "Our aim is to explore how we help our clients be the best investors they can. It was the objective all those years ago when the company wanted to help customers have security for their families. It's the same intent that drives us now to help our clients secure their financial futures, something which is just as important as it was 200 years ago."

Individuals today can no longer rely on a company pension. They are seeking alternative avenues of investment and are doing so from a younger age. This requires a reliable and innovative partner that can help customers easily access, through technology, investment platforms and specialist investment capabilities. "The company wants to help individuals save more and start earlier," says Bruce. "We want to be the easiest firm to deal with and that's driven by helping individuals invest their savings, so they have the financial future they want."

The company services the entire spectrum of investors, which includes institutions, advisers and individual customers. Across these groups, the growing trend towards sustainable investment – something that has been part of the company's ethos for decades – is clear. This has long been a focus for businesses in the UK and abrdn is noticing shifts in behaviour in other parts of the world, including Asia. "Sustainability has not always been at the forefront of the thinking in Asia, but now, having marked 30 years of our investment business in the region, we can use our knowledge and long-term focus on sustainable investing to drive further change," says Bruce. "That is built around education and research to make better investment decisions. You need to have a vision to drive innovation, so it's about identifying positive areas to help businesses transition sustainably. There are companies with considerable funding to invest in the next stage of their businesses – how they do so can be a real positive for this agenda."

The company's efforts to drive positive societal change include the charitable focus on financial education, enabled by technology and innovation. This supports causes that allow people to understand the world and think about ways to avoid financial uncertainty.

It all adds up to a company that spends a lot of time considering the future – the future of its clients, the future of investing and the future of the planet. "All of us in the financial sector have a role to play, and we want to direct capital to the places where it can make the biggest impact. We believe in the power of investment, to help clients become better investors and support the communities we work in.

"Our strong capital resources allow us to invest in the business and our people to produce positive outcomes for all our stakeholders and bear fruit for decades to come."

www.abrdn.com

A history of innovation

The Isle of Man's Strix draws on decades of ingenuity to embed
sustainability into its kettles, appliances and water filtration devices

Eric Taylor was an ingenious inventor. Indeed, he was often so far ahead of his time that it is only now, decades later, that the full potential of his inventions is being realised. Take the windproof, waterproof cotton cloth he developed in the 1930s for instance. This is now used for everyday anoraks but was then so revolutionary it was reserved for Everest explorers and pioneering pilots such as Amelia Earhart.

Another of Taylor's inventions made an even more unlikely journey into everyday use. During the Second World War, the RAF asked him to create a device that would automatically heat flying jackets to protect pilots when planes reached a certain altitude. After the war, he took the same invention and applied it to the heating mechanism of electric kettles. Strix has built a vibrant business on this foundation, and as a world-leading supplier of kettle controls has a 56 per cent market share by value, all while developing and improving appliances in every sector, from filtration to heated taps. "We were founded in 1951 by Eric Taylor," says CEO Mark Bartlett, "and that tech is still made here in our own factory in the Isle of Man, and it is used in almost every electric kettle you will ever use anywhere in the world. The way we produce it has changed, but the technology – the product itself – is very similar."

Strix's success has been recognised in the form of four Queen's Awards, either for enterprise or export, confirming the influence of this unusually innovative business. For many years it was run by Eric's son, Dr John Taylor, also a famous inventor, before he sold it to a private equity firm. More recently, Strix was listed on the stock exchange – a moment, says Bartlett, that transformed the company by unlocking investment and the vast potential of employees. The company built a bespoke factory in China, where Strix has a strong presence, and began a string of acquisitions that allowed it to set a growth target of doubling in size over five years to 2025.

With its place in the kettle market firmly cemented, Strix has sought to extend into other water-related fields, helping the company to

"We are trying to make a fundamental difference in the way consumer goods work"

embed its commitment to sustainability, something that informs all research. "If you look at where we are heading now, we have diversified from kettles," says Bartlett. "We have water filtration, which is essential for sustainability: it removes plastics and provides safe drinking water for those parts of the world where it is needed and is used in farming to remove viruses and bacteria from animal drinking water. Our third sector is appliances. With these products we are trying to make a fundamental difference in the way consumer goods work, whether it's doing things a lot faster or by consuming much less water or energy."

These innovations include the Aurora Water Station, a freestanding appliance that can provide filtered chilled or true boiled water in seconds. Another is the Dual Flo, a kettle that only dispenses the amount of water you require. "The UK is estimated to waste £300 million of water every year by boiling too much water through over-filling or boiling twice when we get distracted while making a cup of tea," says Bartlett. "We are seeking to raise awareness of the issue and help change it. The new kettles limit the amount of water you use, and we are working to educate the consumer so they can save a considerable amount of water and household energy just by changing appliance."

The Aurora Water Station is a particularly smart creation that will satisfy anybody who is looking for speed, convenience and safety – such as the 86 per cent of the US market that still does not own an electric kettle, preferring to boil water on the stove top. "The Aurora is like a coffee machine that provides boiled water in ten seconds from room temperature," explains Bartlett. "It's not plumbed, it's freestanding, and it actually boils water, unlike many hot taps that only get to 98 degrees. You can get a system that does water that is chilled, boiled and everything in between for less than £200. That's convenience at an affordable price."

Hot taps are another growing trend, and Strix has recently completed the acquisition of Billi, an Australian company that occupies the premium market and sells mainly to the UK, Australia and New Zealand. Smart acquisitions such as this help to significantly accelerate the growth plans, always with a commitment to sustainability at the company's core. Strix Group has recently achieved net zero status, and Bartlett knows that its products can make a significant difference.

"When it comes to research and development, any product we design will include a sustainable element, whether it's reducing the amount of water it uses or the amount of energy we use, or by providing safer drinking water. All of these things are very high on our agenda," he says. "As a business, we are doing more in the community, too. We have a strong commitment to diversity and 60 per cent of our employees are female, including 28 per cent of our senior managers."

It seems extraordinary that the device developed by Eric Taylor for the RAF 80 years ago is still used in kettles sold in more than 100 countries, something that provides Strix with extraordinary reach as well as an innate understanding of the potential of innovation. Bartlett believes there are more markets they can break into, such as the US, and growth will be driven by pioneering new products like the Aurora and the Dual Flo.

"We have just launched ISEO, a stylish new water filter kettle that uses LAICA's bi-flux water filters to reduce chlorine and other tap water impurities, and is an important addition to our range," explains Bartlett. "We continue to innovate because that's what we do. It makes life easier for the consumer and harder for our competitors to follow."

www.strix.com

Driving change

With repairing and recycling at its core, Copart gives vehicles a new
lease of life while taking the automotive industry into the future

Copart is a global leader in vehicle remarketing and
recycling, facilitating the reuse of millions of
vehicles worldwide, promoting sustainability and
contributing to the circular economy.

Founder and Chairman Willis Johnson has led the
company's growth for over 40 years, growing from a single
salvage yard to a public company valued at more than $43
billion. Co-CEO Jay Adair's visionary approach pioneered
Copart's patented online auction, now the world's largest
vehicle remarketing platform, and, alongside Willis, grew
Copart's presence across the globe. More recently,
Co-CEO Jeff Liaw has accelerated success by focusing on
customer, innovation and operational excellence.

With operations in 11 countries and buyers in over 190,
Copart sells more than four million vehicles annually. The
company works with progressive insurers to resell total-loss
vehicles (known as write-offs), providing its global buyer
base with the opportunity to buy vehicles for repair and
dismantling. "In the US and the UK, a significant portion
of vehicles sold go to buyers in developing economies,"
says Jane Pocock, CEO of Copart UK and Ireland.
"That facilitates mobility and economic opportunities for
populations that might otherwise struggle to own vehicles."

Copart UK works with the top 22 insurance companies
and thousands of traders, remarketing accident-damaged
and used vehicles to its buyers. The company ensures that
vehicles are properly assessed and categorised according
to the ABI Code of Practice.

The company also supplies parts from dismantled
vehicles. With its recent acquisition of The Green Parts
Specialists, Copart is now reducing the need for new parts
production and associated carbon emissions, as well as
integrating the business to offer efficient parts distribution
to insurance repair networks and Copart's buyer base.

With Pocock at the helm since 2019, the UK business
has gone from strength to strength. She has established a
diverse team and has accelerated growth for the business
and its teammates. Pocock believes that having a female
UK CEO conveys a key message of equality and diversity.
"We now have women in many roles that have traditionally
been male dominated, including drivers and engineers, and
have almost reached parity on our gender split," she says.
"I'm so proud of the team; they go the extra mile from
helping in emergencies, such as flooding, to settling
a policyholder's claim. I encourage a collaborative and
supportive culture. We have a true customer-first approach."

Copart delivers its Environmental, Social and
Governance strategy through its Copart Cares campaign,
which focuses on five key streams: customers, buyers, the
environment, teammates and good causes. "Succession
and personal development are actively encouraged
through mentoring, apprenticeships, driver academies
and a range of roles in different disciplines," adds Pocock.

Sustainability is a core focus for the team at Copart
UK, with formal targets to reduce waste and emissions
under globally recognised programmes such as the
Carbon Literacy Project, EcoVadis and Science Based
Targets (SBTi). Copart recently became a silver level-
accredited Carbon Literate Organisation in record time.

As the automotive industry moves towards automation,
electrification and sustainability, Copart is at the forefront
of the revolution. "We're proud to remain the market leader,"
says Pocock. "Change is challenging but rewarding, and we
know that the combination of our transport network, vast
storage capabilities and amazing teammates enables us to
continually adapt to the needs of our customers."

www.remarketing.copart.co.uk

Diamonds from the future

Eco, ethical and attainable, Analucia Beltran Diamonds' contemporary
designs and collaborations are pushing the boundaries of luxury jewellery

Analucia Beltran's lab-grown diamonds are a feat of technology, and the woman herself is a force of nature. A jewellery designer, diamond expert and experienced TV host, her eponymous, sustainable diamond brand is growing at an unstoppable rate, tapping into the desires of an ever-more mindful customer base. "People now are more demanding and aware," she says. "The youngest demographic, Gen Z, often only want lab-grown diamonds because of the ethical factor. They don't want anything that is mined."

Based in Toronto, Canada, Beltran formed Analucia Beltran Diamonds in 2020 with her brother, Creative Director Lucas Calderon, both of whom were "living and breathing the business" as it grew. She began her career in the diamond industry after hosting live shows and gemstone seminars on cruise ships, which soon led to regular TV appearances. Now, her jewellery company has signed with HSN, the second largest shopping network in the US, reaching over 90 million households. "It's shopping and entertainment, a great fit for our brand."

A more recent partnership is with Canadian gemstone company Korite. Before she launched her jewellery brand, Beltran worked with Korite as a global brand ambassador. Now, she is designing collaborative pieces using her lab-grown diamonds and ammolite, of which Korite is the largest producer in the world. "Ammolite is one of the rarest gemstones in the entire world, a true geological wonder known as the seven colour prosperity stone," she says. "It takes 70 million years to form and has been referred by feng shui masters as the 'Gemstone of the Millennium'."

The close relationship between the two companies comes from a shared sense of ethics in the gemstone industry. "Korite's mining practices are second to none. They're registered as having one of the highest ethical mining practices, recognised worldwide," says Beltran. "For us, it's a beautiful story, marrying together the history of a Canadian gemstone like that and the diamond of the future with me, a Canadian designer."

Beltran drew some of the design inspiration for the collaboration with Korite during a visit to London. "I went to the Tower of London, like a good tourist, and saw the crown jewels for the first time," she says. "I almost cried. They were so inspiring I literally started designing straightaway, completing the Korite collection." These ideas have also fed into Beltran's newly launched charm bracelet collection, which offers something new with lab-grown diamonds.

In another first, Analucia Beltran Diamonds has introduced the VIP Diamond Club, an exclusive service that delivers discounts, early access to new designs and offers at no extra cost to its members. The club currently has thousands of members worldwide. "We're making a community with our customers," says Beltran. "It's something that hasn't been done in the diamond industry before."

As for her next major step, in the coming years Beltran plans to expand the business into retail stores, to reach an even greater number of people attracted by the beauty and integrity of lab-grown diamonds. "By then, people will have seen the brand on TV and cruises, but the goal is to get the jewellery into their hands when they go into the stores," she says. "That is the point at which everything completes full circle."

Considering Beltran's energy, spirit and imagination – not to mention her beautiful designs – it is safe to expect this circle to be completed sooner rather than later.

www.analuciabeltrandiamonds.com

Driven by values

Thanks to its forward-thinking initiatives, Danish fashion and lifestyle brand dbramante1928's high-quality, feature-rich mobile phone cases and accessories are ingrained with social and environmental value

When, in 2012, the dbramante1928 sales team visited a factory the company co-owned in West Bengal, India, the trip left a profound impression on everyone, recalls Daniel Jones, Partner and Chief Brand Officer. It led to Dennis Dress, dbramante1928's CEO and co-founder contacting LittleBigHelp, a Danish NGO that works to help vulnerable, often street, children and women in West Bengal. As a result, the company donates a percentage of its profits from the sale of every product directly to the organisation. An insert in each item explains LittleBigHelp's work and how the customer has contributed. "It's part of our DNA and our mantra," says Dress. "'Great design driven by great values'."

Specialising in affordable, luxurious storage and case solutions for mobile phones, laptops and tablets, these values have long included sustainability. Addressing the environmental issue of waste, including the two billion plastic phone cases sold worldwide annually – many of which are single-use and end up in landfill or oceans – dbramante1928

only uses recovered, recycled and 100 per cent recyclable plastics in its products, including its first-to-market eco-produced power products.

The brand's luxury leather designs are handcrafted by artisans from premium-quality full-grain leather, which is durable and has a long life cycle. The leather is sourced in India and taken from hides generated from the meat industry, which would otherwise go to landfill. Alongside this, dbramante1928's factory provides fair working conditions and is solar-powered and CO_2 neutral.

For Jones, making the case to the retailer of "environmental change without compromise" has been vital. "We had to demonstrate that our product has the same, if not better, price, quality, durability and functionality as today's non-environmentally friendly solutions. Driven by consumer demand, they wanted to take a sustainable approach but didn't have the confidence to do so. As a trusted partner, our product and ethos gave them that confidence."

Since 2020, dbramante1928 has worked with WWF Denmark, part of the World Wide Fund for Nature, on sustainable production, from products and packaging, to distribution and energy consumption. "We have set high ambitions and are committed to delivering on these targets: towards nature and the climate, guided by WWF," says Dress.

As part of this commitment, in 2022, dbramante1928 prevented 21 tons of single-use plastic from entering the environment and removed the equivalent weight of 1,476 million 0.5-litre plastic bottles from landfills or oceans. It also removed the equivalent of 80 tons of CO_2 emissions from its full-grain leather production, using solar energy generated from the panels on its factory roof. Through the WWF, it planted 1,146 million trees in the Rwenzori rainforest in Uganda and supported the development of alternative income for 1,545 local farmers, who now contribute to the protection and restoration of forests and the prevention of the extinction of endangered animals.

In addition, dbramante1928 is a signatory of the UN Global Compact and has set approved net-zero emissions reduction targets, which are grounded in climate science through the Science Based Targets initiative (SBTi). Such activities have earned the brand a gold standard from the business sustainability rating provider, EcoVadis, putting the company in the top 2 per cent globally. Dress, however, is conscious that much work still needs to be done. "We'll keep pushing until we get to net zero," he says. "Tomorrow we will be better than today. Always forward."

www.dbramante1928.com

Towards a cleaner future

In its mission to recycle plastics, Enviroo aims not only to innovate in technological terms, but in social impact, too

"Sustainability is not just for the elite. They're not the only ones responsible for making a difference," says Ahmed Detta, founder and CEO of plastic recycling innovators Enviroo. Detta's aim is to create long-term, measurable and tangible differences through recycling – but this is much more than a run-of-the-mill recycling company.

By focusing specifically on the throwaway material PET (polyethylene terephthalate) that is used in snack vessels and drinks bottles, Detta is on a mission to clarify information for the consumer. "Let's focus on one material so we can say to consumers, look, this bottle will come back 100 per cent as a bottle," says Detta. "The working person cannot necessarily afford the green lifestyle and all that it entails; many people also don't trust that anything is even being recycled. But I want transparency. When our factory opens we will have an open-door policy and a mezzanine floor where anyone can view our production processes."

Detta believes it is Enviroo's responsibility to engage and unite all stakeholders in the recycling journey, and this is the key to obtaining a solution to single-use plastic. "There are now 500 times more pieces of microplastic in the sea than there are stars in our galaxy, and by 2050 fishermen will be more likely to catch plastic than fish," says Detta. "So we are working with a plastic stream that impacts everyone, thus enabling us to collaborate with government agencies, FMCG (Fast Moving Consumer Goods) brands, consumers and charities."

Founded in 2018, Enviroo has already received recognition for its work. Awarded Plastic Recycling Experts of the Year in England at the Global Advisory Experts Awards in 2022, the company will soon be launching a series of plastics recycling plants. "Our goal is to be a net zero business and our plant has been designed to achieve this. CO_2 neutrality is woven into our DNA."

As part of the company's social-impact mission, Enviroo has partnered with Warrington-based charity 4ward Futures to raise awareness about careers in sustainability as viable alternative careers to engineering, law and medicine, for example. The company also recently funded a Master's by Research degree at Lancaster University's Global Centre for Eco-Innovation.

There are major plans, too, to employ former prisoners. "If Enviroo can put in a system to relieve homelessness and return people to the world of work, we will have done something worthwhile," explains Detta. "If it doesn't help every stakeholder, it's not worth doing."

Enviroo is also deep into the process of creating an app that will direct a person to their nearest deposit and return machine. "Here you will take your bottle and choose to either keep the 20p or donate it directly to a homeless shelter where its progress in helping someone can be live-tracked," says Detta. "Over time, your 20 pences grow into maybe a meal a day or a night in a hostel, or eventually some training for that person."

The company's mission is in clear alignment with King Charles's sustainability goals. "His powerful influence means the voice and importance of sustainability will be at the forefront of people's minds and will take centre stage as a priority agenda item," says Detta. "Our new King's passion means that more ethical projects will be endorsed and governments will take climate change more seriously. Sustainability now has its greatest and most iconic champion."

www.enviroo.co.uk

Top of the tree

Cepi provides Europe with the environmental initiatives it needs through policies that support effective forest management, deter greenwashing and encourage renewable bio-based products

The term "sustainability" was coined 300 years ago by Hans Carl von Carlowitz, the father of modern forestry. It is fitting, then, that responsible forest management remains at the forefront of priorities for the Confederation of European Paper Industries (Cepi), the organisation representing the European pulp and paper industry. In the words of Cepi's Chairman and Metsä Group CEO, Ilkka Hämälä, "Our goal is to ensure that forest assets transfer in an even more vibrant, diverse and climate resilient condition to the next generation."

Metsä Group has taken the next step towards more sustainable forestry, publishing in 2023 its principles of regenerative forestry, an integrated action programme to halt biodiversity loss, and set goals to strengthen the state of nature by 2030. Along with the increasing biodiversity of forests, Cepi members play an important role in accelerating the growth of forests. Under the umbrella of Cepi, companies owning and managing forests have agreed to support the European Commission initiative to plant three billion additional trees by 2030. King Charles III has supported similar projects, saying, "Forests are the world's air-conditioning system – the very lungs of the planet".

The King is a noted proponent of the circular economy, a core tenet of Cepi's approach to sustainability, which has doubled recycling and halved emissions in the industry over the past three decades. The organisation is determined to reduce Europe's dependency on fossil-based materials, substituting them for natural ones. "Anything we can do from fossil raw materials we can also do from wood," says Anna Papagrigoraki, Cepi's Sustainability Director.

The European pulp and paper sector has vast expertise in the circular bioeconomy with 139 "biorefineries"– cutting edge paper mills producing a range of bio-based products, including pulp, paper, packaging and innovative textiles, biochemicals and nano-cellulose. The European paper industry is committed to manufacturing evidence-based climate neutral and resource efficient products. This means improving recycled paper collection and developing recycling capacity and efficiency. While more recycled material is used than ever, this "pool" must be replenished from European forests, which the sector works to protect. The industry also aims to make a meaningful difference in sustainable packaging through Cepi's cross-industry alliance, 4evergreen, which has more than 110 members, including some of the largest companies in the world.

www.cepi.org

Travelling light

From luggage wrapping to cups and cutlery, Enviro-Point's cutting-edge biodegradable
and recyclable innovations address the challenge of making travel sustainable

"Finding solutions to the environmental impact of waste isn't as simple as switching everything from plastic to paper," says Graeme Stewart, CEO of Enviro-Point, a British company that creates sustainable solutions for waste management in the travel industry. "Plastic gets a bad rap, but the detail behind the environmental impact data is actually more nuanced. To be carbon neutral, paper would need to be used 23 times. Paper recycling uses 93 per cent more energy compared with plastic recycling, and recycled paper contains 70 more air pollutants and 50 more water pollutants."

Before founding Enviro-Point in 2020, Stewart was already developing innovative services to improve the traveller experience, which were adopted by airports worldwide. He continues to work in the sector, including areas such as gaming lounges, virtual reality retail and pop-up shop infrastructure, applying his hallmark of pairing science with sustainability, which addresses the unique environmental challenges created by the global travel industry.

"You can supply a recyclable product to travellers, but their destination may not support recycling," says Stewart. "Airports, cruise ships and ports deal with large numbers of people, who are segregated for security reasons, leading to high volumes of waste within confined areas, in different locations around the world."

To address these issues, Enviro-Point has partnered with Polymateria, a British startup that has developed material technology to biodegrade plastic in the open environment. When the plastic packaging undergoes prolonged exposure to the elements – over a few months – it transforms to a wax-like substance. This is then biologically converted into carbon dioxide, mineral salts and biomass by micro-organisms in the soil.

"Polymateria's technology is affordable and meets all related quality and safety standards, so we're working with the aviation industry to introduce it to pallet and luggage wrapping, security tamper-evident bags (STEBs), carrier bags, bin liners and even reusable cups and cutlery," says Stewart. "We aim to support airports with a closed-loop waste management system, with improved information signposting and dedicated bins around their premises, and a bespoke collection and recycling service."

Stewart is in talks with the cruise industry, which faces similar challenges. "People travel frequently these days, so it's vital to support the industry in finding affordable solutions that work on a global scale."

www.enviropoint.co.uk

Perfect circles

Albin Kaelin's company epeaswitzerland helps its clients circumnavigate
the complicated route into the circular economy

You cannot simply make a circle out of a line. That is the experience gleaned by Albin Kaelin after 30 years of working on the frontline of the circular economy. Kaelin is founder and CEO of epeaswitzerland, a company that advises businesses on how to overcome the challenges of the circular economy. It supports innovation and research, and with the accreditation as assessor for the Cradle to Cradle Certified certification it offers a complete package for the "Cradle to Cradle" circular economy system, as originally established by William McDonough and Michael Braungart in the late 1980s.

"Cradle to Cradle is about redefining the design of products so all the materials used can be kept in multiple life cycles, maintain quality over those life cycles and are non-toxic. That's the concept and it requires a completely different mindset," says Kaelin. "I made the first Cradle to Cradle product in the world 30 years ago. It's a fabric, and you will have sat on it if you've ever flown on an Airbus A380 in economy class. All our systems are based on linear thinking, which is cradle to grave – a

line, and the line always ends in the garbage bin. That is a concept that has no future."

Based in Switzerland, Kaelin set up his company in 2009, and it has been the recipient of 10 awards in 2022 alone. Its successes highlight both the benefits and challenges of the circular system. A German firm approached epeaswitzerland about designing new packaging for a popular detergent brand. One essential factor, the project's team decided, was that the packaging needed to end up in the same recycling bin as other plastics, even if the recycling process was unique to this packaging – as otherwise it would be too burdensome for consumers to properly dispose it. This required innovation throughout the circle, including with recycling companies to develop specialist technology to identify and separately recycle the packaging. The product is now on supermarket shelves in Germany, and the project team envisages the award-winning packaging in the medium term being made of fully recycled material from within the circle.

Overcoming such obstacles requires innovation and trust. Kaelin explains that epeaswitzerland's team of 20 act as a "knowledge trustee" in the supply chain, right down to gain complete transparency around materials while ensuring this information remains confidential. The company also acts as an "innovation trustee" to help manufacturers and recyclers develop new network partnerships to close the loop. Companies need to transform new techniques, including accounting systems, developed by epeaswitzerland to prove a concept is economically feasible, and this is not possible with a system based on linear thinking.

"We are an accredited assessor for Cradle to Cradle Certified certification," says Kaelin. "We have everything under one umbrella, which is very important as we generate a lot of knowledge for our clients. We have partners in the UK because this is a global enterprise and supply chains are global."

Kaelin is currently writing a book aimed at managers and students who are attempting to navigate the circular economy. "Everybody's trying to make a circle from the line, but you can't just do that. You need to find a solution to create a world without waste," he says. "There is no future if we continue like this. We have to allow future generations to make good-quality, non-toxic products according to their own personal values. That's why we are doing this. I became a grandfather recently, so my heart is burning for the younger generation; but I started this journey 30 years ago."

www.epeaswitzerland.com

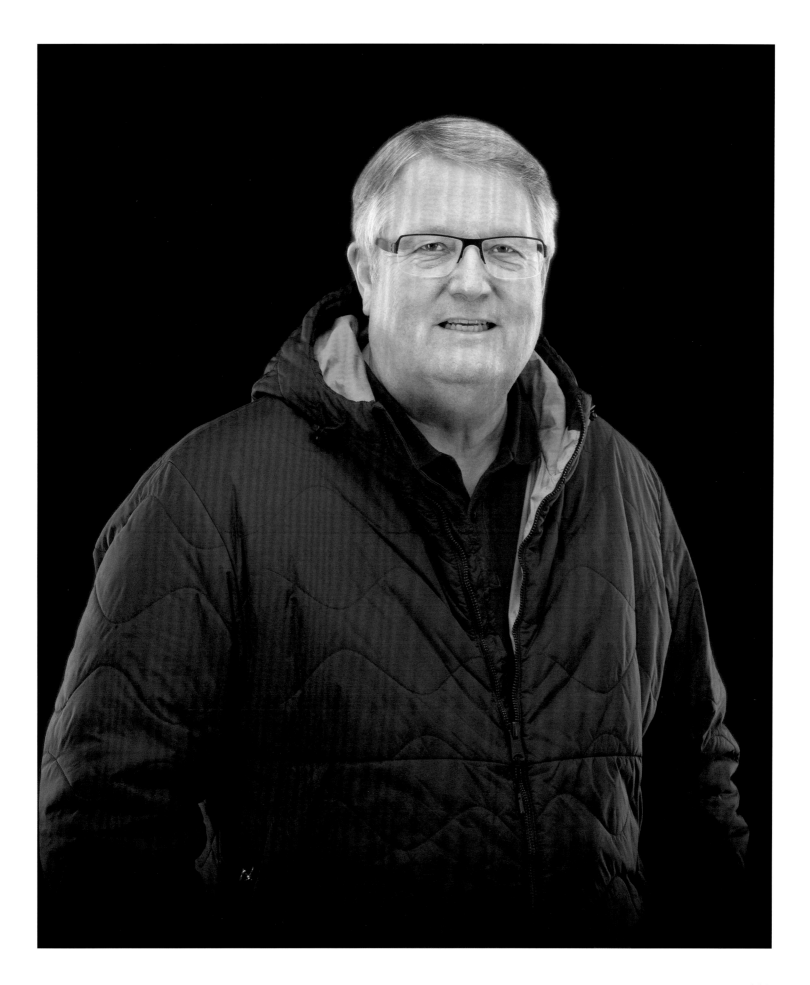

Closing the loop

Faerch manufactures food packaging and recycles it to its
original use, creating a unique and genuinely circular process

P lastic is often seen as the enemy of the environment, but it can be the right material of choice, prolonging shelf life, keeping food safe and reducing food waste. Faerch Group makes it more sustainable by recycling plastic food packaging on an industrial scale.

Part of the AP Møller Group, which invests in companies making a positive impact on society and the environment, Denmark-based Faerch was set up in 1969 and has more than 5,500 employees, operating 32 manufacturing sites globally. Its pioneering work promotes recycling technology and circularity. "We are an integrated recycler and manufacturer of food packaging," says Denise Mathieson, Head of Group External Affairs. "We believe passionately in circularity. Instead of taking more of the world's resources, we should make better use of those we already have."

Faerch's 2018 acquisition of Cirrec, a PET recycler in the Netherlands, led to investment in its first food-tray recycling line, and began a journey towards true circularity in food packaging. Investment in a state-of-the-art second tray recycling line in 2023 saw Cirrec create a world-class facility

and its capacity tripled. "Our next investment will be in 2024 and other recycling centres will follow, with the UK as a possible location, either as a joint venture or a standalone investment," says Mathieson. The recycling will not only enable circularity but also significantly reduce carbon emissions. Therefore, Faerch has set ambitious science-based targets to halve its entire value-chain emissions (Scope 1, 2 and 3) powered by 100 per cent renewable energy by 2030 and reaching net zero value-chain carbon emissions by 2040 (all compared to 2022 base year).

In 2019 UK retailers began to move away from black plastic due to public pressure, and Faerch created a recycling solution for the materials with the award-winning Evolve by Faerch. Food trays are made by recycling the material and can be recycled time and again. Their naturally fluctuating colours are a visual clue to consumers that they are making a sustainable choice. "Instead of being a plastic tray manufacturer that also recycles, our ambition is to be a recycler that also manufactures plastic trays," says Mathieson. "By fine-tuning our technologies and developing specific software, we are the first company to recycle PET trays at scale."

Award-winning Back of Store by Faerch is another innovation for retailers. In 2021, Faerch worked with Tesco to find an end-of-life solution for its back-of-store material waste, then being downcycled into carpets. Its food-grade plastic waste is now recycled and processed at Cirrec's plant for a second life as food-grade packaging. "It was an exciting opportunity to drive circularity with a prominent partner and create a circular closed loop for food packaging," says Mathieson. Its second iteration is Tray 2 Tray by Faerch. This sees household kerbside-collected trays from the Benelux region fed into the European Food Safety Authority-certified recycling process, the output making up the recycled content in the Tesco Core Ready Meals food trays – a first-to-market innovation. To drive further industry change, Faerch is collaborating with the UK Plastic Pact, reprocessing UK kerbside-collected trays to give a second life back into primary food packaging.

"We believe we have a moral responsibility to find a positive end of life for the plastic materials we manufacture and are working collaboratively across the industry to drive that change," says Mathieson, adding that the impact on greenhouse gases from packaging is "a tiny percentage" compared to that of food waste. "We need to educate consumers to understand there are good and bad plastics," she says. "Everyone needs to play their part in taking responsibility to ensure that the packaging they have used is recycled in the most sustainable way."

www.faerch.com

Releasing the potential

FiRe Energy's expertise on energy and infrastructure is meeting economic and sustainable development goals on a global scale

The first time Fiona Reilly stared into a nuclear reactor core was when she was in her early twenties and carrying out commercial work as a newly qualified lawyer. Since then, she has become one of the UK's leading authorities on nuclear power and renewable energy, advising national and international bodies, as well as working with firms and investors through her consultancy, FiRe Energy.

Reilly's company, set up in 2019, works on a range of complex projects involving the worlds of nuclear fission and fusion, and solar and wind power. "With FiRe Energy, I can explore my passion for hugely complicated and unique energy projects that are low carbon and will help us meet sustainability goals," she says.

At the same time, FiRe Energy is also seeking to engage or improve understanding about nuclear power's potential to solve the planet's energy problems. "The biggest challenge we face is climate change and renewables combined with nuclear is the solution to that, while meeting the energy demands of the world we have created."

One high-profile renewables project that Reilly is involved in is the Xlinks Morocco-UK Power Project, which is building an electricity generation facility in Morocco to provide 11.5 gigawatts of solar and wind power, along with battery storage, dedicated to the UK market. The aim is to deliver 3.6 gigawatts of renewable power to the UK every day for 19 hours through cables laid from Morocco, circumventing the coasts of France, Spain and Portugal, to Devon. "I am the UK Strategy Lead, which includes engaging with the UK government, looking at complex cross-country security aspects and anything else that is required to make the project a success," says Reilly. "It's an amazing project with some incredible names working to make it happen."

It is Reilly's conviction, based on her decades of experience in the field, that nuclear needs to be part of a sustainable future. In terms of pure greenhouse gas emissions per kilowatt hour, nuclear is the same as wind and solar, she explains, while in terms of land use it produces far more energy in less space and has a higher capacity factor. Reilly believes that ESG (environmental, social and governance) criteria need to be updated to reflect that reality, particularly regarding the latest generation of power plants. She cites the example of the World Economic Forum's metrics, which map on to the UN's Sustainable Development Goals and are broader than traditional ESG metrics.

Moreover, Reilly feels that countries should be taking greater advantage of nuclear power by recycling the waste. Plutonium and uranium can be recovered to create energy for decades, while medical isotopes can be extracted to assist with medical diagnoses and treatment. Nuclear isotopes are used in so many ways, and "we need to educate stakeholders on their wider use". These are all areas in which FiRe Energy is seeking to drive investment to instigate change.

"People don't need to be scared of nuclear," says Reilly. "Nuclear technology is developing at speed, but the legislation has not caught up with the science. There will always be waste, but the issue is how we reduce it and how we extract the beneficial elements. We have been managing nuclear assets for decades and it is one of the safest industries we have. Now we need to do what is best for society and the future. There have been a lot of studies exploring how well renewables and nuclear complement each together. This has to be the answer."

www.fireenergy.co.uk

Changing fashion

Inspired by her upbringing on a rural ranch in Uruguay, fashion designer Gabriela Hearst uses her understanding of self-sufficiency to underpin her collections with sustainability

It is a long journey from Paysandú in rural Uruguay to New York City, but an even longer one from seventh-generation Uruguayan rancher to the award-winning designer of the dress and coat worn by First Lady Jill Biden at her husband's 2021 inauguration. Gabriela Hearst has done both. Having inherited the family ranch, where she first learned the value of nature and sustainability, she introduced these qualities into the world of fashion as the founder of a label that uses innovative recycled material while maintaining the highest standards of craftsmanship and design. "There is nothing more sustainable than luxury, as it means things are built to last," says Hearst. "But now fashion is changing, and we are all using our trash as valuable raw material."

Hearst founded the Gabriela Hearst line in 2015, which has allowed her to embrace the philosophy of sustainability that defined her life on the ranch, an off-grid existence where nothing was wasted. Since then, she has won dozens of awards, including the 2016/17 International Woolmark Prize for Womenswear, the Pratt Institute Fashion Visionary Award 2018, American Womenswear Designer of the Year 2020, the Frank Alvah Parsons Award for Sustainability 2021, and the inaugural

Leader of Change award for the Environment at the 2021 Fashion Awards. In 2020, she became Creative Director at Chloé. One of her bag designs is in the Victoria and Albert Museum's collection, while Jill Biden's aforementioned ensemble is in the Smithsonian National Museum of American History, and some of Hearst's pieces were featured in The Costume Institute's "In America: A Lexicon of Fashion" exhibition at The Metropolitan Museum of Art.

Hearst is a trustee for Save the Children and the proceeds of profits from all her retail outlets – in New York and a London store designed by Norman Foster – are regularly gifted to charities. She also collaborates with Manos del Uruguay, a non-profit co-operative that works alongside women in rural areas who produce the label's sought-after hand-knits. "I launched Gabriela Hearst on the values of sustainability and long-term thinking. From our first fashion show in 2017, everything we do is based on this," says Hearst. "It's the material we use – linen instead of cotton, merino wool. It's about the impact of that material on the environment and biodiversity, but also who is making the product. I knew if I launched a fashion brand it had to be better than anything else because the world does not need another fashion brand. Whatever I do has to benefit more than myself; the more people it benefits, the better."

When Gabriela Hearst secured a huge hit with the Nina and Demi bags crafted from Italian nappa leather, she chose to limit production rather than use more raw materials than were necessary; the bags are available by request only. The label has eliminated plastic and replaced it with compostable packaging, while developing materials such as aloe-treated linen alongside recycled cashmere and material from Turkish rugs. In 2019, she introduced piqué and twill suits spun from wool from the family's merino sheep farm in Uruguay.

"We strip it down to the basics of beauty and use the brand as a vehicle to find solutions, drive change and spread positive news," says Hearst. "When I started this, people thought I was a Martian, but now they are common practices in fashion. If brands don't change, they will fail because young people are taking note. We want to continue to grow organically and become one of the top luxury brands in the world."

www.gabrielahearst.com

Eco-friendly takeaways

Eco Packaging Products' disposable food and drink packaging has removed plastic entirely, making it perfect for both the environment and eco-conscious consumer

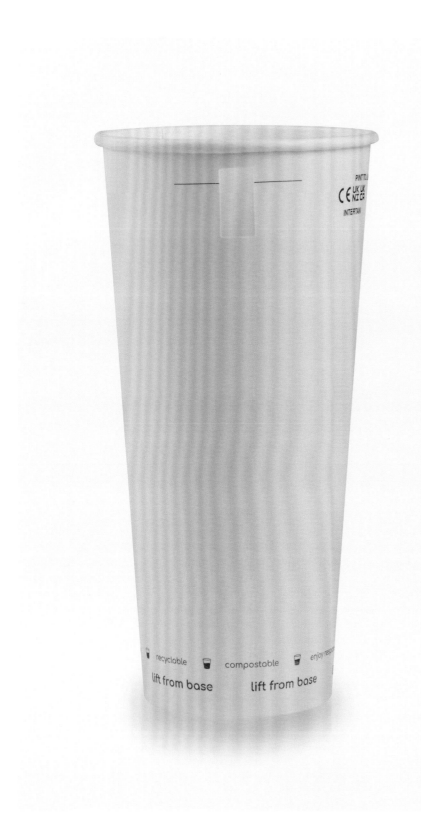

In 2021, a landmark international study published in the scientific journal *Nature Sustainability* classified single-use plastic bags, bottles, food containers and wrappers as the four most pervasive "macrolitter" items in marine environments. Ecological innovator and entrepreneur Ilesh Mawji realised that the solution required a completely different approach to single-use food packaging – one that removed plastic from the mix entirely.

Mawji had already established a successful paper straw company when, in 2020, he co-founded Manchester-based Eco Packaging Products to develop a range of biodegradable and compostable takeaway food packaging. Managing Director Alexander Howarth explains that one of the issues that can arise with eco-friendly food packaging is that a well-meaning business could switch to recyclable packaging, but the consumer may discard it rather than recycle it. "If there is any element of plastic in that packaging, it'll stay in the environment indefinitely, whereas our biodegradable and compostable packaging will naturally degrade."

Cheap takeaway food boxes made from thin cardboard with a plastic coating can be problematic. "But we use a high-quality, responsibly sourced thick cardboard that doesn't usually need additional protection," says Howarth. "When liquid or grease resistance is needed, we can add a plastic-free aqueous barrier coating."

The packaging range, which includes corrugated cardboard food boxes, paper cups and straws and wooden cutlery, too, can be branded. The company also works with clients to develop bespoke products. In 2023, it pioneered fully biodegradable pint and half-pint paper cups with a transparent section to comply with legislation on alcoholic drink quantities. The cups are a game-changer for eco-conscious events such as festivals, while reinforcing Eco Packaging Products as a leader in its field.

"Sustainability is, and always has been, at the heart of what we do and who we are. That extends to the way we do business, so we source consciously from UK suppliers and distributors, to support our community and minimise our environmental impact," says Howarth. "We're a dedicated and inventive team, who are constantly exploring ways to develop genuinely eco-friendly and high-performing solutions for takeaway packaging, which don't compromise on quality, conscience or the consumer experience."

www.ep2.co.uk

Bags of potential

For GoJute International, sustainability goes even deeper than the fully biodegradable bags it creates for leading retail brands

Along the beautiful Cornwall coast, where GoJute International founder Gary Warren spent his childhood, discarded plastic on beaches and in the sea was all too visible. Keenly aware of the damage done by single-use plastic bags, he created an alternative: bags made from jute and cotton.

"Jute bags can be reused hundreds of times and a pure jute bag is 100 per cent biodegradable," says Kat Hardman, GoJute's Brand and Marketing Manager. The jute plant itself has naturally strong fibres and is grown without pesticides or fertilisers, absorbing 15 tonnes of carbon dioxide over a six-month lifespan.

Since it was established in 2006, the company has manufactured bespoke branded or promotional bags for companies including Whittard of Chelsea, the Royal Horticultural Society, Tommy Hilfiger and Iceland. Working with three jute mills in India, GoJute has the capacity to produce 26 million bags per year, and is now the largest manufacturer of jute and cotton bags in Europe.

The advantages for brands who opt for a jute bag are not just related to durability and longevity. Hardman describes them as a "walking billboard of brand and ethics", showcasing the importance of sustainability, right down to the water-based dye used for printing.

For GoJute, the importance of sustainability goes beyond the raw material used in its products. The jute is shipped in a carbon-neutral way, and the company's employees benefit from a package of welfare and education programmes designed to give them a good quality of life. The company has raised millions through charity initiatives, as well as offering support for local schools, and its surplus products are donated to local food banks in the UK.

Thanks to the versatility of the material, GoJute's product range now includes everything from coffee sacks to weed suppressants and vegetable nets. "Changing plastic bags to jute shopping bags is a drop in the ocean of all the things that need to be done," says Hardman, "and that leaves a huge scope of opportunity for any business operating in a sustainable marketplace on the world stage."

www.gojuteinternational.com

Comfort and joy

Helm London's handmade, artisanal candles with evocative fragrances
epitomise the brand's core values of sustainability and minimalism

Smell is one of the most powerful senses, opening an evocative window into past experiences. And, because smell and emotion are closely linked with memory, the aromas we remember from childhood tend to be the strongest. With the scent of freshly laundered linen or comforting cocoa butter, the handmade candles lovingly produced by Helm London are designed to spark such olfactory memories. "Smell is interesting because it triggers these emotional responses in a way that is different to taste or music," says co-founder Carl Tomkinson.

It is something he understands all too well, as the smell of candles takes him straight back to his own childhood. "I grew up with candles as a core memory," says Tomkinson. "My mother always had a candle burning, so it is a real trigger for a comforting memory. There is something very powerful in the scent as well as the experiential element of the candle and the way it burns."

Tomkinson set up Helm London with friend Olivia Watson in 2018, focusing on a desire to create artisanal candles made from sustainable, ethically sourced ingredients. In combination with the company's minimalist aesthetic and personal approach – candles can be customised with a name on the label, or a personal message – the biodegradable, toxin-free high-quality soy wax candles were an instant success. They not only drew attention from retailers specialising in ethical and artisanal home furnishings, but also featured in luxury publications such as *Vanity Fair*, *Tatler*, *GQ* and *World of Interiors*. Tomkinson and Watson have since enhanced their portfolio of beautifully designed candles, branching out into diffusers, essential-oil-based fragrances and scented tealights.

Helm London's success is also down to an innovative approach to scent. There are other fragrant blends, such as Blackberry and Bay; Lime, Basil and Mandarin; and Peppercorn and Raspberry, as well as more familiar aromas such as Vanilla, Citronella and Eucalyptus. Popular creations include candles that smell of fresh linen and cocoa butter, as well as another that combines vanilla with a subtle hint of tobacco.

"Cocoa Butter is our signature scent," says Tomkinson. "We discovered it almost by accident. Olivia was using cocoa butter in her moisturiser, and we wondered if it would work for a candle. It has a comforting, warming smell. I love our Seaweed and Juniper perfume, while our Christmas Spice candle is an all-encompassing festive smell that is extremely popular."

The team at Helm London continue to innovate with regard to sustainability, looking at ways to reuse rather than recycle their glass candle holders. "We are looking at returning the glass so they can be refilled, or sending out refills that are of equal quality to the original candle," says Tomkinson. "We have to maintain our standards and ensure we balance sustainability with the quality and the luxury of the products."

Helm London works closely with artisanal retailers across the UK and Europe, ensuring it supports entrepreneurs with a similar small batch mentality. The next stage will be to expand the company's expertise into the world of skincare. "We want to get the right people and upskill our own artisans to produce amazing, affordable but luxury products," says Tomkinson. "We have been thinking about how to do this properly for a year and are very close to getting it right."

www.helmlondon.com

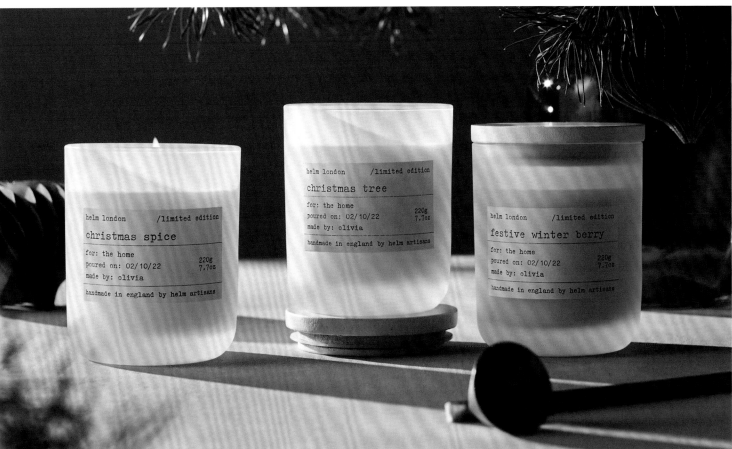

Sustainability made simple

Using Rimm's digital platform, my CSO, small companies have an all-in-one, affordable solution to developing sustainable business models

For small and medium-sized enterprises (SMEs), sustainability can sometimes feel like a quagmire. Smaller businesses do not always have the time, money and experienced staff to execute sustainability assessments and strategies, nor easily afford the sort of fees often charged by consultants. But sustainability is important for SMEs – both in terms of impact on the climate and for a company's reputation and profitability. This is where Rimm comes in.

The Singapore-based company's digital-solutions platform, myCSO, acts as a digital Chief Sustainability Officer, enabling SMEs to record data, monitor progress and set targets around sustainability at an affordable price, from around US$1,000 per year. "Our myCSO platform was set up as an easy and intuitive tech tool for sustainability management, to capture sustainability data in a simple way and apply it across different-use cases from compliance to strategy," explains founder and CEO Ravi Chidambaram. "We serve the wider business ecosystem, including a lot of those smaller companies that have never done these things before, that don't have the expertise or the time and can't afford the expensive solutions."

Chidambaram set up Rimm in 2020, after a career in finance, which included senior positions at Goldman Sachs and Deutsche Bank and founding a successful boutique investment bank in Singapore. But Chidambaram had also become interested in sustainability, originally as an investor and then in academia as Adjunct Professor in Sustainability at Yale-NUS College, Singapore. He created myCSO to solve some of the problems he had witnessed, noting that the marketplace lacked an affordable and easy-to-use tool that was designed to support smaller companies seeking to attain a sustainable business model.

"Sustainability is a young field and there's a lot of noise about it," he says. "People want to do something, but they don't know what that something is and that leads to inertia. We designed a system that is intuitive and builds in some education. We look at how to gather data within your organisation and how to apply that data across compliance or in terms of strategy to identify opportunities for your business. That could include an opportunity to build great products, to access green finance or to become a more sustainable supplier, which might help a company keep key customers. Then you are off and running."

The myCSO platform can benchmark performance on key metrics against peers and set targets, it covers all 69 Global Industry Classification Standards (GICS) and operates worldwide. In developing myCSO, Chidambaram was determined to keep the cost low, as he strongly believes sustainability needs to be more democratic and inclusive. He can offer myCSO's service at a relatively affordable rate because much of the process is automated. But he points out that even the low price should not be seen as a cost.

"It is important for businesses to see myCSO as an investment and not as a cost," he says. "We try to get companies to that mindset, but we also try to ensure the price is attractive. At Rimm, our key principle is one of inclusiveness because, unfortunately, sustainability is currently often restricted to larger companies. We believe that sustainability is all about building ecosystems, and there are many smaller companies that participate in this ecosystem as clients and suppliers. Through myCSO, we can give them quick solutions to interpret performance, set targets and understand where they are in terms of Sustainable Green Environment impact."

www.rimm.io

The green route

Rouute's unique energy harvesting technology transfers kinetic energy from vehicles back into the National Grid, powering the future sustainably

Inspiration can strike anywhere – even while sitting in a car on the M25 between Oxted and Heathrow. That is where Antony Edmondson-Bennett was while he turned over in his mind a problem that he had pondered for years – how to produce clean, sustainable energy from the one thing every city has in abundance: traffic. The solution finally came to him that afternoon on the M25, triggering a process that led to the founding of Rouute in 2017, a company based around the pioneering concept of creating energy through compression pads that can be placed on roads, pavements and even farmers' fields.

"Think of it like a wind turbine, and then take away the propeller," explains Edmondson-Bennett. "We drive our system through compression. Every time a vehicle passes over our system, it triggers a hydraulic motor that drives an alternator to give you power. We can then feed that power back to the National Grid, or it can be used locally. There's no large infrastructure, you can put it anywhere. What I ultimately imagine is a city that can power itself – a real electric highway."

Edmondson-Bennett had been thinking about new ways to meet increasing energy demands since working in the oil and gas industry after leaving the military. His desire was to create something as sustainable as solar or wind power, but with much higher levels of efficiency and reliability. Rouute's compression technology achieves this, and can easily be installed in an existing road with the minimum of disruption, tailored towards the velocity and weight of the traffic. There is even a special version for lorries, which can be laid at lorry stops and service stations, while trials have been held using dairy cattle in the US.

"The cabinet houses the electric and hydraulics in a single unit, which can be scaled up or down so we can go as big or small as needed," explains Edmondson-Bennett. "For the cattle we modified our low-speed compression device. We found that we can generate a lot of power. The dairy farm we are working with has 10,000 cattle and they get moved three times a day, in single file, which means we can generate in excess of 50 to 100kW per animal."

With proof of concept established in a series of successful trials at a number of different sites, Rouute is now ready to be rolled out. As interest grows, Edmondson-Bennett is seeking investors as he prepares to commercialise. Rouute will work best wherever there is heavy traffic, including locations such as drive-through restaurants, service stations, distribution centres, holiday parks and lorry stops. Ultimately, it could prove to be an essential weapon in the battle against climate change. "It's about educating people that there is a new sustainable way of generating electricity that doesn't have an adverse effect on the ecosystem or the natural environment. Rouute allows for a cheaper and more sustainable means of generating power without tearing up the National Grid."

To accommodate current demand with electric vehicle charging, more than £40 billion of investment is needed in the National Grid, explains Edmondson-Bennett, which is not happening. So we need to look at how we meet this demand. "That will be a combination of wind, wave, nuclear and now compression technology," he says. "It's the most sustainable and reliable method there is of producing energy because as long as we have traffic, we have the capacity to produce electricity."

www.rouute.co.uk

Full charge ahead

GRIDSERVE aims to have revolutionised electric charging across the UK's motorway networks by 2024 with its "Sun-to-Wheel" ecosystem

"We're not just charging vehicles," says GRIDSERVE's CEO, Toddington Harper, "we're building an ecosystem called 'Sun-to-Wheel' – a replacement for the modern transport system of 'Well-to-Wheel'. Instead of oil wells, refineries, pipelines, petrol forecourts and combustion engine vehicles, we have solar farms, batteries, cables, Electric Forecourts and electric vehicles. "The energy in fossil fuels is actually stored sunlight from hundreds of millions of years ago, so we skip the millions of years and build solar farms to harvest today's sun energy, with batteries to refine it. It's the same energy, without the environmental impact."

GRIDSERVE delivers the sun's energy into electric vehicles through its Electric Highway – an EV charging network covering more than 80 per cent of Britain's motorways – and award-winning Electric Forecourts, which received the Innovation Award at the 2022 What Car? Awards, the first time a non-carmaker has received such an accolade.

Toddington's interest in sustainable energy emanated from his upbringing. "My father built petrol stations many years ago. After the oil crisis, he set off round the world in search of making a difference, and discovered solar and batteries, which he used to build many of the first solar projects in the Middle East." Toddington and his brother Heston (who also works for the company) were even named after service stations – Heston and Toddington – both of which now have the company's electric charging points installed.

Toddington values and recognises the importance of continuing to push the sustainability message in the race to protect the planet. "GRIDSERVE is on the front foot and running fast," he says. It plans to open some 100 charging locations by the end of 2023, and by 2024 to have transformed charging across the motorway networks, giving people the confidence to drive long distances.

To deliver sustainable energy and move the needle on climate change is "why we run at the speed we do. The odds are against us to reduce greenhouse gas emissions to a level that will prevent temperatures exceeding 1.5 degrees of warming. It is uniquely on our watch to sort it out. History will judge us for how well we respond to this crisis."

www.gridserve.com

Material gain

At Modern Synthesis, creativity and science are converging to craft natural textiles with microbes that are billions of years old

Material designer Jen Keane met bioengineer Dr Ben Reeve while on a quest for material advancement beyond the toxic age of plastic and synthetic fibres. As it turned out, the answer lay in 3.8 billion years of microbial evolution.

Reeve, a scientist from Imperial College, London, had isolated and sequenced a strain of bacteria that could produce nanocellulose, a biomaterial, or natural fibre, that ticked every box in Keane's vision: uncompromisingly high quality, customisable and capable of fulfilling a circular life cycle. Together, they founded Modern Synthesis, a biotechnology company that is using microbiology, material science, engineering and design to reinvent materials.

"Nanocellulose is created by bacteria found naturally in kombucha," explains Keane. "This nanofibre is the strongest, finest form of cellulose, which is the building block of the natural world. Bacteria grow these nanofibres over a period of days – they are stiffer than Kevlar [a strong synthetic fibre], with a tensile strength higher than steel. The nanocellulose is then formed around a natural textile scaffold to create our non-woven biomaterials, which can be used in applications ranging from automotive interiors to footwear and fashion accessories."

This new class of microbial materials eliminates the need for animal- and petroleum-based ingredients, which greatly reduces its environmental impact. The bioreactors used for production take up less land than traditional agriculture, and there is no harm to animals. The microbes feed on sugars from food, which can be sourced from agricultural crop waste. Unlike plastic, these materials can safely biodegrade as part of a closed-loop system that does not degrade ecosystems or shed microplastics.

"Next-gen materials have been gaining momentum for a decade, with over $3 billion invested since 2013," says Keane. "We're now working with leading brands to tailor our materials for use in their products. Because our process is uniquely versatile, we can modify everything from the colour and thickness of the material to its durability in end use.

"We're also collaborating with other innovators in the field to incorporate further microbial ingredients into our process. By pairing cutting-edge biotechnology and design with processes perfected by nature over billions of years, we can create a materially better future for all."

www.modernsynthesis.com

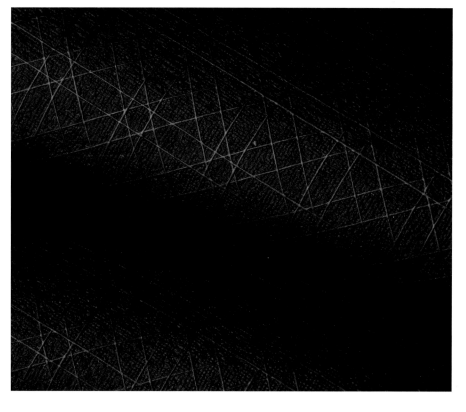

Box clever

With a global reach and local knowledge, packaging producer Tri-Wall
provides it clients with a range of options tailored to their product

When the British government was seeking a partner for the secure transportation of lithium ion batteries – one that could create bespoke packaging, with an understanding of compliance measures – it turned to Tri-Wall. Operating from a string of locations between South Wales and the North East of England, the company has spent decades creating intelligent, multi-material packaging, with an increasing focus on sustainability.

"We are a global business with clients from Japan to the United States," says Gavin Peters, CEO of Tri-Wall UK. "We share our knowledge and expertise to help our clients create a circular economy. By working to Tri-Wall global standards for products and methods, clients can be assured they are getting the same quality everywhere. It's important to communicate; the more we talk to our customers, the more sustainable we can become as we understand their needs."

The company can trace its history back to the 1950s, when New Jersey inventor Abe Goldstein came up with a new type of lightweight,

durable, corrugated cardboard. This now-familiar core product has ten times the compression strength of conventional cardboard but remains light and easy to stack, making it ideal for long-distance transportation. It rapidly replaced timber as the industry's packaging material of choice.

Tri-Wall came to the UK in the 1960s, when Goldstein licensed the invention to different producers around the world. These have now been brought back under the same umbrella by Yuji Suzuki, Chairman and CEO of the Tri-Wall Group, who wants to reconnect Tri-Wall across the globe – driven by a principle of global reach and local service.

As well as its signature corrugated cardboard packaging, Tri-Wall can create packaging using various other materials, including timber, metal and plastic. While cardboard is generally the most sustainable material, that does not always take into account its end use or life cycle. "We have the ability to make a judgement call on what is the best and most sustainable material for each product," says Peters. "We offer our clients packaging that is fit for purpose through our award-winning design department and our unique UKAS-approved dangerous goods laboratory. We use these facilities to create something bespoke and true to the aims of the client's company values, as well as our own."

Tri-Wall UK started life in Monmouth, Wales, and currently employs around 340 people based not only in Monmouth, but also Swansea, Wolverhampton, Manchester, Chesterfield, Northshields and Gateshead. Its recent expansion has been driven by a number of acquisitions, with Tri-Wall taking on several businesses that have a long and rich heritage – for instance, the Manchester business dates back to 1817, and the Wolverhampton plant started out in 1868. These acquisitions have enabled the company to add experience and an in-depth understanding of local customer needs to its offering.

The same high standards are maintained at all Tri-Wall sites – whether in the UK, China, India or the US. This improves sustainability by ensuring quality production can be localised. "Our plan is to continue investing in our current businesses, maximising our environmentally-friendly manufacturing process, one that is modernised for the future of the packaging industry," says Peters. "Continued growth through product and process development, as well as acquisitions, makes us the most rounded packaging manufacturer and supplier, with the ability to provide the right packaging solution, made of the right materials, for our clients' priorities. "We are the best fit for our clients: just around the corner, all around the world."

www.tri-wall.co.uk

Universal message

With Climate Outreach, Noora Firaq is working to engage people from all walks of life with climate change

Noora Firaq is from the Maldives, the palm-fringed frontline of climate change. She now lives in Oxfordshire, bringing her lived experience of climate change to Climate Outreach, where she is Deputy CEO. Climate Outreach is a British charity helping organisations to understand and apply the growing body of evidence on how to effectively engage their audiences with climate change. The research is clear that public engagement is a key part of tackling the issue.

"The Maldives had sufficient fresh water when I was growing up, but now groundwater and freshwater are scarce," says Firaq. "It's 99 per cent sea and 1 per cent land, without higher ground, so it's a very fragile ecology. Around 90 per cent of the islands report flooding annually. The country spends around half of its national budget on climate change adaptation, because it's not just an environmental issue, it's also a humanitarian issue. It affects all aspects of life, including health, security, food and shelter."

Across the globe from her family in the Maldives, Firaq is aware that climate change still feels abstract to many people, so addressing this global disconnect is at the heart of Climate Outreach's work. "To engage with climate change, people need to understand it, relate to it and feel part of the discussion and solutions," she says. "Our work includes helping scientists to effectively communicate climate data to the public, so people can appreciate the difference they can make through lifestyle choices. We work to ensure that those whose livelihoods are affected by a low-carbon future are part of the discussion. We share voices, stories and imagery from the diverse communities and environments affected by climate change who may not feel heard or represented at a global level and who have so much to teach us. Transitioning to an equitable world needs public consent and participation."

Climate Outreach raises funds from donors for projects, partnerships and collaborations with government, policymakers, international bodies, scientists, media, technology innovators, NGOs, other climate organisations and those living and working in affected areas. "You can have cutting-edge scientific solutions and pages of well-meaning policy, but if people don't understand and engage, you can't action equitable, effective, systemic change," says Firaq. "We need to think globally, act locally and communicate universally. We can't do this alone."

www.climateoutreach.org

The complete package

Recyclable, scalable and commercially viable, Pulpex's paper bottle technology is attracting the attention of hundreds of leading brands

Developing paper bottles for the world's biggest consumer brands is not to be rushed. Even a trailblazing innovation will languish in a lab unless it can be delivered at scale – reliably, commercially and sustainably. But the best things come to those who wait, as is proven by Pulpex. As part of a collaboration between UK drinks giant Diageo and venture-management company Pilot Lite, Pulpex and its team of research and development scientists are working mostly with British supply-chain partners to deliver a revolutionary paper-bottle solution, at scale.

"My background is in commercial science at Diageo, which is where the technology at the core of Pulpex was first developed," says Scott Winston, CEO of Pulpex. "When it comes to sustainability, big companies tend to think ahead, as there can be a lot of complexity in implementing change. New concepts also need to be economically viable, have commercial longevity and be scalable. But it's worth the extra time and effort to get it right, as their high turnover means you can make a significant difference to the environment."

Scott and his team had a few key criteria for the concept: it needed to be adaptable, brandable, functional, capable of being integrated into existing factory filling lines, and suitable for single-use and reuse, with minimal end-of-life impact.

The process begins with dry paper, which is turned into wet slurry for moulding. Using chemical and mechanical engineering processes tailored to the end-use product, the interior and exterior of the bottle is coated, strengthened and branded, before being dried ready for filling. Formed from the highest-quality fibres, the bottles are at least 90 per cent paper, with a shelf life of 12 to 18 months. Post use, if not recycled, they degrade readily in the natural environment.

Pulpex's independently verified and patented technology brings together material science, fluid dynamics, AI and CAD (computer-aided design). The company is now creating bespoke solutions for clients' existing packaging lines, and provides supporting maintenance and research and development services. Launched in 2020, Pulpex is already working with corporations including Unilever, PepsiCo, Kraft Heinz, Haleon, Castrol and The Estée Lauder Companies, and has an extensive waiting list of other companies – evidence that patience has paid off for this team of passionate packaging pioneers.

www.pulpex.com

Fantastic bioplastic

The unrivalled team at Titan Bioplastics is creating a new generation of
sustainable plant-based super-plastics tailored to commercial success

"We look at how we can make a commercial impact," says Tanya Hart, CEO of Titan Bioplastics. "As sustainability is a growing part of industry, it's about not being afraid to take a risk."

Titan Bioplastics is a sustainable material engineering company with a focus on recycled and plant-based plastics and bioplastic composites (plastics produced from renewable sources) for commercialisation. With a team offering decades of experience in science, technology, marketing and business development, it has unparalleled expertise, and its bio-based compostable products are revolutionising alternatives to plastic, creating a new generation of sustainable super-plastics.

From Augie Bones, the pet industry's first plant-based dog chew toys, to the first recycled plastic credit card, and with plans to expand into children's toys, the Michigan-based company, founded in 2018, combines material innovations with products that have global marketing potential. "Many small companies have great material innovations," says Hart, "but if you can't commercialise a material at scale to make a market impact, it won't have long-term value. We always ask: can we commercialise? Can this have an impact on the environment? Do we have a viable market product? This is what makes us unique."

At the heart of the business are three initiatives: to support customer-driven projects developing sustainable materials for manufacturing; to produce proprietary "to market" composite innovations, such as Augie Bones; and to further develop sophisticated nanotechnology additive systems. "We're always looking at where the next iteration of commercially viable, sustainable material innovations will come from," says Hart.

The firm enjoys industry recognition, along with investment from Michigan State University Foundation. "With sustainability being so prolific on the global agenda, we have the opportunity to grow tremendously, and the partnerships to make that happen," she says.

A key part of Titan Bioplastics' offerings are high-quality, adaptable-material engineering services that can work in multiple industry sectors. The company maintains close relationships with the producers of the most reputable bioplastic and recyclable materials, "and our development services are tailored to customers' needs, while using existing manufacturing equipment," says Hart. "Sustainability is not a buzzword at Titan," she says. "It is the foundational principle from which all our work derives purpose."

www.titanbioplastics.com

The right move

By using creativity to accelerate the transition to electric vehicles,
WeVee Technologies is helping drivers plug in to an all-electric future

"We are working to become the Spotify of e-mobility lifestyle," says Rahmyn Kress, CEO of WeVee Technologies, the European climate-tech company dedicated to developing, operating and licensing technology platforms that accelerate the transition to e-mobility and sustainable consumption. He and Francesca Spengos founded the company in 2021, but first met two decades ago in the music industry, seeing first-hand the mistakes made as it initially failed to cope with digitalisation and the internet. "We ended up driving blind for some time," says Spengos. "In contrast to the music industry, with the climate crisis there is a clock ticking. We cannot go blind for too long, which is why we have brought in our expertise, our networks, to make change happen fast."

Kress and Spengos have extensive experience in entrepreneurship and sustainability, and a dedication to "creating a more desirable future for generations to come". "The window is there to take advantage, to be environmental activists," says Spengos, "but in a way that makes good business sense for everyone."

Working with industry partners, WeVee assists companies in implementing new legislation like the "salary sacrifice" scheme, to encourage the transition from petrol to electric, reduce overall CO_2 emissions and positively impact their own ESG (environmental, social and governance) rating. The WeVee Corporate Leasing Platform provides a bundled offering of e-mobility-related services, such as leasing, insurance, maintenance and energy solutions for businesses and households. "The employee benefits from converting to an electric way of life with the support of their company and without a loss on their net salary, while the employer saves on national insurance and social security contributions, to name a few," says Kress.

WeVee also offers an app that features personalised e-mobility functions, like charging-station mapping, easy directions, payment and reimbursement, and connected reports, making it a game-changer in the electric vehicle market. With a network of over 450,000 charging stations and a unified payment portal, the app simplifies the charging experience, as well as promoting charging points in rural areas, benefiting local economies. WeVee aims to educate, too, about recruitment of neurodiverse employees and more female involvement in the tech industry. "We want to prove what we're doing is really good business," says Kress, "and should be seen as such."

www.wevee.com

Food and farming

Charles has been a vocal advocate of sustainable farming methods and rural communities for the past 50 years, long before it was common practice to champion such issues

T hroughout his working life, King Charles has championed organic farming, spoken up for sustainable urbanism and emphasised the need for local character and communities to be preserved. In doing so, he has often placed himself in the firing line and faced widespread criticism for daring to challenge what was the prevailing orthodoxy and the conventional way of thinking. However, his thinking has helped to emphasise that these areas, particularly regarding food, farming and the environment, are interrelated and complementary.

He has been a leader in this field for many decades, calling on politicians and business to see the "big picture" to fully appreciate the problems that we all, as humanity, face.

SUSTAINABLE FARMING

Charles's position has always been clear. He believes the future of humanity depends on switching to more sustainable farming practices, which he has always promoted at his private estate of Highgrove and introduced at the farms at Sandringham and Windsor when he took them over. Organic management, he says, enables ecosystems to flourish as nature intended and ensures that we are putting back more than we take from the land. As he explains, "ecological delivery", such as avoiding block cropping and providing trees, hedgerows, wildlife corridors, bird boxes and field margins, is now prioritised on the Sandringham Estate and farm, for instance.

The King assumed overall control of the 21,000-acre estate in Norfolk from Prince Philip in 2017, and was also given responsibility

"Charles has slowly but surely incorporated organic farming methods into the running of the Sandringham and Windsor estates"

Previous page
Charles with Welsh farmers on a tour of Penbedw Farm in Nannerch, Flintshire

Right
Prince William, his father and Ayrshire cattle raised at Home Farm, Highgrove

for the running of the Windsor Estate and Windsor Great Park. Since then, Charles has slowly but surely incorporated organic farming methods into the management of both estates. For example, at Windsor Castle and its Home Farm, The King has explored ways to expand the use of biomass heating (a form of renewable energy that uses wood chippings) on the estate.

For years, like so many fathers and sons who possess sharp minds and have forthright beliefs, Charles and his late father, Prince Philip, clashed over big issues such as organic and genetically engineered food production. Philip, who ran the farms at Sandringham and Windsor before his son, supported scientific advancement as a solution to feeding humanity, while also maintaining that overpopulation was the biggest problem facing the planet and our survival. Charles disagreed.

He spelled out his ambition soon after he took control of the royal estates. "We need to ensure that the land use is not only focused on food production, but that full consideration is given to providing habitats for wildlife," he told *Country Life* magazine. His plan included increasing the number of cattle and sheep at Sandringham – to 500 and 3,000, respectively – to better graze and fertilise the land.

LEADING THE WAY

Now that he is monarch, Charles will inevitably have to be less outspoken, avoiding crossing into areas deemed partisan, and be guided by the relevant government minister as the constitution dictates. However, we have already seen that he intends to use his considerable influence and great convening powers to try to persuade decision-makers to tackle the challenges of the day, such as agriculture and food production.

His views as king remain consistent with those that he held for more than 50 years as the Prince of Wales, and he continues to warn of the dire consequences of not tackling these issues head on and fast. When he first started giving speeches about ecology, biodiversity and sustainability in the 1970s, he was often ridiculed. But it didn't stop him on his quest. Half a century on, he is recognised as a visionary and is widely respected on the issue. He has consistently warned about the use of single-use plastic and on royal tours he would often be pictured planting a tree, giving it a shake and saying, "Have a good life tree!"

Charles has invested personally in organic farming. Since the beginning of the 1980s, when he first took on the responsibility of managing some land in his own right at Highgrove, his Gloucestershire home, and its Home Farm, he has focused on an approach to food production that avoids the impact caused by the conventional system of industrialised agriculture. In Charles's view, that approach had a "disastrous effect on soil fertility, biodiversity, and animal and human health".

In 1985, he converted his farm and Gloucestershire estate to organic farming methods. At the time, he was dubbed an "idiot" by critics. He chose to ignore such criticism, however, and, over time, has been proved right, with his Duchy Organic food brand becoming a major commercial success.

RURAL COMMUNITIES

Alongside championing organic farming methods, he has campaigned on the importance of keeping rural communities alive. The King believes that rural towns and villages need to be both living and working places, and central to this is the part that small farms play.

"When Charles first started giving speeches about ecology, biodiversity and sustainability in the 1970s, he was often ridiculed. Half a century on, he is recognised as a visionary"

When he was in charge of the Duchy of Cornwall, which has now been passed on to his son Prince William, Charles tried to ensure that tenants had continuity through succession, as well as making entry-level farming possible. In 2020, it was announced that he would not be renewing the lease of the land of his Home Farm as he prepared for greater royal responsibilities. But he continues to farm organically at the Sandringham Estate in Norfolk, implementing organic farming methods that strictly limit the use of antibiotics.

Charles demonstrated his support of rural communities by establishing The Prince's Countryside Fund in 2010. And even earlier, in 1979, he set up The Prince of Wales's Charitable Fund to help build sustainable communities. Attending a reception in the gardens of Clarence House to celebrate 40 years of the fund in July 2023, The King announced a new initiative, the Coronation Food Project. This aims to reduce food waste by ensuring that produce that would otherwise have gone to landfills is redistributed to those in need through partner charities and organisations.

Although he probably cannot speak out publicly so much now that he is king, Charles still cares deeply about farming, food production and the communities that support the industry. A farmer at heart, he will use his influence to stand up for what he believes in.

Indeed, at one of his last official engagements as the Prince of Wales at Dumfries House in Scotland, on the day before the Queen's death in September 2023, Charles spoke of being vindicated about the risks of intensive agriculture. "One of the reasons I went organic 40 years ago was because I felt there was an overuse of antibiotics," he said. "And I felt that if you overdo it, you end up with resistance. Anyway, that's happened. I was told I was a complete idiot for even suggesting going organic." Vindicated indeed.

Opposite
A photocall at Shipton Mill, Gloucestershire, where heritage wheat from Charles's nearby farm at Highgrove is used in the mill's flours

Above
Charles visits the Farming Life Centre, Buxton, Derbyshire, in 2015 as patron of The Prince's Countryside Fund

Bubbles of joy

Mooboo is not just a bubble tea brand that has seen success in the UK, it is also a community
with a business model that allows others to share the passion and connectedness it creates

Bubble tea has become a colourful addition to the British high street in recent years, presenting a new experience for those tired of traditional beverages. The inventively flavoured tea, which comes with edible toppings such as tapioca pearls, originated in Taiwan in the early 1980s, but has become widely available in the UK thanks to specialists Mooboo. In 2022, the business celebrated its tenth anniversary and opened its hundredth store, making it the largest bubble tea franchise operator.

"We are trying to make the product accessible," says Eric Khaw, founder and Managing Director of Mooboo Bubble Tea. "We can recreate the same experience with other drinks, including caffeine-free teas. It's a friendly product for many tastes and is classed as vegetarian."

The bubble in bubble tea comes from the chewy tapioca pearl, which is made from the cassava root, a woody shrub that grows in South America. The first bubble teas saw the tapioca pearl introduced to black tea – the bubble was sucked up through a thick straw. Over time, the drink has evolved as makers have become more creative. Toppings include fruit-flavoured balls and jellies, while the tea can be black, milky or green with numerous additional flavourings, from chocolate to mango. There is a vast menu with more than a thousand combinations of flavours and taste sensations to choose from, so customers can mix and match.

"The principle of the product is really something you can drink and eat at the same time," says Khaw. "The first time you try it, it blows your mind. It completely changes your perception of what constitutes a drink. In fact, it is also known as a dessert drink. One of our most popular creations is a crème brûlée-flavoured tea."

As the drinks can be prepared in many combinations – they can be hot, cold, fizzy, or iced – there is much complexity to consider, but everything is carried out by Mooboo's computerised system. After the customer makes an order, the computer tells the server exactly how to make the drink, which ensures greater consistency. To develop and refine this system, Malaysian-born Khaw drew on his experience and expertise in IT.

Another significant influence was the franchise model adopted so successfully by companies such as McDonald's. Khaw wanted to take a similar approach but make it more accessible, allowing ordinary people the chance to run their own business and become part of the Mooboo story. "The franchise business can sometimes seem expensive and rigid, requiring a high level of investment," he explains. "Mooboo's has been inspired by a very successful model like that of McDonald's but on a smaller, more accessible scale. We want anybody who is interested in this business to find an affordable package."

The result of this accessibility is that the majority of Mooboo's franchise holders are family businesses, rather than shareholders or big international companies, which has provided Mooboo with more than 100 locations across the UK. "If anyone shows an interest in starting a bubble tea shop, our team will help in any way they can. The experience of the freedom and excitement of owning and running your own franchise is life-changing."

When Khaw set up the business in 2012, bubble tea was little known in the UK. He vividly recalls spending ten minutes with customers trying to explain the concept, persuading those who were sceptical to sample the product. Now, with bubble tea cafés a fixture in many towns and cities, children and teenagers are persuading their parents and even grandparents to try the drink for themselves. No region is immune to the colourful combination of taste and flavour, which is something Khaw welcomes. "Parents can be happy for their children to choose anything from the menu," he says. "None of our drinks have alcohol in them. As well as being vegetarian-friendly, there are caffeine-free and halal options. Everyone is welcome to come for a drink. Mooboo serves the whole community."

The concept of community is important to Khaw, and he is especially passionate about the one he has developed among

"The freedom and excitement of owning and running your own franchise is life changing"

customers, staff and franchise holders. By encouraging family investors, for example, he strongly believes this will further strengthen the sense of community within the business.

"We are trying to bring the best product to the consumer, but it's also about the people running the business," explains Khaw. "That is what makes the difference. Growth relies on our community-driven approach – the idea that we are the business around the corner. We want to grow the business and the community at the same time."

Khaw believes the current structure allows Mooboo to develop in the right way, without the influence of shareholders, and create more opportunities for work. In recognition of its growth, training and support systems for a network of British franchises, Mooboo is one of the companies on the 2023 Elite Franchise Top 100 (EF100) list. The ranking is an achievement that acknowledges the huge strides that have been made in the past decade, as Mooboo continues its mission to bring bubble tea to the British market.

"We are proud to be a British company," says Khaw, who has plans over the next four or five years to bring the manufacture of the ingredients themselves in-house, so the business does not have to rely on a third party, giving the company an opportunity to further innovate their own products. "That is a big investment in equipment but also people, so we are exploring that operation, looking for the expertise of those who can do this work.

"I am proud to come from the Far East, but everything we develop at Mooboo is for the local market. I want bubble tea to be accessible to everybody."

www.mooboo.co

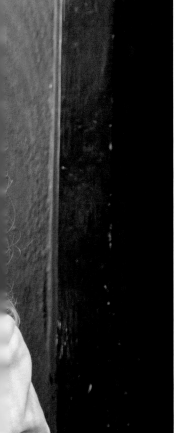

Helping efficiency take root

ProducePay is rethinking the field-to-retail cycle so that everyone can reap the rewards of a more efficient fresh food industry

When Pablo Borquez Schwarzbeck created ProducePay ten years ago he did so with a personal understanding of the challenges experienced by farmers around the world. Schwarzbeck was a fourth-generation Mexican farmer, and his initial intention with ProducePay was to support farmers by giving them access to capital that would help them bridge the difficult period between sowing and harvest. That has since evolved into a company that supports farmers by building relationships with retailers, ensuring fair pricing and improving efficiencies in the food cycle so less food and energy is wasted.

"We are organising the farmers and giving them a basis to go to market together, almost on a communal basis, to get fixed prices for their produce," says CEO Patrick McCullough. "We have agronomists in the field who can objectively quantify the quality of produce and communicate that upstream. We want to avoid rejection [of unwanted produce], which causes waste, and we want to reduce the time from field to mouth, when so much produce is kept in cold storage, as this is bad for the produce and for the environment."

ProducePay uses technology to drastically shorten the traditional field-to-retail cycle. The company estimates that it has already removed three days from the typical nine-day cycle in some markets. This means produce spends 41 per cent less time in cold storage, while rejection is reduced by 80 per cent. This results in food being fresher and healthier, with a fair price for farmer and consumer. McCullough believes further improvements are possible.

"We're focused on fixing the existing perishable produce system, which is terrible for the environment because of cold storage refrigeration, so any waste and inefficiency is very costly," he explains. "There are so many middlemen and speculators in this cycle because they gravitate to anywhere there is price volatility." This comes at the expense of the produce, which spends longer in warehouses, fridges or trucks. Shortening the time from harvest to consumption means the fruit or vegetables can grow for longer, so they will be riper, fresher and

"We ensure farms don't wait two months to be paid – we step in and help"

healthier. "One of the big failures of the current system is we pick too early. Tomatoes should be brilliantly red and perfectly flavourful, but when you see them in the supermarket they are like orange bricks. We think we can address this with a more efficient distribution system."

The company's approach is predicated on the conviction that solving existing price volatility will give growers and buyers the stability to change behaviour. Food is the most volatile commodity on the market, with prices fluctuating wildly because of a poor link between supply and demand. ProducePay uses the collective power of the farmers to lock in fixed-price guarantees from major retailers months in advance. This gives farmers the confidence to farm more effectively, while ProducePay's agronomists monitor quality and ensure that other important social factors, such as water access and labour rights, are not abused.

"We believe we are supporting those farmers by allowing them to consolidate supply, but we also worry about environmental and social issues in farming," says McCullough. "There are a lot of bad actors in farming. I don't think they set out to be bad actors, but they find they are pressured by price volatility and end up making bad decisions. We don't want to see that in the farming sector."

ProducePay began operating in Mexico, where the bulk of food goes to the US, and then expanded into South America, working with farmers in Chile, Colombia, Peru, Ecuador, Costa Rica and the Dominican Republic, again largely serving the US market. The company is now also working with farmers in Spain and Morocco, as well as retailers in the UK, France, Italy and Germany.

Headquartered in Los Angeles, California, ProducePay was founded with the intention of providing short-term loans for small farms, to bridge a difficult period in the farming cycle. This comes at the start of the season, when there are upfront costs – labour, seeds, fertiliser – but no return until long after harvest. While ProducePay still offers this capital advance service to farms, its focus is now on making sure farmers are paid more quickly after harvest. "We ensure farms don't wait two months to be paid – we help handle their financial concerns over that whole cycle," explains McCullough. "We step in and help. We focus on helping them trade so they can make more money. Eventually that will put them in a low credit-risk position. We have had 100 per cent return rate on our capital advances – they all come back every year."

At the heart of ProducePay is a desire to support farmers and the planet by modernising the industry. McCullough believes this is essential if we are to solve the issue of food scarcity. By reducing the

lag between supply and demand, the food cycle will become more intelligent and efficient, drastically reducing waste and ensuring more nutritious food ends up on more plates.

"What we talk about all day is how to apply tech so our partners can have the most efficient industry," says McCullough. "We want to redesign the vertical so efficiently that our capital isn't needed and we can make our original business model extinct. Compare food with energy. When you construct a large wind or solar energy plant, you normally have a 20- to 30-year purchase agreement with a very credit-worthy buyer who is committed to buying that energy at a certain price. We don't have that with produce, even though many of these retailers are investment-grade. But we are working to convince them to give us that assurance, offering a price at an earlier time so we can get more efficient pricing and scale the food supply much quicker. We don't plant enough to support population growth, and food hardship will get worse until we address that."

www.producepay.com

A refreshing approach

Ahmad Tea has stirred up the market with its affordable,
high-quality blends – and its sense of responsibility to suppliers

The story of Ahmad Tea began in 1986 when Rahim Afshar and his two brothers, Karim and Ebraham, started selling tea caddies from a small store, the family's tea shop, on Southampton's London Road, later renaming the company after their father. Ahmad Tea has now expanded into more than 90 countries, with its teas available across the world, from the US to Japan.

"Our mission is to inspire a love of tea," says Gary Winslade, Ahmad Tea's UK Business Development Manager. "If we persuade tea drinkers to trade up to our tea, they will realise that something they love every day can be even better."

Every year, Ahmad Tea donates no less than 20 per cent of its profits to charitable causes, but is now also setting its sights on improving standards across the whole tea industry. It ensures that farmers receive fair prices and offers assistance to workers, particularly the women who rely on the tea trade to support their families.

As well as loose tea, the company offers popular fruit and herbal teas. It has a strong gift selection, too, working with the Royal Botanic Gardens, Kew to create a range of caddies that can be found in Harrods and other department stores. There is also a luxury range called Galerie du Thé, which comprises "the finest and rarest teas we can find," says Winslade. It is vacuum packed at source so it is as fresh as possible.

Ahmad Tea's ability to provide an ideal tea for many different markets has allowed the company to enjoy unimaginable growth since those early days operating out of the Southampton store. The company's big break came with expansion into Spain, followed by regions as diverse as the Middle East and Eastern Europe. With its high-quality but affordable products, Ahmad Tea seeks to attract customers who are curious about sampling premium teas but might be put off by price.

"We believe that everybody should have the right to enjoy good-quality tea. We want to engage people who are ready to trade up but don't want to double their expenditure," says Winslade.

"Our speciality is blending, and we source the highest quality tea from around the world and then blend it, which provides consistency." Indeed, Rahim Afshar, the company Chairman, still personally checks every blend, and refuses to sell anything that he would not drink in his own house. His tea tasting team samples up to 500 cups of tea a day to ensure consistent quality, and each blend is checked up to seven times from the tea bush to the teacup.

The company's desire to improve standards in tea does not just apply to taste; Ahmad Tea wants to be an example to other tea companies. As well as paying farmers the best price, its support for women working in the tea gardens includes providing sanitary products and other essentials. "The goal is to enhance the reputation of tea and its value in the eyes of the consumer," says Winslade. "By supporting the supply chain, we are trying to elevate the profile of tea. We are happy to pay more for tea at source because we will get a better tea, while giving the farmer the true value."

Ahmad Tea has found that, once you persuade people to try a better quality tea, they will never go back. Its aim is to inspire even more customers, alongside setting higher standards for tea distributors.

"Tea is taken for granted," says Winslade. "We want to reawaken the passion and the respect we have for tea in other people across the world."

www.ahmadtea.com

Setting the standard

From a rural ranch in Oregon, the highly certified Shaniko Wool Company
is fighting for the revival of the US textile industry

"Before Charles became King, my husband and I used to say, 'Who will be the Prince Charles of America?' Who will help us save our wool production in America, because it's been devastated," says Jeanne Carver, founder and President of Shaniko Wool Company, located in the high-desert interior of Oregon. Carver launched Shaniko Wool to scale the supply of wool produced in the US certified by the Responsible Wool Standard (RWS). In 2017, her Imperial Stock Ranch, of which Carver is an impassioned steward, became the first ranch in the world to be certified by this highly rigorous comprehensive benchmark.

Since 2020, Carver has worked with academics to develop a research model to measure the environmental impacts of the Shaniko Wool Farm Group ranches, confirming the positive impact on the ecosystems provided by their farming methods. "On Imperial Stock Ranch, we harvest beef, lamb and wool, while capturing 60,000 tonnes of carbon a year, putting that into our soil while producing the commodities that feed and clothe humankind," she says. "We have a net-positive impact on nature and now, through these measurements on each Shaniko Farm Group ranch, our customers can understand our impact. They can pair that knowledge with our high-quality merino wool to give a verified positive story to tell their customers, showing how we can all have a positive impact on nature."

Carver, working with her late husband Dan who passed away in 2021, has farmed the historic ranch since the 1980s. The ranch had been founded by the pioneering Richard Hinton, who was born in a wagon on the Oregon Trail in 1852, as his family headed to the fertile valleys west of the Cascade Mountains in what was then the Oregon Territory. Wanting to be a stockman instead of a farmer, in 1871 Hinton headed back east across the mountains to Oregon's high-desert interior. Here, he established a homestead claim, brought in sheep and cattle, established farm fields and constructed assorted buildings as his holdings grew. By 1900, he was the largest individual owner of land and livestock in Oregon and one of the biggest sheep operations in America. He established sheep, cattle, grain and hay production – four commodities that remain integral

347

"On our family ranches, we produce the commodities that feed and clothe humankind"

to the ranch more than 150 years later. The Carvers still farm every field he created and the historic headquarters are a National Historic District.

This was the legacy that the Carvers sought to maintain when they acquired Hinton's Imperial Stock Ranch. They also understood the importance of nature and introduced farming techniques to preserve the soil, encourage plant growth and maintain the delicate balance of a healthy ecosystem. This included allowing animals to forage and graze, but controlling where they did so, to prepare and fertilise fallow fields naturally. "Grazing animals stimulate plant communities and growth, which, through photosynthesis, draws CO_2 back into the soil from the atmosphere," explains Carver. "We need grazing animals, so we began to devise and implement a total conservation management plan. This is now called regenerative farming, and we've been doing it since 1989." Another important element was protecting the creeks, precious sources of water in this semiarid region. Such was the success that salmon started to return to the creeks in greater numbers each year to spawn.

The Carvers' livelihood was threatened in the late 1990s when their long-standing wool buyer closed processing to go "offshore". From then on, it was a fight to keep sheep on the land, not just for them but for the entire US sheep industry. "The infrastructure for textiles in the US was devastated. Between 1996 and 2000, 26,000 sheep producers went out of the sheep business, and we now have less than ten per cent of the textile industry we once had," she says. "Sheep give us food, clothing and shelter, and ask for nothing in return. Wool is a miracle fibre that has been at the core of textiles for more than 10,000 years. That matters. And it's no accident that sheep and lambs are so symbolic in religions throughout the world. These are things we must honour."

Carver set about developing local networks, finding weavers, spinners and knitters around Oregon who could add value to her wool. She also found outlets for the meat through local restaurants. "I began the journey," she says. "I didn't know anything, but I persevered. Mainly, I didn't know I couldn't do it. At the time, wool had little market value. Textiles had largely migrated to cotton and synthetics, but, within a year, I put my first wool product on the market. I found regional textile artisans, women within 120 miles, who were creating items I could sell. I found local chefs to buy our lamb. We never looked back. These products, attached to place, resonated with authenticity."

Thirteen years after Carver picked up the challenge to preserve sheep on their ranch, she received a call from Ralph Lauren in New York. The company sent representatives cross-country to Oregon to meet her and learn about the historic ranch and her wool. As a result, her wool was used in the Team USA uniforms at the 2014 Winter Olympics in Sochi. She was also recognised by the Pratt Institute of New York as a female farmer changing the fashion industry. More recently, in 2023, Carver received the American Sheep Industry Association's Innovation Award.

Shaniko Wool Company expands Carver's work, and now provides wool from ten long-established ranches, partnering with multiple brands and providing the finest certified merino and merino-cross wool to the market in a range of microns. "We are the first and, so far, only farm group in North America that meets the Responsible Wool Standard," she says. "In 2022, we also aligned with the Chargeurs Group standard, and are now certified to NATIVA Regen, as well as to the RWS." More and more brands are demanding the wool they source be third-party-audited to these global standards. And grower groups around the world are responding. Carver says, "These wool production standards de-risk brands from association with animal abuse and even degradation to landscapes. As a champion of wool, these values align perfectly with what King Charles has espoused his whole life."

www.shanikowoolcompany.com

A local drink

Budweiser Brewing Group is driving the drinks industry forward, creating a responsible and inclusive drinking culture while brewing in harmony with nature

"Our purpose is to 'Dream Big to Create a Future with More Cheers'," says a spokesperson for Budweiser Brewing Group UK&I. "For centuries, the experience of sharing a beer has brought people and cultures together. We take natural ingredients and brew them sustainably right here in the UK to bring people together over the nation's favourite beers."

The responsibilities that come with producing beer are ones that the UK and Ireland arm of parent company AB InBev takes seriously. As the producer of some of the most popular beers in the UK – including Budweiser, Corona and Stella Artois – the company wants to ensure consumers can make informed decisions about their alcohol intake and to produce the best and most popular beers on the planet. There is also the ambition to do all of this sustainably.

The Belgian-based multinational's approach to sustainability begins at home. Beer is as homegrown as any beverage can be, traditionally brewed close to where it is consumed. That tradition is maintained at Budweiser Brewing Group, where breweries are the pride of their communities, using barley from local farms and employing local people, thus supporting agriculture and local economies. It also creates shorter supply and logistics chains, producing fewer emissions.

Central to British beer consumption is the British pub. Budweiser Brewing Group works closely with pubs to support pub culture as a business priority through initiatives and campaigns, including a campaign focused on getting home safely after a night out, 'Get Every Bud Home'. "Throughout Covid and the recovery, we have supported hospitality through donations, voucher schemes and campaigns that encouraged the public to get behind their local," says Budweiser Brewing Group.

The company is also focused on creating a safer and more inclusive night-time economy. "We want every experience with beer to be a positive one, and enjoying our products responsibly is an important part of this. Our goal is to create a nation of smart drinkers," says Budweiser Brewing Group. "We've run programmes called 'City Pilots', which aim to reduce alcohol harm by giving support and advice to people locally. We produce non-alcoholic versions of many of our beers, offering consumers the opportunity to moderate while still enjoying their favourite brands."

Sustainability is a major driver for the brewer. Beer has always been made with natural ingredients, and those used in Budweiser Brewing Group products are 100 per cent natural. Packaging, featuring the Budweiser Brewing Group 'Natural, Local, Renewable' logo, is bringing further transparency to UK customers, showing the product's journey "from seed to sip". This is part of Budweiser Brewing Group's ambition to achieve net zero brewing status across its value chain. The ambition is supported by a range of activity that includes brewing with 100 per cent renewable electricity from solar power and wind turbines. In addition, the brewer's primary and secondary packaging, as well as the majority of its tertiary packaging, is plastic-free in the UK. In London, the company's Kentish Town brewery achieved net zero brewing in 2022.

"We want to be the world's most sustainable brewer," says Budweiser Brewing Group. "And we are getting there one sip at a time."

www.budweiserbrewinggroup.co.uk

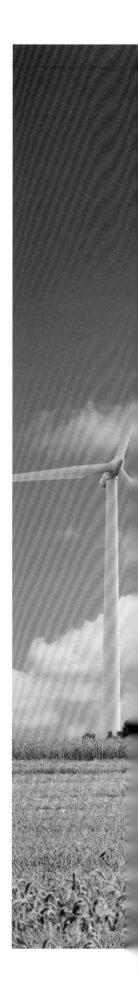

Working in harmony

One of the world's largest chemical producers, BASF is leading the way
with its harmonious solutions to sustainability in the agricultural sector

When The King, as the then Prince of Wales, wrote a book about sustainability and agriculture in 2010, he titled it *Harmony: A New Way of Looking at Our World*. The word "harmony" has become important in contemporary farming, as experts seek to find the ideal balance between the health of the land, the wealth of the farmer and the food needs of society – which is why BASF describes farming as the "biggest job on earth".

"The Biggest Job on Earth platform opens a space for our community and the entire industry," says Neil Kay, Vice President of Western Europe for BASF Agricultural Solutions. "We need to show governments and policymakers what can be done with the right guidance and appropriate incentives – together we can really drive positive change if you invest in the right place.

"We have worked with some farms for 20 years to support biodiversity, showing that it is possible to have a sustainable and profitable farm that supports the soil and the environment around it. It can be done harmoniously."

BASF's roots are in chemicals. The company was founded in Ludwigshafen, Germany, in 1865, to make dyes but has since expanded into a huge global business, supplying raw materials to the automotive, pharmaceutical and construction industries, among others. An important early breakthrough was synthetic fertiliser, an innovation that would become a key driver in the development of industrialised society, supporting the nutrition of billions of people. Agriculture is still a core sector, and the company produces a portfolio of products to help farmers increase yields and the quality of their crops in a sustainable way.

The production of more food to satisfy the demands of an expanding population is one of the challenges that UK farmers face today, alongside logistical issues and the unpredictable, more extreme weather brought about by climate change.

"Our work is about giving farmers a platform to explain farming procedures and the challenges they are having to overcome to get food on our table," says Kay. "We live on an island. We can't acquire more land, but we do need to increase productivity and protect the industry to ensure food security."

It will take a variety of solutions to solve this problem, involving genetics, seeds and chemistry. BASF is predominantly a research and development company, and has created a range of digital innovations to this end. In 2020, it committed to helping farmers reduce CO_2 emissions per tonne of crop by 30 per cent within a decade. "We set out very clear targets about what we want to do around R&D and climate change, and we are looking at ways to reduce emissions per crop and increase our sales of accelerator products," explains Kay.

"Accelerators are solutions that make a substantial sustainability contribution in the value chain." They include projects such as farms that focus on biodiversity, or digital applications that allow barley growers to generate accredited carbon certificates. "We are supporting growers to do the right thing, as well as create new revenue streams where they can trade the carbon they have eliminated."

BASF uses a phrase, adds Kay, about "finding the right balance for success". In other words, solutions need to be sustainable in terms of the environment, profit and the planet. "Every innovation must have the appropriate balance, not just for today but for the future."

www.agriculture.basf.com

Cheesemakers of choice

Butlers Farmhouse Cheeses is leading a renaissance of British cheese, embracing the new with tradition and four generations of expertise

The Butler family has been making award-winning cheese since 1932, starting with its classic Farmhouse Lancashire, still made by hand from an old family recipe. That delicious Farmhouse Lancashire is now available throughout the country in national supermarkets alongside more recent creations, including soft blue cheese and goat's cheese. This 90-year-old family business, however, is not all about tradition. Gillian Hall, owner of Butlers Farmhouse Cheeses, explains that success comes from balancing history with a spirit of innovation. A business cannot prevail if it only looks backwards.

"We reflect on what my parents and grandparents did, which are the traditional ways, the craft and essence of what we do," explains Hall. "We ask where that traditional craft adds value, which is making cheese by hand in open vats, which adds flavour. But where are we able to add technology to increase speed and efficiency and add even more value? We reflect on the best of the past, keep the essence and embrace the new."

This pioneering approach has seen Butlers Farmhouse Cheeses partner with local universities to use AI and machine learning

to examine data around grass, animal feed, milk and climate, to work out which combination of conditions has produced the best cheese in terms of yield, consistency and quality. This has seen the company introduce a soft continental-style blue cheese, Blacksticks Blue, the first of its kind made in the UK, alongside Sunday Best, the classic Farmhouse Lancashire – both of which have won Great Taste Awards in recent years – and popular brie-like soft cheeses such as Button Mill. Other innovations include a direct-to-letterbox delivery service and the introduction of 100 per cent recyclable packaging.

"People don't necessarily want a traditional cheeseboard now," says Hall. "They might want to find a way to share. We wanted to create a cheese that you could put in the oven so two or three people could dip their bread in the same piece of cheese – that was our British brie, Button Mill. People still want to buy British, and that's where we have done a lot of work in the past 20 years. We receive support from the universities, we practise and practise, and we get direct feedback from chefs, consumers and supermarkets. That has allowed us to create products that are handmade and consistently of very high quality."

Throughout the decades, Butlers Farmhouse Cheeses has learned to weather external forces such as the disruption caused by the Covid pandemic. In doing so, the company understands that Butlers Farmhouse Cheeses is part of a local ecosystem, an essential element of what Hall describes as circular sustainability. "We want to have a sustainable business for the family and the 100 or so people who work for us," she says. "In rural areas, you are a big part of the community. We look after our community, and we all rely on each other. The benefit of being a family business is that you can build on the foundations that went before you – you benefit from that hard-won credibility."

Hall hopes this is what she can pass on to her two sons, who are the fourth generation. "If you have survived four generations, you need a pioneering spirit. With the platform of a stable business you can take risks in the knowledge that not everything will work. We are leading the British cheese renaissance from Lancashire, pioneering and pushing the boundaries."

www.butlerscheeses.co.uk

The taste of Cornwall

With a heritage more than a century old, Rodda's Cornish clotted cream
has found favour across the globe while remaining true to its roots

In 1890, Eliza Jane Rodda invited some guests to afternoon tea at her rural Cornwall home. She served them clotted cream made from surplus milk produced by the Guernsey cows on her farm. The clotted cream was an instant hit with the visitors. The story goes that one of them liked it so much he took it home with him, and the interest started to grow from there.

Rodda's Cornish clotted cream has now been part of the family business for five generations, with Nicholas Rodda the current Managing Director. In those early days, it was sold in local shops. Things changed for the Rodda family when Nicholas's grandfather, William, then aged 16, made a trip to London to sell the cream to hotels in Park Lane, as well as high-end stores. "There was no great marketing plan," says Nicholas. "His killer line was, 'My mum says you have to open the jar, taste it, and then tell me what you think'." This emphasis on taste and quality has been the company's ethos for the past 130 years. "William used to say that we have to make the cream good, because our name is on the side of the pot." Although the business has adapted to new technologies, Rodda's Cornish clotted cream is still made using milk from local farmers, then gently baked the way it has always been. Cornish Clotted Cream is one of the few British foods to have been awarded a Protected Designation of Origin (PDO). This means that the public can be reassured about its authenticity and its Cornish origins.

The plan is to keep Rodda's in the family for at least the next 100 years, and Nicholas's son is already learning the ropes. "We are woven into the tapestry of the county," says Nicholas. "At one time, we had three generations of the family working in the business. You get that continuity and also a sense of pride at being embedded in the Cornish community."

With customers including major UK retailers, independent food shops, hotels and restaurants, and selling internationally as far afield as Hong Kong, the company is well-positioned for the future. As Nicholas says, "Eliza Jane could not have envisioned in 1890 that her clotted cream would end up around the world."

www.roddas.co.uk

Leading by example

EcofashionCorp was founded by the eco-lifestyle entrepreneur
Marci Zaroff to develop green apparel and home brands

"To meet the most fundamental of human needs for food, water, air, shelter and clothing, we need a healthy planet, with balanced, sustainable ecosystems," says the US eco-pioneer and entrepreneur Marci Zaroff. "Around 35 years ago, I realised the importance of regenerative, organic and biodynamic agriculture in supporting the needs of the planet so that it, in turn, can support us. In the early 2000s, I met Prince Charles, who I found hugely inspirational at a time when there were not many of us advocating this holistic approach."

Zaroff, who coined the term "ecofashion" in 1995, went on to found four clothing and lifestyle textile brands under the umbrella of EcofashionCorp (EFC). Each brand uses non-toxic dyes, and sources only sustainable, regenerative and/or circular materials, from communities where the welfare of the people and the planet are prioritised.

Since then, Zaroff became a Henry Crown Fellow of The Aspen Institute, and has received countless awards, the most recent of which include the Real Leaders Impact Award in 2021 and 2022, the MUSE Design Award in 2022, and selection as one of 2023's top 20 New York Moves Power Women.

MetaWear is the manufacturing heart of EFC. It produces clothing for the group's fashion labels Seed to Style and YesAnd, and its Farm to Home lifestyle brand. MetaWear also offers a private label and bespoke manufacturing service to businesses worldwide. It is committed to fashion that has a positive impact across all price points, without compromising on quality or style, and with state-of-the-art traceability systems. For Zaroff, traceability is more than a buzzword, it is a tangible pathway joining years of collaborations and supply-chain partnerships. Her groundbreaking RESET cotton farming project is a prime example. "I've been working with cotton farms in India for decades, helping them to adopt financially viable organic and biodynamic farming practices, with climate action and women's empowerment at the core.

"I've also worked with international teams to help establish industry certifications, including the Global Organic Textile Standard, in the late 1990s. Now, through EcofashionCorp and my consultancy and advocacy work, I can share these solutions with a growing number of businesses, brands and consumers who are, at last, scrutinising the term 'fashion statement' and seeking to give it new meaning."

www.ecofashioncorp.com

Researchers without borders

CGIAR's international network of scientific research centres is tackling
one of the world's biggest challenges: food security in a climate crisis

Around the world, nearly 350 million people are affected by extreme hunger – a number that will increase by 189 million if the world warms by 2C, and 1.8 billion if the temperature rises by 4C, according to the UN World Food Programme. Agriculture is a major contributor to climate change, but it is also affected by changing and unpredictable weather patterns. Global agricultural productivity growth has declined by more than 20 per cent due to climate change – 30 per cent in Africa – but the UN estimates food production needs to increase by 60 per cent to meet demand by 2050.

CGIAR has been tackling the complex, evolving challenge of food and nutrition security for more than 50 years. This international organisation runs gene banks, invests in research and innovation to boost crop yields and mitigate the impact of climate change, and works with governments to develop better agricultural policies, with a focus on smallholder farmers of the Global South. The Board Chair is Professor Lindiwe Majele Sibanda, a farmer, scientist and policy advocate from Zimbabwe, who has first-hand experience of these challenges. "Agriculture is both a problem and a solution to climate change," she maintains. "We need to improve productivity and it's clear we do this through adaptation and mitigation."

After El Niño in 1997, CGIAR saw huge declines in productivity in east and Southern Africa. The declines continue in most smallholder farms. "The yield of the seeds we had used for generations has declined, partly because the rainy season is more erratic," says Sibanda. "We need different varieties of seed because of the shift in season, we need more diversity in crops and livestock, and we need crop varieties that are drought and disease resistant. This needs investment, education for farmers and a new way of doing business, as soil quality is being diminished through overplanting, drought and monoculture farming."

CGIAR comprises a network of 15 research institutions across the globe, with more than 9,000 staff working in over 80 countries. It operates 11 gene banks, which safeguard the world's crop diversity for future generations. Governments can request seeds to restore indigenous plants or try new climate-appropriate varieties, while institutions can use them for research to develop more resilient or nutritious types. CGIAR supports farmers with crop and livestock management, using technology such as weather apps to better plan crop preservation, or aligning on when best to plant different crops based on seasonality.

There have been considerable successes already. Almost half the world's wheatland is sown with varieties that come from research by CGIAR scientists, while its work on modern crop varieties has reduced infant mortality by a third across the developing world – averting between three and six million infant deaths per year. CGIAR has provided wheat seeds for several African countries, allowing for heat-tolerant wheat production and mitigating the challenges presented by the Russo-Ukrainian war. As a result, Zimbabwe and Ethiopia will move from being net importers to net exporters of wheat.

Sibanda notes that, with more investment we can reduce emissions and adapt to climate change in a climate-smart way. "The returns are ten to one," she says. "We have a catalogue of climate-smart innovations, such as technologies for seeds and livestock, but the challenge is upscaling. We need investment to take the solutions to farmers globally, and to adopt and adapt them for every local area, culture and climate. Fortunately, we are located in most of these countries, so we can work with farmers and their partners to drive the change needed before it's too late."

www.cgiar.org

Farming with efficiency

Solinftec's artificial intelligence manages millions of acres of land globally
to optimise agriculture without destroying the planet in the process

The world's population is estimated to reach almost ten billion by 2050, placing increased pressure on already stretched food supplies around the globe. For Britaldo Hernandez, co-founder and CEO of Solinftec, this presents an unprecedented challenge for a company that is devoted to supporting agriculture through technological innovation. The company's ALICE AI platform now manages more than 27 million acres of agricultural land in 12 countries, leading to a 30 per cent increase in productivity while reducing the impact of agriculture on the environment.

Solinftec controls 94 per cent of sugar-cane market share in Brazil, as well as being used in row crops, fibre, citrus, coffee and forestry markets. "We are focused on the huge technical problem of helping to feed ten billion people in 2050," says Hernandez. "We will have to produce more food in the same area of land without destroying the environment, and technology will provide the solution. We are creating AI and machines that are more compatible with nature."

Solinftec utilises an AI platform called ALICE that was developed alongside farmers and producers to ensure it meets their needs. "We are inside their farms, and we believe we have credit when it comes to solving their problems as we work exactly where the problem is. We aren't outside the gates of the farm. We are connected to them in all operations, from planting to harvest." The company even has its own farms, which are used to test and improve the AI and robotics that Hernandez believes constitute the future of farming.

ALICE offers complete management of the agricultural ecosystem to meet the challenges of day-to-day farming. It receives and processes more than half a billion pieces of data drawn directly from the field each day. This allows farmers to make more informed and timely decisions while ensuring agricultural practices focus on maximum efficiency and sustainability. Working in conjunction with ALICE, the fully autonomous Solix is a robotics platform launched by Solinftec that is able to "do the scouting", giving farmers real-time information. It works 24/7, carrying out spot applications as a sprayer and attracts and kills pests with light pulses.

Hernandez believes that sustainability as well as food security will come from technologies that create efficiencies and eradicate waste. Solinftec helped its customers avoid the emission of 1,365,591 tons of carbon dioxide between 2012 and 2021 – a reduction equivalent to the planting of more than 167 million trees or the use of 3,890,573 electric cars. "Any solutions that optimise agriculture will have an important impact when it comes to the environment, which is why we believe that being a more efficient producer will directly improve environmental matters. Our producers use significantly fewer chemicals and have less tillage, which means less carbon is released from the soil; and it limits the use of heavy machinery on the farm."

Hernandez highlights the importance of working alongside food producers to provide and refine the tools they need to feed the world, as this stimulates innovation and tests ideas. He also salutes his colleagues, who he says prosper in a creative work environment. "We are a collective that respects the individual, and everything comes from creativity," he says. "When I guarantee people can be themselves, I guarantee their creativity. This culture produces very good ideas and means that people do more when it comes to profitability, but also tackle the ethical problems, as we know that we are doing good for the environment and for the world."

www.solinftec.com

Nature works

Through trade, technology and training, with a biodiversity focus, De La Tierra
helps farming communities across the globe experience tangible benefits

Farming techniques that promote biodiversity are environmentally friendly, but their successful adoption depends on economic viability. Set up in 2012, De La Tierra promotes such techniques through three pillars of activity: supplying fresh produce, consultancy, and implementing waste reduction technology.

A project the company designed for Innocent Drinks in Spain is illustrative of its work. It involved planting wildflower strips between rows of orange and apple trees and reducing pesticides to encourage pollinators and natural enemies. Not only is this beneficial for insect life, but it also increases fruit production and profitability. "The wildflower species that we chose had to reflect the local climate and attract beneficial insects," says Athanasios Mandis, founder and Director of De La Tierra. "We had to engage with local farmers: the wildflower strips couldn't be wider than the tractor wheels, or the flowers would get crushed. This co-production needs to happen to encourage adoption."

De La Tierra strikes a balance between such in-depth local research and standardised methodologies to support the agrifood sector with sustainable practices. "There is a big collaborative effort by the agrifood industry to address socioenvironmental challenges within supply chains," says Mandis. "There is an awareness to do the right thing, and a recognition that the challenges are too big to solve alone. It has to be in partnership with other supply chain actors."

Food supply chains are interdependent, therefore improvements must be made by all parties together, from the transnational companies to smallholders, academics, civic organisations and consumers. "When we are discussing any solutions or methods, it is not a top-down approach. There is a need for participation and engagement with local actors." Nature-based solutions such as the Innocent Drinks project works for those on the ground. "If you want to get systemic, transformative change, the farming community has to experience tangible benefits."

De La Tierra also offers training, supporting farmers in Malawi to implement Quality and Environmental Management Systems. It resulted in successful Rainforest Alliance and British Retail consortium audits and thriving mango and banana farms. "For me, that was an example," says Mandis, "of how anything can be achieved with the right approach, training and engagement."

www.de-la-tierra.com

Tasting notes

Based in the world's perfume capital, luxury distillery Comte de Grasse
harnesses the science of the fragrance industry to make cutting-edge spirits

Just north of Cannes on the Côte d'Azur is the historic town of Grasse. For centuries, it has been the global epicentre of fine perfumery, but now there is a new collective in town with a rather more spirited approach to bottling the botanicals that thrive in the sunshine and gentle maritime breeze – gin-maker Comte de Grasse.

"In the history of perfumery, there was a period of decentralisation in the sourcing of botanicals as it was cheaper overseas," says Georgina Boden, Brand Manager for Comte de Grasse distillery, which was set up in 2017. "Comte de Grasse's founder, Bhagath Reddy, as a foreign entrepreneur, wanted to ensure that we were giving back to a local economy that gave us so much. A commitment to resettling agricultural families' lands was one such initiative."

The distillery's 44°N gin, which has already won numerous awards including Gold at The Gin Masters 2020, encapsulates the warmth, energy and flavour of the French Riviera with notes of citrus, cade, mimosa, rose centifolia and immortelle. Its sibling, 06 Vodka X Rosé, marries fragrant organic rosé wine from Provence with French winter wheat.

The distillery itself is housed in a 17th-century perfumery, painstakingly restored to its former glory – both architecturally and as a hub of botanical innovation. Sustainability also permeates every other aspect of production. "Our methods bring together modern extraction techniques that utilise cutting-edge science," says Boden. "This includes ultrasonic maceration, low-temperature vacuum distillation and CO_2 critical extraction, which helps maximise our energy efficiency. We're committed to supporting sustainability locally by forging partnerships in the community, working with farmers to regenerate interest in botanical agriculture, and sourcing 80 per cent of our botanicals from the region. We also collaborate with a social integration association, to create opportunities for unemployed people to return to work."

As well as making a difference today, Comte de Grasse is mindful of the future. Its master distiller, Marie-Anne Contamin, a lecturer at the University of Nice, works with the university on a sponsorship programme that allows spirit technology PhD students to drive innovation at Comte de Grasse in return for access to a research lab just ten metres from the distillery. This collaboration is nurturing a new generation of botanically inspired innovators.

www.comtedegrasse.com

Feeding everyone

Sustainable Planet is poised to help feed
a growing global population with the
environmentally friendly superfood,
the water lentil

The pressure on planetary resources is set to intensify. One major pressure is on food. According to UK cross-government research, around 795 million people face hunger every day, with two billion lacking essential nutrients; it is estimated by the United Nations that 50 to 70 per cent more food will have to be produced in the next 25 years to feed the world's population of ten billion by 2050. Even if more agricultural land were available, however, increasing protein would cause further deforestation, biodiversity loss and soil degradation, as well as requiring more fresh water and releasing more greenhouse gases, worsening climate change.

Such challenges require innovative thinking and new technologies. One potential solution is being provided by Sustainable Planet, a UK-based high-impact agri-tech company. Founded in 2021 by Sven Kaufman and Susan Payne, its mission is to provide a soybean alternative, a fast-growing, protein-packed, planet-friendly aquatic plant known as the water lentil, or duckweed. "The company was launched to offer solutions to three compelling global problems: food security, climate change and regenerative agriculture," says

Payne. "We can address all these issues in one company using one plant." The water lentil is important because it can be grown on non-arable land, and it is climate positive as a carbon sink. "Unlike other protein plants, it reduces carbon emissions in the atmosphere and nitrates in water. It ameliorates saline eroded soils by drawing up salt like a vacuum cleaner," says Payne. "We are currently growing it on salt flats in Mozambique, even using saline water. The business brings jobs and higher incomes to farmers in Africa and the Middle East. It's an organic superfood that is very easy to grow using natural fertilisers, and it's scalable as well as highly impactful."

Sustainable Planet with its academic partners has the technology to extract protein from the water lentil so it can be used in all variety of human foods, with byproduct used to boost animal feed alongside grains, a role otherwise reserved for soybeans. This plant-based protein-rich food also helps address malnutrition. When comparing water lentils with soybeans, the figures are startling: soybeans produce four tonnes per hectare per annum, requiring fresh water and arable land; water lentils are grown on non-arable land and yield 30 to 80 tonnes per

hectare per annum, climate dependent, using 15 times less water, and contain more protein and nutrients. They also release large amounts of oxygen, which helps to mitigate the impact of climate change.

For Sustainable Planet, the challenge is to raise funding quickly to meet growing global demand and unleash the potential of the water lentil at scale. The company has completed tests in eight countries in four regions and is now training people to work on repurposed lands. "One of the company's most impactful aspects is addressing 16 of the 17 UN Sustainable Development Goals, starting with the training and employment of potentially thousands of subsistence farmers who can increase their incomes by three to five times," says Payne. "We have the technology and we have the team on the ground. We have been offered non-arable land in various countries to grow protein. With more funding, we can replicate our model to provide protein products, like protein bars, pasta and sports shakes, at scale. Growing water lentils is more sustainable than any other protein source for global food supply, for farmers, for repurposing and regenerating land and for the planet. Healing lands, helping lives."

Fresh starts

Jonathan Tole Consulting is on a mission to unlock the potential of agri-food businesses by helping them use technology better

When Jonathan Tole's grandfather ran a mixed farm in the West Midlands, technology could not have been further from the agenda. "Everything was done by hand," says Tole. "It was probably old-fashioned even then." The experience of growing up around cattle, sheep, pigs and corn nevertheless taught Tole a lot about the industry he wanted to work in.

After studying horticulture with a focus on crop and food production, Tole worked in various fresh-produce roles in the UK, Poland and Spain. Change and technology were constants, and he saw first-hand how innovation can transform a business.

In 2017, he set up Jonathan Tole Consulting (JTC) to bring this knowledge to people in the industry by developing technology-led solutions that work for them. "I love the potential of technology to transform the efficiency of food production," says Tole, "and I understand how it can be applied to agri-food businesses."

JTC often works with companies to introduce systems that give an overview of inventory and costs, which can generate better insights into snags and expenses in the chain, and help boost profitability. "Because I understand the real-life world of agri-food and farming, I can see the challenges of every role and process," says Tole.

AI and machine learning will help the industry understand how crops perform in different conditions, and how to improve. Robotics and automation will also replace some manual tasks. But we are not there yet. "Technology is moving fast, and the industry is under significant cost and environmental pressures, while consumers are demanding more. We are at an interesting juncture."

A key part of Tole's role is helping businesses manage change, even when they are keen to embrace it. "There is a change curve," he says. "People must learn a new way of operating, which takes time. I support them with that." He also helps startups to get the best out of technology to take their company to the next level and create a business model that will succeed.

Tole hopes to take these lessons beyond the UK. As long as his work is making a difference, he believes, it could be anywhere. "I want to help businesses become better than they were before," he says. "It is more of a mission than a job."

www.jonathantole.com

Passing on knowledge

Danish label Knowledge Cotton Apparel, a champion of organic fashion and style, traces its production to keep consumers informed

Mads Mørup grew up learning from his father, whose textiles business had a strong emphasis on the human and environmental impact of the industry – long before this outlook became mainstream. Mørup had always looked at the fashion sector through this lens, and decided to set up his own brand. "We are called Knowledge Cotton Apparel because of the legacy I got from my father," he says.

Mørup founded Knowledge Cotton Apparel in 2008 in his home country of Denmark. It creates classic menswear and womenswear, as well as collections for kids, with a strong emphasis on the use of natural fibres. "Our products have 99 per cent traceability from field to warehouse," explains Mørup. The company is also carbon positive, offsetting emissions from transportation with projects related to conservation and renewable energy. A recent project boosted regenerative farming in India, that is, growing cotton without pesticides to improve the long-term soil health and farmers' yield. It earned the brand the coveted Regenerative Organic Certified status for its cotton.

Since the company's beginnings, consumer habits and understanding of sustainability have changed. "Back then, people didn't really know what sustainable manufacturing was," says Mørup. "It was harder for them to understand a complex supply chain like ours." Now, he says, there is "a bit of a movement" towards quality products that will last and have a known provenance. Consumer awareness has increased.

As an early adopter of sustainable practice, Mørup says that Knowledge Cotton Apparel will benefit. "As new regulations come in, there has been a lot of greenwashing in the industry. Our position will get stronger with more competition, as we will always be known and recognised as one of the first movers."

Knowledge Cotton Apparel is on sale throughout Europe in its own eco-friendly boutiques, as well as selected online retailers and department stores. The company intends to increase its market share in the coming years. Like the Knowledge Cotton owl trademark, a symbol of wisdom and nature, the company "has a vision of what is going on," says Mørup, "and where we should go in the future."

www.knowledgecottonapparel.com

Recipe for change

Matriark Foods upcycles surplus vegetables and off-cuts into
healthy products while diverting edible food from landfill

Every year, around 33 million tonnes of perfectly edible vegetables never make it to the table in the US. "Agricultural food waste is one of the top contributors to greenhouse gases," says Matriark Foods founder and CEO Anna Hammond. Since 2018, the New York-based organisation has been transforming the way food is sourced and produced. It works with vegetable manufacturing facilities and farmers, sets up the compliance to reclassify off-spec produce and remnants as ingredients, before creating healthy products for food service (schools, hospitals, corporate cafeterias), retail and emergency food providers. While reducing the environmental impact of waste, it offers farmers and businesses another stream of income. "Selling to us saves them from paying to send it to landfill, which is a good business model for everyone."

The model can be used anywhere. "We are not doing anything new," says Hammond. "People have used their resources to the full for thousands of years, although less so for the past 80 years of agriculture and food production." The name Matriark is partly inspired by Hammond's grandmothers, who lived through the Great Depression and "never wasted anything. There was always room for one more at the table." The first product was a vegetable broth concentrate made from the tops and bottoms of celery, carrots and onions – "We're doing what every good home-chef does, just on an industrial scale." More recently, the company has launched a range of tomato sauces for retail, followed by, in 2023, a vegetable stew in a shelf-stable carton for foodbanks and emergency food providers.

The products have a verifiable positive environmental impact: they are Upcycled Certified, meaning that at least 10 per cent of the ingredients would have gone to landfill, and are Carbon Neutral Certified, so each product has a full Life Cycle Analysis against which carbon credits are paid. "Our goal is to make it possible for everyone to participate in mitigating climate change through their eating," says Hammond. "This approach aims to advance resilient, local supply chains for food security and help meet one of the UN's Sustainable Development Goals, which is to cut food waste in half by 2030."

www.matriarkfoods.com

Responsible eating

With its cultivated beef burger, food technology company
Mosa Meat is on a quest to be kinder to the planet

Following almost a decade of research, the first hamburger grown directly from animal cells was served in London in 2013. The innovators behind that breakthrough now run Mosa Meat, a company formed three years later in Maastricht, the Netherlands, whose founders believe cultivated burgers will bring huge benefits to the planet, its inhabitants and the agricultural industry.

"It started with a concern for food security and for the climate," says Maarten Bosch, Mosa Meat's CEO. "The demand for meat will increase massively in the next decade and that will have a huge impact on the ecosystem. We have a population problem and are being confronted by the limitations of the existing system."

Bosch explains that Mosa Meat focuses on beef because the cow is particularly inefficient, converting only 15 per cent of the nutrients it consumes into food for humans. Mosa Meat can replace this with a system that can produce up to 80,000 burgers from a single 0.5 gramme sample of meat taken from the cow under anaesthesia. This is kinder to the animal, better for the planet and would produce affordable, healthy, tasty beef for millions, perhaps billions, of people around the world. Once the beef has been perfected, the company aims to apply the technology to other types of meat as well as poultry.

Mosa Meat intends to license its technology to other companies, so they can use it in their own factories, which would rapidly increase the pace of change. Singapore is the company's first target market, with the UK and EU to follow soon after. Bosch believes that the new food technology companies are already more transparent than traditional food producers and insists that this new technology will not be to the detriment of Britain's farming community.

"We know farming is an important topic to The King and that some farmers see us as a threat," he explains. "But we are already working with farmers on a project to see how this technology can enhance the role of the farmer, who will remain a very important part of the chain as they have the essential knowledge and assets. Local infrastructure is so important for us, and this is an opportunity that we want to embrace and which we want farmers to embrace, too."

www.mosameat.com

Model of resilience

Regrow Ag utilises climate impact modelling to help farmers
secure the future of their business and the environment

Growing up in Ukraine, Anastasia Volkova witnessed the impact of climate change on the farmland around her. Hot, arid summers and sudden rainstorms made farming increasingly unpredictable. After obtaining a PhD in aerospace engineering, Volkova thought of a solution – software that would use satellite technology to provide farmers with actionable agronomic insights. In 2016, she turned her idea into a company, enabling farmers to make data-based management decisions to maximise their harvests, despite the increasingly volatile weather.

By 2021, Volkova was solving a bigger problem: as the agrifood sector contributes around a third of global greenhouse gas emissions, was it possible to incentivise farmers to adopt climate-friendly practices that would reduce emissions and sequester more carbon in the soil? Volkova acquired a startup that specialised in soil carbon tracking and modelling, and together they became Regrow Ag, a US-based company that leverages both remote sensing technology and scientific models to create unprecedented opportunities for farm emissions reductions.

Regrow works alongside major food and agriculture companies to provide data about emissions in their agricultural supply chains, which they have not previously been able to accurately calculate. Intelligent models demonstrate the potential future impact of adopting more sustainable practices – such as planting cover crops – and identify those that offer the best environmental outcomes. "We monitor more than one billion acres and that means we can see the patterns. We can look at where to invest and explain what to prioritise," explains Volkova.

Working towards net zero goals, the companies can then work with their farmer-suppliers to provide incentives for adopting these approaches. Regrow's models also allow farmers to predict the impact of changes to the land, which means they can adapt and develop climate resilience.

The commitment to sustainable change in agriculture gives the Regrow team a clear and unified vision. "We're very focused on what we're trying to achieve," says Volkova. "If we farm badly, we make the climate worse, which makes farming harder, which means we can't feed ourselves. We want to make it as easy for them as possible, so everybody has the best information and the best tools to work with."

www.regrow.ag

Source of life

Coconut water brand Vita Coco champions the feel-good factor with refreshingly real ingredients and a company ethos that balances profit with purpose

The idea for Vita Coco came from a chance encounter 20 years ago in a New York bar when friends Michael Kirban and Ira Liran met two Brazilian women. When they asked the Brazilians what they missed most about their country, the reply was "coconut water". Not only did Liran go on to marry one of those women, but the idea for the beverages company was born.

The friends realised there was an untapped market elsewhere for the packaged drink, which was ubiquitous in supermarkets in South America. When they brought the first batch to the bodegas of New York, it sold out fast. "They knew they were on to something," says Tim Rees, Managing Director of the EMEA (Europe, the Middle East and Africa) region. Founded in 2004, the company now sells in more than 54 countries and is the largest coconut water brand in the UK. "Coconut water is an amazingly versatile drink, which has grown in popularity as consumers have become increasingly health-conscious. It is lower in sugar than orange juice but has more vitamin C, as well as naturally occurring electrolytes."

With some three million coconuts cracked per day and the category's predicted growth of 20 per cent a year, a secure, sustainable supply chain is essential. Vita Coco aims for the lowest carbon footprint possible, teaching organic farming methods to farmers in Sri Lanka, Brazil and the Philippines, such as using the coconut husks in place of fertiliser. "Coconut trees live for 50 to 60 years, and their yield gets lower as they get older. We work with farmers on regenerative farming, supplying them with coconut seedlings so they can grow the next generation of trees."

This is all part of The Vita Coco Project, which focuses on: empowering the farmers and their families to increase their annual yields, and operate and grow sustainably; enhancing community facilities; and educating the farmers and their children. So far, the project has built over 30 classrooms, and aims to raise one million people in their farming communities out of poverty, and plant ten million seedlings by 2030.

Closer to home, the brand has partnered with local educational charities in London, teaching children about running ethical businesses and offering work experience to underserved children. In addition, Vita Coco has earned B Corporation certification, demonstrating its commitment to balancing profit with purpose.

www.vitacoco.co.uk

Pick of the crop

Focusing on the future of agriculture, UK-based Unium Bioscience provides farmers worldwide with high-tech, low-cost natural solutions to maximising crop production

"Crop production when aligned with nature has a wonderful ability to look after itself, with a little support," says John Haywood, co-Director, with Dr Nigel Grech, of Unium Bioscience. "Unfortunately, we have been reliant on artificial fertilisers and the crop-protection chemistry – and they can spiral us in the wrong direction."

Founded in 2017 and based in Howden, East Yorkshire, Unium utilises methods based in plant physiology to maximise crop production. Haywood sees Unium's mission as finding sustainable and affordable alternatives to throwing chemicals and artificial fertilisers at agricultural problems, instead "bringing the cycle back to nature". The challenge is, "How do we maintain and enhance the farmer's production in an environmentally sensitive way?"

Working with researchers specialising in crop physiology, Unium looks to support the plants' metabolism with natural products, biological solutions and nutrition. "There are no cure-all solutions; its about working hand in hand with the crop and the experience of the farmer," says Haywood. Unium products are rigorously tested and trialled before being marketed. "We're data driven and transparent about that data, but a lot of the decision-making has to take place on the farm," he explains. Unium supplies data on crops and suggested treatments and, based on trials, shares all the data with growers so they can make informed decision, with the aim of an 85 per cent odds of success.

Social media has seen a real boon in the industry, allowing information to be shared quickly by influencers for the benefit of other interested farmers and growers. "One influencer described on video the tremendous improvement from one of our biological seed treatments compared to untreated. He had seen the crop emerge stronger and greener, and we followed the crop to yield when he registered a 0.8 tonne yield increase. That represents a £220 gross margin, or a return on investment of 18:1. The following afternoon we sold out of that product."

Unium has plans to expand across the Americas, Asia, central Africa and Europe with strategic partners, working with new crops such as soy, citrus, nuts and grapes. "It's an exciting time because people want improved nutrient management and that means change," says Haywood. "High prices and product scarcity are forcing this. It drives science-based innovation and that's what we are about."

www.uniumbioscience.com

Recipe for success

Pearl Brasserie, a Dublin fine-dining restaurant for over 20 years, has uncovered the secret to its enduring appeal

When Pearl Brasserie opened in 2000, there was no social media to promote it. Its owners, French chef Sébastien Masi and his wife Kirsten, relied on word of mouth to let the Dublin public know about the brasserie, the first to open in Ireland's capital. They named it Pearl after the first gift Sébastien bought his wife: pearl earrings. And the personal touch is one of the reasons the couple believe it is such a resounding success.

"When you choose to spend money in a restaurant instead of eating at home, it is the whole ensemble that matters," says Sébastien. "The food is important, of course, but so is everything else – even the glassware."

The brasserie is now more of a fine-dining experience than it was back in the early days. Yet its enduring popularity speaks for itself, even thriving during the economic downturn and surviving the pandemic. "We have a lot of recommendations and return visits," explains Kirsten. "One of the nice things about being open for so many years is that people who used to come with their parents when they were children are now bringing their own children."

Nestled between five-star hotels in the Georgian part of Dublin, the multiple-award-winning brasserie, which has been in the Michelin Guide since 2001, serves modern French cuisine with a Japanese twist. Its proximity to the business centre and government buildings means it is perfectly placed for work lunches as well as family celebrations, with a menu that ranges from à la carte to surprise tastings and vegetarian. The basement location, full of nooks and crannies, offers discretion to business clients and celebrities alike. "It's luxurious, comfortable and spacious," says Sébastien. "People get a bespoke service, and from the moment they enter they are cocooned."

Since the brasserie opened the team has grown from just four staff to around 40, and it has also undergone refurbishment. Times may have changed but the approach, however, remains the same, from the attention to detail to the use of the best produce. "Any restaurant is only as good as its last meal," says Kirsten. And this one is firmly embedded in Dublin life.

www.pearl-brasserie.com

CHAPTER SIX

A VISION OF MODERN BRITAIN

Social harmony

As the Head of State, King Charles has a strong sense of duty and a drive to continue serving the nation and its people

W hen the time comes to evaluate Charles's legacy, one must examine his public role in its entirety. Charles has devoted his whole working life to service and duty, supporting his mother, the late Queen, when she was head of state, and ably stepping up now that he is king. He has become a hugely successful global philanthropist, and it is his status as a pioneer of national and international interests and issues for which he will be best remembered.

His role has changed somewhat since his accession. As king, he has already encountered some frustrations, and it can sometimes appear that he is simply presenting his government's decisions, rather than giving voice to his own ideas and opinions. It is also true to say, however, that as monarch he has a leading role to play in all aspects of national life, more so than ever, helping provide continuity and social harmony throughout the country. As Head of State, King Charles is effectively the official embodiment of the country, its unity and legitimacy – a living national symbol on its unbroken continuity.

NATIONAL SERVICE

In our parliamentary system, his powers are largely ceremonial, but as a master of "soft power" his role is vital. The King greets important foreign guests, particularly visiting heads of state, and often hosts a banquet in their honour at Windsor Castle or Buckingham Palace.

On a national level, his role is equally essential. As the country's figurehead, the monarch promotes social harmony and speaks for and to the nation at times of crisis, as the Queen did in her reassuring "We will meet again" address during the 2020 lockdown. The sovereign also leads the country at times of celebration, such as the broadcast of the Christmas message, providing a shared sense of stability.

As Head of the Church of England, Charles is the Defender of the Faith and Supreme Governor of the Church of England, titles that date back to the reign of Henry VIII. On the advice of the Prime Minister, The King appoints archbishops, bishops and deans of the Church of England, who then swear an oath of allegiance and pay homage to the monarch. His role is titular, with the most senior clergyman, the archbishop of Canterbury, the effective spiritual leader of the church.

As sovereign, The King is also Head of the Armed Forces, and his father, brothers and sons have all served. He has a long and close relationship with the military, both in the UK and in the Commonwealth – one that he maintains through regular visits to service establishments and ships.

While as monarch, Charles must remain strictly neutral with respect to political matters. Behind the scenes, he still has the right to be consulted, the right to encourage and the right to warn his political leaders. He maintains a special relationship with the sitting prime minister, meeting with him or her on a regular basis.

CHARITY AND COMMUNITY

It is through his charities, and the work carried out on his behalf by the wider family, that The King interacts and directly helps his people most. Members of the Royal Family have links with hundreds of charities, professional bodies and public service organisations, and it is through this royal patronage that the monarchy also encourages voluntary action. This was demonstrated most clearly by "The Big

"As monarch, Charles has a leading role to play in all aspects of national life, helping provide continuity and social harmony throughout the country"

Previous page
Founder of The Prince's Trust, Charles hosts the charity's 2019 awards ceremony, in London in 2019

Above
The King welcomes Joe Biden at Windsor Castle during the US President's visit to the UK in July 2023

Opposite
With French President Emmanuel Macron at the Arc de Triomphe, Paris, on his first state visit to France as king

"It is through his charities, and the work carried out on his behalf by the wider family, that The King interacts and directly helps his people most"

"By 2001, The Prince's Trust was supporting 25,000 young people each year and had established itself as a national charity with an impressive scale and impact"

Help Out" aspect of the coronation celebrations, whereby Charles urged people across the country to volunteer in their communities on that weekend's extra bank holiday.

Charles has been described as "the greatest charitable entrepreneur in the world" – helping to raise more than £100 million a year when he was Prince of Wales through his 17 core charities. This all began in 1976, when Charles had a bold idea after leaving active service with the Royal Navy. Determined to improve the lives of disadvantaged young people across Britain, he founded The Prince's Trust.

With record unemployment and spiralling inflation, young people had been largely abandoned. Charles used his severance pay of £7,400 to fund 21 pilot projects, which were started around the country through the distribution of grants. Examples included the hiring of swimming baths in Cornwall to train young lifeguards and helping to establish a self-help bicycle repair scheme.

As unemployment rose above three million, many young people felt they had no stake in society. In response, Charles's charity set up the Enterprise programme in 1983 and within three years, 1,000 young people were backed to start a business. An intensive

42-week programme with a mix of challenges later developed into the hugely successful 12-week Team programme, which was launched in 1990.

By 2001, The Prince's Trust was supporting 25,000 young people each year and had established itself as a national charity with an impressive scale and impact. Mass unemployment seemed a thing of the past and the trust turned its attention to the long-term jobless, those in greatest need of support.

The economic crisis of 2008 and the austerity measures that were subsequently brought in by the government had a devastating impact on young people, leaving one in five 16- to 25-year-olds out of work. The trust responded by tightening its belt and helping more young people each year, despite the challenge of raising more than a million pounds each week. As of September 2020, the trust had supported one million young Brits.

If Charles's role is set to evolve with his elevation from prince to king, it is safe to say that the beliefs and sense of duty that he has demonstrated to date all point to a monarch for whom service and leadership will go hand in hand.

Delivering life-saving therapy

With world-leading innovators at the helm, Oxford biotech company Evox Therapeutics
is spearheading a new class of drug-delivery systems to target previously untreatable diseases

When Antonin de Fougerolles was born three months premature in 1965, he did not have any real hope of survival. In fact, no child born in Canada that early had ever survived. But survive he did, thanks to the medical expertise of the Montreal hospital that kept him alive against all odds.

"I spent the best part of two years going in and out of hospital and had speech therapy for years – but now I speak before hundreds of people on a regular basis," says de Fougerolles. "It puts life in perspective and from an early age I felt fortunate to be here and that as a result I should do something with my life. I had a clarity around what is important. Some inspirational teachers changed my outlook, that is why I now do charity work around education as that can radically affect one's course in life."

Having owed his life to science, de Fougerolles decided to devote his life to it, originally as an academic and then in pharmaceuticals where he felt he could make the biggest impact by discovering and bringing new drugs to market. The most recent stage of his career has brought him to Oxford-based biotech company Evox Therapeutics, where he has been CEO since 2017. In this role, he helps engineer exosomes, the body's natural delivery system, enabling a wide variety of drugs to reach previously inaccessible tissue to treat rare diseases.

"You read a lot about new genetic medicines, but these treatments need to get into cells to be active," explains de Fougerolles. "Making those drugs is not the problem, it's getting them to the right places. At Evox, we are advancing drugs to treat rare diseases using a new natural delivery system in a very safe and effective way.

De Fougerolles brings with him more than 25 years of biotech experience and huge successes – "Being naturally curious, I am also involved with several other startup bio-techs, helping create a UK network. So many people I meet are using a drug I developed, including members of my own family." He developed around half a dozen different drugs after leaving Harvard before becoming the

founding Chief Scientific Officer of a small startup. That company was Moderna, where de Fougerolles led the team that developed the mRNA chemistry and lipid nanoparticle drug-delivery system that was later used for Moderna and BioNtech/Pfizer's breakthrough Covid-19 mRNA vaccine – mRNA technology is believed to have saved the lives of at least 16 million people to date.

"I was CSO, which meant I ran all the science and invented the chemistry," says de Fougerolles. "I was the first person to demonstrate that this method of drug delivery worked. I worked on pandemic preparedness 12 years ago to develop mRNA as a vaccine platform and got that into development. Most vaccines take years to produce but for Covid we already had this technology."

Following the extraordinary impact of his work in mRNA, de Fougerolles wants to tackle other problems facing the world. As well as his role at Evox working with innovative pharmaceuticals and drug-delivery systems, he is keen to harness some of the science used in biotech to create pioneering solutions for other challenges facing the world, such as climate change.

De Fougerolles notes the important work done to raise awareness about climate change by King Charles, especially his long-term perspective towards saving the planet. "I am still looking to change the world," says de Fougerolles. "mRNA is in the rearview mirror for me but there is more to do, from climate to degrading plastics – a whole slew of fields where bioengineering can play a role. There's a lot of ingenuity and smart people working on so many projects, thinking long term rather than short term. King Charles has been able to talk about this since the 1960s in a way a politician can't, starting the conversation and opening a few doors for others."

As someone who benefited from a handful of inspirational teachers, de Fougerolles is a strong believer in the power of education and works with Big Change, a charity co-founded by Princess Beatrice. "Big Change looks at new ways to educate and mentor people, particularly the under-privileged," he says. "In the UK, education is all about test-taking but that's not really what life is about. We are looking for alternative ways to educate people and we want to influence governments to find alternatives."

De Fougerolles also talks with enthusiasm about his work with Helfie. The Australian company uses AI to screen more than a dozen different diseases in seconds through an app, and nearly 80 per cent of human health conditions are expected to be screened in this way. Each screening costs less than £2 and "it could save people's lives," says de Fougerolles. "It can differentiate between Covid, asthma or

other lung ailments, just by talking into a microphone. You can photograph a mole and it will tell you if it is high risk for melanoma. It can measure vital signs using AI and will help you seek a second opinion. You could scan the entire population of Australia for skin cancer in under an hour.

"In some areas of the world, there's great phone coverage but poor healthcare – this will revolutionise that, just as it will somewhere like the US where the costs of seeing a healthcare professional can be off-putting."

Much of what de Fougerolles does with Evox and elsewhere is about supporting the biotech ecosystem. "It's not just about developing these individual companies, it's about mentoring people in the UK and building a vibrant biotech ecosystem," says de Fougerolles. "I have a lot of experience I can share, so people don't repeat the same mistakes. Ultimately, I want to leave the world a better place than when I arrived."

www.evoxtherapeutics.com

A second life

Recycling Lives is a recycling company built on
the principles of doing good – environmentally,
socially and commercially

As a child, Steve Jackson would visit his father Terry's scrapyard in Preston, Lancashire. He noticed that some of the people who worked there had difficulties. They had fallen on hard times or experienced problems with mental health, leaving them homeless or struggling to survive. This experience formed the principles for Jackson's Recycling Lives, a unique organisation that is both a successful recycling business and a charity. It employs ex-offenders, providing them with skills, responsibility, opportunity and purpose.

In 2008, CEO Jackson restructured his father's company, which was originally founded in 1977. Since then, it has managed to support vulnerable individuals while protecting the planet and turning a profit. "We began this journey with the starting point of doing good and everything has followed from that," says Executive Chair Andrew Hodgson. "Our social purpose attracted household names, which allowed us to win large contracts."

The company is the largest processer of end-of-life vehicles and waste electrical appliances in the UK, working from multiple sites across the country, from north to south. "We have become very effective at extracting material and see that as one of our purposes – to recycle 100 per cent of what we receive," says Hodgson. "By the end of 2025, we will be putting nothing into landfill and we want to ensure 100 per cent of the material in the UK stays in the UK."

Using circular economy solutions, Recycling Lives is intent on transforming the sector. It aims to innovate more with the recycling of raw material, all the while making sure the essence of the company – "our commitment to people and the environment" – is retained.

Alongside recycling raw material for the benefit of the economy and environment, Recycling Lives strives to support vulnerable people. The company begins this process through the prison system, where prisoners recycle flatscreen TVs, allowing them to learn the basics of the job, as well as experience the responsibilities and benefits of employment. The philosophy is centred around getting people into "a sustainable circle of

"We began this journey with the starting point of doing good and everything has followed from that"

opportunity", with the understanding that stable employment gives people a chance to turn their lives around and reconnect with friends and family. It also has a positive impact on society through a reduction in crime and placing less burden on health and employment services. As a charity, Recycling Lives helps place ex-offenders with other employers, too, who have a similar approach to supporting vulnerable people.

"We have workshops in ten prisons," explains Hodgson. "We take 1.5 million flatscreen TVs every year through our prison workshops. Every time somebody buys a TV, the manufacturer needs to prove it has been recycled on a one-for-one basis, and we work with the TV companies to provide that evidence." The prison workshops are run by the charity and generate some of its funding. "They enable us to instil some basic principles required for work around personal responsibility and health and safety," says Hodgson. "As the prisoners come towards the end of the sentence, they will move to a Category D prison, which means they might get releases on a temporary licence. They will then come to work in one of our local facilities to get more experience of our working conditions and allow us to demonstrate they can function. This is all to prepare them for the work environment."

This system has brought huge success for individuals, for society and for Recycling Lives. "Because we have great experience working with individuals, we can take some of the more challenging and difficult cases," says Hodgson. "Ex-offenders have a 60 per cent reoffending rate after 12 months; those with Recycling Lives have a 2.5 per cent reoffending rate. A lot of them don't have functioning families, so we become their family. We have people who have been through the most awful experiences, and they tell us they wouldn't be alive without Recycling Lives. We put our arms around them when they have nobody else."

Recycling Lives achieved the environmental gold standard B Corp status in 2022 and opened a site in Scotland after acquiring Glasgow-based John R Adam & Sons. One of the organisation's core skills comes from the ability to recycle effectively. The company generates more than 600,000 tonnes of high-quality shredded steel a year and is the largest end-of-life vehicle processor in the UK, responsibly recycling upwards of 180,000 cars a year. With its goal for zero landfill, the company puts very little of this into landfill. That means elements such as gold, copper and silver can return to circulation, to be used in batteries for the next generation of electric vehicles.

"Once you extract that material from the earth you want to keep it in circulation," says Hodgson. "The mining process harms the planet and its people. We give people a second chance, and we want to do the same with the material. It's just chemical elements and that doesn't diminish over time, but the reality is that when we extract steel with magnets there are invariably impurities. However, we have less of these than anybody else – what people call impurities we call by-products, and we are getting better and better at extracting them."

The plan now is to go further, with Hodgson "looking at other places in the world to see if there's anywhere our model can work" – and deeper, by employing individuals from disadvantaged communities before they commit an offence. "There is circularity with materials and the effect on the planet, but also with people," he says. "King Charles has often talked about the importance of community when building better futures for people, and we are seeking to break the cycle by reaching young people before they offend.

The ability to help people while doing good for the planet is why customers, investors and employees are drawn to Recycling Lives, says Hodgson. "We now want to show broader business community what we are doing, as we believe other industries can learn from our model."

www.recyclinglives.com

Closing the skills gap

The Skills and Education Group is an
enduring champion of social mobility, helping
provide the training and qualifications for
individuals to succeed

Social mobility is a passion close to King Charles's heart, and he has
supported the concept for decades through initiatives such as The
Prince's Trust, which has long advocated for apprenticeships and
skills training. Although the trust was founded in 1976, the Skills and
Education Group can trace its history back even further, to more than
110 years. Founded as the East Midland Educational Union in 1912, it
has since evolved to become a member-led charity. During this time, it has
strived to improve the lives of individuals by championing professional
education and skills-oriented organisations, providers and learners.

"Our members are colleges, social enterprises, charities and local
adult education services, and our mission is to support the advancement
of our members through skills education," explains Paul Eeles, Group
Chief Executive. "We help with the professional development of our
workforce in our 62 membership organisations through training
programmes, and we champion social mobility, putting 40 per cent of
our surplus into our foundation to support young people and adults to
stay in education or to go further in their learning. This could be people
who need the bus fare to get to college or who need equipment for their
training, whether it's a new laptop or knives for a trainee chef."

Since the foundation was formed in 2019, it has awarded 540 grants
totalling just over £174,000 in sums of between £200 and £1,000.
These grants are made possible through one of the core activities of the
organisation, which is to provide professional qualifications. The
Skills and Education Group offers 340 Ofqual-regulated qualifications
in a range of industries, with more than 20,000 qualifications awarded
each year through hundreds of further education centres and general
trading providers. All qualifications are designed with the input of
industry professionals who work with the group to an agreed set of
learning outcomes. Their responsibility is to develop content that is fit
for industry and will allow an individual to prosper in the workplace.

Trades that benefit from the work carried out by the Skills and
Education Group include the drinks and motor industries. The British

"Primarily it's about making a difference to people through the vehicle of skills and education"

Institute of Innkeeping Awarding Body (BIIAB) joined the group in 2021, licensing pubs and bars as well as offering a huge range of qualifications for those working in the drinks industry, from mixology to health and safety. The organisation also trains MOT testers, ensuring cars are safe and keeping roads and drivers free from unnecessary danger. An online element takes the form of a Membership Hub, which provides a network for users to access a wide variety of training and development opportunities, as well as many additional resources.

"We deliver qualifications and assessments in more than a dozen different sectors," explains Scott Forbes, Chief Operating Officer. "We award alcohol certificates so people can sell drinks and we are the market leaders in that. And we support people who are training to be mechanics. We do everything from welding to counselling and this helps people from a broad range of industries to take control of their own professional development."

Activities such as these connect to the foundation's central mission and the social mobility element of its work. "Our income – our commercial business – comes from the qualifications we offer, and that funds the grants for the foundation," says Forbes. "It all works to the benefit of our members. They pay a membership fee and for that they receive support and advice, professional development and the opportunity to access grants for their learners."

Adult learning and professional development have faced significant challenges in recent years, from cuts in central funding to the impact of the increase in the cost of living. This has made the work of the foundation even more important, and it now offers grants to those learners whose life circumstances may require extra support. "We have an application process for a learner who applies for a grant," says Forbes. "They will fill out a form and the relevant tutor will give us a statement outlining what the student needs in terms of additional support and why they are a compelling case for us to consider supporting their learning."

This assistance can take the form of laptops, printers, course books, stationery, tools and toolboxes, hairdressing equipment, course fees and transport costs, as well as living and childcare costs. The foundation can support students to attend educational events, including visits and seminars that help with learning outcomes. It also holds annual awards and represents the further education sector at a national level.

The work of the Skills and Education Group aims to develop a more productive and resilient workforce. This can mean helping adult learners with a mid-life career change or it can mean providing opportunities for continued career development. Apprenticeships – which King Charles has long said should be valued as highly as academic qualifications – are a particularly effective method of learning. And for those who want to go to university, the group offers an Access to Higher Education Diploma, which helps 2,000 learners progress to university each year.

"Primarily, it's about making a difference to people through the vehicle of skills and education," says Eeles. "We recognise that people have a contribution to make at any age and through our product range and our foundation, we can bring a voice to that conversation about social mobility.

"I see social mobility as about making a difference to people's lives, so they are equipped with the skills and knowledge that will empower them. We want people to be able to deal with changes in their circumstances on their own terms, and we want to help grow the sectors we serve and the work we do to the overall benefit of learners of all ages."

www.skillsandeducationgroup.co.uk

Acts of kindness

Renowned for compassionate and expert palliative care, Sue Ryder is now reaching thousands of people across the UK with bereavement support

As one of the UK's best-respected charities, Sue Ryder has benefited from royal support for over 35 years. Queen Elizabeth II was a former patron, and King Charles III, in his role as Prince of Wales, was a patron of the Sue Ryder Hospice in Cheltenham since 1986. He made regular visits over the years, spending time with patients, staff and volunteers.

Sue Ryder has been supporting people during the most difficult times of their lives for nearly 70 years. For most of that time, the charity's focus has been on delivering expert palliative care for those with a terminal illness, through specialist doctors, nurses and carers, as well as providing specialist care, rehabilitation or support to those with a neurological condition. The charity is also regularly involved in larger conversations around funding, workforce, practice and policy at a senior level in both the wider health sector and the political arena.

In recent years, to address a growing demand, Sue Ryder has diversified its offer to include bereavement support. As Heidi Travis, Chief Executive of the charity points out, due to the ageing population in the UK, we can expect that by 2030 there will be an additional 140,000 deaths a year, with many of these requiring the specialist end-of-life care that Sue Ryder has provided for decades. "There will always be a need for this," she says, "not only from a medical standpoint, including pain and symptom management, but also focusing on the practical, psychological and spiritual needs of a person at the end of their life and the loved ones around them. When someone is in our care, we look to support the family, too, both emotionally and with as many of the end-of-life practicalities as we can.

"We are passionate about giving people the quality of care they deserve. Through our services, we empower people to make their own choices about their care. That is always at the forefront of our thinking, so if somebody at the end of their life wants to die at home, we want to provide a service to enable them to do so. We are always looking to ensure we can provide more care for more people, in the way they want to receive it."

Sue Ryder launched its bereavement offering in 2015 with the setting up of its Online Bereavement Community to provide support for friends and family to help them manage and understand their grief. "People often feel alone in their grief, and they struggle to talk to others about it, so our bereavement community offers peer-to-peer support for those going through the same experience," says Travis.

The charity has more than 150,000 people a year using its online community and even more who visit the online bereavement information pages. "We know from talking to bereaved people that, for some, peer-to-peer support is not enough, and so to address this need we have introduced our Online Bereavement Counselling service. This offers people who are struggling with their grief six free video sessions with an expert bereavement counsellor to help make sense of their feelings."

Sue Ryder has continued to diversify its bereavement help and has introduced Grief Guide, a self-help platform with content and tools to help people through the process. In 2021, the charity launched the Grief Kind campaign to help encourage the nation to be better at supporting people who are grieving. Research found that people were shying away from having conversations about grief, which left the bereaved feeling isolated and alone.

As part of the Grief Kind campaign, Sue Ryder created a range of special resources, including a set of contemporary sympathy cards that people can order when someone they know experiences a bereavement. "As many people don't know what to say to someone who is grieving, the cards come with advice on how to open up meaningful conversations about grief," explains Travis. There are four cards in a pack so that people can send them at different times, for example when someone they know has first been bereaved or at difficult times like anniversaries.

> ## "Our bereavement community offers peer-to-peer support for those going through the same experience"

The cards feature words such as "I don't know what to say, but I am sending you so much love" and "You never need to lie when I ask you how you're doing".

Another initiative to help people through bereavement and encourage open conversations on the subject is Sue Ryder's Grief Kind podcast, hosted by author Clover Stroud. The episodes feature celebrity guests who share their first-hand experiences of bereavement and discuss how those close to them helped them during their most vulnerable and difficult moments. "The podcast really resonates with people who have lived with grief, because our guests have been through their own difficult experiences and want to help others," says Travis.

The Sue Ryder website offers bereavement advice, too, from what to do in the first couple of days, months and years, what to say or what not to say, to how you can recognise the role that culture and religion plays in the grieving process. Available to watch on the website are Grief Kind classes, which offer advice from trained bereavement counsellors who address the public's most frequently asked questions.

Sue Ryder is a charity that is always changing to meet the needs of the people it supports. "We are recognised as setting very high standards," says Travis. "The services we provide have changed over the years, but every organisation needs to be able to adapt and respond to the needs of the people it supports, otherwise it will fall by the wayside. The people we support are at the heart of what we do as an organisation, and we will continue to deliver services that best help the people we serve."

www.sueryder.org

Network of support

From mental health to learning disabilities and home help, Care Horizons' mission is to offer people the highest level of support and empathy

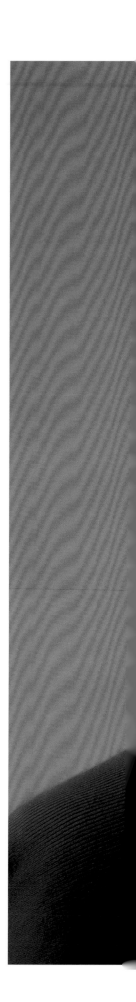

Care Horizons is one of the most cherished specialist healthcare providers in the southwest of England. The Bristol-based business puts its success down to looking after the wellbeing of everyone involved. "We take the time to speak to not only our clients, but also our staff members, too," says CEO and Managing Director Vierka Hiscock.

This progressive approach benefits everyone, she says. "The people who work for us say how privileged they are to do what they love. And it's very rewarding to hear that."

The organisation specialises in supporting people with mental-health conditions, including those with autism and learning difficulties, or complex needs that require live-in care. Care Horizons aims for clients to remain in their homes where possible, so they can enjoy their independence while help is given to connect them with the community. The team also works with relatives and other care providers to provide the best outcome.

On a personal level, Hiscock saw the importance of compassion and understanding when her son was diagnosed with ADHD (attention deficit hyperactivity disorder). "As a child he was labelled as naughty; people didn't realise that he was just bored," she says.

Hiscock moved to the UK from Slovakia in 2005, working as an accountant and business manager in care services, but over time she felt the need to shift away from focusing on profit. "I became fed up with working with numbers," she says. "I like meeting people and learning about their lives to see how I can help them. For example, we had a client who we helped after his mother passed away. He became house-proud and started going out on a scooter on his own. At Christmas, every single home on his street sent him a card because they liked

him so much. It was incredible to see the sparkle back in his eyes."

Staff receive ongoing training to help them respond in the best way to their clients' needs, which may include mental-health conditions that span eating and bipolar disorders, addictions, or schizophrenia. Meanwhile, carers who specialise in conditions such as Parkinson's and dementia are on hand to provide care for those who require round-the-clock assistance. There is also a big emphasis on helping people with learning disabilities reach their potential while in a safe and supportive environment. A full assessment is made as soon as a client contacts Care Horizons. The team then decides if that person needs residential care, supported living, or simply extra help with everyday living in their own homes.

The business has doubled in size since Hiscock took over in 2017 and has included the opening of a hub in May 2023. "Sometimes our clients are lonely, so the social hub is for people to come here and read or socialise," she says. "And we're also setting up a small gym in our building." The social club is set to include group classes such as shopping and cookery, as well as support for those looking for voluntary roles and preparing for job interviews. Care Horizons excels at making people feel part of the community again.

As the world becomes more tuned into the significance of mental health, Care Horizons is leading the way. "As well as treating people as individuals, we consider their past, because the past is important in understanding the present," explains Hiscock. "Any one of us can have mental-health problems at any point in our lives."

www.carehorizons.co.uk

Stronger together

The success story of Wigan Borough charity Compassion in Action stems from an all-encompassing service embedded in the local community

Back in 2006, Pam Gilligan's passion for bringing people together to help each other began with a coffee morning. The venue, St Mary's Church Hall in Lowton, Wigan, Greater Manchester, soon became too small for the demand. With dedication and determination, she sowed the seeds for a charity, Compassion in Action, asking then-MP Andy Burnham for help in putting down roots to secure the organisation's first premises.

"From the very start, my vision has been to unite people, who are the heart and soul of this charity," says Gilligan. "The services we provide are delivered across four key pillars – Practical, Physical, Mental and Social – which is the definition of whole-person care. Every project we undertake evolves from our mission statement: 'Heart prints of love... Meeting the needs of the people'."

With the valued support of its partners, including Wigan Council, PGL Pipelines, rugby club Leigh Leopards, local businesses and members of the community, Compassion in Action has stayed true to Gilligan's belief that, 'Together, we can make a difference'. Nowhere is this more apparent than at its community outlet in Lowton and distribution centre in Atherton, and at its thriving Community Village of Inclusion in nearby Leigh. For adults with learning and physical disabilities, and the elderly, the village offers an environment that breaks through the barriers of isolation, allowing friendships to form and community bonds to be forged through volunteering. Practical support, such as furniture, clothing, food and access to warm spaces, or "Heat Retreats", is provided to those in need who are referred by the charity's partner agencies.

In 2014, the charity was the proud recipient of The Queen's Award for Voluntary Service. Gilligan explains how the example of the late Queen Elizabeth II's resilience has helped her to navigate present-day challenges. "Unity in the community is the answer to surviving the economic crisis. We all need to support our new monarch and government as they explore ways to best help us."

In line with the charity's pillars, there is never a closed door: Compassion in Action is constantly looking for innovative ways to break generational cycles of poverty. It nourishes and nurtures young people through skills training, volunteering and apprenticeships.

Having recognised a need for local non-clinical mental health services, Compassion in Action unveiled its therapeutic intervention counselling service in 2015, which has since supported more than 5,600 people. Meanwhile, its pioneering residential facility, Oasis House, launched in 2020. This "first of its kind' service relieves pressure on the wider healthcare system, preventing the need for clinical intervention among those in mental-health crisis or mental distress. Offering five-night stays, it is a place for celebration and recognition of people's strength, resilience and ability to achieve goals.

"Whole-person care includes creating opportunities for social connection," says Gilligan. "As a Bronze Award holder of the Armed Forces Covenant Employer Recognition Scheme, we host a weekly brunch for the borough's valued veterans. Our community events and lunches are a fertile ground for new friendships to blossom." No child is forgotten at Easter or Christmas, either, "with our long-standing appeals ensuring Easter eggs, brand-new toys and a full Christmas lunch are delivered to every family referred to the charity."

From its unique Community Village of Inclusion to its commitment to delivering well-evidenced whole-person care, Compassion in Action gives hope in times of despair.

www.compassioninaction.info

Nurturing global citizens

With utmost professionalism and expertise, Academic Families matches international students with the best UK boarding schools for their individual needs

Parents often entrust their child's education to a school many thousands of miles away, and that is where Academic Families comes in. The agency places international pupils from more than 40 countries at boarding schools across the UK. "Many of our clients are high-net-worth individuals, accustomed to making big business decisions," says Managing Director Lorna Clayton, who founded the company in 2012. "But no business decision is more demanding than deciding what's right for your child's education."

The Academic Families team has experience living overseas, so they possess a deep understanding of the challenges involved. "Everything we do is child-centred," says Clayton. "And there's no greater reward than hearing from families that our approach works and that their child is thriving in their new school. We recommend what we believe is best for the child, and to the standards we would want for our own children."

Clayton believes British schools are among the best in the world. "A British education is a pathway to success," she says. "There are more than 450 British boarding schools to choose from, offering a wide variety of curriculum styles. There's a school for everyone, and we will identify the right school for your child."

Academic Families also provides guardianship care for students at UK boarding schools. The team has an intricate pairing system to ensure children are placed with the right host family, fostering enriching relationships that often last beyond school careers. "One alumnus was so grateful for all the support he had received from his host family that he brought his new wife to meet them when he returned to the UK on his honeymoon," says Clayton.

In 1998, Clayton founded a Kenyan education charity, Assist a Child to School, which funds and places underprivileged students in education. For this work and her services to young people, she was awarded an MBE in 2023, in The King's first Birthday Honours List.

"It's always been important for me to share my knowledge and do my best for children," says Clayton. "British schools offer a holistic approach that produces well-rounded, resilient individuals. A British education is the best gift you can give your child."

www.academicfamilies.com

A haven for rehabilitation

With Ascot Rehabilitation, Dr Ali Al-Memar has created a much needed facility for those on the path to neurological recovery

Rehabilitation for neurological conditions can be tough, and Dr Ali Al-Memar wanted to help. Having left Iraq in 1989, he worked his way up through the NHS, becoming a consultant neurologist in 1998. He worked in that role in London Hospitals St George's, Kingston and Queen Mary's, beginning private work in the 2000s. It was then he found that those seeking private sector neurological diagnoses often had to travel widely to different locations for tests.

"I got together with colleagues working privately and said, 'Why don't we establish a company to provide diagnostics?" says Dr Al-Memar. "The idea wasn't to make money; it was to help patients." He started Wimbledon Neurocare, which grew to cover the southwest and some of central London and taught him the financial side of running a business. "But I began to realise there was something missing," he says. "We saw patients throughout their journey, but not their rehabilitation." And given the lack of rehabilitation facilities in many places, he realised people were prepared to travel for quality care.

A former nursing home in Bagshot, Surrey became the site for Ascot Rehabilitation Hospital, which Dr Al-Memar set ups in 2012. Registered with the Care Quality Commission, the unit offers inpatient care, with outpatient and outreach care provided from two central London locations. Available therapies include speech and language therapy, physiotherapy, occupational therapy and neuropsychology, and complementary therapies such as creative movement therapy, yoga and tai chi.

Ascot Rehabilitation relocates in late 2023 to a new state-of-the-art hospital in London SW16 equipped with the most advanced technology. It will be the first smart hospital to operate from. "We have a commitment to quality and have appointed people who are very sympathetic to our patients and offer a personal touch," says Dr Al-Memar. "We also keep prices reasonable." Treatment is offered for conditions such as traumatic brain and spinal cord injury, stroke, neurological and muscular skeletal conditions, and post-operative and amputee rehab.

Ascot Rehab is expanding to offer outpatient care for children, including those with autism, and has invested in robotics and new technology. "For ten years we have proved we provide fantastic rehab."

www.ascotrehab.com

Powering change, saving lives

As technology drives the smart homes revolution, the charity
Electrical Safety First plays a vital role in keeping safe

One in ten people in the UK have first-hand experience of an electrical fire or shock caused by an electrical appliance bought online, according to Electrical Safety First, a charity that campaigns to ensure the domestic use of electricity in the UK is as safe as possible. With the world moving increasingly towards electrification, there is a real risk such dangers would increase without the organisation's hard work and technical expertise.

"We are all passionate about our mission, as we help save lives," says Chief Executive Lesley Rudd. "We provide safety advice, and we campaign on behalf of the public and electrical trade professionals to improve legislation and raise awareness of the dangers presented by electricity. We advocate for safer electrical installations and products, and we have a technical team who provide expert advice and guidance on how people can protect themselves."

The charity has enjoyed significant successes in recent years. Thanks to one of its campaigns, electricity in private rented accommodation must now be checked every five years – legislation that will be extended to the social renting sector. In addition, funding from Electrical Safety First has helped people have portable heaters and electric blankets professionally checked and replaced, if dangerous, ensuring their safety and warmth during the colder months. Another national campaign drew attention to the fires resulting from poor quality or the misuse of electric-scooter and electric-bike batteries. An Electrical Safety First laboratory test showed one such explosive electric-bike battery fire (pictured opposite, bottom right).

Electrical Safety First's 2023 report "Battery Breakdown" outlines the fire risk of lithium-ion batteries in people's homes, particularly with electric scooters and bikes. "People charge them at home and there can be major problems," says Rudd. "At the moment, manufacturers can self-certify, but we want there to be a requirement for third-party certification because these batteries have the explosive potential equivalent to six hand grenades and can catch fire very quickly." The report offers recommendations to government and related bodies.

Following years of experience working in the sustainable-energy sector, Rudd is a strong advocate for greater electrification but worries about ignored, overlooked and unforeseen dangers, particularly when it comes to housing being retrofitted, or when people have poor access to charging points for electric vehicles. Another fear is the lack of regulation for online marketplaces – Electrical Safety First is pressing for them to be treated the same way as high-street retailers.

Rudd believes vulnerable people should be entitled to free electricity checks, just as they receive free gas checks from energy suppliers. She also notes that while health-and-safety regulation applies to the workplace, the definition between home and work is increasingly blurred, making this area more important than ever. With all such issues, Electrical Safety First engages government and industry, increases public awareness and publicises guidance.

"We are only a small charity, but we punch above our weight," says Rudd. "We get our campaigns into the national media, which raises consumer awareness and puts pressure on the government to act on dangers facing UK citizens. International governments have sought our advice, and we are in regular conversation with politicians, civil servants and industry in all four home nations. Our focus is electrical safety, and saving lives is what motivates me and my colleagues every day."

www.electricalsafetyfirst.org.uk

Family values

Luckley House School's small size, Christian ethos and flexibility
combine to benefit pupils as well as their families

Surrounded by woodland and boasting a state-of-the art theatre that was opened by Prince Edward in 2017, the co-educational, independent Luckley House School in Wokingham, Berkshire, combines the best of the British countryside with modern facilities and a contemporary, flexible outlook towards education and children's pastoral needs.

The school was founded more than 100 years ago on its current site, initially operating as a girls' school until 2015, when it started to welcome boys. Following the arrival of that initial cohort of six boys, admissions are now divided almost equally between girls and boys. The shift to a co-educational approach epitomises the adaptability of a school that embraces the future.

"We have a small school ethos, which means we treat everybody as an individual and can offer a tailored approach to learning," says Areti Bizior, Headmistress. "There is a lot of flexibility in terms of what we offer our pupils and their families, both in terms of their

academic career as well as their daily routine. For instance, we can help pupils if they need to stay for supper or come in early for breakfast. That flexibility is due to our size, and it brings us and our pupils some real benefits."

Supported by a dedicated and talented academic staff, there are around 375 pupils at the school, some 40 of whom are boarders. Boarding is available for those who only wish to stay during the week alongside a cohort who board full time. Many of the latter come from overseas, which also helps create an international feel at the school. The school arranges trips for boarders at the weekends, in addition to the wide range of excursions for study and leisure, from cultural outings to ski holidays and enriching visits to more far-flung destinations such as South Africa and Kenya. The school's Whitty Theatre, meanwhile, provides a professional environment for pupils to take part in music and drama, at the same time learning technical and stage management skills.

Outside of the classroom, the children have space to play sport and explore the natural environment. As well as the extensive woodlands and a nature trail, the school's grounds include ziplines and beehives. There is a popular ecology club for pupils interested in the environment, and the school has received a prestigious Green Flag award in the international Eco-Schools programme, which is designed to raise environmental awareness among young people. Run in the UK by the charity Keep Britain Tidy, Eco-Schools helps improve the school environment, focusing not just on litter, but also biodiversity, citizenship and healthy living.

The school offers a range of scholarships for gifted pupils, as well as means-tested bursaries for underprivileged families. All fees are inclusive of tuition, text books, lunch and break refreshments and most after-school activities. The school has an excellent academic record, but it also endeavours to deliver a well-rounded education in line with its Christian ethos, "which provides a framework for our ethos of family values and respect".

"We want pupils to pass the entrance test to ensure they will thrive in our environment, and we expect good passes for A-level, but that test is not the only basis on which we make decisions around entry," explains the Headmistress. "There is also an interview and we take a wider view to make sure that school and pupil are a good fit for each other."

www.luckleyhouseschool.org

Real world ready

AAT (The Association of Accounting Technicians) opens up access to finance careers for everyone, equipping accounting professionals with real-world skills

The power of apprenticeships to transform lives is something King Charles has promoted for many years. The ethos of apprenticeships – to gain qualifications while learning the technical application – is integral to the work of AAT, the world's leading professional and awarding body for accounting technicians. A qualified accounting technician has the practical and technical skills that add value in any workplace, but people do not necessarily need to have gone to university to become one.

"It is the most authentic professional accounting body for diversity and inclusion, whatever your social or educational background," explains CEO Sarah Beale. "Our qualifications are accessible to all and provide a practical grounding in what it is like to work in accountancy and bookkeeping. Our members come equipped with real-world skills, ready to add value and improved productivity at their employer's workplace or their own businesses."

For more than 40 years, AAT has delivered status and tailored support to its now 124,000 members and students around the world, helping school leavers, graduates or those changing career later in life gain access to professional accountancy and bookkeeping careers, and then continually progress. AAT works to attract those who might not have previously considered accountancy or bookkeeping as an occupation, including the less privileged, promoting the value these skills bring to any career or entrepreneurial opportunity.

"Professional isn't how you were born, it's how you behave," says Beale. "The professions were late waking up to the benefits of vocational learning, but if you sit down with employers, they see the value. This route brings huge social and economic benefits, and if we can set those hard-to-reach cohorts of society on a rewarding career path, it will solve a lot of socioeconomic problems. Any savvy employer wants better diversity of thought and representation in their workforce because frankly, it's good business, as well as doing the right thing. AAT provides an opportunity for all to gain beneficial skills and rewarding careers that they may never have thought possible. After all, it's why we were formed in the first place."

www.aat.org.uk

Eliminating the threat

Security consultancy AVORD is making its world-class technology accessible to all, improving the cyber risk rating for small business

Brian Harrison, CEO and co-founder of AVORD, admits there is something unusual about a job that sees him occasionally retire to a darkened room for a couple of hours so he can "think like a bad guy". Harrison, however, is an expert in security, which means having to predict and anticipate any weaknesses in a client's defences that have the potential to be exploited by an inventive enemy that includes armies of super-fast AI hackers, alongside resourceful human opponents.

"I love the sector and making order out of chaos," says Harrison, who set up the company with Chief Operating Officer Howard Pritchard in 2017 after working as a consultant for large organisations such as Lloyds Bank and the Post Office. "With AVORD, we wanted to bring security to the masses. We wanted to start a company that was approachable to companies of all sizes because for big corporations, their weakest link is usually the smaller suppliers. Our prices are a lot lower than the major security consultancies, which means we are able to work with small businesses and universities and help them support the larger companies. They are all connected in some way."

AVORD promises transparency, affordability and flexibility, with Harrison involved at every level of the business, from finance to strategy and human resources, to ensure the company delivers on its promises. But for him, this is more than just a business.

He speaks of a desire to use it as a vehicle to create opportunities for young people, citing as inspiration the work of The Prince's Trust, which reflects The King's commitment to training and social enterprise. Harrison intends to create academies, which will support underprivileged young people and provide them with opportunities and a pathway to a career in security. In this way, the company can upskill those keen young minds that might otherwise be overlooked, benefiting the UK and the wider business ecosystem.

"We want growth," says Harrison, "but we want to educate the UK and Europe about the importance of security. I want to introduce our academy to bring in that training. Education is part of everything we do – educating young people and small companies so that businesses of all sizes can learn and grow."

www.avord.co.uk

Sense of community

At Plymouth Marjon University, students learn about inclusion and community as a force for good, from grass roots-level football to elite

Football has the potential to change lives, not only for professionals, but also for those at a local and community level, such as Sunday league referees, players with disabilities and children's team coaches. Plymouth Marjon University supports football at both professional and community level, often combining the two in an approach that is in keeping with the university's origins. Marjon began life in London as the two separate colleges of St Mark and St John, both of which catered for the underprivileged. After merging in 1923 to become the College of St Mark & St John, known as Marjon, it moved to Plymouth in 1973, receiving full university status in 2013.

"It's 50 years since we moved from London and that's an anniversary we are excited about," says Caroline Westwood, Dean of the School of Sport, Exercise and Rehabilitation. "For us, the institute is so well placed to support all facets of inclusion and disability in sport and football across our region. We do a lot of work in the community right

up to high-performance sport. The FA supported us to introduce a high-performance centre for female football, which has seen a lot of success including some who have played for the Lionesses, such as Katie Robinson, who is now at Brighton."

The university holds "Train like a Lioness" days for local primary schools and works closely with national and regional FAs to develop players of all ages for local women's teams. The university has also established a very strong relationship with local football club Plymouth Argyle, where students often undertake placements that see them working on match and performance analysis – the sort of hands-on experience a student would struggle to receive at a bigger club.

Teaching staff include former professional Dr Ian Stonebridge, who retired through injury, and Senior Lecturer Aaron Cusack, who was on Plymouth's books as a youngster. In both cases, grants from the PFA allowed them to return to education, receive formal qualifications and remain involved in the sport, contributing to the game they love. Such an approach aligns with another of the university's ambitions, which is to retain more talent – coaching, teaching and playing – in the South West.

This is helped by the university's role as one of nine FA Women's High-Performance Football Centres (WHPFC), which allows Plymouth Marjon to provide an educational and community-based setting to recruit, develop, deploy and produce quality coaches and inspire player development. In addition, the university has created a dual career pathway so students can continue to study while playing, and has used its formal partnership with the Plymouth Argyle Community Trust to allow students to get involved in community coaching.

"The journey that a lot of our students go on, whether they are fans, coaches or players, is around community," says Senior Lecturer Dr Phil Brown. "A lot of that is about using the power of football to do good, which aligns with our own historical values. Football is the hook, it attracts people and allows us to work with issues around disability, employment and gender. Football is a grass roots activity, and that voluntary effort is so important. We do coach development, we do futsal with Devon & Cornwall FA, we work with those who have disabilities and prosthetics – which is all part of our inclusion and community programme. It's about that community development work. Exceptional talent will go on to fame and fortune, but community work has the potential to change lives."

www.marjon.ac.uk

Plant the seed

Savage Cabbage is one of the UK's leading brands of natural CBD wellness products, providing support to many loyal customers

In 2016, Jade Proudman was at her lowest ebb. Her large intestine had failed, she had been rushed to hospital and had 11 emergency surgeries in 13 months. "It was all quite dismal," she recalls. "Then, just as I was beginning to feel I'd turned a corner, I woke up one morning and found I couldn't move my legs or my feet. I was diagnosed with reactive arthritis and in extreme pain. I even asked my husband to help me end it all, to overmedicate me."

Proudman's husband flatly refused. Instead, he advised her to take CBD (cannabidiol) products, derived from the hemp plant. Proudman ordered a care package from a certified US CBD brand and immediately felt a profound sense of uplift. "Within 24 hours I felt the fog had been sucked out of my head – I had total clarity. I knew this was life-changing and I needed to talk about it."

As a result, Proudman founded Savage Cabbage, finding no structure in place for those who wanted to learn more about the

benefits of CBD. Savage Cabbage was initially formed as a support network. "There were a lot of people asking questions and no one answering them," she explains. Proudman took it upon herself to become the person who could provide those answers. "I'm a trained social worker, so I felt that need to provide support," she says. "I felt that if you were aware of a problem and did nothing about it, you were complicit in that problem. That's the social worker within me."

Savage Cabbage – the name is intended to tackle pejorative descriptions such as the "devil's lettuce" – grew rapidly, mainly by word of mouth; today, Proudman speaks of "micro-communities" in 44 countries. It swiftly became a business, and one of the early UK CBD successes, largely through the profound connections that Proudman was able to build with her increasingly loyal customers. Today, Savage Cabbage provides an authentic, authoritative voice, with Proudman able to advocate in meetings at Westminster.

"Hemp is a wonder plant," she says. "You can not only extract the oil and consume it, but its fibres are also used in everything from construction to housing insulation. It has benefits for the entire planet. Hemp sequesters carbon; the plant rejuvenates the soil. If we had a proper established farming community for hemp in this country, we could help to invigorate our economy and our ecosystem."

Proudman believes that in post-pandemic times, there is an increased desire for natural wellness. "We're living through a social and economic crisis," says Proudman. "Health systems aren't as good as they should be – what is out there that can help mind, body and soul?"

"We all have an endocannabinoid system within us," she explains. "It was discovered in the 1990s, and it turned out that a lot of health issues we face could be down to endocannabinoid deficiencies. Your body has receptors for CBD. It's a natural tool that could help make us feel younger and healthier. Once I started utilising these products daily, I noticed a significant difference of self."

According to Proudman, the practical benefits of CBD are in coping with conditions from anxiety to pain, even sleeplessness. "It's important to me that our message is being heard – and I'm not going away."

www.savagecabbage.co.uk

Best of British

The British School of Monaco blends Britain's cherished education system with the cultural diversity of Monaco to create an ambitious institution for students

The British education system has been fine-tuned over centuries and is now admired for its academic rigour and global cultural resonance. The British School of Monaco takes the finest aspects of the British system and adapts them to the needs and context of international students in the principality. "We believe the British education system is one of our greatest creations and we draw strength from that," says Luke Sullivan, an educator who founded the school with his wife, Dr Olena Sullivan-Prykhodko, in 2022. "Our international families join us from around the world knowing what we stand for." The school's grounded approach is wrapped up in its motto: 'Wisdom in Humility'.

Accredited as a Cambridge and Pearson International School, with UK-trained teachers, the institution delivers a nurturing and flexible education that gives pupils a sophisticated understanding of the English language, a love of literature and rooted values. Its learning characteristics of "Reflection, Resilience, Adaptability and Balance" underpin each lesson. The school's "secure, compassionate and expertly crafted educational setting" receives glowing reports. "Our children's excitement to share their daily experiences are a testament to the remarkable environment you have created," writes one family. "Thank you for creating an environment in which our children can learn, grow and flourish," writes another.

The British School of Monaco is opening its secondary school in September 2024 and plans to deliver an education for 250 children from age three to 18. Further schools, adapted to the specific needs of host countries, may follow. It currently offers a bespoke, secondary "Individual Programme" of one-to-one lessons to 20 students, which is particularly suited to elite athletes. A third component is the Modelex Education Centre, which provides individual, after-school and holiday tutoring alongside top-flight UK and US school and university entrance guidance.

Obtaining permission to open the school was challenging. "We underwent a rigorous process to obtain the permits," says Luke. "The experience itself embodied the school's values of 'integrity and responsibility for oneself, respect and generosity for others, and courage and curiosity in life'. With the regular reinforcement of these values, the diverse parent body shares in a clear universal philosophy. Family-run and values-based, we deliver the pinnacle of British education in the heart of Monaco."

www.britishschool.mc

Space to grow

Since 2012, the Manchester Youth Zone has had a transformative effect on the lives of countless local young people

"Young people in deprived areas like north Manchester are often excluded from the benefits that the city affords, because of a lack of representation and access to arts, sports and business opportunities, despite having the talent, diversity and drive to succeed," says Amanda Naylor OBE, CEO of the Manchester Youth Zone. "Our role is to help them navigate barriers of discrimination, crime and poverty, bridging the gaps and supporting them to contribute and thrive."

By showing more than 4,500 children a year the opportunities available to them, and bringing the corporate world into the charity sector through social-value programmes, the Manchester Youth Zone (MYZ) is changing lives and ensuring young people reach their potential.

The MYZ is part of the OnSide network, which provides a safe environment for young people to discover their passion and purpose, gain support and guidance from experienced youth workers and meet friends. At MYZ, young people can make use of the sports hall, dance studio, boxing gym, fitness suite, climbing wall and 3G sports pitch. To nurture creativity, they can design, develop and produce their own work in the music room, art area, allotment or sensory room. Its facilities include an enterprise and careers space, where they can create products on 3D printers, develop a website and build a social-media presence. There is also support to work towards specific jobs and qualifications. MYZ provides further programmes to tackle children and young people's poor health outcomes, address youth violence and support mental health.

The organisation is open from morning till night, seven days a week, and every session includes a free hot meal, providing essential support for a population impacted by cost-of-living challenges and poverty. Parents and carers have their own support from the MYZ through specialist family workers, who provide family sessions and emotional and practical support on the many issues impacting families.

"Young people have lives, relationships and complications outside MYZ, so our support doesn't stop at the front door; we develop place-based support where we are needed," says Naylor. "We provide vital immediate support, but also give young people and their support systems the tools, strategies and experiences that will empower them for life."

www.manchesteryz.org

Learning and beyond

From Alnwick Castle to Husky Advance, St Cloud State University's student programmes are inventive, engaging and relevant for society today

It is a long way from Alnwick in Northumberland to St Cloud in Minnesota. But these two distant and very different locations in the northeast of the UK and midwestern US have developed a close connection over nearly 50 years, thanks to the St Cloud State at Alnwick university programme. This sees students from St Cloud State University live and learn at Alnwick Castle, a historic site that has been a location for film and TV, including the Harry Potter series and *Downton Abbey*.

The programme is part of an innovative approach to study that has been embedded at St Cloud State over decades. The university was founded in 1869 to train teachers and has since expanded its programme to offer more than 260 undergraduate, graduate and pre-professional programmes, across five colleges and two schools along the Mississippi river.

"We have been in existence for more than 150 years and started with a mission to serve the people, the state and the greater good by providing teachers to what was one of the more rural parts of the country," says Dr Robbyn Wacker, St Cloud State University President. "We had a mission and, no matter how we have evolved over time, that has always been our approach as we seek to serve Minnesota, the US and beyond."

As well as the Alnwick programme, a sense of St Cloud State University's global outlook can be gleaned from its 131,000 alumni found around the world – Wacker has recently returned from an alumni dinner in Nepal with almost 50 former students. Students are attracted by the range of St Cloud State's offering and its capacity to offer exceptional learning in a university that is still small enough to create a strong sense of community. "We have more than 10,000 students and, as we say to students, this is the perfect size to create a community, but with the education and sporting programmes you would associate with a larger university," says Wacker.

The university innovates with a framework called "It's Time". It features constantly evolving programmes and imaginative teaching methods to nurture graduates during their post-university life. It means opening the university to mature students seeking professional training or a career change; and embracing more engaging styles of teaching so students can take part in lab work, simulation and 3D printing. The result creates a vibrant campus with graduates well placed to prosper in the 21st-century workplace.

Environmental studies and sustainability programmes are an essential, newer element. "We also have a programme called Huskies Advance, which creates opportunities for students in subjects they are passionate about but may not be embedded in their major, so you could pick a topic on sustainability when majoring in business," explains Wacker. "Our ambition is to continue to reach the highest standards in education while meeting societal needs."

With society changing at a rapid pace, the idea is to adjust to that. "'It's Time' is guided by the concept that we can't continue to be the same university we were ten years ago," says Wacker. "Our programmes need to evolve, and we need to engage in different ways of teaching and supporting students to give them a customised approach to learning to ensure their success. We want our students to graduate into high-quality careers and have the confidence and skillsets to be fluid. That's why St Cloud State University is committed to providing programmes that are relevant and engaging."

www.stcloudstate.edu

Building Iraq's future generations

The world-class British University of Iraq in Baghdad aims to bridge
the gap between education and employment

One of the challenges facing Iraq is the increasing number of university graduates who are unable to find work. Driven by the unemployment figures, Professor Victoria Lindsay decided to take on the responsibility of providing young Iraqis with a quality, British-style education. "The unemployment statistics in Iraq are horrendous," she says, "with 35 per cent unemployed. And a great many of those are graduates because the degrees with which they're graduating don't meet the country's needs." Moreover, when Lindsay spoke to business leaders in Iraq, she found a reluctance to hire young Iraqis due to a perception that foreign graduates were better equipped for the workplace.

Having left her job as the first female Director of the British Council in Iraq in 80 years, Lindsay became Founding President and Vice-Chancellor of the British University of Iraq. To undertake the project of founding this new educational establishment, she recruited a group of academics and former diplomat John Tucknott to chair the board, securing investment of $90 million dollars for her ten-year plan. The team acquired land in Baghdad to build the first carbon-neutral educational institution in Iraq, using UK architects and construction companies.

The Iraqi Minister for Higher Education accepted the proposal for the university's foundation in January 2023. Its curriculum will include subjects not available elsewhere in Iraq, covering renewables and energy transition, among other UK-accredited courses. "These are high-quality degrees in subjects such as geoscience and geophysics. Our students will be the only people who have degrees of that quality in Iraq – they are the future."

Lindsay believes the university will be important in terms of research, for example, into agricultural innovation, which is vital to Iraq's economic success. "How do you grow things when you have no water? Because you need to find a way, otherwise you are dependent on other countries. It will also bring Iraqis together, regardless of faith or ethnicity."

Lindsay believes the British University of Iraq could be replicated elsewhere, to immense benefit. The UK government could do this – "the soft power, the legacy, is huge". For now, she says, "We have great hopes and are ready to get to work and build what we all expect will be a world-class university."

www.buiraq.co.uk

Rising to the challenge

The National Association for Able Children in Education works with schools to improve provision for the brightest children while raising standards for all

"We know that pulling from the top is more effective than pushing from the bottom," says Rob Lightfoot, CEO of the National Association for Able Children in Education (NACE). Founded 40 years ago, NACE is an independent education charity that works with schools across all ages and sectors to support more able students, raising standards across the school. Lightfoot first encountered NACE as a secondary-school senior leader, when he saw first-hand the impact the approach had on both learners and educators.

Addressing the needs of more able learners can raise achievement for a much wider group of learners as it increases the challenge for all. "At the heart of our vision is the intent to improve schools and outcomes for all pupils through a particular focus on the needs of the more able learners," says Lightfoot. "Nearly 500 schools have been accredited with the NACE Challenge Award since 2006 and with them we see a rising tide effect because increasing challenge raises expectations and improves education for all learners."

NACE's Challenge Framework provides a structure for schools, or a framework for school or departmental self-evaluation, which then supports school leaders' action plans to bring about long-term sustainable school improvement. This can be accompanied by staff training. Once a school has applied the framework, NACE auditors can provide external accreditation with the Challenge Award. Alongside the option to apply for the Award, NACE member schools can access ongoing support through resources, webinars, research and networking opportunities.

The work of NACE is particularly beneficial for those from less privileged backgrounds, helping to raise aspirations and increase opportunities for these learners. "With disadvantaged learners you need to utilise every second of every lesson to improve their chances of social mobility," says Lightfoot. "Business sponsors can work with us to support disadvantaged learners. We have sponsorship models for businesses that wish to support schools with high numbers of these learners, and we can then supply our services to them for free."

Part of NACE's mission is to help schools to equip young people with the resilience, ambition and independence to prosper in the workplace, whatever their background. "We need our most able students to be creative, problem-solving thinkers for the future of our country – and business leaders should be interested in helping us develop those skills."

www.nace.co.uk

School of thoughtfulness

Students' wellbeing and happiness are at the heart of
the education offered by St Lawrence College in Kent

When staff and students were asked to come up with a social vision statement for St Lawrence College, they chose their words carefully. "A caring community of kindness, positivity and respect" was the result – and the Head, Barney Durrant, says this is exactly what parents will find there.

"It has always been a very rounded school, looking to develop the whole child," he says. Founded in 1879, the mixed school in Ramsgate, Kent, serves around 600 children aged three to 18. Around 40 per cent of those are boarders, the rest day pupils. "The size of the school means that every single child is well known by staff."

The school takes proactive and preventative measures – boosted in challenging times – to ensure pupils' mental health and wellbeing. Peer mentoring, peer support and community events help to foster a sense of belonging. St Lawrence College is a "High Performance Learning" school, which empowers every child to achieve academic success and focuses heavily on extracurricular activities such as sport, art, music, drama and volunteering. "Getting involved in the community and making a difference there has a positive impact on mental health," says Elle Matthews, Assistant Head. "There is a real culture of supporting and looking after each other." The school encourages open discussion about wellbeing, and housemasters receive mental-health first aid training. St Lawrence College also uses STEER tracking, an evidence-based tool to identify young people with hidden vulnerabilities.

Feeling valued for who they are plays an important role in students' happiness, says Durrant, which is why on International Day students are encouraged to wear traditional dress, speak about their cultures and share typical food. "We have about 30 different nationalities within the school. Helping them feel secure and comfortable boosts their self-esteem, and we know this brings higher academic results, better life chances, and improves their overall experience of school."

Highlighting and celebrating these differences fits with the outlook of St Lawrence College. "We are part of a local community and a global community, creating the leaders of the future," says Durrant, "whether that is leading countries, large organisations or charities."

www.slcuk.com

Giving students a voice

Queen Ethelburga's Collegiate is among the highest performing independent schools in the country, creating an environment in which pupils thrive

When the students of Queen Ethelburga's Collegiate in York approached their annual Speech Day, several went to staff with a suggestion: could they showcase their home countries and attend in national dress? Principal Dan Machin thought this was a great idea. Not only would this highlight the school's diverse intake, but it also exemplified the way the school encourages students to take the initiative.

"We have always been very open to making sure that our students talk to us about what we can do for them," says Machin. "That's a very important part of what we do. We are not the school where we expect students to fit in; we want students to tell us what they want and then we make sure they achieve it. We give them a voice and support their ambition because that's how you get the best out of people. It makes for a more positive and diverse environment that serves the students a lot better."

Queen Ethelburga's is a co-educational independent school set in more than 220 acres of beautiful North Yorkshire countryside. It was founded in 1912 and accepts children from three months to 18 years.

The school was rated at the highest standard by the Independent Schools Inspectorate and both of its senior schools have strong academic results. The Collegiate has four schools divided into early years and primary (Chapter House); middle school (King's Magna); and two senior schools (The College and The Faculty), where students can study GCSEs, A-levels and BTECs. Day students are drawn from the local population and there is a large international student body, attracted by the school's imaginative approach to education.

Daniel Machin himself has been at the school for 18 years. "When I joined, we were a lot smaller and we have tried to keep that small school feel even as our student numbers have grown," he says. "Because we are now a larger school, we are able to run more courses and activities, but we are focused on not losing that personalised approach."

The school prides itself on its capacity to provide an individualised approach whether that is pastoral, study or careers. "We don't ever want to lose sight about what it takes to look after the individual."

www.qe.org

Soothing mind and body

Plenaire's skincare range is informed by a core philosophy, to create physical and mental wellbeing and be a force for good

Namrata Nayyar-Kamdar, founder of UK skincare brand Plenaire, understands the significance of good mental health, having experienced post-natal depression after the birth of her second child. Recognising that mental-health issues can often first arise in early adulthood, she wanted to help young people develop lifelong, calming daily habits, so she launched Plenaire to provide a simple and effective skincare routine around which to do so.

"I hope to encourage young people to be kind to their skin and themselves. A regular skincare ritual offers us a few moments to ourselves each day, so it's the ideal time to connect with our physical and mental health, taking pleasure in looking after both," she says. Designed for any gender and skin type, each product is a multitasker, crammed with quality, natural, multisensory ingredients. Instead of being absorbed in a complex skincare regime, people can just focus on themselves.

Before setting up Plenaire in 2020, Nayyar-Kamdar had a successful career in brand management and product development for high-profile corporates. Her marketing experience and clinical knowledge of the skincare and beauty sector now inform her own products and core ethos, which is not just about feeling or looking good, but also about doing good. "Brands are part of popular culture, so I believe we have a responsibility to be a force for good," she says.

From the cult classic Violet Paste Overnight Blemish Crème and Droplet Lightweight Moisture Gel to its delicate Rose Jelly Gentle Makeup Remover and indulgent Skin Frosting Deeply Hydrating Mask, each product sends a gentle message of optimism and encourages self-care. Vegan and cruelty-free, the range is formulated in small batches in Suffolk using only clean ingredients and no parabens or sulphates, making it perfect for delicate and sensitive skin. The packaging, developed with leading waste management experts, uses a recyclable BPA-free monomaterial polymer, making it foolproof to recycle kerbside, and there is an incentive scheme for recycling the containers.

"Plenaire is a certified B Corporation and a carbon-neutral business," says Nayyar-Kamdar "Our sustainability commitment is also verified by Provenance, an innovative platform that traces products' origins via blockchain technology. Independent verification helps to develop better brand trust in this era of greenwashing." For Plenaire, it is "important for young people to know that we, as a brand, are also true to them".

www.plenaire.co

A model global school

At the British International School of Zagreb, with its English-style education, students from across the world receive both academic and cultural enrichment

After the Croatian War of Independence, Martin-Tino Časl wanted to create a private school in Zagreb fit for ambitious and talented students. Starting with language and illustration lessons, the Kreativan razvoj primary school attracted pupils from more than 80 countries. Časl soon realised teaching in English was most effective, and the school adopted the English National Curriculum.

Parents from that institution encouraged Časl to start an international British school and, in 2013, the British International School of Zagreb was born. It proudly became the first school in Croatia to offer the Cambridge Secondary (IGCSE) and Cambridge Advanced (International AS- and A-level) qualifications. They can be used to enter any university in the world. "We very much appreciate the British educational system," says Časl. "Just as you have the Premier League for football, the Cambridge qualifications are the best of their kind."

The multicultural school offers small classes of no more than 15 and a rich range of extracurricular activities designed to bring out pupils' potential. In the afternoons, they can choose from fitness, basketball, football, table tennis, gymnastics and swimming. "I knew from my own background and experiences that there are many kids with interests like I had growing up," says Časl. "You just need to give them a chance to fulfil their wishes.

"We are very proud of our students. Some have gone on to study at Ivy League universities, Stanford and Berkeley in the US, and at King's College London and the London School of Economics, to name a few."

Facilities include an indoor pool and dining hall, serving three meals a day. Since 2021, boarders have also been accepted to the school. Uniform is compulsory and the school day runs from 9am to 4.35pm Monday to Thursday, ending at 3pm on Fridays. There is a security guard and 24-hour electronic surveillance to keep pupils safe.

The school is a very pleasant environment for children, set in a residential area with no traffic. There is a strong focus on socialising. In the cafeteria, eight chess tables provide an opportunity on rainy days for games between teachers and students. "Everyone is very happy here," says Časl. "It is not unusual to see some pupils upset at the end of term because they are sad to leave."

www.britishschool.hr

A pathway to Oxbridge

With its Get the Edge programme, Avernus Education gives talented students the best chance to gain admission to the UK's top universities

British universities are among the very best in the world in global ratings, and the standard and competition to gain admission to them has never been higher. That makes it increasingly important for the most gifted students to find ways to excel in every area that will be examined by a university admissions team to give them the best chance of success. That is where Avernus Education comes in.

The company realises that reaching Oxbridge or another of the G5 universities – Imperial College London, University College London, King's College London or the London School of Economics – now requires the sort of commitment, skill, organisation and self-belief equivalent to obtaining an executive-level job. Avernus has the expertise to guide students and parents through this challenging and complicated admissions process, ensuring students develop the skills and attitudes the best universities require, while identifying the most effective personal pathways for students keen to pursue fulfilling studies and careers in the distinguished areas of law, medicine, STEM and the humanities.

Avernus Education was co-founded in 2022 by Mike Strickland and Daniel Possener, experts in education with a passion for the British education system. Strickland, the Head of Education, came to Avernus with extensive experience of British and international education spanning several continents and multiple curricula, including a period as House Master at Harrow International School Hong Kong. Cambridge graduate Possener is an NCFE-accredited educator with experience in law as well as having worked with prestigious schools and consultancies in both Hong Kong and the UK.

Together, they created Get the Edge, a programme designed to support talented students through the rigours of the UK university application system. The programme offers comprehensive university application mentorship and includes Oxbridge and G5 university private tours, academic and extracurricular enrichment and enhancement, public-speaking training, personal statement masterclasses, university admissions test mentoring, academic competition masterclasses, virtual internships with leading companies, online courses, bespoke webinars, interview preparation and residential courses at the University of Oxford. The latter includes the chance to study for an EPQ – Extended Project Qualification, a self-guided project – in a residential summer masterclass at Brasenose College Oxford. This will deliver a qualification worth half an A-level, which is highly valued by leading universities, in just four weeks of study at one of the world's great colleges.

At the heart of the programme is a mentorship model that sees students receive individualised support in every aspect of their journey. Avernus creates a Personalised Student Pathway for each individual covering everything from university selection strategy, test preparation and personal statement support, to extracurricular mentoring, interview practice and summer camps. The process is overseen by knowledgeable senior consultants and advisers, one of whom will meet a student to personally oversee their pathway and university application.

The core mission of Avernus is to help students receive the appropriate advice, tools and support to succeed. With average Oxbridge acceptance rates at 15 per cent, compared with Avernus rates at 52 per cent, and average London acceptance rates at 35 per cent, compared with Avernus at 85 per cent, the programme is working. Whether that is an ambitious international student looking to study at a G5 university, or a student seeking to stand out in when applying to other UK universities, Avernus helps top students achieve their goals.

www.avernuseducation.com

The business champion

The King's Awards
for Enterprise, like the
Queen's Awards before
them, provide the perfect
opportunity to honour
business innovators
and best practice

King Charles has always encouraged a balanced approach to business combined with a benign, holistic approach to science and technology. For him, good business practices and a sustainable economy go hand in hand with a harmonious society and saving the planet.

A long-term proponent of encouraging the private sector to find solutions for the world's problems, he has urged business leaders to take collective action to tackle climate change by reducing emissions and adopting greener working practices. For many years, he has spoken publicly about the importance of sustainable investment into the regeneration of forests and in support of the world's oceans.

PRIVATE SECTOR POWER

More recently, he saw the Covid-19 lockdown and its immediate aftermath as crucial. He introduced his Great Reset initiative – the economic recovery plan that he launched at the World Economic Forum in June 2020 in response to the pandemic.

The Terra Carta initiative that he went on to establish in 2021 provides a roadmap to 2030 for businesses to move towards sustainable markets, enabling them to harness the power of nature with the transformative power, innovation and resources of the private sector. Its aim is to encourage three major market transformations: firstly, a shift in corporate strategies and operations; secondly, a reformed global financial system; and thirdly, enabling an environment that attracts investment and incentivises action.

The overall goal of the initiative is to support an informed transition to a climate-neutral, inclusive circular bioeconomy through a multi-

"Helping to inspire the growth of new businesses has long been one of Charles's passions"

Previous page
During his state visit to France, The King attends a showcase of Britsh culture and business in Bordeaux

Above
King Charles gives his support to the Scottish whisky industry by officially opening a distillery, 8 Doors, in John O'Groats in 2023

Opposite, top
The royal couple meet traders and business owners at Covent Garden market in London's West End

Opposite, bottom
Recipients of the 2023 King's Awards for Enterprise line up for a royal handshake at a Buckingham Palace reception

"Charles has thrown his weight behind the newly named
King's Awards for Enterprise, honouring outstanding
achievement by UK businesses"

stakeholder approach. Charles believes it is not the lack of capital that is holding us back, but how that capital is deployed.

Charles, as the Prince of Wales, first made a speech on the issue in 1970, when he called for more recycling and a reduction in the reliance on cars and aeroplanes. Since then, he has doubled down on businesses.

By 2013 his language in speeches had hardened, as he told an audience of leading financial officers from companies such as GlaxoSmithKline, Burberry and Network Rail that the world was "consuming our children and grandchildren's inheritance in order to fuel today's short-term, untenable economic growth".

He has consistently argued that world leaders must seize the opportunity of a global economic slowdown to adopt a renewable, regenerative and inclusive standard that supports biodiverse and resilient ecosystems. He has called on humanity to recognise the true value of biodiversity and the fundamental interdependence of all living things.

"We must invest in nature as the true engine for a new economy," he said at a digital forum in March 2021, "a circular bioeconomy that gives back to nature as much as we take from her in order to restore urgently the balance we have so rashly disrupted."

The fact that he is now king hasn't restricted him and he remains pro-business and pro-environment, although determined not to let companies off the hook when it comes to the environment and sustainability. Indeed, the first time I met him after he had acceded to the throne was on 16 November 2022, at a reception to promote small businesses that he hosted at Buckingham Palace.

As he stepped out from the White Room, where he had been chatting to business leaders including billionaire Peter Jones, star of the television series *Dragons' Den*, he spotted me. I bowed my head and addressed him, "Your Majesty", and he asked how I was. This event was typical of him using his convening powers to bring together, in this case, small business with government ministers and financers.

AWARDING EXCELLENCE

Helping to inspire the growth of new businesses and for them to operate in a sustainable way has long been one of Charles's passions. He established Business in the Community more than 40 years ago, in 1982, and it has made a real impact up and down the country. The organisation's Seeing is Believing programme has taken 25,000 business leaders around the country to witness the challenges faced by people running businesses in different areas. The programme also supports "Business Connectors", senior managers who can share their depth of understanding about their local community to help break down local barriers and deliver greater social and economic resilience.

As monarch, Charles has also thrown his weight behind the newly named King's Awards for Enterprise, honouring his late mother's legacy in awarding outstanding achievement by UK businesses. Formerly known as The Queen's Awards and founded in 1966, the programme awards British businesses and other organisations who have excelled at international trade, innovation, sustainable development or promoting opportunity. The King's Awards are presented by His Majesty, on the advice of the prime minister, and are the most prestigious official awards for British businesses. The recipients are permitted to use The King's Awards emblem for the next five years on their products and to promote their services.

Charles has advocated a constructive relationship between business and the world's environmental challenges for more than 50 years, culminating in the establishment of the Sustainable Markets Initiative at the World Economic Forum in 2020. His ambition is to build a co-ordinated global effort to enable the private sector to accelerate the transition to a sustainable future.

"We need nothing short of a paradigm shift," Charles told the World Economic Forum. The old ways, within the financial markets and in big business, need to be overwritten by "a higher-purpose mission putting people and planet at the heart of global value creation". Of that, King Charles has no doubt.

Genius invention

ORCA Computing's scientists and engineers are on a mission to make quantum computers scalable, integrating current technology for real-world applications

"We have to tell our customers that it's a complete departure from how we currently think about computing," says Richard Murray, CEO and co-founder of ORCA Computing, whose aim is to develop and commercialise quantum computing systems. "The Nobel Prize-winning physicist Bill Phillips said that quantum computers were as similar to conventional computers as conventional computers are to an abacus."

ORCA Computing was founded in 2019, after Murray met co-founders Professor Ian Walmsley, then Pro-Vice-Chancellor of research at Oxford University and now Provost of Imperial College, and Dr Josh Nunn, whose work on quantum memory and use of photonics (the delicate process of isolating single strands of light) heralded a new direction for quantum computing. "If you think that a lightbulb produces trillions of photons per second, you'll appreciate that generating just a single photon is an incredibly hard thing to do," says Murray.

Drawing on 30 years of scientific research and technological breakthroughs, their aim is to significantly reduce the complexity, cost and time it takes to scale up quantum systems – to turn what has hitherto seemed like a remote, future prospect into a feasible reality for businesses. Murray describes the company as "a perfect marriage between cutting-edge science, business and applications". Although it has offices in Krakow, Toronto and Seattle, ORCA's headquarters is in London – where the industry is seen as "booming and UK-centric, with a great future".

One advantage of ORCA systems is that they function at room temperature; others freeze qubits (the basic units of quantum information) to near zero, requiring cumbersome, expensive equipment. ORCA Computing also uses standard telecommunications equipment, such as the same optical fibre components that carry internet traffic. "Before ORCA, you couldn't use that for quantum computing," says Murray.

These strokes of practical ingenuity enable ORCA Computing to hold its own alongside giants such as Google. "Ingenuity really does give you an advantage. This is a field where you're trying to do things that no one has done before," says Murray. "Key to our ability to compete and be disruptive against big corporate rivals is groundbreaking discovery. This started with our invention of the quantum memory and continues across multiple areas of machine learning, lasers and electronics." Quantum computing is the "moonshot of our generation", he continues, which will not only revolutionise research and development in the fields of climate change, pharmaceuticals and AI, but also be more sustainable than conventional computing.

"People don't realise how energy intensive the use of any digital device is," says Murray. "If you use Machine Learning or AI, such as ChatGPT, there's a warehouse full of computers churning all the data. Sending an email uses one gramme of carbon dioxide, more if you attach images. It amounts to a huge carbon footprint. Quantum computing helps offset that. Our systems require vastly less energy because the information is stored as light, which is less energy intensive, but also because many calculating scenarios take place simultaneously."

It is remarkable how much ORCA Computing has achieved, delivering quantum computers to customers such as the UK's Ministry of Defence and clients across the High Performance Computing and Energy sectors. Here, "it's about looking for more sustainable approaches that allow us to continue to adopt new digital technologies, but without increasing our carbon footprint," says Murray. In the vision for a less energy-hungry world, ORCA is playing a starring role. "Things once thought impossible are now possible."

www.orcacomputing.com

Crystal clear

As vinyl-wrapped door manufacturer Crystal Doors proves, on the road to net zero, strict sustainable values breed a resilient and thriving business

After winning the prestigious Queen's Award for Enterprise in 2021, in recognition of sustainable development, Crystal Doors owner Richard Hagan found himself face to face with Prince Charles at the award's reception. Hagan is a passionate environmentalist who has taken Crystal Doors on an empowering journey towards net zero, and the future King was eager to hear his story.

"When I got to the castle, I found that I was sat at place one on table one," says Hagan. "I thought they put me there because I was having the vegan meal, but the prince came straight over to talk about what we had done with Crystal Doors. That underpins how important sustainability is for him. He told me that he had been talking about it for 50 years. He has been far ahead of everybody."

Hagan founded Crystal Doors in 1994 in the North West of England, manufacturing vinyl-wrapped doors for the kitchen, bathroom and bedroom, before expanding to make similar products for schools, hospitals, prisons and shops. The company uses quality materials, offers a wide choice of designs and can deliver a 24-hour express turnaround.

But this is more than just a very successful and innovative company (proof of which is the astonishing 16 awards it has won in just three years). In 2015, Hagan installed a 980kW biomass burner at the Crystal Doors factory in Rochdale. After being told by the local authority that the biomass burner was not environmentally friendly and needed to be removed, he decided to research the topic to prove otherwise. Not only was Hagan vindicated by the result, but this "crisis to climate change hero" moment kick-started Crystal Doors' journey towards net zero.

His ambition grew as he began to realise the scale of the problem facing the planet. The biomass burner was followed by a state-of-the-art dust extractor to create cleaner air, and the introduction of solar panels and insulation. Next came a commitment to recycle 99 per cent of waste and use recycled materials. The company uses bicycles and

OUR FOCUS GOALS

13 CLIMATE ACTION

Take urgent action to combat climate change and its impacts

By achieving carbon neutrality by 2022, we're doing our part to limit global warming and show that small businesses can make a big difference.

12 RESPONSIBLE CONSUMPTION AND PRODUCTION

Ensure sustainable production and consumption

We're doing our part by finding and developing alternative materials that support the circular economy and are made of recycled content

7 AFFORDABLE AND CLEAN ENERGY

Ensure access to affordable, reliable, sustainable and modern energy

We're supporting the transition to sustainable energy by generating our own solar power, improving energy efficiency and adopting clean energy technologies.

"I have taken 50 per cent of our turnover and invested it in sustainability"

100 per cent electric vehicles, while the supply chain has been rigorously vetted for sustainability. Hagan has pursued every opportunity to create a cleaner, greener business.

This achievement has only been possible because of his decision to sacrifice short-term profits and personal wealth for investment. "My understanding of wealth isn't what we amass ourselves but what we give to others, and those with the most wealth have the most responsibility," he says. Rather than pass initial costs on to the customers, Crystal Doors has continued to match competitors on product, price and service. Now that investment is bearing fruit in the shape of significantly reduced overheads and operating costs, while Hagan is seeking to make Crystal Doors an employee-owned co-operative, so everybody shares equally in its success.

"We have reduced energy use by 75 per cent per door," he says. "Being an eco-warrior is about business resilience and Crystal Doors is thriving. Because of the hard work we have done, we have been able to absorb energy price rises and are much further along that journey than competitors. I have taken 50 per cent of our turnover and invested it in sustainability – that is what it takes, but for many big companies it is shareholder profit first."

The most recent achievement, in April 2023, saw Crystal Doors receive accreditation as a B Corp company. B Corp is a non-profit organisation that offers certification to companies that demonstrate the highest standards in five different categories: governance, workers, community, the environment and customers. Hagan was impressed by the rigour of the process, which demanded exceptional levels of accountability and transparency. He was delighted to see the company awarded exceptional scores in two areas in particular: environmental issues and community engagement. This went towards a combined score of 130 across all categories. Crystal Doors needed 80 points to qualify for B Corp certification; most businesses score around 50.

That is a testament to Hagan's commitment and conviction. He recognises that his approach remains unfashionable, with many business leaders less keen to invest in supporting the planet or local community. However, he believes his peers are open to the idea of a circular economy and this is how he explains his philosophy to others. "Business leaders understand the concept of the circular economy. Nature has no waste; it is all circular. We had to go through the pain of adaptation for eight years. It wasn't easy but it's not a huge amount of time in the grand scheme of things. The more I gave, the more I got back. It opened up new networks, and now Crystal Doors is in a strong and happy position. Employees are proud to work for us and we can increase our turnover. That means we can make great profits and take income from companies that aren't as environmentally friendly. For eight years, we have put others before ourselves and now we have the rewards."

Hagan will continue to educate and agitate for change, appealing to both consumers and businesses to make the changes required to create a sustainable future. "I want to be a global advocate for sustainability," he says. "I want people who had never really thought about the green stuff to see what it is possible to do. I want them to say that if this little guy with a company in the North with 35 staff and a £3 million turnover can do it, maybe they can, too.

With consumers, it's about lifestyle. It means understanding how to offset properly and to use locally sourced products. Everybody has the responsibility to be net zero. We are one world, one planet. King Charles is happy to say that, and it's a great chance to talk about this as we mark his 75th birthday in his Coronation year."

www.crystaldoors.co.uk

The road to success

Gray & Adams' refrigerated trailers have been transforming food transportation
for 65 years, with each vehicle tailored to the customers' needs

In an old stable block in Fraserburgh, Aberdeenshire, a small vehicle-repair business called Gray & Adams was founded in 1957 by the father of James and Peter Gray. Today, that Scottish company has evolved to produce industry-leading temperature-controlled trailers from a 50-acre complex nearby. Gray & Adams trailers are trusted by the likes of Co-op, Marks & Spencer, McDonald's, Waitrose, Warburtons, Tesco and Sainsbury's to safely transport perishable goods around the country. In addition, the company has brought exciting new ideas to food transportation, among them a double-decker trailer for refrigerated transport – innovation that received The Queen's Award for Enterprise in 2020. And, as many of Gray & Adams's designs are bespoke, the company carries patents on many of its designs, including one for the Farmlay trailer.

"It's essentially been the same core technology since the 1970s, but with a lot of refinement," explains James, who is joint Managing Director of Gray & Adams with his brother Peter. "Customers want to be more environmentally friendly, or they want their vehicles to last longer. They might tell us they have two or three vehicles doing something, but can we make a single trailer that does it all in one?"

As befits a company that designs and builds motor vehicles, the inventive team at Gray & Adams never stands still. The Fraserburgh site is constantly being improved, redeveloped and expanded. One new manufacturing building meets the huge customer demand for double-decker trailers, while a car and commercial vehicle repair centre has been recently completed, freeing up an older set of buildings. These will be replaced by a new manufacturing facility to further streamline the process and enhance innovation and manufacturing capabilities. "We are always getting customer requests for improvements and refinements in cost and efficiency," says James. "There are always new materials and components, and we have to experiment with them."

This innovation includes electrification. Two approaches are being explored by the major manufacturers: one is the use of axle-driven

442

generators to feed the refrigeration unit; another is to cover the trailer roof with solar panels. "These are in the early days and our customers are experimenting to see what works best for their products," says James.

The ability to innovate according to clients' unique needs is in Gray & Adams's DNA, ever since the company started out manufacturing mobile shops for local grocers. Early attempts at food preservation saw trailers kept cool using dry ice. Later came the introduction of refrigeration, a concept that transformed food delivery. These early refrigerated units had just one function, but Gray & Adams became experts at creating dual-purpose vehicles; one of the earliest was for transporting grain to Scottish whisky distilleries and returning with full bottles and barrels.

Today, Gray & Adams still has its roots in Scottish tradition through the manufacture of specialist mobile larders for the treatment and storage of game in the field. The royal estate of Balmoral is one client. "For Balmoral, we make game larders with two compartments: one where the birds or deer come in for preparation, and a chilled section," says James. "We have a steady business making these Game larders more or less on demand, as each one is custom-made depending on needs."

When King Charles, then Prince of Wales, visited the Fraserburgh site for the company's 60th birthday in 2017, he was able to witness the innovation for himself, and James is quick to note the importance of the Royal Family to the company and the community. "The royals are very supportive of the region," he says. "I have a huge admiration for them, and there is so much they do that isn't known or publicised. They are held in very high esteem here." James and Peter were therefore especially proud to receive OBEs in the 2023 New Year Honours list.

Royals aside, most of the company's work is with the larger supermarket chains and food and drink distributors. Innovations include the award-winning double-decker trailer, which works by loading the first level, then raising it by hydraulics and wire ropes so a second level can be filled. This has increased capacity by 70 per cent, massively reducing the number of vehicles on the road to the benefit of the environment. The company also makes a single trailer that can maintain three different temperatures, a concept extended to double-decker trailers. Some double-decker vehicles have been adapted to be serviced by a standard loading bay, improving efficiencies as clients do not need to access a specialist bay. Most of the trailers can be used for at least ten years if looked after, and some might do up to three million miles in total, which is important for the company's sustainability priorities, as is taking care of clients. "Whether a client is ordering one trailer or 101, we treat everybody the same and that's the philosophy the company is built on," says James.

James and Peter have both worked for the family firm for their entire working lives, spending holidays and weekends at the Fraserburgh site from a young age and gaining experience in all areas of the business. James's sons, one daughter and grandchildren now work for the company, too. This family approach gives the company longevity and consistency, qualities valued by the 700-plus employees, some of whom have been at Gray & Adams for several decades. The company has a thriving apprenticeship scheme and is about to open a new training centre where teachers include retired employees, passing on their knowledge to the next generation.

The family legacy allows Gray & Adams to call upon a wealth of experience and an understanding of change and how it can be achieved. Each new idea leads to further improvements and refinements. "Our customers make a request, we get on with it, and each new idea has benefits we can bring to our other customers," says James. "Responding to our customers' needs has always been at the heart of what we do."

www.gray-adams.com

Going for gold

Proudly independent, east London-based Baird & Co trades, manufactures
and refines bullion, providing tangible assets to wide-ranging clients

In good times, people use gold to make beautiful objects; during more challenging periods, they turn to gold as a reliable investment. Whatever the national economic mood, for more than 50 years the family-owned London bullion merchant Baird & Co has been buying and selling this precious metal. It also runs the UK's largest gold refinery, which can take gold of low purity and refine it to 24 carats for clients that span from private investors to the Royal Mint.

The business was set up in 1967 by the late Tony Baird and is run by his wife, Executive Director Lorena Baird, and son, Director Alex Baird. "As a young man, Tony was fascinated by gold coins and became well known for collecting them," says Lorena. "He then began to trade gold, starting with ancient coins and gold Krugerrands."

The natural progression for the company was to start making bars and then build a refinery. "If Tony was still alive, he'd have continued going backwards and invested in a gold mine, because if you have

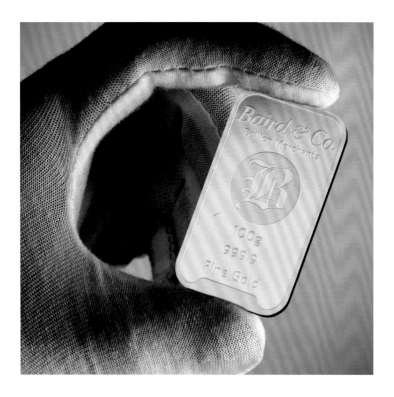

access to your own mine, then you have a guaranteed supply of the metal," says Lorena. "We are now chasing my husband's dream, but in a slightly different way."

Following her husband's death, Lorena began to use her 25 years of corporate experience to modernise the business, winning a Queen's Award for Enterprise for achievements in International Trade, in 2018. One key element of the company's success was improving the sourcing of gold – not only securing a steady supply, but also ensuring it was transparent and ethical. That led Baird & Co to invest in the welfare and upskilling of miners in Africa.

"We have established new supply chains in Africa to comply with new regulations," says Lorena. "We are trying to help the miners with better practices, such as no longer using mercury to split the gold as it causes huge environmental damage. We work with the miners, pay them a fair price and ensure they meet the rules and regulations. That allows us to have a positive impact on the community and environment while guaranteeing a secure source of gold."

A consistent supply of gold will enable Baird & Co to expand its manufacturing capability while developing staff through an apprenticeship scheme aimed at supporting the community in this disadvantaged corner of east London.

As well as the refinery, Baird & Co has a retail premises in Hatton Garden, home of the British gold and jewellery industry. This allows Baird & Co to service walk-in customers, who, like all of the company's more than 20,000 clients – indeed, like all "goldbugs" over the centuries – are enticed by the tangible quality of gold. Gold can be touched and transported, and as such is much more than simply numbers on a computer screen.

"It means our customers are so varied," says Lorena. "We have grandparents who buy a gold sovereign for a grandchild's 21st birthday, and we have investors who believe gold is the best way to protect their wealth against shocks such as war or inflation."

People invest in gold at all levels in many different ways, explains Lorena, which is why Baird & Co deals with everyone from private clients to family offices and corporate clients. "Whenever there is instability of any kind, we get more interest, and during the good times people want special items. There are so many people who believe in the power of gold."

www.bairdmint.com

Electric dreams

Auto Electrical Supplies is a specialist provider of automotive
wiring protection that has won admiration for its overseas trade

"Winning The Queen's Award for Enterprise in International Trade has catapulted us further than ever before," says James Fawkes, Chairman of Yorkshire-based Auto Electrical Supplies (AES). "It stands for excellence and we're so proud to be part of such an elite bunch."

A company that began in 1992 in Fawkes's garden shed now exports to 37 international markets, and is a global leader in the distribution of products that protect critical wiring in commercial and off-highway vehicles. AES employs 20 people across three businesses: AES Export launched in 2014, and AES USA Corp, based in Illinois, opened its doors in 2016. AES is a high volume stockist and the UK's leading global distributor and exporter of Harnessflex conduit systems and aftermarket products used within the automotive industry. Building on its strong global presence, the company has expanded further, opening a new facility in India in 2023.

"We stock the full Harnessflex portfolio, plus thousands of other aftermarket products," says Managing Director Richard Norris. "The key is knowing the products and building relationships with customers. We've had customers using us for 30 years. I was a local lad who came in pretty much at the beginning, was promoted and treated well here for decades."

"We like recruiting from the local community, and we like to develop their skills," adds Fawkes. "We bring them in and pull them up and then recruit more from that community."

AES also takes sustainability seriously. "We have hugely increased capacity and warehouse space," says Norris. "We've had solar panels installed and have multiple electric vehicles, as well as electric charging points for visitors and staff, and we've enhanced our recycling systems."

The recognition that the company received in 2020 with a Queen's Award for its strong international presence has since been a cause for huge celebration at AES. "We know what the Royal Family means to people around the world," says Fawkes. "It has put a British company on the world stage and it's a massive feather in our cap. All I can say is, thank the Lord for sheds."

www.aes.group

Healthy eating

The Nutrition Society was founded to support the nation's diet during wartime, and advances the study of nutrition and its role in health today

When The Nutrition Society was founded in London in 1941, wartime rationing was in place, and nutritionists had a significant role to play in ensuring that people ate a balanced diet during this time of shortage. While some nutritional advice has changed since then, much of the early research by Society members still forms the basis of our diet today.

"The work of our founding members helped shape the first dietary guidelines," says Caroline Roberts, a public health nutritionist and the Society's Science Communications Officer. "Many of these we still use today."

At the same time, our lives are now very different to how they were in those war years. "One aspect that has changed is our food environment," says Roberts. "There are many more processed foods available and people are not as physically active as they used to be."

Another change is the sheer amount of misinformation in circulation. Roberts points out that anyone searching for evidence-based nutrition information may find themselves inundated with inaccurate information, especially online. Nevertheless, the Covid-19 pandemic has seen an increased public interest in health matters. As a UK charity whose mission is "to advance the scientific study of nutrition to promote human and animal health", the Society has long supported a change in statute to protect the title "nutritionist", which, if successful, will benefit professionals and the public alike. At present, anyone can call themselves a "nutritionist", while the title of "dietitian" is already protected by law.

As part of its mission, the Society publishes six journals, including the prestigious British Journal of Nutrition, which showcase scientific research, and organises regular conferences to bring experts together. The Society's 2,900 members from 87 countries benefit from access to professional development training and support for international travel to develop global evidence-based nutrition programmes. "These opportunities benefit career progression enormously," says the Society's President, Professor Julie Lovegrove.

Celebrating 80 years of nutritional research and its dissemination, the Society's 2021–2026 Strategic Plan lays out its latest ambitions in support of the UN Sustainable Development Goals, including an e-learning platform and addressing global nutritional challenges. "UK scientists and nutritionists are among the best trained in the world," says Lovegrove. "They have the expertise to influence training elsewhere, and thus contribute to improving global nutrition."

www.nutritionsociety.org

Perfect chemistry

Penman Consulting's chemical-industry expertise is in demand across the world, and ensures that everyday products can be used safely

In 1996, Mike Penman received an MBE for his services to environmental safety while working at British chemical company, ICI, in collaboration with the Department of the Environment. He then worked in the US and Europe, before leaving the corporate world to found Penman Consulting with his wife, Sue, in 2007. Penman Consulting assists corporations with scientific expertise to meet global regulatory requirements for the chemicals that go into their products, enjoying such success that his company was awarded one of the first King's Awards for Enterprise, in International Trade, in 2023.

"The King's Award is very satisfying because halfway through my career I received an MBE and now, as I come towards the end of my career, we have a King's Award," says Penman. "I went from the UK to work around the world, then came back home to develop a business out of the skills I had gained."

Penman Consulting provides specialist regulatory services to the chemical industry on health and environmental matters. Although it largely goes unnoticed by the consumer, the chemical industry is one of the world's largest, producing the essential components for almost everything we use in day-to-day life, from fridges to paint to shampoo. Ensuring the chemicals are safe for use remains a core motivation of Penman Consulting. The company has a team of 60 across Europe, India and the US. To handle large amounts of data, Penman has developed specialist software, Active Steward, gaining a unique edge in chemical regulatory affairs management.

"These chemicals and their combinations can be very complex and there are strict regulations to manage safety," says Penman. "We are writing dossiers, regulatory submissions, assessing chemicals and organising innovative testing. There's a huge prescription on the amount of data that is required."

The company has a broad spectrum of customers and, says Penman, is sensitive to the needs of them all. Most of the work is around regulation, risk assessment, generation and interpretation of data. "People come to us from all over the world to access our expertise as we are recognised as being close to the regulators and close to industry."

The work undertaken by Penman Consulting is essential for any industry or company that seeks to move towards a circular or green economy. Any changes in raw material – known as feedstock – alters the industrial process and creates what, in chemical terms, will be a new product, requiring assessment and regulation. Similarly, recycling invariably means using raw materials that are less pure. This can have an impact on humans, animals and the planet, something that needs to be understood and acted upon to help industry and society achieve non-hazardous material cycles.

"Substitutions can be beneficial, but you need to know what the new chemicals will do," explains Penman. "There's a huge amount of work that needs to be done to demonstrate that what we are doing is safe, because there is no point in having a circular economy if it produces new concerns." Penman Consulting aims to build its business in the circular economy by supporting industry in its green transition. "The King has been promoting sustainability issues for a long time. We gained a citation for international trade because our exports have increased significantly over two years. Compared to other King's Awards winners we are still minnows, so it was wonderful to be recognised at this stage in our development."

www.penmanconsulting.com

Blazing a trail

Quality and innovation are the guiding principles of Brian James Trailers, which has seen record international trade over the past years

"It's been a tough few years what with the pandemic, the extraordinary cost increase of raw materials and energy, as well as export shipping costs, but, despite this, and thanks to our colleagues and business partners, we've ended up navigating these choppy waters," says Lewis James, CEO of Brian James Trailers, which designs and makes car trailers for the automotive and construction sectors. "And we are incredibly proud to receive one of the first King's Awards for Enterprise."

The win in the Award's International Trade category in 2023 reflects how the Northamptonshire-based company has become a major exporter, with 60 per cent of its high-quality products sold across Europe, Australia and New Zealand. Although the brand is well-known for its links to the motorsport industry, more than half of the business is now in the commercial sector, which includes the manufacture of tipper trailers, plant trailers for diggers and other equipment, as well as general-purpose trailers. "The construction industry is where we see the biggest growth in the coming years," says Nick Brown, Chief Operating Officer. "We're focusing here and in further increasing export sales, which have grown dramatically in the past three years."

Now led by the grandson of company founder Brian James, the family-run business has been going strong in Daventry for the past 40 years. A workforce of some 200 people is employed over the five sites in the manufacture of trailers designed using advanced computer software. Brian James Trailers has not only been innovating and gradually broadening its product range, but has also made significant investments in recent years. "Two new factory buildings and additional precision manufacturing equipment, including more robot welding and laser-cutting machines, has helped the business meet the incredible upsurge in market demand," says James.

A former recipient of a Queen's Award for Enterprise in International Trade in 2018, Brian James Trailers has numerous accreditations to its name, including certification from the ISO (International Standards Organisation) for its quality management systems. As another mark of quality, Brian James trailers come with a five-year chassis warranty, which the company says is part of the reason why its trailers are the first choice of professional users worldwide.

www.brianjamestrailers.co.uk

The feelgood factor

From goat to garment, Brodie Cashmere's sumptuous clothing has
a modern spin, not only in its design but in its traceability, too

A highly distinctive yet timeless brand with Yorkshire roots, Brodie Cashmere is known for its luxurious cashmere and soft cotton silk pieces. The family-owned outfit launched more than 10 years ago and has gone on to shake up the cashmere market with its fabric quality, contemporary colours and unique prints. Founder and CEO Anne-Marie Holdsworth, who comes from a family of Leeds cashmere traders, designs the garments in-house with style input from friends and family, choosing only the best fibres produced by traditional craftsmen from Scotland to Mongolia. "It is this attention to detail that means each piece is safe to wash in the machine and won't pill," says Holdsworth.

The stock graces 1,600 retailers worldwide and the company has a regular presence at fashion trade show Pure London. So it is no wonder that Brodie Cashmere won the 2022 Queen's Award for Enterprise in International Trade and was also nominated by Drapers for Brand of the Year in the 2022 Sustainable Fashion Awards. "This was amazing and completely unexpected as we were up against major brands like Superdry with huge reach," says Rush.

"The time we're really trying to grow online is also when people are wanting to know more about sustainable and ecologically sound brands," adds Rush, Head of Marketing and Communications at Brodie Cashmere. "If the good message is also coming from the top – from the Palace – it is a sign that we can support each other."

Sustainability is integral to Brodie Cashmere's world – Holdsworth wants to "slow fashion down. For us, the responsibility doesn't end as soon as we sell a jumper; considering the afterlife is always just as important." As members of the Sustainable Fibre Alliance (SFA) – which works to improve the impacts of cashmere production in Mongolia – the company helps to preserve the pasture condition and water sources so that wildlife numbers are protected, while looking after the lifestyle of the nomadic herders. SFA offers educational programmes, range land training and assistance with accessing further markets.

"We try to be regenerative as opposed to just sustainable, says Rush. "So we say 'sustainable' is not really improving anything – you're keeping everything at the same level – whereas 'regenerative' is aiming to restore the planet."

www.brodiecashmere.com

Resilience in the workplace

Birmingham-based Shelforce manufactures windows and doors of the highest quality, which the business attributes to an outstanding workplace culture

Visitors to the Shelforce factory in Erdington near Birmingham have described it as one of the happiest and most inspiring workplaces they have ever seen. This is quite a change from ten years ago, when the business – which today manufactures high-quality double-glazed windows and fire doors for local authorities, government tenders and commercial projects – was close to collapse.

Since then, Shelforce has had a transformation, which not only saw it achieve a record turnover, but also receive a 2023 King's Award for Enterprise. This is an incredible achievement for any factory, but what makes it even more significant is that Shelforce has a commitment to employ people with disabilities, with 75 per cent of staff having some form of impairment.

"When we won the King's Award, it was quite emotional because we could see how we had grown over the past ten years," says Business Manager Howard Trotter. "It's been life changing.

"We want other businesses to look at us and ask why we have been so successful. The reality is, it is because resilience doesn't come from the building or the balance sheet, it comes from the people – and the most resilient people are the ones who have battled through the hardest challenges, such as being blind or deaf from birth. We want to show other businesses this approach works. It's not just profitable, it has social value."

When Trotter arrived at Shelforce in 2013, the company was struggling. Its closure would have been a sad end to a business that had charitable roots, having been established in 1839 by the Royal School for the Blind as a workplace for visually impaired people.

But Trotter was determined to create a financially viable business. He had to prove to clients that the products that came out of the factory would be of the best quality and at the same time rebuild the self-belief of the workforce, encouraging workers to take responsibility for the factory's output and operations.

Trotter believed a change in workplace culture was needed. Making reasonable adjustments for some staff, "I told them we had to show we could produce quality products and they embraced that responsibility. They want to be treated like everybody else, and it was about evolving the culture so everybody had responsibility."

Part of this change was in de-emphasising disability. "We don't talk about disability. Our view is that we all have imperfections of different kinds, so what we need to do is make the best of the abilities we have as we compete in the open market."

The workers had huge desire and resilience, explains Trotter, as well as excellent practical skills. Together, they reorganised the factory to create a more efficient system, and each improvement brought benefits that increased confidence. In 2021, Shelforce was named Business of the Year by Birmingham Chamber of Commerce, and the business continues to grow.

Trotter hopes the story of Shelforce will be an inspiration to others. "I have learnt over the last ten years that if you are disabled you have had to live with challenges your whole life, and one of the most important assets in any business is resilience," he says.

"People with disabilities are incredibly resilient. A lot of people leave compassion at the factory door, but we bring it on to the factory floor. We don't want to let anybody down and every success is one secured by the whole family, not any individual."

www.shelforce.com

The green valley

Through the creation of green infrastructure, Cenin is turning a corner of Wales into a renewable energy hub

When it comes to renewables, Welsh infrastructure company Cenin is a force of nature. By combining multiple forms of green energy – and developing the infrastructure to support this – it has injected new life into rural communities. The inspiration came during a visit to Austria that Director Martyn Popham made in 2005. "I saw difficult areas utilising natural resources to create economic value and benefit the environment and realised this could be applied to our area," he says.

Founded in 2011, Cenin now runs multiple low-carbon developments across South Wales, all built on cutting-edge green technology. National attention came in 2021 when Cenin won a prestigious Queen's Award for Enterprise in Sustainable Development, thanks to its outstanding impact on reducing emissions. The company's business hub, Parc Stormy, based in Bridgend harnesses power from wind, solar and waste to save 200,000 tonnes of carbon per year.

As well as contributing towards the fight against climate change, Cenin's projects benefit the community. "They give a lifeline to local people by creating employment," says Popham. "We're proud that we've attracted a lot of investment, and landowners and local councils want to collaborate with us."

At Parc Stormy, Cenin has an educational facility for schools to learn about the green economy. Popham explains that it is about helping people to understand there are prospects in this industry for innovative thinkers and you do not necessarily need to be academically gifted or come from a privileged background.

In this way, Popham hopes to have the same impact on future generations that King Charles III had on him when he visited Dumfries House, part of The Prince's Foundation, where young people are trained in real-life skills. "The King was ahead of his time. A lot of my values are aligned with his; I've just adapted them to a different environment."

With more innovative projects to come, Cenin is a success story, both for British business and in combating climate change. "We only have one planet and I believe we have a bright future," says Popham. "We need people to understand there are ways of living well, it's simply a case of doing it differently."

www.cenin.co.uk

Engineering excellence

Family-run with a passion, DK Engineering is the one-stop specialist
for Ferrari owners, from turn-key renovation to race-ready preparations

For David Cottingham, it all started with his passion for XK Jaguars. In 1963, he bought a lightweight XK 120 that he restored and raced. Eventually, the demands on his time that this entailed became so great that he and his wife, Kate, decided to take the plunge and go into the classic car business full time. In 1977, they founded DK Engineering, lending their initials to the company name.

James Cottingham, the youngest son of David and Kate, now heads up the company as Managing Director and Lead Acquisition Consultant, while following in his father's footsteps behind the wheel in races. He spends every day working alongside his parents to sell, store, restore and service a plethora of motor vehicles, or prepare them for competition. "The scale of the business in terms of the quality and quantity is unparalleled – nobody else in the world offers the same range of service," says James. "We are among the biggest in all these different sectors and the only company that does all of them. We are unique in that sense."

Just about anybody who owns a classic Ferrari will have come across DK Engineering. From a purpose-built facility in Chorleywood,

Hertfordshire, specialist staff work on some of the rarest and most beautiful examples of automotive craftsmanship ever seen. While Ferraris are the company's speciality, it works on other marques, including Lamborghini, Porsche, Jaguar and Maserati. It helps that the UK is at the centre of the classic car trade, explains James. "The majority of restoration and sales experts are in the UK. It's an industry that is based in this country because of our engineering background. This is the country that pioneered the restoration of these classic cars. We are a car-driven nation and have the best events, namely the Goodwood Members' Meeting, Festival of Speed and Revival meetings, The Classic at Silverstone and other racing events at Brands Hatch, Donington, Oulton Park and Snetterton."

James's favourite car is the Ferrari F40. "There is so much history around the brand and there is something creative and artistic about it. There has been a real surge of interest, with people meeting up at shows, races and rallies. It's a huge community and it is continuing to grow."

www.dkeng.co.uk

Industrial might

A small business with global objectives, European SprayDry Technologies engineers high-performance plants and machinery for industries ranging from foods to pharmaceuticals

The recipient of The Queen's Award for Enterprise in International Trade in 2015 and 2022, European SprayDry Technologies (ESDT) has proved small businesses can have a global reach, and it is putting this to good use for the planet and the next generation of engineers.

ESDT designs and supplies high-quality bespoke spray dryers, fluid bed dryers, evaporators, powder processing plants and all associated ancillaries, predominantly to clients in the food, chemical, pharmaceutical and dairy sectors across the UK and internationally. Its engineers and process designers collaborate with the world's best manufacturers and fabricators to create cutting-edge, reliable, user-friendly products that meet clients' precise specifications and ESDT's exacting criteria in performance, energy efficiency, quality and environmental responsibility.

"As a small business, we can be more flexible and accessible than larger organisations, while upholding the same high quality," explains Mike Gorsen, ESDT's Managing Director. "We have a deeply embedded understanding of the thermodynamics, engineering and physics of spray drying. This expertise is readily accessible to our clients during the design process and if they have any subsequent queries – which isn't always the case with larger companies." ESDT is also ensuring this knowledge passes to future engineers by creating opportunities for apprentices, school leavers and graduates.

The company is pursuing an equally proactive approach to nurturing the planet. During the early days of the Covid pandemic, it introduced technology and practices to enable its engineers to work remotely with clients, and has continued with this approach to minimise company travel and lower its carbon footprint.

"Energy efficiency is another area of sustainability we're focused on," says Gorsen. It's difficult to recover heat from the spray-drying process, and spray dryers also heat up buildings around them, which then often require cooling. So ESDT is exploring ways to utilise air source heat pumps and photovoltaic solar panels to create some of the heat needed for spray drying and, at the same time, produce a cooling effect to reduce temperatures in surrounding buildings. "As engineers, we love resolving technical problems, so it's particularly rewarding to be working on a solution to the issue of energy efficiency in this industry, as it will benefit us, our clients and the planet."

www.spray-dryer.com

Safety drive

JMDA Design's car seats have played a significant role in child safety for over 30 years while winning prestigious awards for innovation

Car safety seats have saved innumerable children from death and life-changing injury over the past three decades, an incalculable improvement helped by the work of JMDA Design, a British company founded in 1991. In that time, JMDA's co-founder, Derrick Barker, has been responsible for over 120 designs of child car seats for dozens of leading manufacturers, transforming the industry through innovations designed to increase functionality and safety.

The company's achievement was acknowledged with the receipt of a Queen's Award in 2019 for International Trade and its founders were honoured to attend a reception at Buckingham Palace, hosted by the then Prince Charles. "This recognised our contribution to child safety globally," says Cherril Barker, Derrick's wife and co-founder, with responsibility for finance and marketing. "We have contributed significantly to the child car seat industry, giving us a sphere of knowledge that is unprecedented. We work with the large brands because they know we have the knowledge to deliver the finished product. These are highly regulated pieces of equipment – and they need to be: a child's life is at stake. That's why people come to us."

With partner offices in China and Italy, JMDA has developed a global capacity to service the needs of the industry. The company's design and regulatory know-how is unparalleled, with Derrick having a secondary role sitting on a body that informs and refines regulatory changes. This expertise has led to opportunities in related fields of safety and children's products, including wheelchairs, stairlifts, baby monitors and strollers, recognised by four prestigious Red Dot Design Awards from 2016 to 2020.

The couple stepped away from JMDA in March 2023, but Derrick will continue to offer advice, while Cherril switches her focus to charitable work. "We have developed huge influence over the industry because of our history of success, our strong networks and our experience," says Derrick. "This has created a global centre of excellence that is now embedded in our senior team. There's a very moral angle to what we do. We are mindful of the importance of our work and that explains the care we put into designs to ensure they are safe. We have played a major part in the statistical reduction of injury to children over that time. You can't protect everybody, but you can substantially reduce the risk."

www.jmdadesign.com

A new leaf

Smartleaf's patented technology is tackling food
waste by ensuring salads stay fresher for longer

In 2017, a survey carried out by the Waste & Resources Action Programme (WRAP) found that people in the UK throw away 40 per cent of the salad bags they buy every year. Smartleaf inventor Scott Phillips knew he wanted to do his bit to tackle this food waste. Salad is often thrown away because it tends to be purchased without a particular meal in mind and is frequently forgotten at the back of a fridge, either unopened or having only been used once. The purpose behind Smartleaf technology is to make that forgotten bag of salad last longer.

"People often forget about their salad and it goes to waste," says Managing Director Jo Phillips. "But by sanitising it, you remove all the microbes that can cause moulds or spoilage, and we have heard stories about the salads still being fresh two weeks later. We are the first to commercialise this process." Smartleaf technology tackles food waste by extending the shelf life of bags of salad, keeping them fresher for longer. As food waste generates ten per cent of global greenhouse gases, this is an important step forward for fresh produce spoilage in the home.

Smartleaf is a gentle, sanitising treatment that can keep salads fresh for longer than traditional methods of salad washing. Baby leaves such as spinach and rocket are more than 90 per cent water. The patented method works by lightly misting the leaves with electrically charged water droplets small enough to penetrate microscopic holes on the surface. This cleans the leaves, removes bacteria and keeps them safe to eat while retaining their natural flavour and hydration. By reducing the bacterial loading, spoilage is kept to a minimum and the salad lasts longer using only natural substances. In 2022, this innovative and radical technology won Smartleaf a Queen's Award for Innovation.

"Our big contribution to sustainability is tackling food waste," says Phillips. "People don't see salad as a long-lasting product, and it drives a lot of waste through the chain because of that final stage where consumers just put whole bags in the bin." With plans to get Smartleaf salads stocked by more retailers, Phillips and her team are keen for as many customers as possible to try this uniquely fresh produce for themselves.

www.smartleaf.co.uk

The goodness of vanilla

LittlePod is reintroducing the world to the taste and benefits of real vanilla, and helping preserve the rainforests at the same time

Britons love vanilla. It is one of the nation's favourite flavours. Yet 97 per cent of all vanillin used in the West is artificial, so most people do not know about real vanilla. An enterprising Devon-based company is determined to change that.

Founded in 2010, LittlePod is dedicated to promoting real vanilla – and its importance to the world's rainforests. "Real vanilla comes from a delicate, beautiful rainforest orchid," says Janet Sawyer MBE BEM, LittlePod's founder and Managing Director. "It is labour-intensive to grow, and it takes up to five years from planting a crop to producing cured vanilla pods. But growing vanilla sustainably is a powerful way to preserve our rainforests."

In 2023, LittlePod received the King's Award for Enterprise (Sustainable Development). It recognised LittlePod's determination to forge impactful global connections that contribute to sustainable agriculture. The award was presented by the Lord Lieutenant of Devon David Fursdon, who said, "Isn't it fantastic that a small company in a village in East Devon can reach out and have an impact on the world while doing social good at home."

From early on, the company has spearheaded its Campaign for Real Vanilla, founding a pioneering vanilla orchard in Bali. Farmers led by Dr Made Setiawan work with a sustainable polyculture model. Vanilla orchid vines are grown on a mixture of rainforest planting, including coffee and cacao trees. "At first the area was barren," says Setiawan. "Now, our orchard is rich in biodiversity, and we're working with the Indonesian government to help more farmers adopt LittlePod's polyculture model."

"Rainforests are the lungs of Earth," says Sawyer. "When people buy quality LittlePod products, they're helping to support indigenous farmers who are preserving rainforests, improving the air we breathe and making the world a better place."

The company is committed to meaningful social enterprise, offering employment, training and mentorship to young people from southwest England and beyond. "They've improved themselves and improved LittlePod. Now they're out in the world, advocating for us and telling our story," says Sawyer.

Sawyer is keen to leave customers with an intriguing thought: "If we could make an incursion of just 1 per cent into the artificial vanillin market, we could double the demand for real vanilla worldwide – and help the planet."

www.littlepod.co.uk

Everlasting design

Sustainability is built into NaughtOne's British-made, modern commercial furniture, from the timeless designs to the commitment to repurposing and recycling

From the craftsmanship and the tailoring to the upholstery and customer service, there is true heart in the 18-year-old North Yorkshire-based NaughtOne, which designs and makes high-performing commercial furniture with a residential appeal. "We craft and manufacture timelessly relevant designs, applying a British design philosophy that transcends our Yorkshire roots," says Nadean McNaught, Managing Director.

"The products stand out because they can wear many 'clothes and faces'," she says. "We are different in that we offer lots of choice. We create something that is unique to the customer, something that is bespoke."

Designing for modern spaces, some of NaughtOne's major clients include Amazon, Microsoft and PayPal. The company philosophy is that because everything starts with a genuine human need, design should have absolute simplicity and be in accordance with those needs. Sustainability goals, too, are inherent in everything brought to market. "Our Ever chair and sofa range is based around circularity," says McNaught. "It is the first furniture we made where we didn't use any chemicals to fuse the product together, and where all parts can be taken apart and recycled at the end of its life." Products launched since Ever have followed suit, with circularity in mind. "Our Take-Back programme means we help customers recycle properly, and we repurpose components, reducing the amount of raw materials we use," she says. "For us, it's more than our accreditations; it's about growing our business in a way that makes us proud."

Winning The Queen's Award for Enterprise in International Trade, in 2019, is a testament to the company's global success. It has showrooms in Chicago and London, and employs nearly 100 people across the world. "After the pandemic, we saw fantastic growth in the UK, as well as across Europe and the US," says McNaught. "In line with our sustainability ambitions, we aim to produce products locally wherever possible, and so expanding production into new markets, such as India and China, meant we were able to support those markets, while reducing product miles travelled and carbon emissions."

www.naughtone.com

Flying start

Simply Start makes the entrepreneurial journey less bumpy by providing the
right mentors, service providers and investors in one common marketplace

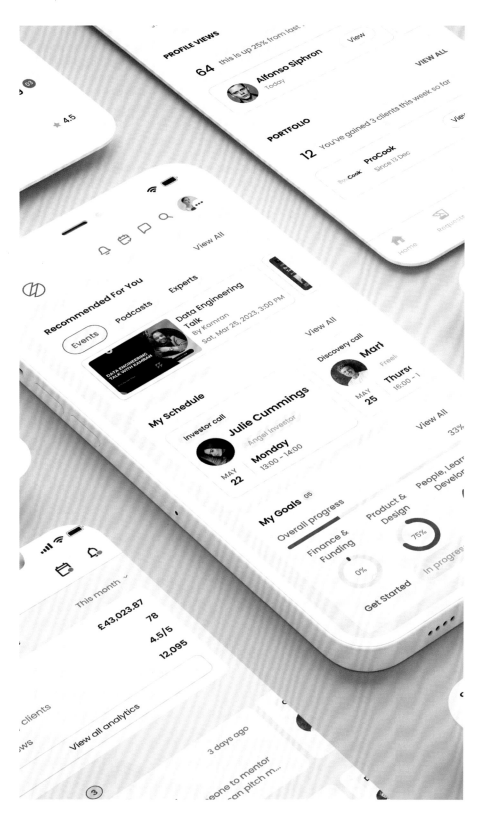

Around half of all businesses fail in the first five years is a statistic that Jason Shoker, founder of Simply Start shares. Simply Start, however, aims to make the startup journey easy. Through an all-in-one marketplace, it connects entrepreneurs to all the experts and resources they need to run a successful business.

"There are all sorts of reasons businesses struggle, especially in the first few years," says Shoker. According to business owners, reasons for failure range from funding running out to having the wrong investors, being in the wrong market, a lack of research, bad partnerships or ineffective marketing, among others.

Simply Start aims to help with this and more, fixing the biggest problems faced by startup entrepreneurs. These include having to go to different places to find the right and relevant mentors, board advisers, investors, freelancers, service providers and resources to build their businesses, at the same time ensuring they are vetted and trusted. Startups also have to try to compare different price proposals from suppliers and manage ongoing mentoring and funding services, all of which can be very time consuming.

For many companies, access to Simply Start's all-in-one business online marketplace is a game-changer. The marketplace matches startups to a whole plethora of business mentors, suppliers and funding services, while providing the necessary collaboration tools within the platform to help startups track and manage their progress. The aim of the platform is to also make ongoing business recommendations to help sustain companies and see them grow.

"Although Simply Start has been designed to solve common problems facing entrepreneurs," says Shoker, "it also offers huge benefits to other users, such as mentors, board advisers, investors, services providers and freelancers, in terms of high-quality, engaged networking and targeted, actionable business opportunities."

The anonymous data acquired from such a platform can also facilitate the analysis of wider business trends and inform strategic support for businesses at a governmental level. Indeed, Shoker sees potential for Simply Start in addressing the $1 trillion startup ecosystem, and hopes Simply Start can help all those involved to get started in business much more simply – and go on to succeed.

www.simplystart.com

Research in practice

The renowned James Hutton Institute implements its outstanding food, energy and environmental research in hundreds of projects worldwide

Based in Scotland, the James Hutton Institute knows that as the world feels the effects of global warming, the issues of food security and sustainable agriculture will become increasingly important. This non-profit research organisation is developing new technology and crops to make farming more sustainable, ensure food supply in a changing climate and create resilient communities. Its scientists, for example, have developed blackcurrants that do not need winter frosts to produce fruit, fast-cooking potatoes, diesel alternatives for tractors and even a "climate positive" gin, among hundreds of other innovations.

However, the cross-disciplinary institute, which was set up in 2011 and employs some 500 people working on over 200 projects at any one time worldwide, does not just focus on crops. "A lot of our problems are about human behaviour, not technology," says Chief Executive Colin Campbell, who explains that ensuring public awareness is key to long-term improvements.

One of the projects, in Orkney, is aimed at establishing a community run "vertical farm", and a scheme in India provided school toilets that could run on renewable energy and recycled water technologies. "The key to success however, was the social scientists engaging the community and training them to operate it themselves," says Campbell.

Based in Dundee and Aberdeen, the Hutton collaborates on research in more than 20 countries, and much of its work "on the ground" is in India, sub-Saharan Africa and China. The organisation is also proudly Scottish: "A huge amount of our research is in Scotland, funded by the Scottish and UK governments."

It is perhaps no surprise that the James Hutton Institute – named after one of Scotland's most famous scientists – was awarded The King's Award for Enterprise in Sustainable Development, in 2023. "In the past there was massive success in improving agricultural production, but there has also been damage to the environment, and so now we take a much more holistic, integrated approach," says Campbell. "It's about producing food, water and energy and regenerating our land and nature at the same time. That's a tricky thing to do."

www.hutton.ac.uk

The X factor

With its X-POT water-filtration system, Vexo International is on a mission to protect households, businesses and the environment

"We're basically polishing water 24 hours a day," says Darren Wilkinson, founder and Chief Executive of Vexo International, the energy-saving solutions specialists. He is talking about X-POT, Vexo's water-filtration system, the effects of which on a heating system can be dramatic, both for users and the environment.

X-POT was developed and manufactured by the Bedfordshire-based company to restore water cleanliness and improve commercial heating and cooling system performance and life cycle. Water rushing through radiators often contains corrosive metals and corrosive bacteria. Over time, these build up and block the pipework, resulting in efficiency losses and leaks, "which are expensive to fix and harmful for the environment," says Wilkinson.

The brand's filtration system solves the problems by directing water from the heating system into a magnetised chamber, drawing out any metals inside. Water then passes through a second non-magnetic fine filter, where particles of hematite, biofilm and limescale are captured and eliminated.

Wilkinson recalls how installing an X-POT at a care home transformed lives for residents who were complaining of being cold and of leaking radiators. Within a week of a local mechanical contractor installing an X-POT, the complaints ended. "By winter," he says, "many residents kept their doors open as the heat from the radiators was so hot – even though there was snow outside."

Easy to retrofit, the X-POT improves a building's energy efficiency, in keeping with Vexo's emphasis on operational sustainability and its mission to help mitigate the climate crisis. "Repair call-outs are reduced, and you save on gas as you burn less," says Wilkinson. It is why, working with global strategic partners, such as Skidmore in North America or BSS and Travis Perkins in the UK, X-POTs are installed everywhere from Alaska to New Zealand, in locations from Westminster Abbey ("I did the survey myself," says Wilkinson) to football stadia, theatres, hospitals – even chocolate factories, where the X-POTs help keep assembly lines at a constantly cool temperature.

Vexo won The Queen's Award for Enterprise in Innovation in 2022, but Wilkinson says his contribution is small compared to those who have supported Vexo since its founding in 2010. "We turn up every time for our customers," he says. "That can't happen without our team, our supply chain and certainly our customers."

www.vexoint.com

The art of packaging

Wrapology's sustainable packaging ensures brands communicate
their story with the least amount of environmental impact

"Often, packaging is the first point of physical interaction with a brand. Packaging communicates the brand values: the materials used, how it feels and functions. The quality of workmanship mirrors the integrity of the product. Packaging is not just information on contents and brand," says Annika Bosanquet, who in 2001 co-founded Wrapology and what later became the family business. "Even the sound of packaging creates part of the experience, enhancing customer engagement."

Wrapology is a pioneer of a holistic, sustainable approach to packaging, putting the environment at the core of global supply-chain thinking. With more than 20 years of innovation in processes, materials, inks and, recently, digitisation, Wrapology has kept at the forefront of the global packaging market.

To minimise its impact, Wrapology uses a combination of approaches, such as value engineering (making the product smaller or using fewer materials), alongside sustainable manufacturing values (including the principle of mono materials for easier consumer kerbside recycling). "Not only does this reduce costs for everybody, it also delivers the options of the least amount of unnecessary handling for logistics and warehouse personnel and, in turn, reduces the amount of carbon used in the product life cycle," says Bosanquet.

Since production is shipped to over 22 countries, she notes that saving just a few millimetres on the depth of an advent calendar can make a cargo container-sized difference to the transport of a shipment, as well as reducing road freight, helping to lower budgetary, logistical and environmental impact. "It is essential we reduce the environmental impact of packaging and do everything we can to support businesses to reach net zero carbon by 2030," says Bosanquet. "This doesn't have to be at the expense of brand impact: we are approaching a new era of exciting commercial developments of materials, such as fabrics made from wood and using plant waste instead of plastics for packaging fitments."

To deliver the finest quality packaging for global luxury brands, Wrapology offers significant experience in material management and logistics, receiving the 2022 Queen's Award for Enterprise in International Trade. For localised control and transparency of production, Wrapology has teams in China, Hong Kong, Europe and the UK. "Recent investment in automated digital technology gives clients more control over an even more efficient and seamless transition, from initial concept to the final unboxing experience," says Bosanquet.

www.wrapology.com

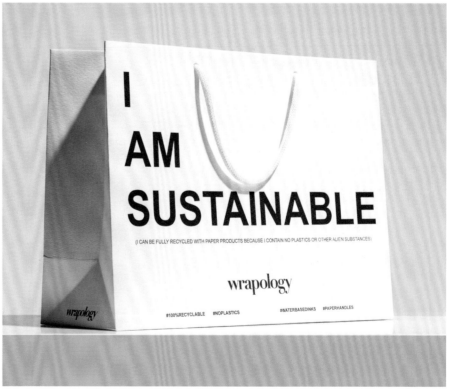

Building a railway legacy

Railway engineering company Xrail has developed a reputation for international trade excellence by breaking into new markets worldwide

"Now is an exciting time for a British company to be involved in international railway solutions," says Munir Patel, CEO of engineering company Xrail. "Britain has a long railway legacy and a wealth of expertise we can share with other countries that are developing their railway infrastructure. Saudi Arabia alone is set to build 8,000km of railway by 2050."

Patel is a London Export Champion, Chair of the Export Committee in the Railway Industry Association, and works closely with the Department for International Trade. Following a 17-year career with Transport for London, he founded Xrail in 2011. The company provides consultancy services, engineering solutions and project management support to main line railways and metro systems. It has expertise in the design, installation, testing and commissioning of new railways, as well as in maintenance, improvement and obsolescence management for existing railways.

"We established an early foothold in the Middle East, initially in Dubai and then Saudi Arabia, where we provide signalling systems, technical buildings and 24/7 support for a high-speed line from Mecca to Medina," says Patel. "The line was built by a Spanish company, which – after hearing about our performance in other Middle East projects – asked us to take over the maintenance services for the line; and then on the back of our performance in Saudi, asked us to do the same for the state-of-the-art Madrid–Levante line."

Xrail employs a 220-strong team in the UK, Spain and Saudi Arabia, and is exploring further opportunities in Taiwan, Turkey, Serbia and Australia. It received The Queen's Award for International Trade in 2022 for outstanding international growth over the previous three years. Overseas sales grew by 2,281 per cent during that period and the proportion of total sales exported increased from 9 to 73 per cent.

"Our focus is on building international relationships and using our expertise to develop and generate tangible value for our clients," says Patel. "In Saudi Arabia, in addition to our general maintenance teams, we have four British engineers training 12 local apprentices, which is a groundbreaking initiative in the country. Equally, we learn from our projects, clients and partners and are as passionate about reinvesting this knowledge and experience in the UK." A pioneer of the industry, Patel leads the way for other British railway suppliers to explore burgeoning markets.

www.xrailgroup.com

The modern monarch

A new Royal Family is emerging under the guidance of The King, as the celebration of His Majesty's official birthday demonstrated

As King Charles proudly rode out to inspect his soldiers of the Household Division for Trooping the Colour on 17 June 2023 to celebrate his official birthday, he was at last the lead actor in what for Brits has become a familiar annual stage show.

Now Colonel-in-Chief of the Household Division, Charles, whose real birthday is 14 November, rode on horseback throughout the two hours of military parade, reviewing and saluting his troops, his face barely visible due to the bearskin cap on his head and its chin strap. His late mother, Queen Elizabeth II, had last rode in the trooping in 1986.

George II started the tradition in 1748 when he moved his birthday celebrations to coincide with the annual military parade, as he thought it would be too cold for the public to be able to celebrate in November, his actual birth month. The ceremonial event itself dates back even further to the reign of Charles II in the 17th century, when regimental colours trooped in front of soldiers so they could recognise their unit in battle.

RIDING HIGH

Now it was Charles's big day. He was accompanied on horseback by his son and heir, Prince William – the Prince of Wales and Colonel of the Welsh Guards – and two of his siblings, Princess Anne, who is Senior Colonel of the Household Division, as well as Colonel of the Household Cavalry's Blues and Royals, and Prince Edward, the Duke of Edinburgh, who rode as Colonel of the London Guards, the army reserve battalion of the Guards Division, which was formed as a product of the military reforms in 2022.

"The Clarence House way is slowly but surely being introduced"

Previous page
King Charles and Queen Camilla wave from the balcony of Buckingham Palace after the Trooping the Colour parade

Opposite
The King sets out on horseback wearing his Welsh Guards uniform, in the company of his son William (left) and brother Edward

Above
A display of pageantry as regiments from the Household Division march along The Mall, joined by the Royal Family on horseback

Above
The Queen and the
Princess of Wales ride
in a carriage at the
parade, wearing
colours that represent
their regiments

Opposite
Members of the public
watch the RAF flypast
soaring above The
Mall, culminating in
the red, white and blue
of the Red Arrows

"In honour of the new king, 18 Typhoon fighter jets also drew out 'CR' for Charles Rex in a mesmerising display"

Queen Camilla, wearing a stylish scarlet military-style coat dress by Fiona Clare inspired by the Grenadier Guards, of which she is Colonel, rode in a carriage to Horse Guards with the Princess of Wales, dressed in green as a nod to her role as Colonel of the Irish Guards, with Prince George, Princess Charlotte and Prince Louis. Once again, it was Louis who delighted royal crowds when he pulled faces at his siblings and covered his ears and nose, making it appear as though he had smelt something unpleasant. At one point during the flypast, the young prince posed while pulling off a military-style salute.

The flypast featured 70 aircraft from the Royal Navy, British Army and the Royal Air Force in a six-minute spectacle. Crowds looked on in awe as Hurricane and Spitfire jets took to the skies and soared above Buckingham Palace. In honour of the new king, 18 Typhoon fighter jets also drew out "CR" for Charles Rex in a mesmerising display. A squadron of Red Arrows, the world-renowned RAF Aerobatic Team, then brought the event to a close as they ejected red, white and blue smoke into the sky above.

CHARLES IN CHARGE

For Charles, it was another first, as the first king to appear at the birthday parade since 1950, the last year George VI attended. With each royal landmark event his position as monarch becomes more established. The transition from the late queen to the new king now complete, there is a new "slimmed down" monarchy in play under Charles. Indeed, there were fewer royals on the main palace balcony, just Charles's team of working royals.

No Harry or Meghan, no Prince Andrew. The Clarence House way is slowly but surely being introduced, with Queen Camilla acting as his main enforcer. Mindful of the years of public service his late mother's first cousins have given to the crown, Charles has treated the Dukes of Kent and Gloucester with great respect, encouraging and inviting them to attend official receptions at the palace and family events. On the eve of Trooping the Colour, he went to see Princess Alexandra, the Queen's cousin, and a family member he has always been close to, as she had been poorly.

The King cares about his wider family but realises that changes must and will be made for the sake of the monarchy. It is not so much about have a streamlined monarchy – a notion that his own sister, Princess Anne, said "doesn't sound like a good idea" in an interview with CBC News – as it is about efficiency and expense.

What matters to The King is that the monarchy is cost-effective. Cuts must be made but not necessarily to the budget. For Charles, it is about getting value for money, for the monarchy and the people it serves.

Left
His Majesty's "slimmed down" version of the monarchy view the flypast from the main palace balcony

Connecting the world

With a global telecommunications infrastructure built on over 160 years of innovation, Alcatel Submarine Networks is an industry-leading provider

When the first transatlantic telegraph cable was sent by Queen Victoria to US President James Buchanan on 16 August 1858, it heralded a breakthrough moment in the formation of global communication, allowing an almost instantaneous connection between the US and Europe. Those undersea cables laid beneath the Atlantic Ocean were manufactured at a Thames-side factory in Greenwich, London, to which Alcatel Submarine Networks (ASN), founded in 1983, can trace its history. Operating from the same location – alongside other sites around the world, such as France and Norway – ASN produces the high-tech submarine cables that are essential for modern communication.

"Even today, 99 per cent of international data traffic is transmitted via underwater cable, rather than satellite," explains Taj Bhambra, Managing Director of the Greenwich site. "In terms of output, we have laid around 700,000 kilometres of cables under the sea, which is enough to circumnavigate the globe almost 18 times. Effectively, every person

on the planet who is connected to the internet is using equipment that in some way comes out of Greenwich, where it all started. So there is a huge sense of pride in our history but also our future. We talk about connecting people and connecting the world and are quietly proud of what we have achieved."

Cables laid by ASN allowed the world to function during the pandemic, as work, education and shopping gravitated online. It is also a measure of the company's status and accomplishments that in 2022 it received its eighth Queen's Award for Enterprise, in recognition of excellence in international trade and outstanding three-year growth in overseas sales. Rooted in British traditions of innovation and industry, the French-owned subsidiary is also part of Finland's pioneering Nokia Group.

ASN leads the global market in terms of transmission capacity, which it increases through the addition of new cable-laying ships and the creation of more efficient cables. The company's fleet of vessels lay several different kinds of single-core fibre cable, with varying levels of protection depending on the conditions on the seabed. Those close to the shore end and in the most turbulent parts of the ocean will be "double-armoured", or wrapped in several layers of steel wire. Others can be buried a few metres beneath the seabed. ASN is also exploring the development of multi-core fibre to increase transmission ability and meet the ever-increasing global demand for connectivity. Submerged equipment, from repeaters to branching units and terrestrial power feeding equipment, is produced on site in Greenwich, in tandem with the project management and marine operations teams housed there.

Innovation is part of what makes ASN so successful. As well as communications, the company supplies technology for other sectors, including oil and gas. Sensors developed for these industries can be placed on the sea floor to create a 3D picture of an oil field, which enables more efficient extraction. ASN is committed to climate action and these sensors will be integrated into repeaters to measure changes in sea temperature, aiding scientific research and therefore helping the journey towards sustainability. "We take a long-term view," says Bhambra. "We are custodians of a wonderful company and will leave it for the next generation. As a business we have been around for 160 years, and plan to be around for much longer. Alongside that commitment to innovation, we are looking to be more efficient, more sustainable and more environmentally conscious."

www.asn.com

In good hands

AP Security not only has 30 years of expertise in a
range of services, but also puts mentorship at its core

"My family and I are very much royalists, we love what they do, so I feel very privileged to have been involved in the late Queen's pageant, working security on The Mall," says Diane Mulkeirins, Director at AP Security, one of the largest independently owned security companies in the UK.

Founded as an events company in 1991, AP Security provides consultancy, on-site crowd management and other services. With offices in Hertfordshire and Sussex, it launched its Manned Guarding division in 2012, which ushered in further specialisms, including corporate security, mobile patrols and CCTV. The company now employs up to a thousand people.

"We are very keen on our own social responsibility as a company," explains Mulkeirins. "A lot of people pay lip service to it, but we aim to be givers. People and charities come to us for help if they cannot afford security, and then we will work a resolution that suits the client. We have also been working closely with the charity Dare2Dream, whereby we go into schools and mentor students over about four months.

"Because there is so much pressure on kids these days to produce, to go to university, we show them they can have a career path and it doesn't have to be in that academic arena, per se. They can achieve financial security as, for instance, a director, by starting out as a security officer."

Some AP Security employees are doing Open University courses, but everyone is supported to learn and train, whether it is a Level 2 NVQ or NEBOSH (National Examination Board in Occupational Safety and Health). The company's own training school was also set up to upskill those with careers in the security industry or to help new recruits.

AP Security recognises that while society is working towards equal opportunities for women in the workforce, the security sector is still weighted towards men (only ten per cent of people in the industry are women). However, AP Security wants to change that, not only with its school programmes, but also with its recruitment drives.

"A lot of young girls come along to training and they ask lots of questions, and we give them the opportunity to find out what their role could be. We recently worked with a number of people from all ages on a personal safety course, where we showed them how to read a situation and learn from a situation. It is a programme that we offered for free."

As part of their charity work, the team raise funds for the Children with Cancer Fund. "We've called our efforts 'Around the World in AP Days' and are all walking as many miles as we can, plotting our distances to get 'around the world'. It will take a while, but it is keeping us all fit, as well as raising money."

Another of the company's commitments is as a signatory to the Armed Forces Covenant, a pledge acknowledging that those who serve, or who have served, in the armed forces should be treated with fairness and respect. AP Security achieved the Silver Award in 2022, and it is now going for gold.

"We're happy as a company," says Mulkeirins. "We have employees from a lot of diverse backgrounds, many ex-military men, but they all come together under the AP banner. They all have to be licensed and Level 3 First Aid trained. These guys are tough, but they will look after you, too."

www.apsecurity.co.uk

Cooked to perfection

With ambitions to be indispensable in every kitchen, MEATER's wireless thermometer is transforming the cooking of meat, fish and poultry

From a simple family meal to a convivial barbecue with friends, nothing can ruin the experience quite as much as undercooked or overcooked meat. And if the cook is busy focusing on the meat, the rest of the meal might get overlooked. To solve this problem, friends Joseph Cruz, Teemu Nivala and Wen Nivala tried to use a wire-connected meat thermometer, only for the wire to get damaged and, before they noticed, the meal ruined. This led the trio – all of whom had hardware and software engineering experience – to design MEATER, a wireless smart meat thermometer that can be monitored via a dedicated app.

"They looked at the meat thermometer and thought, 'Why can't this be wireless?'," says Daniel Hartshorn, MEATER's Head of People. "After doing some research, they realised there was nothing like this available. You can get an instant read with a meat thermometer, but they are hard to use and you need to know what you are doing. MEATER is very simple to use and can be used for all kinds of meat, fish or poultry. We believe that we are democratising high-quality food through technology."

Founded in Leicester in 2015, MEATER also has offices in the US and Taiwan, from where it gains valuable feedback about different global markets. It was launched following a wildly successful crowdfunding campaign – the target of $180,000 was achieved in 48 hours – and has gone on to take the culinary world by storm. The meat thermometer market is worth $900 million in the US alone, with huge potential in other parts of the world where meat consumption is high, such as Australia, Latin America and Europe. MEATER's versatility, from grilling a couple of chicken breasts to barbecuing a whole pig or cow, also means it can be used for kombucha, a fermented tea.

The kombucha usage was discovered by one of MEATER's customers, many of whom have become avid fans of the product, constantly finding new ways to employ the technology. These fans include leading chefs on both sides of the Atlantic who are excited by the potential. "One chef in the UK trained under Alain Ducasse," says Hartshorn. "He has explained that MEATER allows him to share some of his more complex recipes with a wider audience, as it gives

users the confidence to successfully cook at a high standard, which makes them want to do it again and again. Then they can think about some of the other elements, such as aesthetics or side dishes."

The company continues to listen to its users as it grows, seeking to improve, refine and update the thermometer with new software. MEATER maintains a unique hold in the market but aims to become as important a utensil in any kitchen as the wooden spoon or spatula. Meanwhile, innovation includes an entirely new product that Hartshorn describes as another "world first".

"We feel we have a substantial edge in terms of the technology," says Hartshorn. "Our competitors are trying to catch up with what we have already achieved, while our R&D department is already cooking up some extraordinary follow-up products. You have to innovate and invest. We have shown there is a huge market and appetite for the product and our journey is very much about the customer, as we know we wouldn't be here without them."

www.meater.com

Keeping it local

Celebrating an area's character is of prime importance to the City Pub Group, as is being central to the community

When we want to celebrate an occasion – of national, local or personal importance – we often do so in a pub. People in the UK have gathered in pubs for decades, and while pubs have changed over the years, they remain the centre of any community, where people can meet and enjoy the company of friends – and strangers. Many of the finest are in cities, and the best of these are often owned by the City Pub Group, a group of pubs mainly in the South of England and Wales that offer a unique experience based on a shared philosophy.

"City Pub Group is a collection of individual pubs, each catering to their local territory," explains Clive Watson, who co-founded the company in 2011 and is Group Chairman. "There aren't many places where people can meet their friends or people from the same area who share their interests and tastes, and the pub creates that space."

It goes without saying, Watson is a passionate fan of the British pub. "We don't impose our brand across the great cities of England and South Wales – we want to create places that people identify with and feel are their own. That is what underlies it. It's very much about local beer and local food, and allowing our managers to engage with local events and charities. Our staff have support as they are part of a wider team, but they can do things they know locals will enjoy."

It is an approach that saw the group's pubs celebrate the Platinum Jubilee in 2022 with street parties and live music. Similar events were planned for the Coronation of King Charles, according to what was locally appropriate. This acknowledges that what works at The Tivoli in Cambridge (opposite, bottom left and right), a grand old Art Deco cinema converted into a bar, offering food, shuffleboards, indoor golf and two roof terraces overlooking the River Cam, will be different to what is required at Potters, a handsome traditional pub in the heart of Newport in Wales.

The City Pub Group gains its understanding of local habits by building clusters of pubs – seven in Cambridge, four in Norfolk, four in Bath and Bristol, several in London, plus more in other pockets of the South East, South West and Wales. This allows staff to work across the group and enjoy career progression while retaining their knowledge and love of community.

Pubs have had to adapt to survive. For the City Pub Group, that means having pubs with rooms, such as the elegant 15-room Aragon House in Parsons Green, west London (so named because Catherine of Aragon stayed there after separating from Henry VIII); the recently opened Pride of Paddington, ideal for the short trip to Heathrow on the new Elizabeth Line; or The Oyster House (opposite, top right) overlooking Swansea Bay in Wales.

It also means putting on events – from bingo to pub quizzes – as well as serving great food, hot drinks, non-alcoholic beers and wines, plus beers, spirits and wines from local producers. In Bath, the group's new Bath Cider House (opposite, top left) has become a magnet for cider lovers, while Daly's Wine Bar in the City of London has turned into a long-standing landmark. In addition, the company runs six brew houses in different cities that draw on regional brewing heritage.

Watson reflects on the main influence behind setting up the company and its future growth. "The reason we started City Pub Group is that we love our different cities and their characteristics, and we felt there weren't enough pubs that celebrated those things. We want to create great pubs for all these great cities in the UK."

www.citypubcompany.com

Natural performance

Born out of the need for a high-performing, environmentally sound deodorant, AKT London's premium, natural balms are shaking up the industry

It was while performing in the West End in London that Andy Coxon and Ed Currie took on the challenge of finding a good deodorant. The pair performed in eight shows a week in the same costumes, and they could not find any product that would keep them fresh throughout their gruelling schedule. "No matter what we tried, they stained our costumes and did not give that all-day protection they promised," says Coxon.

In addition, they found the deodorant industry outdated. "Everything is pink and flowery for women, and black, silver and 'fire' for men," says Coxon. So they started experimenting with formulas that would prevent odours, smell more appealing than existing deodorants and most importantly, perform as they did. The process took three years, until in 2018 "we nailed it" and The Deodorant Balm by AKT London was born – natural, plastic-free and gender-free.

What had started as a way of solving their own problem quickly snowballed. "We sent samples to every single performer in the West End, launched a Kickstarter, and everyone went absolutely nuts for it," says Coxon. When the pandemic hit, closing theatres, they focused full-time on their business, with a mission "to give you the confidence to step onto your stage – whatever that may be – and perform".

AKT's Deodorant Balm has since won awards from *Tatler*, *Harper's Bazaar*, *Marie Claire*, *Cosmopolitan* and more. They offer five gender-neutral fragrances with names inspired by scenes in a script such as Orange Grove and After Thunder, while the plastic-free, aluminium tubes and caps are recyclable. "A recent survey found that 71 per cent of beauty consumers are looking for sustainable options," says Coxon. "They are searching for those products that are making a difference and being innovative – but many big brands still rely on plastic." Plus, he explains, "aerosols now pollute more than cars in this country and 80 per cent of consumers are unhappy with their deodorant."

The success of AKT's Deodorant Balm suggests an appetite for something new. Following expansion into the US, the company is extending its range of products. "We get so much feedback from people saying this is the best deodorant they've ever used and that it's changed their life," says Coxon. "Hearing that makes it all worthwhile."

www.aktlondon.com

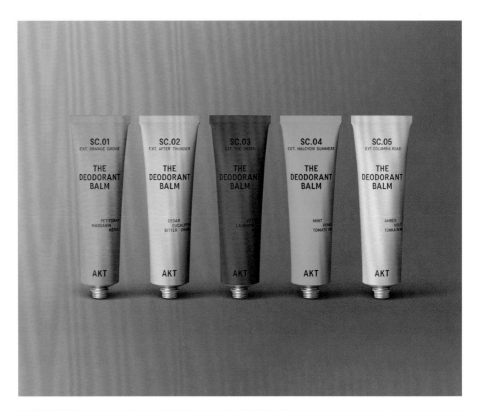

Best in show

Avant Garden has taken garden wares to new heights with its online
offering of bronze sculptures, water features and garden furniture

"Exclusivity is key. Nobody else is doing what I do," says Nick Martel. "And now I've taken it further afield, it's growing all the time." Martel has been running Avant Garden, a unique online, high-end garden shop, since 2000. Selling bronze sculptures and statues, with almost 600 different pieces in the collection, Avant Garden offers everything from 6ft-tall stags to exotic birds, and from exquisite water features to dancing ballerinas. The company also provides garden furniture by the century-old, family-owned British manufacturer Barlow Tyrie, which perfectly complement the bronzes. "Barlow Tyrie only uses the finest teak, marine-grade stainless steel and brass fittings," says Martel. "Everything is the best."

Martel's horticultural roots stretch back generations; his grandparents on both sides were horticulturalists and his parents ran a nursery and garden centre in Guernsey. While Martel is well known on the island for the calibre of his work, in recent years he has expanded the business, with a customer base now stretching the globe. Avant Garden has been found at prestige events as the National Game Fair at Ragley Hall, Warwickshire, the Royal Horticultural Society's Chelsea Flower Show and the Spirit of Christmas Fair at Olympia. "We're branching out and investigating possibilities," says Martel. "The whole business has changed – it's been really rejuvenating and a joy."

The company's evolution from a bricks and mortar shop in Guernsey to an online-only retailer with a worldwide market has meant that the quality of Avant Garden's products has been put to the test, so they can withstand a wide range of elements. "Everything is tried and tested here," says Martel. "Guernsey is extremely tough weather-wise because you have high salt, high humidity, high sun, and so things are going to fade, corrode, rust or break down one way or another." Bronze, however, "just goes on forever".

The 100 per cent bronze statues – made in Europe by sculptor Ben Wouters – are not only beautiful in terms of design and elegance but double up as a truly sustainable option to become embedded into families for generations. "Some people just end up discarding stuff," says Martel. "Whereas what we produce can be handed down. They become proper works of art, and, once people realise that and they enjoy the experience, they become hooked."

www.avantgardenbronzes.com

Face value

A stalwart of the high street, FatFace's inimitable style is
a huge success story across the UK and North America

"We have been honoured to work with The Prince's Trust over the past 15 years in a variety of different ways, whether it's getting young people to design products with us or participating in the Palace to Palace bike ride," says FatFace CEO Will Crumbie. FatFace has forged a close relationship with the Trust and been inspired by the partnership. "When you see the output and the transformation that happens with these young people, it's phenomenal. They bring so much energy and ideas and excitement."

Over three decades, FatFace has presented an exciting front for British fashion, bringing its multichannel lifestyle clothing proposition to the UK and across the pond. Alongside a thriving international digital business, the company has over 180 stores throughout the UK and Ireland, as well as more than 20 in North America, and a recent launch into Canada.

FatFace began in the ski resorts of France in the late 1980s, with two friends selling t-shirts and jackets to fund their love of skiing. The pair were savvy enough to record the addresses of their customers. They noted that many lived in west London, which is where they opened their first shop, in Fulham. Since then, FatFace has become a high street favourite and great British success story, employing more than 2,000 people. In 2016, FatFace entered the US market and opened the first Canadian store in 2023.

Stemming from its strong connection to The Prince's Trust, FatFace works with young designers who have emerged from the charity's Tomorrow's Talent programme. In addition, the company has partnered with the Trust to raise funds for International Women's Day, celebrating the achievements of women across the world, including its own female staff. Overall, the FatFace Foundation has given more than £2 million to good causes in the past 13 years.

The brand has embraced a commitment to sustainability, placing it at the heart of its business. FatFace has been carbon neutral for more than two years and is now on a mission to achieve net zero status. "For us, sustainability is a guiding principle supported by the direction The King has taken," says Crumbie. "One of our mantras is about creating a community, so inclusion is very important to us. I would really love it if the next CEO came to us after starting out as a store manager or from a more junior role. That's something The Prince's Trust has taught us."

As part of its multichannel strategy, FatFace still invests in physical stores even as the online business expands. The brand has now evolved from its origins in extreme sports to sell everything from printed dresses to babygrows, but always with a clear product DNA: considered style, trusted quality, sustainably sourced. "The product is essential in our world," says Crumbie. "You have to get that right. It is about being at the edge of what you can give your customer; you need to give them something exciting and that means continually refreshing what you do. Our opportunity lies in getting that beautiful product in front of even more customers."

Next is FatFace's focus on North America. "Canada combines the Britishness of the Commonwealth with an American influence that is very exciting for us. North America has been a successful market and we believe there's much more to come."

www.fatface.com

Going the extra mile

Leading by example, National Windscreens is a driving force for good sustainable practice and customer service

"We're an industry where people talk a lot of about ESG [Environmental, Social and Governance], but if I'm honest more could be done," says Mike Rotin, Director of National Windscreens, the UK-wide vehicle glass repair and replacement specialist. "We want to address that and lead the way for our industry."

Simple things can have a big impact, he explains, from vegetable oil fuels that can now be run in diesel vehicles to the electrification of cars, particularly in the cities. "It's about getting the ship pointing in the right direction and trying to bring everyone along on the journey."

Rotin feels he has a vested interest in the process of sustainability, of reducing the carbon output of every element in his work. "It's not a cost-driven exercise – it's very important that we set the standard for future generations. I have grandchildren and I dread to think what things could be like when they're adults. It's a real issue."

Set up as a membership organisation in the 1970s, National Windscreens has been working with its members to align its values with those set out by the Cary Group, a leading car care services provider with whom the company has worked since 2018, offering sustainable solutions for the repair and replacement of vehicle glass. National Windscreens also works with major insurers to "drive some different behaviours around sustainability", and Rotin is heartened by the positive response he has received from the sector.

Time was when windscreens were simply things to look out of, to keep the wind at bay. Today, they contain multiple technologies – cameras, sensors – with further developments to come. "We're seeing windscreens with touch-screen technology, driverless cars. The world is going to really change in terms of the technology that's there." For Rotin, the challenge is to ensure that when a vehicle with a damaged screen comes into one of their workshops the complex systems it contains remain intact. "There is a real focus on the quality and care of the workmanship, repair and replacement – the onus is on us to make sure we're giving the consumer their vehicle back with these safety systems operating as intended."

The onus is also on the customer to ensure that a chip in a screen is repaired quickly so that it does not develop into an outright crack. Screen replacement carries its own carbon cost. "We're working with insurers as to how to get the consumer to get that repair done as soon as possible – maybe by reducing the excess payment on repairs as both a commercial and environmental incentive."

Customer service and the customer journey are key to National Windscreens. The company has invested heavily to ensure that customers receive the highest quality service, from training technicians in customer support, to ensuring its centres are comfortable environments conducive to talking through with customers about why repair is better than replacement, to get the message to trickle down.

Rotin hopes that good service and a determination to go the extra mile in terms of good sustainable practice can be an example to others. "We're challenging the business to forget the old ways. It will require investment, but if you don't do anything at some point, someone's going to tell you what to do. I'd rather be in control of our own destiny than have a regulator come along with a big stick and tell me to do it."

www.nationalwindscreens.co.uk

On the ocean wave

Reinventing holidays at sea, P&O Cruises is on an evolving journey
to offer extraordinary travel experiences in a distinctively British way

Whenever a P&O Cruises ship enters a port, it flies the Union Flag proudly as it brings British guests to different corners of the world. This quintessentially British company was founded in 1837 and is now synonymous with cruising. In one poll, when asked to name a cruise company 97 per cent of respondents answered P&O Cruises. But more than this, P&O Cruises believes it represents the best of Britain – literally flying the flag around the world. No more so than with the company's two newest ships, Iona and Arvia, which lead the company's efforts towards a more sustainable future.

"They are the largest ships ever designed and operated in Britain, and they use liquefied natural gas, the cleanest fossil fuel available and a real step forward for the industry," says P&O Cruises President Paul Ludlow. "That met with a lot of praise, and it is a real testament to the investment we are making towards sustainability. We have two of the most innovative ships operating anywhere in the world, we fly the Union Flag wherever we go, and we see ourselves as representing Britain around the world. We take British people on holiday in a familiar environment while they explore the world."

That means P&O Cruises has become adept at predicting what British people want from their holidays, often having to think several years in advance of current trends. This approach considers the five core ingredients of any great holiday – dining, entertainment, destinations, service and partnerships. The company works with the best of the best across these pillars including chef and restaurateur Marco Pierre White, drinks expert Olly Smith, chefs Shivi Ramoutar and José Pizarro, as well as pop stars Gary Barlow and Nicole Scherzinger. The company also has partners such as *Time Out* travel and entertainment guides, Salcombe Gin, The Tidal Rum and a new headline sponsorship with BAFTA Television Awards.

"If you are going to be an expression of Britain, you have to be relevant to Britain and that relevance changes constantly," explains Ludlow. "People's tastes are always evolving and that in turn changes what they want from the holiday experience. We need to reflect that and be ahead of trends. We want our guests to have a great holiday – filled with memorable moments and experiences they can talk about proudly."

It is an approach that has reaped rewards – with a very high rate of repeat guests and an evolving and younger demographic. Different itineraries attract different guests – from a 99-night round-the-world cruise to very popular Caribbean and Mediterranean destinations, short breaks around northern Europe, the scenic Norway fjords and much more. On-board elements are adapted correspondingly. P&O Cruises constantly improves, refines and fine-tunes its offering, while strengthening relationships with governments and tourist boards across the world, which appreciate the economic, social and cultural value provided by British guests.

"It's about never sitting back," says Ludlow. "We need to think like a challenger not a market leader, looking for anything that will help push us forward. Our ambition is not just to grow within the cruise space, but the holiday market in general, so we pay attention to those wider trends and see that as the opportunity for growth and improvement. Whether it's on-board or on-shore experiences, service or sustainability, we constantly look outside our space to keep moving and to stay desirable."

www.pocruises.com

Solace for the skin

Made from natural fabrics, Solpardus swimwear is ethically
produced and the perfect partner for those with sensitive skin

Swimwear should feel as fabulous as it looks. This simple maxim inspired Freya Bickford to start her own swimwear company, Solpardus, making beautiful bikinis and swimsuits from fabric made from bamboo, as well as soft linen trousers, shirts, dresses and hats. Freya formed the brand because of her psoriasis, a skin condition that was agitated by the artificial fabrics used by most swimwear manufacturers.

The Solpardus story began in Cornwall during lockdown. Stress had caused Freya's psoriasis to flare up, and she was keen to safely get some sun on her skin. "I have had psoriasis since I was 11, and I know that, for me, spending small amounts of time in the sun helps massively," she explains. "Do it safely and you could reap the benefits."

While looking for her swimwear, Freya realised that everything she owned was synthetic, and harsh against her sensitive skin. She wondered if there was anybody selling natural alternatives to the synthetic materials that swimming costumes are made from. "When I couldn't find any in the UK, I decided to make them myself."

Using fabric made from bamboo and her sewing machine, Freya created her own bikini. It was a success, and her company was born, with a focus on simple, timeless designs and the highest-quality materials and finishes. She named the company Solpardus, meaning "sun leopard" in Latin, after coming across a positive message on social media.

"I saw a woman talking about her psoriasis," says Freya. "She was saying that when it starts to heal in the sun, you have lost the pigment, so you have this pattern that is like a leopard print on the body. Previously, I would get embarrassed or self-conscious and try to cover it up, but I could now see that this actually shows how far I have come. When you are over the hump of the flare-up and starting to heal, it's special."

While the label's designs are ideal for people with skin conditions such as psoriasis and eczema, or for those recovering from cancer treatment, they are also perfect for anybody whose skin is easily irritated by synthetic material or who simply prefer the feel and philosophy of natural textiles. Until the 1950s, swimwear was made from cotton or wool, and Solpardus is putting the focus on the use of natural materials once again. Bamboo fabrics are already used elsewhere in sportswear; and with the plant requiring considerably less water to grow than other natural materials, it is a more eco-friendly option.

The company works with small British businesses, ensuring "less continuous purchasing, less waste, less disappointment". Biodegradable, sustainable buttons made from British milk are produced in Gloucestershire, while a business in Brighton sources Indian silk sari scraps, otherwise destined for landfill, but given a new lease of life as Solpardus drawstrings. All Solpardus garments are then proudly manufactured, both ethically and sustainably, in London.

Freya hopes that Solpardus will help more people think about the relationship between clothing and skin. With further products in the pipeline, she wants to encourage conversations. "We want to work alongside skin charities to ask what people both want and need from their fashion choices. Solpardus is great for the skin. It's comfortable, but it also encourages confidence," she says. And it empowers the wearer, too. "Our aim is for no one to have to choose between comfort and style. When you look good you can feel amazing, and it's incredible the health benefits this can offer, especially for skin."

www.solpardus.co.uk

The change maker

With experience shaping company strategy of the largest corporates,
Cintamani Group is well-placed to support business leaders to success

When top businesses need help with strategy and development, they turn to Corporate Strategies and Executive Coach Ngan Nguyen. With 15 years of business guidance experience, including working for management consultancy firm McKinsey & Company, Nguyen is the first choice for many Fortune 500 companies. "It's about looking at what organisations are trying to achieve and helping them create the impact they want," she says.

Based in London after a decade in Boston, Nguyen set up consultancy business Cintamani Group in 2017, working with a hand-picked team who share her vision. "We're a small firm, and we're selective about the projects we work on, so we can really deliver impact and value for our clients," she says.

The business is named after the Cintamani Stone, a gemstone that in Buddhist mythology is said to unlock wisdom and higher knowledge. Similarly, Nguyen's integrated approach combines holistic principles with cutting-edge, science-based research and sound business strategy to reinforce the ultimate goal of having a positive influence on the world. "We want to work with clients who have an inspiring mission, so we can be the catalyst to bring together the right people and partners to help them thrive."

Nguyen guides her team towards the best result while managing the client relationship. "It's about delivering what is needed at the company level, alongside adding value and being aware of the needs of the market," she says. A recent project involved working with the International Association of Women, a global organisation that encourages collaboration and conversations that support equity and the professional development of women worldwide. "The mission is to help the membership thrive – to dream, rise and lead."

Establishing a positive workplace is important. "I'm conscious of making sure we grow and implement the strategies and tools we recommend to clients internally," says Nguyen. "Our goal is empowering people, our greatest assets, to work at their best. Happy people live up to their skills and can do more."

Nguyen has a philosophical approach about the future. She wants her business to grow slowly and build a solid foundation, rather than chase revenue and risk sacrificing people's development or lifestyle. "As I build this business, I'm learning that it's about the journey and not the destination," she says.

www.cintamanigroup.com

As right as rain

Protecting the public from downpours for more than six decades,
Fulton's famous umbrellas are intertwined in British heritage

"I remember once seeing film of The Queen visiting Canada," says Nigel Fulton, CEO of Fulton Umbrellas, whose company supplies the Royal Family. "It was gale force, the crowds were on the runway, umbrellas turning inside out, lying broken on the ground. And the camera pans to The Queen emerging from the plane with a Fulton umbrella, the Birdcage. And I'm thinking, oh God, please let it hold out. But it stayed rock steady over her shoulders. I was so delighted."

Fulton needed to have nothing to fear. Unlike some more expensive designer umbrellas, Fulton's are meticulously engineered and rigorously tested in wind tunnels to cope with the worst of the elements. "If our umbrellas can't stand up to the wind, they'll end up in the bin," says Fulton. "I've seen umbrellas retailing at £400; beautiful fabric, walnut handles, but the frames are cheap and nasty. The ribs will break at the first gust of wind."

The story of the company began in 1956, when Fulton's father Arnold set up a workshop in Whitechapel, London. With a degree in mechanical engineering, and a passion for taking an everday object and analysing every aspect to make improvements, he decided to specialise in umbrellas, acquiring his first major client, Selfridges, in 1957. Today, Fulton enjoys 30 per cent of the UK market share, with clients including John Lewis, Paul Smith, the National Gallery, Fortnum & Mason and the Wimbledon Tennis Championships.

Fulton shares his father's passion to create the lightest, most compact, most resilient brollies in the world. However, times have changed since the 1950s, when you could have any colour umbrella you liked "so long as it was black". Today, Fulton umbrellas come in a range of prints and styles, with a particular emphasis on sustainability, leading the field in making much of its fabric from recycled plastic bottles.

The team at Fulton continue to upgrade their umbrellas, incorporating discreet yet telling improvements of materials, mechanisms and fabrics. But while such details preoccupy and fascinate Fulton, he acknowledges that these subtleties are not always obvious. "I'm glad people don't notice some of these things because it means there isn't an issue. For us, it's a case of buy once, not ten times."

www.fultonumbrellas.com

Aiming for the stars

Space Forge is fundamentally changing the way materials of the future are manufactured, by sending them into space

Making semiconductors is a notoriously tricky business. The deliberate introduction of impurities to these valuable materials, known as "doping", allows us to control their conductivity, and therefore apply them in a variety of uses from phones and aeroplanes to healthcare and navigational equipment. Cardiff-based scaleup Space Forge aims to take all the delicate processes involved – made even more difficult by aspects such as gravity and unwanted substances present in the atmosphere – and instead carry them out in the one place that lacks those factors completely: Low Earth Orbit.

"The way that most space companies use space is as the ultimate high ground," explains Chief Executive Joshua Western, who co-founded Space Forge in 2018. "But two of the most underused aspects of space in terms of how we use it are microgravity and a high-purity vacuum. Just by being there, you start with a much better manufacturing baseline than Earth, which allows you to create more than 100 different types of materials."

Once in orbit, the manufacturing facilities aboard Space Forge's satellites will afford its clients the ability to fashion these exotic materials completely autonomously. To start with, the company is concentrating on supplying compounds for the next generation of semiconductors. "They are very challenging to grow," explains Western, "deposited on substrates literally atom by atom. It's a slow process, and usually a hot one, too, running at about 1,000C. Earth's gravity prevents us from creating the purest of compounds, in space that isn't a problem; you're able to grow much purer crystal structures, which effectively reduces the energy use associated with these chips."

As such, chips manufactured using substances assembled in orbit have the potential to unlock new efficiencies in power usage back on Earth. Their potential to boost sustainability across a range of sectors is immense, believes Western. "We're not that far away from being able to deploy these semiconductors into 5G mobile towers, electric-vehicle car chargers, aerospace systems, or into the National Grid to improve electricity transmission, so less energy is wasted in getting energy from power stations into people's homes."

That only works, however, if Space Forge can get the materials down to Earth in one piece. Fortunately, Western has a plan for that. After the satellite is de-orbited, the craft unfurls an umbrella-like parachute that allows it to float back down to the surface at a gentler pace than most other man-made objects that re-enter the atmosphere. "Not to get too much into the kind of science and engineering of it," says Western, "but it's best described as Mary Poppins from space."

Targeted landing zones for Space Forge satellites include in the Australian outback, a section of the Welsh coast and a patch of the Atlantic Ocean off Portugal. All that remains is a successful launch and retrieval operation. After a false start in January 2023 due to a fault on the Virgin Orbit rocket carrying Space Forge's satellite, the company has been preparing for its next attempt at reaching outer space in early 2024.

"We've started producing semiconductor substrates on the ground, conducted high-altitude drop tests, subjected the craft to simulated micrometeorite impacts – in fact, we've really run out of things to do on the ground," says Western. All that remains for Space Forge is to reach the final frontier. "It's all hands on deck to finish our next mission, which should be on a launcher in the next few months."

www.spaceforge.co.uk

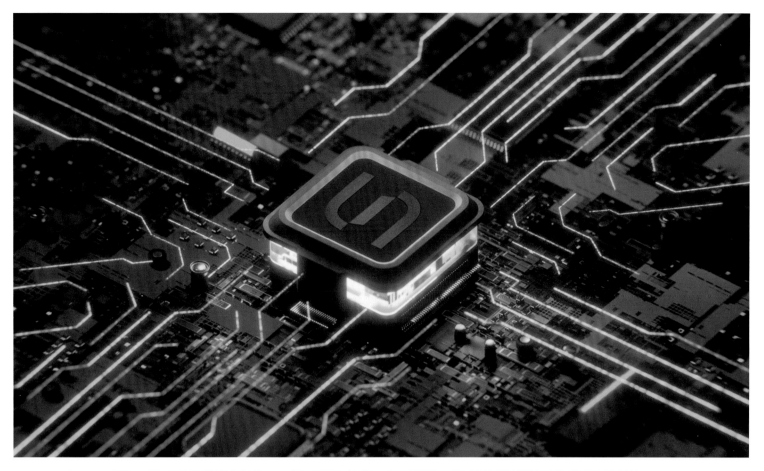

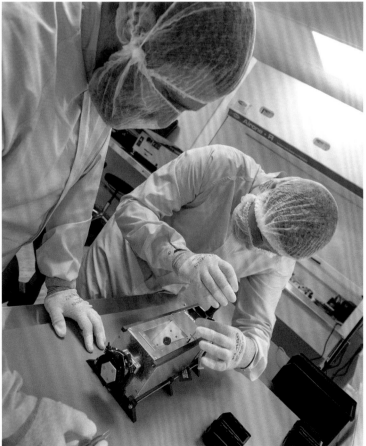

Causing a stir

Tea Cups London's quintessentially British tea sets are infused with rock and roll spirit, made using quality vegan-friendly materials

For touring rock musicians, the long hours spent travelling from gig to gig can lead to a hankering for the comforts of home. The three siblings who form the British-Italian band Miccoli have been writing songs and playing live for years – but when they are not performing perfect three-part harmonies on stage, their dressing-room conversations invariably revolve around their yearning for a proper cup of tea.

"We were always on the road and got fed up drinking tea out of plastic and paper cups," says Alessio Miccoli. "We were all of the opinion that tea tastes better out of proper china, but in every canteen in every arena we were getting paper or Styrofoam cups. When we couldn't tour during lockdown, we wanted to do something creative, so we turned to our second love, which is tea."

And the result, Tea Cups London, was established in 2020. All three siblings – Alessio, Adriano and Francesca – poured their collective energy into the project, initially researching fine bone china to find a vegan-friendly alternative. "Utilising a natural composite material instead of animal bone ash, Tea Cups London has crafted elegant tea sets, maintaining the delicate, translucent and

pearl-like qualities of fine bone china, all without using animal products," says Alessio.

The trio have collaborated on the designs, seeking out classic children's book illustrations, such as John Tenniel's whimsical work on *Alice in Wonderland*, or EH Shepard's evocative drawings of Winnie-the-Pooh, and creating beautiful patterns of them to adorn their teapots and cups.

Tea Cups London has also expanded beyond tea cups, offering items such as teaspoons and tea strainers as well as porcelain travel mugs, and the siblings are preparing to launch a range based on their own illustrations, taken from Adriano's drawings of famous city skylines. Products are currently available online and in selected retail outlets, but Alessio says they are targeting department stores that share their love for the classic British aesthetic, vegan-friendly material and tea.

Alessio, Adriano and Francesca have found this venture to be a refreshing and productive outlet for their artistic side. "Our creative juices have truly found a new canvas in this venture," says Francesca. "We are drawing and designing our new line ourselves, incorporating our own music into our adverts, and sharing responsibilities in design,

admin and marketing." We enjoy working together. I guess it has been instilled in us very early on – through the Italian side of our family – to be very family-orientated." Running Tea Cups London together has also allowed its three founders to apply the business skills they learned as musicians to another industry. "Navigating through the realms of writing, recording and producing music is as much an entrepreneurial journey as it is a creative one," says Alessio.

That craving for a good cup of tea when out on the road is something the Miccoli siblings have found to be a common feeling among their fellow musicians. Tea Cups London can even boast members of the rock and roll aristocracy among its fans. "Bringing our own cups on tour has undeniably enriched our experience," says Alessio. "Working alongside our management team, which has guided legendary acts such as Genesis, Phil Collins and Nick Mason, among others, we've found ourselves using our tea cups and 'tea talk' as an icebreaker in backstage conversations, surprisingly sparking interest. We think that tea is definitely becoming the new rock and roll."

www.teacupslondon.com

Protecting privacy

Titan Security Technologies safeguards online communications with a single comprehensive suite of services that users can really trust

Having spent their careers helping people through their jobs in law enforcement and the US military, with the strong sense of personal duty and responsibility that that entailed, Lars Allred and Tracy Hadley Green knew exactly how to provide the physical security that allows people to go about their daily lives in confidence and safety. When the pair decided they wanted to use their skills to help individuals on a global scale, it made sense to focus on cybersecurity. Titan Security Technologies promises ultimate security in a digital world – but it does more than that: the company was launched with a pledge to always do things differently to its peers.

"When we started this company, we were determined to set ourselves apart from our competitors," says Allred. "We know that there are other companies out there that promise privacy and offer secure communications, but they don't always have the best ethics. We wanted people to know they can trust us right from the start by operating with complete transparency. Many security companies sell your information even when they promise they won't, or they have

data breaches even though they claim to be completely secure. We wanted to be different."

Titan Security Technologies, headquartered in the UK, promises superior encryption and protocols that surpass all other security services. The company uses a VPN (virtual private network) to encrypt an internet connection, cloaking online activities and shielding any personal or sensitive data from potential threats. It reduces the risk of identity theft, cyberstalking or unwarranted surveillance. Titan can also provide secure communications, such as end-to-end encrypted email, that can be read only by the intended recipient. Titan cannot access a user's account, demands no personal information – not even email – and accepts cash or cryptocurrency for those who prefer not to use a credit card.

Allred and Hadley Green believe that privacy and security are inalienable rights, so offer a "freemium" model, providing basic services for free to anybody in the world. This reflects a wider outlook that is rooted in ethics and empathy. "One thing we are looking forward to as we grow is to start a non-profit so we can give something back," says Hadley Green. "Titan is all about the global, but we want to use the non-profit to focus on the local and help those in our community who are the most vulnerable. We have both worked with military veterans and with people who have experienced domestic violence. We can help these people with our products to make sure their data is secure, and privacy is guaranteed, but we can help them in other ways. We feel as if we are here to give back to our fellow man."

Titan has plans to expand its range. Products in the pipeline include a secure operating system combining multiple privacy features that will allow a device to be used in a warzone or other situation where security could be compromised. An additional plan is to develop a "security token", which would be like a more secure cryptocurrency – one that, unlike Bitcoin, cannot be traced or hacked. "Titan is security you can actually trust," says Allred. "That summarises everything we promise into a single sentence. People can try and copy the tech, but they can't copy the principles."

www.titansecuritysuite.com

The new space age

Covering more than 200 cities globally, workspace marketplace
Hubble offers companies a flexible solution to hybrid working

Since the Covid pandemic, it is no longer a given that everybody needs to work in an office from nine till five, five days a week. However, for Tushar Agarwal, the question of why companies use permanent office space was firmly on his radar since he co-founded his company, Hubble, in 2014.

A global office rental marketplace, Hubble specialises in finding flexible, furnished office space, available on-demand. "We realised that companies don't want office space – they want a happy, productive workforce," says Agarwal, the CEO.

"Today, some companies have offices that sit empty four days a week. So, they've got to think about letting go of their lease deal and working on a 'pay as you use' basis. We have companies now paying 75 per cent less for office space than they were before – and their employees are happier, having choice as to when and where to work."

With options for office space hire from three days a week to an hour at a time, and covering more than 200 cities worldwide, Hubble mediates between businesses and office providers, helping them to adapt to the new, flexible world of work and working patterns. For example, the reduction in commuting; the weakening gravity of "supercities", with London-based companies now employing people from the regions without requiring them to relocate; and the rise of "digital nomads" – people who travel freely, working remotely via the internet.

At the same time, Hubble understands that workers still want to have a connection with their company. Employees need the sense of belonging that comes from working physically alongside colleagues in creative spaces, as well as having the opportunity to bond with potential clients in face-to-face meetings.

Hubble offers more than 10,000 workspaces, which are available across the world, enabling people to work from any of its locations at any time. Companies buy a pass on behalf of their employees so that they can access a range of networks and places.

Among Hubble's most popular products are Private Day Offices, where clients can hire an entire office for, for instance, one day a week, rather than booking a meeting room or an event space. "This is where we see the world going," says Agarwal.

www.hubblehq.com

Alternative finance

Kuflink Group delivers secure, swift and transparent short-term loans to borrowers and investors through its innovative FCA-authorised and regulated digital platform

"We have become the lender who you can go to, away from the high-street banks," says Narinder Khattoare, CEO of Kuflink, a bridging lender and peer-to-peer platform. "After the 2008 financial crash, our founders thought, rather than keep borrowing money they'd go into the lending and brokering market. Sixty or 70 alternative lenders came to the UK market, and we were one of those providing alternative finance. Since 2011, we have been giving liquidity to borrowers, property developers and landlords."

Kuflink offers flexible short-term loans and is an FCA (Financial Conduct Authority) authorised and regulated online peer-to-peer platform. The loans offered are stringently underwritten, conforming to high standards and invariably secured by UK property. Khattoare explains that the FCA regulation allows the business to go anywhere in the UK and Europe to generate investment. "We are different in that we provide a digital platform where you can scrutinise the valuation report, see the comparables, see the risk rating. There is transparency and speed, and we can see the difference it makes to

individuals. We wanted to make use of people's money rather than have it sitting in the bank. Everyone has been used to zero per cent interest rates for the past ten or 12 years, whereas we wanted to provide a product that really works for borrowers and investors."

In 2022, Kuflink received multiple accolades at the Peer2Peer Finance Awards, including Bridging Lender of the Year, CEO of the Year and Investor's Choice Winner. The award-winning, 45-strong company has invested over £300 million to date across almost a million investments, often co-investing up to 5 per cent alongside the initial investment. "There have been zero investor losses to date, and average returns are around 8 per cent," say Khattoare, noting that FCA regulations advise against investing unless you are prepared to lose money. "The beauty of our business is that we are not backed by a private equity firm or a hedge fund who tend to put criteria in place and stipulate that you do not move outside them. We create the criteria and then test them in the market. If they work, investors will put money in."

www.kuflink.com

Code for the road

Enhancing electric vehicle performance is just one of the areas in which Twelve Oaks Software is delivering bespoke innovation

Small companies can make a huge impact on the world if they have the right combination of innovation, integrity and insight. Twelve Oaks Software is a 20-person software development team based in York that was founded nine years ago and quickly developed an impressive reputation, building software for clients including Barclays and *The Great British Bake Off*. But Twelve Oaks is now seeking to make a real difference to the planet, working with a company in Silicon Valley to develop software that will improve the performance of electric vehicles by optimising how and when they are charged.

"There are a lot of difficulties with the fact nobody knows how to run an electric vehicle fleet," explains Twelve Oaks founder Paul Jervis. "One thing I did was create a server to communicate between the charger and the vehicle to ensure it is more efficient. Companies running large delivery fleets need to learn how to use their vehicles – they need to know where to charge them, when to charge them, how long it will take and how much it will cost. All this needs to be worked out to allow for considerably more intelligent use of the vehicles."

Jervis founded Twelve Oaks because he was unimpressed by the work produced by so many existing software developers. With a focus on quality, communication and delivery, he has built a team of gifted and versatile developers, headed by CEO Matthew Hamilton. The pair intend to keep the company small, so they can provide agility and flexibility for clients while also nurturing and supporting employees. It is a policy that has enabled colleagues to work remotely for Twelve Oaks as they travel around the world or visit family overseas, while also allowing for the greatest cross-fertilisation of talent and ideas. The team's knowledge base continues to deepen as individuals learn from peers and more experienced colleagues. As each coder develops a wider range of skills, they bring increased value to Twelve Oaks' customers.

"We have an excellent quality assurance system where all of the code we do will come back to be examined by other members of the team," explains Jervis. "That allows somebody who is more junior or inexperienced to look at the code and learn from it, while somebody more senior is able to oversee the code and give advice and guidance before it is released to the client."

The company has developed an additional service in the form of an "app audit". This will allow investors to hire Twelve Oaks to audit software before purchasing a tech company; Twelve Oaks' experts will ensure the software is fit for purpose and has a suitable shelf life. The auditors will publish their findings in a detailed report, written in layman's terms, so investors can see whether they are making a wise decision.

As well as working to enhance the performance of electric vehicles, Twelve Oaks' focus on sustainability also extends to ensuring its software is as efficient as possible. "We are cognisant of the electricity usage of software, which is another sustainability issue," says Jervis. "If you have wasteful processes spinning away doing needless work, that costs a significant amount of electricity that needs to be generated somewhere, often using unsustainable sources. We don't want to optimise the use of electric vehicles by creating software that requires the burning of fossil fuels so they can function."

www.twelveoaks.software

Leading the field

With its groundbreaking approach to decommissioning oil and gas wells,
Well-Safe Solutions is pitching to become the best in the industry

The world is transitioning away from its reliance on fossil fuels towards cleaner and more sustainable forms of energy. But this does not mean the skills created and developed in the oil and gas industry are completely redundant, with many workers ready to play a crucial role in the transition process. Phil Milton began his career as an apprentice in mechanical engineering before working offshore for a decade and then progressing through the ranks. Now, he is founder and CEO of Aberdeen-based Well-Safe Solutions, where he uses his knowledge and experience to decommission unwanted oil and gas wells, both onshore and offshore, with a firm eye on environmental wellbeing.

"As we move away from fossil fuels, we need to remove unwanted wells and do so in a way that ensures they are environmentally safe – preventing them from becoming a leak path in the future. As we do this, we must also consider the reuse of wells and reservoirs, and in some cases, they may have the potential to be repurposed for carbon capture," says Milton.

Launched in 2017 with six employees, the business has grown to more than 400 employees, with turnover going from under £1 million to £170 million. "Our vision is to become the well-decommissioning partner of choice for the industry," says Milton. "We are the only company in the UK – maybe globally – that can take a project and deliver all aspects, from the engineering, project management and provision of the asset through to logistics and waste-stream management."

Milton realised he could carve out a niche in the decommissioning market after observing first-hand the inefficiency of the existing piecemeal process, which required numerous vessels and burnt excessive amounts of fuel. After securing investment from partners including Alasdair Locke, Chairman and majority shareholder,

Milton was able to deploy his alternative solution, which put all necessary equipment and manpower on a single vessel, massively reducing the cost and duration of operations, while increasing fuel efficiency. Having proven the concept by successfully decommissioning hundreds of wells in the North Sea via the three rigs that they own and operate, Well-Safe is preparing to deploy its single-asset solution globally. Well-Safe also secures and decommissions onshore gas and oil wells and is developing business in the Netherlands, Germany and other European countries.

"There is a huge opportunity for us and the UK to export this model globally and be at the leading edge of decommissioning," says Milton. "We have opened an office in Australia and have begun delivering engineering studies in Africa, Thailand and Canada. We work within very stringent regulatory requirements to provide a robust but environmentally sensitive solution."

As well as ensuring that a British company is a world leader in the field, Well-Safe Solutions is training the next generation of workers, creating opportunities for young people to build careers and support the transition towards clean energy. Having entered the industry himself through an apprenticeship, Milton understands the importance of developing talent and has created multiple programmes to grow the workforce.

"We have foundation apprenticeships, we have modern apprenticeships, and we have graduate programmes," he says. "We go into schools, colleges and universities to educate students on the decommissioning sector, the work we do to support a just energy transition, and the careers available in oil and gas during this transition. I am incredibly proud of what we have already achieved. It's been a great journey with rapid growth, and we will continue to grow over the coming years."

www.wellsafesolutions.com

Electric avenues

Not content with being the predominant British taxi maker, LEVC is poised to conquer the global electric vehicle market with an expanded product line-up

In 1977, a young Prince Charles was photographed behind the wheel of a special Silver Jubilee taxi in the grounds of Buckingham Palace. By then, the London Electric Vehicle Company (LEVC) had been dominating the British taxi market for almost 70 years. Little had changed in that regard when the prince visited the LEVC factory in Ansty, Coventry, in 2019; but while the taxis built by the rebooted brand retained the same iconic features, now they were rolling off the assembly line ready to take on the world as state-of-the-art, range-extended electric vehicles (or REEV).

Then, in 2023, LEVC launched its cutting-edge digital operating system, Space Oriented Architecture (SOA), which optimises space and brings advances in range efficiency, charging time, connectivity, autonomous capability, intelligent cockpits and much more.

All this should help the vehicles negotiate the city with which they are so synonymous. "London's conditions set a number of challenging requirements," says Chris Allen, Managing Director – not least building a vehicle big enough to pick up several passengers at once, with room for an accessible ramp, while being able to zoom down narrow lanes and maintain a turning circle tight enough for the absurdly small Savoy Hotel roundabout. Achieve all that and this "positions you globally as the only company capable of making vehicles that remain safe, efficient and accessible in the most difficult transportation environments".

Little wonder, then, that LEVC aims to take the global passenger EV (electric vehicle) market by storm and achieve a 20 per cent increase in sales by the end of 2023. It is an opportune time to do so, says Allen, as the global transportation sector embraces green energy and a philosophy of shared mobility. LEVC already has a presence across Europe, with over 30 dealerships, from Spain to Sweden, and Germany to Greece, not to mention a ride-hailing agreement in Paris and importation accords in Azerbaijan, Australia and Japan.

The next stage is to use those locations as launch pads for the new generation of vehicles and "to create the infrastructure and continue the technology that can take on the latest clean air zones and sustainability requirements that make the world a better place".

www.levc.com

Next generation electronics

Pragmatic Semiconductor's groundbreaking technologies are transforming electronics with bespoke, cost-effective alternatives to the silicon chip

It was while talking to prospective customers looking for novel electronic solutions that technology entrepreneur Scott White realised there was a gap in the market. "It became clear there was an appetite for the equivalent of the silicon chip to embed easily into things that aren't electronics," he says. Items such as packaging for consumer goods needed the technology – at the right price.

White set up Pragmatic Semiconductor in 2010 with Richard Price, with the idea of creating low-cost integrated circuits that would be thin and flexible enough to embed in items across multiple sectors. "We developed the technology platform in-house," says CEO White. "And, over the past 12 years, we have taken it from concept to volume manufacturing." The name was deliberately chosen. "It's not technology for its own sake, or the highest performance solution; we find a balance between functionality and cost-effective delivery."

With institutional and strategic investment of more than £150 million in place, Pragmatic Semiconductor has now installed its first commercial fabrication line, in Sedgefield, County Durham, and the company is growing. "Over the next decade, we expect to deploy 100 fabrication lines around the world with this technology, which is still globally unique."

Customers, from consumer brands to electronics companies, can use the technology to create bespoke solutions to their needs. "Most of our business has evolved into our 'foundry' model," explains White. "We provide a design kit that allows customers to develop their own functionality using the basic building blocks of our technology, then we manufacture it for them." This means the technology can be used for a greater range of applications than if the company had to develop every single use case.

"We've seen customers moving to reusable packaging models where timely identification of the individual package is critical," says White. Accessible healthcare is another key area, as the technology enables wearable "smart patches".

The production cycle time is 24 hours, "dramatically shorter" than the three months it typically takes to manufacture silicon chips. "Over time, more of our lines will be dedicated to large customers for on-site production," says White, "giving them a unique solution for strategic control of their electronics supply chain."

www.pragmaticsemi.com

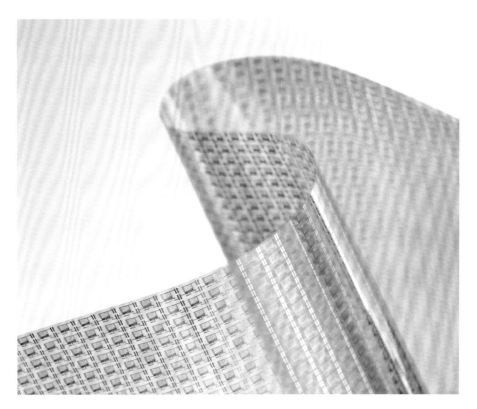

Timeless style

Really Wild Clothing champions all that is beautifully British, a brand in which refined city styling meets wild heritage

In the 20 years since Really Wild Clothing was founded, the brand has changed along with the women who wear its products. "We very much started as a country brand," says founder and designer Natalie Lake. "But we quickly realised that the women we were designing for were interested in taking that theme of heritage clothing (tweeds, wools and classic style) and wearing it in the city as well."

Today, Lake's collections are a reimagination of contemporary, heritage designs. Embodying craftsmanship with luxury fabrics, they are made to last, with seasonal appeal all year round. What remains unchanged is the quality and attention to detail. Peel away the collar of a navy-blue blazer for an unexpected flash of colour or stitching detail that elevates it above the ordinary.

With limited pieces handcrafted by artisans from Scotland to Spain, the London fashion house is the last word in luxury. Its origins remain firmly rooted in the countryside, perfectly combining hardy Scottish tweeds and knitwear with the most delicate Liberty silks to create a timeless yet instantly recognisable look. The brand has broken down the barriers between town and country.

Fabrics are sourced from stalwarts of British design, including wool and tweed from some of Scotland's oldest mills. In this way the brand supports homegrown craftspeople and ensures that their techniques and expertise live on for future generations, while also protecting jobs.

The sustainable approach has won Really Wild Clothing fans among celebrities, royals, aristocracy and businesswomen alike. "Our modern, classic designs are made to last, not to wear for one season and then discard," says Lake. "Although the designs have evolved and got better and more relevant, the quality has remained our absolute constant."

Versatility is one of the defining features of the collections. Quality, natural fabrics that layer effortlessly and pared-back silhouettes translate seamlessly into everyday life.

Along with a flagship store on the King's Road in Chelsea, the label plans to open more shops and sell to an increasingly avid online following. While quintessentially British, it also aims to bring its signature style to a wider international market. Overall, says Lake, it is about "listening to our customers and developing our designs".

www.reallywildclothing.com

In the frame

Pictorum Art Group is making it easier for a new generation of art collectors to access the market

The relationship between art and luxury has forever run parallel, interlinking occasionally over a shared innate quality. Over time, the concept of what constitutes art or luxury has diversified. With the art world becoming more complex, Pictorum Art Group brings together experts in art investment, curating and appraisal to make the experience of collecting art less daunting. "We are working to eliminate that sense of intimidation new collectors experience when they enter a gallery or the art market," says Matthew Navin, Pictorum CEO.

In the modern marketplace, a lack of visibility, funding and knowledge has, says Pictorum, caused an absence of quality representation opportunities for emerging artists. Pictorum's expert advisers seek out artists who are truly passionate and dedicated to developing their practice. The organisation's groundbreaking approach is to be the artists' eyes and ears at the right place, build their knowledge, support them financially and help establish them, to create a more ethical and inclusive environment for the future.

Pictorum's core centres around collaboration, modernisation and creativity. It takes pride in establishing lasting relationships with organisations that share the same synergy and ethos. Since 2021, Pictorum has partnered with institutions including Sotheby's Institute of Art. "In an industry where the rulemakers are no longer the tastemakers, collaboration is the only way to initiate disruptive change," says Sanaa Sachdev, Operations Director.

The company was founded in 2018 by Matthew, alongside brother and co-founder Jackson Navin, as Pictorum Advisory, the investment arm that acts as an incubator and patron for talent. Building on rapid success in the UK, the group now comprises five complementary brands that are collectively transforming the experience of owning and investing in art.

The group's flagship contemporary art space, Pictorum Gallery London, opened in 2022, and is now celebrating the launch of its most recent brand, Duveen + Vollard, a premium art-logistics service provider. Other brands include Articul8, a publication that reports on art world trends, from global news to auction insights, and Artelligence, an art tech platform that collates this information to offer detailed analysis to art market stakeholders. With plans to expand to India, the doors to innovative, transparent art investing are wide open.

www.pictorumartgroup.com

The built environment

Charles's passionate views on town planning, architectural design and construction methods are all part of his wider philosophy of modern living

harles was sitting at his desk in a comfortable, dark-grey leather chair surrounded by papers and his handwritten letters. We shook hands and I told him that I felt his visit to Vanuatu, the island nation in the South Pacific Ocean, that day had been a triumph. It was April 2018 and The King, then the Prince of Wales, was immaculately dressed as ever, sporting a lightweight-wool Anderson & Sheppard tailored suit and silk tie, and a silk pocket handkerchief. Not one to take praise very well, he nonetheless smiled warmly and said, "Yes, I was very touched by the warmth of the welcome."

Our conversation was wide-ranging. One minute we were discussing the future of the Commonwealth, the next climate change, but when we discussed the built environment and Poundbury, Charles's traditionalist village in Dorset, he became more animated. Poundbury is unfairly described by some as a sort of "feudal Disneyland", but in reality it is a growing and diverse community where people have settled and now work and live. It has developed over time and has now realised The King's vision.

THE POUNDBURY PROJECT

I told him that I had visited Poundbury three times on media days arranged by his then Clarence House office and, essentially, approve of the concept. Poundbury is a living example of what The King believes the urban environment should be – providing those who live and work there with a home and not just a "house".

In 1993, when he created Poundbury, a new-build town with a mix of Georgian, Victorian, neoclassical and even Greco-Roman-inspired building design set on the edge of Dorchester, Dorset, it followed the principles for architecture and urban living that The King had expressed in his well-received 1989 documentary and best-selling book, *A Vision of Britain*. Under the direction of its lead architect and planner, Léon Krier, who worked closely with Charles, its design is based on traditional architecture and New Urbanist philosophy, and followed the principles of legibility, flexibility, durability and affordability.

While it still divides opinion today, there can be no doubt its mixed-use design has created a thriving community. At its heart are homes, public amenities, retail spaces and other business facilities together with open areas, all designed as a walkable community that prioritises people rather than cars. Poundbury's 4,600 residents live in a mix of private and affordable housing, and some 2,600 people working in the town's more than 250 shops, cafés, offices and factories.

A CRITICAL VOICE

Charles has never been afraid of being controversial when it comes to subjects that matter to him. In May 1984, he famously denounced a proposed extension to the National Gallery as "a monstrous carbuncle on the face of a much-loved and elegant friend" at a royal gala evening at Hampton Court Palace to mark the 150th anniversary of the Royal Institute of British Architects (RIBA). Further speeches followed in which he accused architects of being more destructive than the Nazi air force, with no consideration for the impact his comments had on their reputations and careers. He said some planners and architects have consistently ignored the feelings and wishes of the mass of ordinary people in this country.

"To be concerned about the way people live; about the environment they inhabit and the kind of community that is created by that environment should surely be one of the prime requirements," he said at the RIBA event. "What have we done to it [London] since the bombing during the war? What are we shortly to do to one of its most famous areas – Trafalgar Square? Instead of designing an extension to the elegant facade

Previous page
On site at Charles's Welsh home, Llwynywormwood, renovated with an emphasis on craft and sustainability

Right
Poundbury in Dorset, Charles's vision for a new-build town, featuring a revival of historic street patterns and architecture

Above
Charles pays a visit
to Poundbury in 1999
with lead architect and
planner Léon Krier (left)
and developer Andrew
Hamilton (right)

Opposite
A tour of Poundbury
as a model town, led
by Charles for a group
of MPs, officials and
members of the Urban
Land Institute

"Never has there been a monarch with such an enduring interest in the built environment, nor one with such clear opinions"

of the National Gallery which complements it and continues the concept of columns and domes, it looks as if we may be presented with a kind of municipal fire station, complete with the sort of tower that contains the siren. I would understand better this type of high-tech approach if you demolished the whole of Trafalgar Square and started again with a single architect responsible for the entire layout."

There is no doubt that some architects were irritated by his interventions, and claimed it set back modern architecture a decade as planners would not approve anything like it again. In his defence, most of the public backed Charles rather than the modernist architects. If anyone had read the full text of his speech instead of just the headlines, they would have seen that Charles was advocating many of the core beliefs of the day.

Once again ahead of his time, Charles championed sustainable planning in the construction industry. He also supported increased access for those with disabilities, the importance of community consultation and resident-led housing co-operatives, and the revival of historic street patterns and traditional housing types, such as terraces and courtyards.

Charles was stepping into the political limelight more and more. Rather than shy away from controversy, he was drawn to its flame, confident enough in his own position to speak out on issues that mattered to him. He felt it was his duty to raise the debate on big issues and that it was important to challenge politicians, to live up to what would otherwise be empty promises.

This go-getting attitude resulted in clashes with the Conservative government of the time, led by Margaret Thatcher between 1979 and 1990, particularly over the Tories' inner-city policies. As a result, Charles was accused of meddling in political affairs and overreaching his constitutional position. If anything, the criticism only encouraged him to go further, especially regarding what he saw as the need for the rebirth of inner cities.

Charles wanted to offer more than rhetoric and established his organisation Business in the Community (BITC) to support those deprived of services. He pushed the prime minister to meet with local leaders of his outreach programme, which she eventually did, hosting a lunch at Number 10. Although, like the Queen, Charles was supposed to be non-partisan in politics, he found some of Thatcher's policies to be divisive and uncaring and was motivated to act.

A UNIFIED VISION

It has understandably exasperated Charles when he has been accused of jumping from one topic to another. It is only when you examine all that he does in detail that the integrated and interrelated picture of his life's work becomes clearly visible. "Perhaps I should not have been surprised that so many people failed to fathom what I was doing," he noted in his trailblazing book *Harmony: A New Way of Looking at Our World*, published in 2010. "So many appeared to think – or were told – that I was merely leaping from one subject to another – from architecture one minute to agriculture the next – as if I spent a morning saving the rainforests, then in the afternoon jumping to help young people start new businesses."

His influence in the planning system increased over time. Some developers and architects, who did not want to offend him with their important planned projects, even showed Charles their proposals before they were submitted for planning permission.

Never has there been a monarch with such an enduring interest in the built environment, nor one with such clear opinions. Charles has been known for intervening on major planning decisions, and while some insist it is not his role to do so, he has continued to find solutions for the challenges of urban growth, the housing shortage and the building of new, sustainable communities. His passion for the built environment is unwavering and his role in the discussion is important – on almost every issue of substance relating to our cities and the environment, he has largely been right.

"Charles was confident enough in his own position to speak out on issues that mattered to him"

Opposite, top
A tour in 2015 of the House of Dorchester chocolate factory, one of more than 250 businesses now based in Poundbury

Opposite, bottom
Charles views the construction and preservation work for the new Museum of London in West Smithfield in 2021

Above
A look at plans for Knockroon, a housing development Charles initiated in 2011 on the edge of his Scottish estate Dumfries House

Engineering sustainability

With more than 40 years' experience in its field, CPW is a leader in sustainable engineering for both old and new buildings

At first glance, the ornate cloisters of St John's College, Oxford, and brutalist high-rise housing estate Broadwater Farm in Tottenham might not have much in common. Yet both are projects undertaken by international consultancy CPW, which specialises in identifying and tackling the challenges of decarbonisation. Through innovative zero-carbon new builds and renovations, the company is transforming environmental building services.

"There is a stereotypical image of an engineer being fixed in their ways, but we aren't like that. We force ourselves to adapt and change," says Director Carl Standley. "Over the past 15 to 20 years or so, we have pushed things a lot harder than our peers when it comes to sustainability. We were one of the first UK companies to train in the German Passivhaus system, which was then new to the UK market. This approach to low-energy building design focuses on passive engineering techniques, creating a super-insulated building that needs very little heating in winter and uses electricity efficiently, resulting in very low operating costs."

This commitment to change reflects CPW's origins – a company set up in 1978 by three engineers, Couch, Perry and Wilkes, who were disillusioned with the blasé approach of the industry. They initially worked on projects in the healthcare sector but moved into other fields. In 1997, it was time for a new generation of leaders, and five partners took over, though the original founders continued to be involved.

One of the new executive team's first decisions was to create an apprenticeship scheme to develop CPW's own pipeline of talent, one that would understand and embrace the company's values. This has proved to be incredibly successful, with over 70 per cent of trainees staying for ten years or more. Company Director Carl Standley joined as a trainee, showing the potential pathway for progression, and CPW has since opened offices elsewhere in the UK, and in Poland and India, in both cases through employees who set up offices in their home countries.

CPW's forward-thinking approach, such as with the apprenticeship scheme, has allowed it to be an acknowledged expert in sustainability,

an issue it was raising with customers as early as 2004. For the company, it is an agenda like The King's, who has been discussing these issues for decades, says Mark Morris, one of the five successors. "We understand how difficult it has been. We've been to meetings and talked about sustainable design and been completely ignored and cast aside because it wasn't fashionable. But now everybody is rightly interested."

As a result CPW is now an industry leader, both in designing low-energy buildings such as the University of Leicester's pioneering medical school, and decarbonising existing buildings and estates. The university's George Davies Medical Centre is one of the largest Passivhaus-certified buildings in the UK, meaning its energy efficiency reduces the structure's ecological footprint. It has won several awards, including the 2018 Energy Awards' Public Building Energy Project of the Year. "With full certification we reduced the existing building energy usage by over 80 per cent," says Innovations Director Neil Foster.

"What's really important is the aftercare. When you commission a building it does very well at the start, but then people start to fiddle with the controls and things go downhill. So, we return to the building quarterly for three years post-occupation to look at how it is performing and make tweaks and improvements. We see if we hit our predicted targets, learn about what has actually worked, and simplify concepts. It's all part of our belief in the importance of keeping the brain flexible and learning from everything we do."

While CPW has designed several low and zero-carbon buildings, including offices, homes, warehouses and even the Ben Ainslie Racing HQ in Portsmouth, a significant element of the company's passion and expertise now goes towards decarbonising existing structures and estates. This can be exceptionally challenging, but the work will have a major impact for decades – perhaps even centuries – to come.

Take the case of St John's College in Oxford, an estate that includes buildings dating from 1555. "The college is committed to decarbonise in ten years," says Foster. "It requires being empathic and working alongside conservationists to preserve these fantastic, listed buildings. We have learned a lot already and been able to take this knowledge to other clients to help with their estates in completely different fields."

Other examples of these are Broadwater Farm, a regeneration project of 296 net zero carbon homes, and Kettering General Hospital, where CPW is decarbonising existing hospital buildings while putting in place the infrastructure for new ones. This requires replacing the decades-old, steam-powered heating system with a more energy-efficient, modern equivalent – in this case, a hybrid heat pump – without disruption to

hospital services. The new system needs to be future-proofed, so it can be replaced when an even more energy-efficient solution comes along.

Embracing complexity is integral to CPW, from supporting charities and social enterprise schemes to investing in individuals and diversity. In 2022, it won the UK Employer of the Year at the Investors in People Awards. "Everybody from trainee to director understands the principles of sustainable design," says Director Dave Gambell. "We have opened our field of vision and are bringing in different people to help expand our own approach to sustainability. There is a passion through all the ranks, spending a bit more time to get it right and making sure the younger generation develop our ethos even further.

CPW has signed up to initiatives such as the Terra Carta, launched by The King, which places sustainability at the heart of private enterprise. "Our message to the industry is clear," says Gambell. "We are responding to the environmental impact of construction. Let's save our future by solving our past."

www.cpwp.com

Building a brighter tomorrow

Headquartered in London, hotel owner and developer 4C Group is on a mission to delight guests and investors, operate sustainably and make a positive impact within the community

When Al-karim Nathoo's father, Bashir, emigrated from Tanzania to the UK in the 1970s, he found a warm welcome as well as incredible opportunities in his new home. It is apposite that following this friendly reception, he chose hospitality as the sector in which he would build his own business, operating a number of hotels as part of a growing portfolio that began with a single bedsit and now encompasses holdings on four continents.

The company's name, 4C Group, playfully hints at this family business's smart ability to foresee opportunity. "We have a clear vision of what we want to achieve and are very passionate about growing the business and to be recognised as a market-leading hotel operator and developer," says Al-karim, who is CEO. "We have a clear strategy and are quite measured in our approach. We don't necessarily want to be the biggest, but we do know our market. Hotels are our passion project."

As well as owning and operating hotels in the UK, the Middle East, East Africa and Canada, 4C Group, which formed in 2010, has now sought to bring its experience and commitment to residential and mixed-use developments. In 2022, 4C Group partnered with Regal London to deliver The Haydon, a residential tower of 87 apartments in Aldgate, in the City of London, an area that is experiencing a rapid transformation. The building is due to complete in Q2 2024. The company has also acquired land in Camden, north London, for a mixed-use development that includes serviced apartments, offices and affordable housing.

"Currently, there is a lot of buzz around 'hybrid hospitality' – this intersection of living, eating, meeting and working," says Al-karim. "We operate in a very competitive landscape and to stand out we focus on our key attributes. For our hotels, that means creating a positive guest experience. We have always tried to be innovative and on the cusp of new technologies. We are also very committed to providing new opportunities for our people to grow, developing our own talent."

It is essential to the company that its buildings are part of the local neighbourhood, with support provided to the community. "My father is still very involved in the business, and he always says it is important for us to leave the world in a better place than how we found it – that is his raison d'être. Profit is important, but it's not the only thing."

This philosophy has inspired 4C Group's work in sustainability, with the company seeking to ensure that best environmental practices are adhered to where possible. This is seen, for example, in The Haydon development and the newly opened Canopy by Hilton London City, a 340-bedroom hotel where responsible initiatives are woven into the infrastructure and amenities. The hotel was recently awarded Excellent for its BREEAM In-Use status. In addition, 4C Group invested in building and supporting the local neighbourhood with its own community centre and hub, now known as the Portsoken Community Centre.

"Sustainability is a core pillar for us," says Al-karim, who also sits on the Advisory Board of the Energy and Environment Alliance, a not-for-profit coalition of hospitality sector leaders who work with experts to really focus on this issue. "That is something we really embrace. Consumers are becoming more environmentally conscious and that is one area that really sets us apart. We promote environmental responsibility and showcase the sustainable practices we adopt as we continue this journey."

www.4cgroup.co.uk

Setting new standards

The efficiency of its 3D concrete printing technology has enabled
ChangeMaker 3D to transform major building projects throughout the UK

When Natalie and Luke Wadley, the founders of ChangeMaker 3D, make big decisions, they often do so in the most informal of surroundings: the sofa, a kitchen table, or Friday night round the firepit. It is an unorthodox approach that suits this most unconventional of companies. And ChangeMaker 3D – a pioneer in the world of 3D concrete printing, and named Best 3D Concrete Printing Company in the UK in 2022 – is unconventional not only in the way it is introducing new technologies and ideas into the famously conservative construction industry, but also in its vision of success, which seeks to improve the lives of individuals and the planet rather than simply record a profit.

"We want to use this new technology as a force for good," explains Natalie. "It isn't just about being a successful business. We want a business that is about more than making money – it is doing good and being sustainable in every sense. We want our robots on as many infrastructure projects as possible in the UK, training disadvantaged people and using a technology that reduces carbon. Construction is still a male-dominated space and there's a lot to do in that area as well. We are introducing different types of thinking, and that provides an opportunity for diversity."

Natalie and Luke met at school as teenagers, and their long relationship has given them trust and an intuitive understanding. They left their jobs and sold their house to raise funds for ChangeMaker, which was initially conceived to build homes using 3D printing technology. "We wanted to out-print poverty, building 3D-printed houses and training people from disadvantaged communities to use the technology to build their own houses," says Natalie.

The benefits of 3D printing for construction are many. Alongside providing the opportunity for individuals to acquire new skills, bringing local economic benefit and enabling community regeneration, it is cheaper, faster, more efficient and safer than traditional methods. It is also better for the environment, using technology that delivers a 20 per cent reduction in carbon emissions with its trademark brand Printfrastructure, whose tagline is: "We are here to Printfrastructure like our planet depends on it".

By 2020, the company was ready to pivot into infrastructure. Important contracts were secured with the United Utilities Innovation Lab in the North West, and HS2. "They wanted to use their spending power to be sustainable, and they became our early adopters," says Luke. "They are clients but also advocates, they have put money into projects that have taken us forward because they can see what we are doing and how important it is. That's why the relationship has worked."

Natalie and Luke see themselves as integrators as well as trailblazers. The company works with tech innovators to find the best technology, helping to refine and improve the robotics. The company takes its message of improved productivity and sustainability to construction firms and infrastructure projects. Ultimately, the pair want to return to housing, but their ambitions do not stop in the UK.

"We want to be international," says Luke. "We want to reinvest, look at disaster relief and support developing countries around the world. We built a water chamber in three-and-a-half hours using our technology – that can be done in every village in every developing country where water is going to become increasingly valuable. We want to design out carbon, and print in a way that is more sustainable and has productivity enhancement, using technology that gets faster and more accurate all the time."

www.changemaker3d.co.uk

Better spaces and places

A proponent of biophilic design, Charlotte Findlater creates
healthy homes that respect, and bring people closer to, nature

Humans have a fundamental need to connect with nature, but many of us live in a built environment. Design studio Charlotte Findlater helps clients to re-establish this vital connection through a holistic, multi-sensory, biophilic approach to architecture, property development, interior design and ecoscaping.

"I've had an affinity with the natural world since childhood," says Charlotte Findlater, who set up her studio in 2021. "I spent most of my time outdoors, surrounded by wildlife and nature. Wandering through the countryside, my eye was often drawn to the architecture of buildings and their place within the landscape, and I became curious about the symbiotic relationship between humans and nature, and the way the built environment affects this."

Later, as a property developer, it became clear to Findlater that a sustainable, circular and environmentally friendly approach to architecture and design was both possible and necessary. "I felt that such an approach needed to encompass every step in the creation, or

renovation, of a built environment: architecture, construction, interior design and ecoscaping. Someone said to me, 'Charlotte, jump and the universe will catch you', and that was the push I needed to establish my biophilic design business using this approach and to focus on my advocacy work in this field."

Findlater and her team work with forward-thinking clients on groundbreaking luxury builds, refurbishments and renovations. Projects range from individual private homes to larger commercial and hospitality spaces. Every element is carefully considered: the materials and build methods, the relationship between the building, landscape and human health and the impact of the project on the planet.

Clients are encouraged to consider the toxicity, carbon footprint and impact of each item used on a project. "Every stage of the life cycle is considered," says Findlater. "What are the positive or negative effects of its manufacture on the environment and local community? Could an existing item be repurposed and used? How will the item affect their wellbeing? And does the item later have the potential to be recycled or repurposed?" Another prompt is for clients to focus on the "beautiful, multi-sensory experience of being in nature" and what it means to them. "We infuse the space with design features that revive that experience for them, through the choice of materials, colours, lighting, furnishings, artwork and plants."

The studio aims to achieve B Corp Certification, reflecting Findlater's desire to reach the highest of social and environmental standards, transparency and accountability. It does so by nurturing relationships with artisan craftspeople who share an understanding of, and commitment to, an approach to creating spaces that deepen the symbiotic relationship between humans and nature – with the overall aim of enhancing the health and wellbeing of both. Charlotte Findlater also supports the UN's Sustainable Development Goals, one objective of which is to ensure the protection of the planet and its natural resources.

"When we're in nature we feel good, so we need to let more of this positivity into our built environment, while also reducing our negative impact on nature," says Findlater. "This applies to building design, materials and furnishings – which can all be chosen more mindfully, with a timeless, 'less is more' approach that values each item for its positive effect on us and the planet. By adopting this mindset from the start, as a project develops so too does the client's connection with nature and the space itself. It is a privilege to witness this gradual transformation."

www.charlottefindlater.co.uk

Planning for the future

UK construction giant Galliford Try is optimising its effect socially
and environmentally with a new approach to building methods

There are times when sustainability simply means saying no. This is something Stephen Slessor, Managing Director of Galliford Try Environment, has come to embrace as the construction company balances the requirements of clients with the needs of the environment.

The business operates across the UK, with a focus on infrastructure and building projects in sectors such as education, defence, roads, rail and water. Slessor leads the division of Galliford Try that is a leading partner to regulated companies in the water sector. "In that sector, we can often refurbish or improve the network – finding solutions that extend the life rather than building something entirely new," he says. "So our first question these days is: 'Do we even need to build anything? Can we maximise existing assets?'"

The business now has an entire team focused on asset optimisation, tackling the challenges of ageing infrastructure, climate-change resilience and funding pressure. "It means there are times when the best thing to do is nothing at all," explains Slessor. "It can be counterintuitive, but it can create better relationships and is better for the environment."

It is an approach that demonstrates the progressive nature of Galliford Try. From being a traditional design-and-build contractor, whose origins date back to 1908, the group has had great success into extending its capabilities into capital maintenance and asset optimisation. These were recently bolstered by the acquisitions of NMCN's water business in 2021, and MCS Control Systems and Ham Baker engineering in 2022. Galliford Try is today one of the UK's leading construction groups, with 3,700 employees.

"We work across the UK and our people are all part of their own local communities. That's why social value is embedded within our decision-making," says Slessor. "Typically, we can add up to 30 per cent social value for every pound we spend. We invest in training and in our local economies. We have a big focus on making people's lives better."

From 2012 to 2021, Galliford Try reduced its Scope 1 and 2 emissions by 65 per cent, and is committed to reducing its clients' direct emissions. "As our operations head towards net zero, we are developing new goods and services that will help our clients reach net zero, too," says Slessor. It is why the company sees old methods of construction as a last resort. As well as the focus on refurbishing and refreshing existing assets, Galliford Try uses digital solutions to build smarter, using AI to do capital maintenance and asset management. It is a proactive outlook that will reduce the burden over time.

"We recognised a few years ago that, to be successful in the future, we had to change how we deliver projects," says Slessor. "We have developed partnerships that complement our skill sets and are like a one-stop shop. If a client has a complicated water-treatment project, they can come straight to us and we can deliver it from start to finish in an environmentally friendly fashion." Asset optimisation helps reduce power consumption, and Galliford Try has found solutions that can reduce power usage by up to 20 per cent. "That is good for everybody, including the bill payer," says Slessor. "There's a strong ethos in the company about making sure we do things properly, not just in terms of delivery, but for the environment and the social good as well."

www.gallifordtry.co.uk

Appendices

About the publisher

St James's House boasts a bold visual identity, one that has established us as a global leader in publishing and communications. Working across the spheres of royalty, government, charity and commerce, we specialise in providing organisations from around the world with unparalleled access to hard-to-reach audiences and markets.

Each of our high-quality publications features intelligent and engaging editorial along with considered and contemporary design – a combination that puts us at the forefront of the publishing industry across a wide range of sectors. We provide our partners with the chance to be part of a tangible product that not only tells their story, but also gives them unique and privileged access to high-profile international events, launches and celebrations.

Our portfolio includes official publications for Her Majesty The Queen's 90th Birthday Celebration at Windsor, the RAF's centenary celebrations, the Royal British Legion's centenary and the Platinum Jubilee Pageant.

We are passionate about creating beautiful books, memorable events and striking publicity campaigns that provide our clients with long-lasting benefits and an enhanced global presence.

"I would like to thank you immensely for being a key partner in the Platinum Jubilee Pageant. It is hugely appreciated, not only by those of us involved in staging the event, but also by Buckingham Palace and the government"

Sir Nicholas Coleridge CBE,
Co-Chair, Platinum Jubilee Pageant

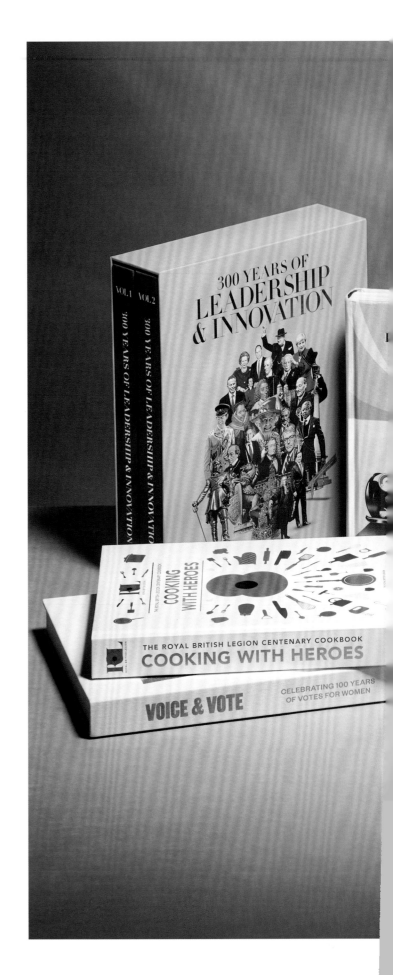

Acknowledgements

ROBERT JOBSON, AUTHOR

Robert Jobson is a number one *New York Times* and *Sunday Times* best-selling author and royal correspondent, who has chronicled the story of the House of Windsor for more than 30 years and is internationally recognised for his in-depth knowledge of the Royal Family.

Robert is Royal Editor of the *London Evening Standard* in the UK and Channel 7's *Sunrise* in Australia, and Royal Contributor for ABC's *Good Morning America*. He is a regular on Sky News, the BBC, ITV and Channel 5.

His best-selling books include *William & Kate, the Love Story*; *Diana: Closely Guarded Secret*; *Prince Philip's Century*; and *Charles at Seventy: Thoughts, Hopes and Dreams*. His latest book *Our King – Charles III: The Man and the Monarch Revealed* was published in April 2023.

ARTHUR EDWARDS MBE, PHOTOGRAPHER

Over the past four decades, wherever the Royal Family have travelled, Arthur has gone with them. He joined *The Sun* newspaper in 1974 and has captured more than 200 royal tours across some 120 countries, as well as seven royal weddings, five royal funerals and eight royal births.

From Queen Elizabeth II's tour of Australia and New Zealand to the White House, Arthur has photographed the Royal Family's key moments, capturing images that are cherished by millions and will continue to be viewed and savoured for years to come.

Often referred to as the House of Windsor's favourite snapper, Arthur was presented with an MBE by the Queen in 2003 for "outstanding service to newspapers". When Queen Elizabeth met him the following week, she jokingly asked him why he wasn't wearing his medal.

CREDITS

Photography
Arthur Edwards, Adobe Stock, Alamy, Getty Images

Climate Outreach: Aerial photograph of Malé in the Maldives by A Shuau/Obofili (page 324, top)
Gabriela Hearst: Daniël Bouquet (page 310); Gabriela Hearst (page 311)
Solpardus: Tessa Bricknell, Headcake Photo (page 490)
Wrapology: production, Wrapology; photography, Ryan & Robert (page 464)

Other images are the copyright of individual contributors and organisations.

Contributor
Poonawalla Group: Written by Mohammed Luqman Ali Khan (pages 184–87)

Sponsors index

4C Group	522
abrdn	288
Academic Families	404
Advanced Hydrogen Technologies Group	248
Ahmad Tea	344
AKT London	482
Alcatel Submarine Networks (ASN)	474
Alchemie	276
All Steels Trading	249
Alta Semper Capital	196
Analucia Beltran Diamonds	296
AP Security	476
AquaSource	254
Ascot Rehabilitation	405
Aslan Renewables	148
Association of Accounting Technicians (AAT)	410
Auto Electrical Supplies	446
Avant Garden	483
Avanti Communications	166
Avernus Education	426
AVORD	411
Avuke	188
Baird & Co	444
Barker College	144
BASF	352
Bouchaine Vineyards	170
Brian James Trailers	450
British International School of Zagreb	425
British School of Monaco, The	416
British University of Iraq	420
Brodie Cashmere	451
Budweiser Brewing Group	350
Butlers Farmhouse Cheeses	354
BVI Finance	146
Candriam	255
CarbonTRACC	258
Care Horizons	400
CATS Global Schools (CGS)	190
Cenin	454
Cepi	302
CGIAR	358
ChangeMaker 3D	524
Charlotte Findlater	526
Chartwell International School	197
Cintamani Group	492
City Pub Group	480
Climate Outreach	324
Climate Strategy & Partners	244
Climate X	259
Cole & Son	176
Compassion in Action	402
Comte de Grasse	363
Concourse	206
Copart	294
Corre Energy	260
CPW	518
Crown Goose	207
Crystal Doors	436
Culture Trip	227
dbramante1928	298
De La Tierra	362
DK Engineering	455
Dwi Emas International School	218
Eco Packaging Products	312
EcofashionCorp	357
Electrical Safety First	406
Ensembl	229
Enviro-Point	303
Enviroo	300
epeaswitzerland	304
ESG360°	267
Esprit	192
European SprayDry Technologies	456
Evox Therapeutics	384
Faerch	306
FatFace	484
Finance Incorporated Limited	149
FiRe Energy	308
Fischer	246
Fulton Umbrellas	493
Future Carbon Group	250
GA R&D	152
Gabriela Hearst	310
Galliford Try	528
GB-Sol	261
Global PMI Partners	214
GoJute International	313
Gray & Adams	440
GRIDSERVE	320
Helm London	314
Hemswell Coldstore	262
Herconomy	150
Hubble	500

Sponsors index

Instituto Superior de Engenharia
do Porto (ISEP) — 200
International Curriculum Association — 194
James Hutton Institute, The — 462
JMDA Design — 457
Jomadasupe — 215
Jonathan Tole Consulting — 366
JTI UK — 198
K2 Corporate Mobility — 280
Kantar — 202
Kippa — 226
Knowledge Cotton Apparel — 367
KogoPay — 180
Kuflink — 501
Lady Primrose Fragrances — 204
LEVC — 506
Linly Designs — 208
LittlePod — 459
Luckley House School — 408
Manchester Youth Zone — 417
Marge Carson — 208
Matriark Foods — 368
MEATER — 478
Megger — 284
Minesoft — 210
Mission Zero — 263
Modern Synthesis — 321
Mooboo — 336
Mosa Meat — 369
Mpowa — 252
National Association for Able Children
in Education — 421
National Windscreens — 486
NaughtOne — 460
Nephila Climate — 256
Nutrition Society, The — 447
Oaro — 264
Offshore Solutions Group — 265
Oliver Wyman — 222
ORCA Computing — 434
P&O Cruises — 488
Pacha Group — 212
Pearl Brasserie — 373
Penman Consulting — 448
Pictorum Art Group — 509
Plenaire — 424
Plymouth Marjon University — 412

Poonawalla Group — 184
Pragmatic Semiconductor — 507
ProducePay — 340
Pulpex — 325
Queen Ethelburga's Collegiate — 423
Really Wild Clothing — 508
Recycling Lives — 388
Refilwe Monageng Trading Enterprises — 151
Regrow Ag — 370
Resource Solutions — 216
Rheinmetall Defence UK — 223
Rimm — 316
Rodda's — 356
Rouute — 318
Savage Cabbage — 414
Shaniko Wool Company — 346
Shelforce — 452
Simply Start — 461
Skills and Education Group — 392
Smartleaf — 458
Solinftec — 360
Solpardus — 490
Space Forge — 494
Spectrum Markets — 224
St Cloud State University — 418
St Lawrence College — 422
Strix — 290
Sue Ryder — 396
Sustainable Planet — 364
Tea Cups London — 496
Titan Bioplastics — 326
Titan Security Technologies — 498
Toucan Hill — 170
Tri-Wall — 322
Twelve Oaks Software — 502
Unium Bioscience — 372
Vale Verde International School — 228
Vexo International — 463
Viberg — 225
Vita Coco — 371
Well-Safe Solutions — 504
WeVee Technologies — 327
WMF Energy — 266
Wrapology — 464
Xrail — 465
Yacht.Vacations — 220
Zenith Bank — 140